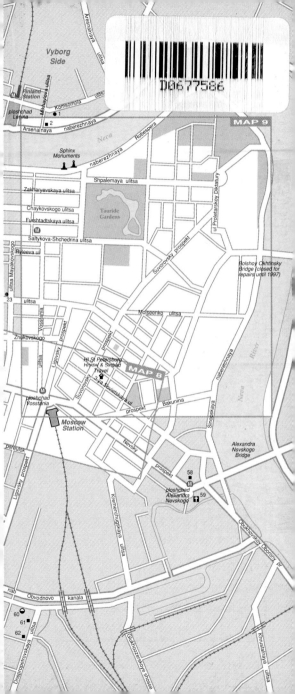

Vyborg
Side

Finland
Station

ploshchad
Lenina

Mekhovaya ulitsa

Arsenalnaya ulitsa

Komsomola

■ 1
● 2

Arsenalnaya

naberezhnaya

Neva

Robespera

naberezhnaya

MAP 9

Sphinx
Monuments

Shpalernaya ulitsa

Zakharyevskaya ulitsa

Chaykovskogo ulitsa

Furshtadtskaya ulitsa

Saltykova-Shchedrina ulitsa

Ryleeva ul

ulitsa Mayakovskogo

● 23

ulitsa

Zhukovskogo

ulitsa Vosstaniya

Ligovsky prospekt

Suvorovsky prospekt

Tauride
Gardens

Suvorovsky prospekt

ul Proletarskoy Diktatury

Bolshoy Okhtinsky
Bridge (closed for
repairs until 1997)

Moiseenko ulitsa

prospekt

Hi St Petersburg
Hostel & Sindbad
Travel

3-ya Sovetskaya ul

MAP 8

Bakunina

naberezhnaya

Neva River

ploshchad
Vosstania

Suvorovsky prospekt

prospekt

Moscow
Station

Nevsky

prospekt

Sinopskaya

Alexandra
Nsvskogo
Bridge

Kremenchugskaya ulitsa

58 ■
ploshchad
Alexandra
Nevskogo

59

Ligovsky prospekt

pereulok

Obukhovskoy Oborony pr

Krustalnaya ulitsa

nab

Obvodnovo

kanala

● 60
■ 61
■ 62

Dnepropetrovskaya ulitsa

Glukhoozerskoye shosse

D0677586

Map 1   Central St Petersburg
(see previous page)

PLACES TO STAY

 2   Holiday Hostel
 3   Hotel St Petersburg
     Гостиница С.-Петербург
 6   Hotelship Peterhof
     Гостиница Петергоф
22   Hotel Rus
     Гостиница Русь
43   Hotel Helen-Sovietskaya
     Гостиница Гелен-Советская
58   Hotel Moskva
     Гостиница Москва
61   Kievskaya Hotel
     Гостиница Киевская
62   Hotel Zarya
     Гостиница Заря

PLACES TO EAT

 4   Kalinka Stockmann's
 8   Kafe Fregat
     Кафе Фрегат
10   1001 Nights
     Ресторан 1001 Ночь
16   Club Ambassador
     Клуб Амбассадор
29   Senat Bar
     Сенат Бар
30   Le Bistro Café
     Кафе - Бистро
49   Restoran Na Fontanke
     Ресторан на Фонтанке
51   Montreal Steak
54   Mollies Irish Bar
     Молис ирландский бар

OTHER

 1   Kresty Prison
     Кресты Тюрма
 5   Morskaya Pristan (Landing)
     Морская пристань
 9   Hermitage Theatre
     Эрмитажный театр
11   Japanese Consulate
     Консульство Японии
12   French Consulate
     Консульство Франции
13   Marble Palace
     Мраморный дворец
14   Summer Palace
     Летний дворец
15   Engineers' Castle
     Инженерный замок

METRO STATIONS

NICK SELBY

Bronze Horseman (Peter the Great)

St Petersburg

a Lonely Planet
city guide

Nick Selby

St Petersburg
1st edition

Published by
Lonely Planet Publications
Head Office: PO Box 617, Hawthorn, Vic 3122, Australia
Branches: 155 Filbert St, Suite 251, Oakland,
CA 94607, USA
10 Barley Mow Passage, Chiswick,
London W4 4PH, UK
71 bis rue du Cardinal Lemoine,
75005 Paris, France

Printed by
SNP Printing Pte Ltd, Singapore

Photographs by
Nick Selby, Roger Hayne, Kari Voutilainen, Grant Faint,
Markus Lehtipuu, John Noble

Front cover: Tsars Symbol, St Petersburg (Grant Faint,
Image Bank)
Front gatefold: Top: Headed to Market (Nick Selby)
Bottom: St Petersburg (Kari Voutilainen)
Back gatefold: St Petersburg courtyard (Nick Selby)
Title page: Beloselsky-Belozersky Palace (Nick Selby)

First Published
Feburary 1996

National Library of Australia Cataloguing in Publication Data

Selby, Nick
St Petersburg

1st ed.
Includes index.
ISBN 0 86442 326 8.

1. St Petersburg (Russia) – Guidebooks. I. Title.
(Series: Lonely Planet city guide).

914.74530486

Nick Selby

Nick was born and raised in New York City. He worked for five years as a sound engineer, but after 3½ years in a two-metre-by-two-metre cubicle mixing music for an American soap opera, he decided that anything – *anything* – would be a step up. In 1990 he took a job as a morning DJ at Warsaw's first privately owned radio station, Radio Zet, and soon afterwards did a stint as a creative director at a multinational advertising agency there (a post from which he was unceremoniously sacked). With another American expat, he set up a small publishing company in St Petersburg, and in 1992 he wrote *The Visitor's Guide to the New Saint Petersburg*, published by Fresh Air Publications. Since travelling around Asia and all too little of Australia in 1993, he now spends his time travelling and writing with Corinna, his wife.

From the Author

Many thanks to Eugene Patron, Steven Caron, Natasha Dovorets, Elena Vvedenskaya (twice), Lloyd Donaldson, Shannon Farley, Jan Passoff, Petri and the staff at the Helsinki Eurohostel. Also thank you John Noble, John King and Richard Nebesky; and at LP Australia: Andrew Tudor for coping and Jane Fitzpatrick and Lindsay Brown for staying calm; Charlotte, Andrea and Rachel at LP UK; Angela Wilson, Bernard Goldstein, Marlies and Mutti, Nancy, John & Ben, Regina Shoykut, Carolyn Djanogly, Tom Brosnahan, Rande and Kathleen at Travel By Design, Miami Beach; the Artilleriestrasse: Reiner, Sabine, Anja, Fetah & Gino, Herbert; and of course, Corinna.

This Book

This first edition of St Petersburg was written by Nick Selby in the course of his research for the first edition of Lonely Planet's *Russia, Ukraine & Belarus*. It drew on the introductory and Leningrad chapters of LP's *USSR* which were written by John Noble & John King.

From the Publisher

This book was edited and proofed by Lindsay Brown and Lynn McGaurr with help from Jane Fitzpatrick, Nick Tapp, Katie Cody, Anne Mulvaney and Suzi Petkovsky. Chris Klep drew the maps with assistance from Andrew Tudor, and Rachel Black did the design and layout with help from Tamsin Wilson. Richard Nebesky and Kolya Cowall proofed the Cyrillic, Lou Callan edited the Language section, Dan Levin produced the Cyrillic font and Simon Bracken and Andrew Tudor designed the cover.

Warning & Request

Things change – prices go up, schedules change, good places go bad and bad places go bankrupt – nothing stays the same. So if you find things better or worse, recently opened or long since closed, please write and tell us and help make the next edition better.

Your letters will be used to help update future editions and, where possible, important changes will also be included in a Stop Press section in reprints.

We greatly appreciate all information that is sent to us by travellers. Back at Lonely Planet we employ a hard-working readers' letters team to sort through the many letters we receive. The best ones will be rewarded with a free copy of the next edition or another Lonely Planet guide if you prefer. We give away lots of books, but, unfortunately, not every letter/postcard receives one.

Contents

Maps

Introduction

If Moscow is Europe's most Asiatic capital, St Petersburg is Russia's most European city. Created by Peter the Great as his 'window on the West' at the only point where traditional Russian territory meets a seaway to Northern Europe, it was built with 18th and 19th-century European pomp and orderliness by mainly European architects. The result is a city that remains one of Europe's most beautiful: where Moscow intimidates, St Petersburg enchants.

The vistas of elegant buildings across the wide Neva River and along the canals and avenues recall Paris, Amsterdam and Venice. But St Petersburg's beauty, happily little harmed by Stalinist reconstruction, is of a brand all its own.

The jolly onion domes of Moscow seem almost passé here, where a more Western outlook was taken at every stage of planning and construction. Even the colour of the city's buildings: the green and gold of the Winter Palace, the red beside the Anichkov Bridge, the blue of Smolny Cathedral, reflect a stylistic allegiance more to the courts of Europe than the Kremlin. The buildings' playful Baroque façades simply exude the riotous opulence of tsarist Russia. Today, despite their well-publicised problems, residents feel enough affection for their city to call it simply 'Piter' and visitors' taste buds are now receiving a much improved welcome from new private and foreign restaurant ventures. Reform and transformation is giving the city a facelift that's about 73 years overdue.

The spirit of reform is so alive here it's palpable; small Russian-owned businesses are popping up everywhere, Western businesses are following suit (cue Pizza Hut, McDonald's and the rest), and even the city itself is getting in on the money train by (get this) accepting corporate sponsorship of street signs. That's not your imagination, that street sign does say 'USA Today'. And the deification process has turned 180 degrees: the Order of Lenin plaque at the ploshchad Vosstania metro station was replaced with a Marlboro cigarette ad.

St Petersburg is chock-full of history: from here two centuries of autocratic tsars ruled Russia with the splendour and stubbornness that led to their downfall at the hands of its workers and soldiers in March 1917. Here that same year, Lenin came back from exile to drive his Bolshevik Party to power.

The city's two centuries as Russia's capital bequeathed it an artistic and entertainment scene which still leads Russia today. Russian ballet was born here and the 19th-century flowering of Russian music was centred here. Nijinsky, Tchaikovsky and Rimsky-Korsakov, to name but a few, spent important periods here. Pushkin was educated in, exiled from, re-admitted to and killed in St Petersburg; Dostoevsky set *Crime and Punishment* here, and Akhmatova penned her moving poetry about life in what was then Leningrad.

At one end of the cultural spectrum today are the Hermitage, one of the world's great art museums, housed in the tsars' superb Winter Palace, and the Kirov Ballet, which has recently overshadowed Moscow's Bolshoy. At the other end, St Petersburg has produced many of Russia's top rock bands; wealthy young Russians spend sultry summer evenings partying in dozens of Western-style nightclubs, or at rave parties that run all night long, with laser shows, top dance hits and DJs imported from the UK, Sweden or, in many cases, Africa.

St Petersburg's latitude, level with Seward, Alaska; and Cape Farewell, Greenland, gives it nearly 24-hour daylight in midsummer but long, grey winters. From June to August, when temperatures usually reach 20°C, the city is absolutely packed with foreign and Russian tourists. From December to March, when the Neva is ice and temperatures rarely exceed freezing, the long nights have a twinkling magic; the sun lazily lobs itself skyward at around 10 am and decides to call it a day around 3 pm.

Facts about
St Petersburg

HISTORY

Alexandr of Novgorod defeated the Swedes near the mouth of the Neva in 1240, earning the title Nevsky (literally, 'of the Neva'). Sweden took control of the region in the 17th century and it was the desire of Peter I (the Great) to crush this rival and make Russia a European power that led to the founding of the city. At the start of the Great Northern War (1700-21) he captured the Swedish outposts on the Neva, and in 1703 he founded the Peter & Paul Fortress on the Neva a few km in from the sea. After Peter trounced the Swedes at Poltava in 1709 the city he named, in Dutch style, Sankt Pieter Burkh, really began to grow.

Peter the Great

Those Swedes weren't exactly pushovers; Peter's trounce was the result of no small measure of ruthlessness. And as one may suspect, the rapid growth of St Petersburg from a muddy mess to a lavishly constructed world capital was not accomplished through the Russian peasantry's eleemosynary views towards their Tsar.

Peasants were drafted as forced labour, many dying as a result. To raise money to construct the city, Peter taxed everything he could think of including beards and coffins and imposed the infamous 'Soul Tax' on all lower class adult males. Architects and artisans were brought from all over Europe. Canals were dug to drain the marshy south bank, and in 1712 he made the place his capital, forcing administrators, nobles and merchants to move here and build new homes. What's more, anyone entering the city would have to bring building supplies with them – wagons were checked at the city line.

The upper classes were also thrown into a tizzy by Peter's edicts on their performance: aristocrats could either serve in the army or the civil service, or lose their titles and land. Previously bequeathed birth status counted for little, as state servants were subject to Peter's new Table of Ranks, a performance-based ladder of promotion with the upper grades conferring hereditary nobility. Some aristocrats lost all they had, while capable state employees of humble origin and even foreigners became Russian nobles.

Peter mobilised Russian resources to compete on equal terms with the West, eclipsing all but the most powerful nations of the day, a startling achievement. His territorial gains were small, but the strategic Baltic territories added ethnic variety, including a new class of German traders and administrators who formed the backbone of Russia's commercial and military expansion.

He was also to have the last word on the authority of the Church. When it resisted his reforms he simply blocked the appointment of a new patriarch, put bishops under a government department and in effect made himself the head of the Church.

By Peter's death in 1725 his city had a population of 40,000 and 90% of Russia's foreign trade passed through it. The south bank around the Admiralty had become the centre.

Peter died without naming a successor. Had it not been for a government structure built on the Table of Ranks and a professional bureaucracy with a vested interest in its preservation, Peter's reforms might well have died with him.

After Peter

Peter's immediate successors moved the capital back to Moscow but Empress Anna Ioannovna (1730-40) returned to St Petersburg. Between 1741 and 1825 under Empress Elizabeth, Catherine the Great and Alexander I it became a cosmopolitan city with a royal court of famed splendour. These monarchs commissioned great series of palaces, government buildings and churches, which turned it into one of Europe's grandest capitals.

Catherine II (the Great)

Of Russia's female leaders, none is more famous, and infamous, than Catherine II. Born Sophie Fredericke Augusta in what is now Szczecin, Poland, on 2 May 1729, Catherine was the daughter of the German prince of Anhalt-Zerbst. At 15, young Sophie went to Russia to marry Peter, Empress Elizabeth's nephew and heir to the Russian throne (later, Catherine said of Peter: 'I believe the Crown of Russia attracted me more than his person'). On Elizabeth's death, Christmas day 1761, Peter became Peter III.

Peter III was not only widely disliked, but he was widely disliked by powerful members of his military who soon felt, as did his wife, that perhaps his wife should take over. This was accomplished in June 1762, when a party of officers (led by the brother of one of Catherine's lovers) arrested and subsequently killed Peter, and Catherine became ruler of Russia.

While many claim that Catherine was something of a sex fiend (rumours persist that she 'had more lovers than a serf had hot dinners' and that she got a 'charge' from bestiality), it would seem that she was the target of some deft propaganda by jealous male members of the court. Her diaries are said to list fewer than ten lovers, though some do run concurrently, which seems to put her somewhere to the more conservative side of... well, Madonna, anyway.

Catherine as Leader Catherine's legacy stems from her constant self-education and love of culture. She was a big fan of Enlightenment, and brought Russia forward by leaps and bounds in terms of Westernisation. She established, in 1767, an Assembly of Deputies to draft new laws, and wrote the *Nakaz* – instructions or guidelines. She instituted wide-scale reforms in the military as well as the peasantry, and encouraged industrial and agricultural growth and trade.

This is not to say that Catherine was a bleeding heart. Her reign saw expansion through naval victory at Çeşme (Chesma), which ended in a 1774 treaty giving Russia control of the north coast of the Black Sea and 'protectorship' of Christian interests in the Ottoman Empire – a pretext for later incursions into the Balkans. In Poland she adroitly installed a former lover as king, and expanded her control over what is now roughly present-day Lithuania, Belarus and western Ukraine. She showed ruthlessness during the rebellion of 1773-74, led by the Don Cossack Yemelyan Pugachov, who claimed that he was Peter III. Pugachov's rebellion, which spread from the Ural Mountains to the Caspian Sea and along the Volga, was Russia's most violent uprising to date. Hundreds of thousands responded to his promises to end serfdom and taxation, but they were beaten by famine and government armies. Pugachov was executed and that was it for Cossack autonomy.

But Catherine was benevolent, or at least pragmatic, by the standards of the time. To boost the efficiency of local government, Catherine replaced Peter's 12 provinces with 50 of roughly equal size, each with a governor. The lowest district administrative level was formed by land-holders, newly freed from Peter's compulsory state service.

Catherine's most visible bequest was to bring Russia to the world stage of arts and letters. She freed up regulations and restrictions on publishing and increased the number of schools and colleges. Her vast collection of paintings forms the core of the present-day Hermitage museum collection. And Catherine went on an architectural commissioning spree, inviting dozens of Western European architects to change the face of St Petersburg.

Her palaces are to this day reminders of the wealth, power and opulence enjoyed by the Russian nobility, and Catherine put them up almost as quickly as postwar Soviet engineers slapped together the hideous prefabricated buildings that mar the landscape of so many Russian and Eastern European cities.

Alexander I

When Catherine died in 1796 the throne passed to her son, Paul I. An old-school autocrat, he antagonised the gentry with attempts to reimpose compulsory state service and was killed in a coup in 1801. So much for Paul I.

Paul's son, Alexander I (who had been Catherine's favourite grandson), had been trained by the best European tutors and kicked off his reign with several reforms, including an expansion of the school system that brought education within reach of the lower-middle classes. But he was soon preoccupied with wars against Napoleon which were to dominate his career.

After being defeated by Napoleon at Austerlitz, north of Vienna, in 1805 and then at Friedland, near modern Kaliningrad, Alexander began to negotiate. The Treaty of Tilsit (1807) left Napoleon in charge as Emperor of the West and Alexander as Emperor of the East, both of them (in theory) united against England.

1812

The alliance lasted only until 1810, when Russia resumed trade with England. A hopping mad little Napoleon decided to crush the Tsar with a Grand Army of 700,000, the largest force the world had ever seen for a single military operation.

Rather than meet the Grand Army in Prussia or Poland, Alexander shrewdly drew it into the vast Russian countryside in the summer of 1812, scorching the earth to deny the French sustenance. Napoleon set his sights on Moscow, the symbolic heart of Russia. A bloody but inconclusive battle was joined at Borodino, 130 km west of Moscow, with the Russians withdrawing in good order.

In September Napoleon entered a deserted Moscow; a few days later the city was burnt down around him. Feeling awfully silly standing there amidst the ashes of a city that isn't so hot even when it's built up, and with winter coming and his supply lines overstretched, Napoleon ordered a retreat – he was unable to do anything else. His troops, harassed by Russian Partisans, froze and starved. Only one in 20 made it back to the relative safety of Poland, and the Russians pursued them all the way to Paris.

The Decembrists

Alexander's death without a clear heir in 1825 sparked the usual crisis. His reform-minded brother Constantine, married to a Pole and living happily in Warsaw, thank you very much, had no interest in the throne. Officers who had brought back liberal ideas from Paris in 1815 preferred him to Alexander's youngest brother, the militaristic Nicholas, who was due to be crowned on 26 December 1825. Their rally in St Petersburg was quashed by troops loyal to Nicholas, who threw those who weren't killed into the Peter & Paul Fortress. Nicholas demanded to look each so-called Decembrist traitor in the face before pronouncing sentence, psychologically terrorising many (executing some, while subjecting many others to mock executions, complete with blindfolds and macabre pronouncements, only to be told at the very last second that their sentences had been 'commuted'; after which they were exiled). More than 100 were sent into Siberian exile.

The remainder of Nicholas' reign was as inauspicious as the beginning; though he granted title to peasants on state land (effectively freeing them) and restored trade with England, his foreign policy accomplished little else than to annoy everyone in the Balkans, most of the rest of Europe, and to start the Crimean War, in which England and France sided against Russia. Inept command on both sides resulted in a bloody stalemated war.

Alexander II & the 'Great Reforms'

Nicholas died in 1855. His son, Alexander II, saw the Crimean War stirring up discontent within Russia and accepted peace on unfavourable terms. The war had revealed the backwardness behind the post-1812 imperial glory and the time for reform had come.

The serfs were freed in 1861. Of the land they had worked, roughly a third was kept by established landholders. The rest went to village communes, which assigned it to individuals in return for 'redemption payments' to compensate former land-holders – a system that pleased no-one.

But the abolition of serfdom opened the way for a market economy, capitalism and an industrial revolution. Railroads and factories were built and cities expanded as peasants left the land. Nothing, though, was done to modernise farming, and the peasants found their lot had not improved in half a century.

In the reign of Alexander II (1855-81) and his son, Alexander III (1881-94), Central Asia came under Russian control. In the east, Russia acquired a long strip of Pacific coast from China and built the port of Vladivostok, but sold the 'worthless' Alaskan territories to the USA in 1867 for just US$7.2 million (the US was said to also be in the market for a slice of mainland Siberia, but the Russians apparently asked too high a price for it).

But the loosening of restrictions and rapid change in the make-up of Russian society took its toll. The emancipation of the serfs and industrialisation brought a flood of poor workers into St Petersburg, leading to overcrowding, poor sanitation, epidemics and festering discontent. Revolutionary sentiment was rife, and radicals were plotting the overthrow of the Tsarist government as early as the second half of the 19th century. Alexander II was assassinated in St Petersburg by a terrorist bomb in 1881.

Most of the more reactionary members of society (that is, those expressing dissent of any sort) were rounded up and either executed or exiled, and the reign of Alexander III was marked by repression of revolutionaries and liberals alike.

The Russo-Japanese War

It's hard to imagine this today, but at the turn of the century, St Petersburg's dabbling in Asian affairs created problems. Port Arthur, home of the Russian Fleet during China's Boxer Uprising, was attacked by Japanese forces on 8 February 1904, after Russia refused to withdraw its troops from the region. The Russo-Japanese war which followed was quick, devastating and humiliating to the Tsar's forces.

Even the Trans-Siberian Railway didn't help the Tsar's army to move enough men and supplies from west to east, and Russia was soon losing any territory it defended in the region. After a series of defeats, the entire Russian flotilla that had been sent from the Baltic to the region was annihilated by Japanese forces in the Battle of Tsushima.

Throughout the war, the Tsar's strategy (as has always been the case in Russian military affairs) was to throw as many men (meaning hastily, in many cases violently, drafted peasant men) as he could at the Japanese. In this case, the drafting and subsequent butchering of young Russians caused a huge political backlash, and the series of defeats took their toll in the form of ever increasing civil unrest in St Petersburg. Under the terms of the peace treaty finally signed on 5 September 1905, Russia not only gave up Port Arthur, the larger half of Sakhalin Island and other properties, but also recognised Japanese predominance in Korea.

The 1905 Revolution

St Petersburg became a hotbed of strikes and political violence and the hub of the 1905 revolution, sparked by 'Bloody Sunday' 9 January 1905 when a strikers' march to petition the tsar in the Winter Palace was fired on by troops. The group was made up of about 150,000 workers, who were staging what many say was a peaceful protest (it was being led by Father Georgy Gapon, a priest). It's unclear how many of the demonstrators were killed (most estimates say several hundred, but some say as many as 1000), but what is certain is that the incident served to solidify ties between squabbling opposition factions by giving them a much better idea of whom the common enemy was.

In the months to follow, peasant uprisings, mutinies (most famously that aboard the Battleship Potyomkin) and other protests abounded. Soviets, or 'workers' councils', were formed by social democrat activists in St Petersburg and Moscow. The St Petersburg Soviet, led by Mensheviks (Minority People, who in fact outnumbered the Bolshevik, or Majority People's party) under Leon Trotsky, called for a massive general strike in October, that ground the country to a standstill.

These protests resulted in Tsar Nicholas' grudgingly issued 'October Manifesto', which, along with granting theretofore unheard of civil rights, laid the basis for the Duma, Russia's elected legislature. The Manifesto calmed an angry populace for the time being. By 1914, when in a wave of patriotism or at least anti-German sentiment at the start of WW I, the city's name was changed to the Russian-style Petrograd, it had 2.1 million people. But as soon as 1917, Petrograd would again be the cradle of revolution.

WW I

Tsar Nicholas' ham-fisted leadership during the formative years WW I (by most accounts Nicholas was both a perfectly likable fellow and an execrable leader) and a collapsing domestic policy were the straws that eventually broke the camel's back. After heavy losses in the first year of war, the second saw disasters at every turn, with Russian troops bogged down and suffering badly. While the brilliantly executed Brusilov Offensive, embarked upon after Austro-German forces mounted a spring offensive against Italy, was a military success, it produced an additional one million Russian casualties. Facing total losses of almost two million, and German incursions deep into the Russian homeland, the folks at home were not amused.

The 1917 Revolution

Actually, there were two. With all the confusion caused by the war, along with a breakdown in the chain of command and the increasing influence of the spooky Grigory Rasputin on the Tsar's wife, Alexandra, morale was very low. People were blaming Nicholas personally for failures of the Russian armies (which is what rightly happens if one insists on personally leading troops into slaughter). Political fragmentation had resulted in a powerful reincarnation of the Petrograd Soviet of Workers & Soldiers Deputies, based on the 1905 model. Workers' protests turned into a general strike and troops mutinied, forcing the end of the monarchy. On 1 March Nicholas abdicated about 38 seconds after he was 'asked' to by the Duma. Nick's brother Mikhail (probably shrewdly) declined to take the reigns of power, and the Romanov dynasty of over 300 years officially came to an end. A short time later, Nicholas and his entire family were dragged out to Yekaterinberg, (Boris Yeltsin's home town) just east of the Ural mountains; they were later murdered and buried in a mass grave.

A provisional government announced that general elections would be held in November. The Petrograd Soviet started meeting in the city's Tauride Palace alongside the country's reformist Provisional Government. It was to Petrograd's Finland Station that Lenin travelled in April to organise the Bolshevik Party, and against Petrograd that the loyalist General Kornilov marched his troops in August, only to be headed off by rebel soldiers and armed workers from the city. A former girls' college in the city, the Smolny Institute, became the focus as the Bolsheviks took control of the Petrograd Soviet, which had by then installed itself there.

During the summer, tensions were raised considerably by the existence of two power bases: the Provisional Government and the Petrograd Soviet. The Bolsheviks' propaganda campaign was winning over a substantial number of people who, understandably, thought that the slogan 'Peace, Land and Bread' was a good maxim by which to live (though the Sovs always had a bit of a tough time with that last part). Tensions were high; Lenin thought that the time for a Soviet coup was then. But a series of violent mass demonstrations in July, inspired by the Bolsheviks, was in the end not fully backed by them, and was quelled. Lenin fled to Finland, and Alexandr Kerensky, a moderate Social Revolutionary, became prime minister.

In September, the Russian military chief-of-staff, General Kornilov, sent cavalry to Petrograd to crush the soviets. Kerensky turned to the left for support against this insubordination, even courting the Bolsheviks, and the counter-revolution was defeated. After this, public opinion massively favoured the Bolsheviks, who quickly took control of the Petrograd Soviet (chaired by Trotsky, who had joined them) and, by extension, all the soviets in the land. Lenin (you'll remember he was cowering in Finland through all this) decided it was time to seize power, and returned from Finland in October.

The actual 'Great October Soviet etc, etc', revolution came after Bolsheviks occupied key positions in Petrograd on 24 October. Next day the All-Russian Congress of Soviets, meeting in the Smolny, appointed a Bolshevik government. That night, after some exchanges of gunfire and a blank shot from the cruiser *Aurora* on the Neva (which served to show the navy's allegiance to the uprising), the Provisional Government in the Winter Palace surrendered to the Bolsheviks.

Armistice was signed with the Germans in December, 1917, followed by the treaty of Brest-Litovsk in March 1918 that surrendered Poland, the Baltic provinces, Ukraine, Finland and Transcaucasia to the Germans. This negotiation for a separate peace with Germany enraged (but probably didn't shock) the Allied forces, who would later back anti-Bolshevik fighters in a nose-thumbing effort to punish the revolutionaries for taking their ball and going home. Germany, with its eastern boundaries out of harm's way, could turn its attentions towards Western European annoyances (not that it ended up helping much).

The Civil War

There was wide dissent after the revolution, and a number of political parties sprang up almost immediately to challenge the Bolsheviks' power. And the Bolsheviks found themselves the proud new owners of all the same problems that had plagued governments before them. The power struggle began peacefully in the November elections for the Constituent Assembly, the Socialist Revolutionaries won a sweeping victory, only to have the assembly shut down by a very mad Vlad but before long, a multi-sided civil war would erupt. Trotsky founded the Red Army in January 1918, and the Cheka, Russia's secret police force designed to fight opposition, was established.

The new government operated from the Smolny until March 1918, when it moved to Moscow fearing attacks on Petrograd from within and without. Civil war raged until 1921, by which time the Communist Party had firmly established one-party rule, thanks to the Red Army and the Cheka, which continued to eliminate opponents. Some escaped, joining an estimated 1.5 million citizens in exile.

The privations of the Civil War caused Petrograd's population to drop to about 700,000, and in 1921 strikes in the city and a revolt by the sailors of nearby Kronstadt helped bring about Lenin's more liberal New Economic Policy (NEP).

Petrograd was renamed Leningrad after his death in 1924. It was a hub of Stalin's 1930s industrialisation programme and by 1939 had 3.1 million people and 11% of Soviet industrial output. But Stalin (probably rightly) feared it as a rival power base and the 1934 assassination of the local Communist chief Sergey Kirov at Smolny was the start of his 1930s Party purge.

NICK SELBY

Victory Day poster, Nevsky prospekt

WW II

When the Germans attacked the USSR in June 1941 it took them only 2½ months to reach Leningrad. Hitler hated the place as the birthplace of Bolshevism, and he swore to wipe it from the face of the earth. His troops besieged it from 8 September 1941 until 27 January 1944. Many people (and three-quarters of the industrial plant) had been evacuated. Nevertheless, between 500,000 and a million people died from shelling, starvation and disease in what's called the '900 Days' (actually 872). By comparison the USA and UK suffered about 700,000 dead between them in all of WW II.

Leningraders dropped dead of hunger or cold in the streets and when no cats or rats were left they ate glue off the back of wallpaper. The city was saved from an even worse fate by the winter 'Road of Life' across frozen Lake Ladoga to the east, a thin supply line which remained in Soviet hands.

The Postwar Period

After the war, Leningrad was reconstructed and reborn, though it took until 1960 for the population to exceed prewar levels. The centre and most of the inner surrounding areas have been reconstructed, though the outlying areas (as is the case practically everywhere in Russia) are lined with horrific, cookie-cutter cities of prefabricated apartment blocks that go on forever. Throughout the Khrushchev and Brezhnev years (when you could 'still get bread in the shops'), Leningrad confined its revolutionary activities to the worlds of arts, letters and music, at which it excelled: it was indisputably the Soviet Union's cultural and artistic centre. Many of the period's more innovative artistic contributions, such as rock music, came to the Soviet world through Leningrad.

The 1980s & Gorbachev

After Brezhnev's death in 1982 (it was only noticed in 1984), he was replaced by former KGB director Yuri Andropov. But shortly after the requisite celebrations and hullabaloo that accompanied a Soviet party chairman's installation, Andropov dropped dead. Still not satisfied that Brezhnev's contemporaries were a bit past it, the Supreme Soviet (still staffed by many hard-line Brezhnev supporters) appointed yet another crony, Constantin Chernyenko, who expired even before he could replace the Kremlin curtains, after just 13 months in office.

Seeing the need for some new, or at least circulating, blood, Mikhail Sergeevich Gorbachev was installed in 1985 amidst much unintentionally ironic talk of 'getting things moving again'. Gorbachev launched an immediate turnover in the politburo, bureaucracy and military, replacing many of the Brezhnevite 'old guard' with his own, younger supporters. He clamped down on alcohol sales in an attempt to address a problem that was costing the Russian economy dearly: alcoholism. He also attempted to accelerate the economy and, most important, he announced a policy of *glasnost* (openness). The hope was that he could spur the economy by encouraging some management initiative, rewarding efficiency and letting bad practices be criticised.

Gorby, as he came to be known in the American and British tabloid press, stunned the world by adopting an extremely conciliatory attitude towards the West, and in his first summit meeting with US president Ronald Reagan in 1985, Gorbachev unilaterally suggested a 50% cut in long-range nuclear weapons. By 1987 the two superpowers had agreed to remove all medium-range nuclear missiles from Europe; other significant cuts in arms and troop numbers followed. The 'new thinking' put an end to the Soviet Union's 'Vietnam', the unpopular Afghanistan war. Relations with China improved as well; in 1989 Gorbachev went to Beijing for the first Sino-Soviet summit in 30 years.

Chernobyl & Perestroika

The shock of the Chernobyl nuclear disaster in April 1986 fuelled the drive towards political restructure at home. Gorbachev announced that there would be greater openness in reporting things like disasters. It had taken a very un-glasnost-like 18 days to admit the extent of the Chernobyl disaster to the West, which was underplayed, and even longer to inform the other socialist countries in the Warsaw Pact, and that was after prodding from Scandinavian and European observers who noted huge levels of radiation emanating from the region. It is worth noting that a now unclassified KGB document, commissioned and signed by Yuri Andropov, predicted the disaster on 21 February 1979, more than seven years before it occurred. The document cited, among other concerns,

... design deviations and violations of construction and assembly technology ... occurring at various places in the construction of the second generating unit of the Chernobyl AES ... could lead to mishaps and accidents.

Gorbachev's anti-alcohol campaign brought him nothing but unpopularity and caused huge growth in illegal distilling, and before long it was abandoned. But above all it was becoming clear that no leader who relied on the Party could survive as a reformer. *Perestroika*, or 'restructuring', became the new cry. This meant limited private enterprise and private property, not unlike Lenin's NEP, and further efforts to push decision making into the grass roots, away from the central bureaucracy. New laws were enacted in both these fields in 1988.

The 'Sinatra Doctrine'

The forces unleashed by Gorbachev's laudable reforms were hard to control (to say the least) and precipitated the fall of the Soviet Union. With reduced threat of repression a growing clamour for independence was spurred: first in the Soviet satellite states of Eastern Europe, followed by the Baltic Republics, then Moldavia, then the Transcaucasian republics. The Eastern European countries threw off their puppet Soviet regimes one by one in the 'domino' autumn of 1989. The Berlin Wall fell on 9 November, spurring a whole new market for chunks of asbestos-laden cement. The Brezhnev Doctrine, Gorbachev's spokesperson said, had given way to the 'Sinatra Doctrine': letting them do it their way. Over the next two years, the Soviet Union was engaged in maintaining control of its republics and its borders, sometimes through the use of the army, but it was never able to close the floodgates.

In what was a minor annoyance at the time, in a June 1991 referendum, residents of the city of Leningrad voted to rename the city St Petersburg. They passed the referendum (though it's interesting that the region around the city refused to join in the fun and to this day calls itself the Leningradsky oblast), but the measure was stopped by Gorbachev and only ratified after the events of August 1991 (note the building of suspense). In presidential elections, also held in June 1991, Boris Yeltsin won by a good majority the title of President of the Russian Republic.

1991 Coup

On 19 August 1991, a group of hardline Party loyalists staged what was perhaps the most inept coup of the 20th century. While Gorbachev was on holiday at his Crimean *dacha*, it was announced in Moscow that a 'state of emergency' was in effect; that Gorbachev was feeling quite poorly and would be unable to continue as leader.

A self-appointed Committee of the State Emergency announced that it was in power.

Tanks appeared on the streets of Moscow, and Yeltsin joined a group of protesters at the Russian Parliament's headquarters, the White House. When tanks approached, Yeltsin, in full view of CNN and other television cameras, leapt aboard one and implored the tank crew to use their heads and hold their fire.

Over the next several days in Moscow, the crowds of protesters grew and grew, and the disorganised plotters gradually fell apart, drank a lot of vodka, lost control and gave up.

Showing an astounding ignorance of coup etiquette, the plotters neglected to turn off several avenues of communication with the West. From the 'what on earth were they thinking' department: Western news cameras and reporters were allowed to report almost unhindered, and cellular telecommunications and electronic mail were left intact, while an order early in the coup from the government placed a ban on, among other and of all things, home video recorders.

Swan Lake When Leningrad residents tuned on their televisions and radios and saw and heard 'Swan Lake' they took to the streets in protest. (For some reason Swan Lake is the programme of choice during governmental upheaval in Russia; a curator at the Russian Museum said that the next time he hears it he's hopping on a plane to Finland.) Anatoly Sobchak, a reformer who had been elected in 1989 to the St Petersburg city council, and became mayor in 1990, achieved a new height in obfuscatory oratory when he stormed into the regional military headquarters and talked them out of carrying out their Moscow-issued orders to arrest him.

As hundreds of thousands of Leningrad protesters filled Palace Square, Sobchak appeared on local television denouncing the coup and asking local residents to do the same. Fearful but determined residents spent a jittery evening awaiting the tanks that Moscow had threatened to send in, but they never appeared.

After the Coup

A rather sheepish but healthy-looking Gorbachev returned to Moscow and announced that he was back in power. Yeltsin had been so public a rallying figure that it would have been foolish in the extreme to try and deny it, which is precisely what Gorbachev did by acting as if all was fine and everyone could go home now. Soon after, Yeltsin appeared on television, proclaiming the

Communist Party an illegal organisation, and what
fragile threads remained of a Soviet Union were ripped
apart. On 25 December 1991, Gorbachev resigned, and
the Soviet Union was officially pronounced dead. Next
day, the Russian Federation's flag of red, white and blue
flew over the Kremlin.

The Mid-90s

Today St Petersburg is a cosmopolitan city with a lively
cultural and artistic core. Foreign and Russian business
is quickly setting down roots. St Petersburg is Russia's
biggest port, and a huge industrial centre.

Plans for making St Petersburg a tax-free port went
the way of the dodo, but foreign business in the city is
booming. Corny and over-used as the term may be, St
Petersburg has in fact re-established itself as Russia's
window on the West.

In October 1993, when radical politicians in Moscow
threatened the Russian government, St Petersburg again
remained aloof as the situation in the capital went literally ballistic.

In 1994, the Goodwill Games were (as perhaps all Goodwill Games are) a disappointment in terms of turnout, but
the preparations for them were a huge shot in the arm for
the city, which invested millions of dollars in repairs and
generally sprucing up the place. Roads were patched,
stadiums renovated, buildings painted, parks manicured
and replanted, and English-language signs began sprout-
ing up everywhere. The police and traffic police even
received new uniforms, and since the traffic cops are absolutely everywhere, even that helped the city's image.

And with all Moscow's in-fighting, dirty politics and
entrenched lobbyist sub-culture, more than a few people
are thinking that maybe Peter the Great had the right
idea in moving a tumultuous country's capital northward, to the city on the Neva.

ORIENTATION

St Petersburg sprawls across and around the delta of the
Neva River, at the end of the easternmost arm of the Baltic
Sea, known as the Gulf of Finland. Entering St Petersburg
at the city's south-eastern corner, the Neva first flows
north and then turns west across the middle of the city,
dividing there into several branches and forming the
islands of the delta. The two biggest branches, diverging
in front of the Winter Palace on the south bank, are the
Bolshaya (Big) and Malaya (Small) Neva, which flow
into the sea either side of Vasilevsky Island.

The heart of St Petersburg is the area spreading back from the Winter Palace and the Admiralty on the south bank, its skyline dominated by the golden dome of St Isaac's Cathedral. Nevsky prospekt, stretching east-south-east from the Admiralty, is the main street, with many of the city's sights, shops and restaurants. Nevsky prospekt crosses three waterways cutting across from the Neva to the sea, the biggest being the Fontanka River.

The north side of the city has three main areas. The westernmost is Vasilevsky Island, at whose east end, the Strelka, stand many of the city's fine early buildings. The middle area is Petrograd Side, a cluster of delta islands whose south end is marked by the tall gold spire of the SS Peter & Paul Cathedral. This is where the city began. These two islands, or 'sides' are often abbreviated on local maps and written directions as 'VS' (Vasilevsky Side') and 'PS' (Petrograd Side).

The third, eastern, area is Vyborg Side, divided from Petrograd Side by the Bolshaya Nevka channel (not to be confused with the Bolshaya Neva) and stretching east along the north bank of the Neva.

Name Changes

While St Petersburg is still in the process of renaming many of its streets, in many cases simply restoring the pre-communist names, there have already been such fundamental changes to the names of the city's streets that any map more than three years old is useless. More infuriating, residents sometimes refer to renamed streets, even major ones, by their old name. The box shows street (and other) name changes that were in place in May 1995; newer changes may be found in publications such as the *St Petersburg Press*, the Russian-language and English-indexed yellow pages *Ves Peterburg* and *The Traveller's Yellow Pages*. In this book the new street names are referred to. In the case of two, Kamennoostrovsky prospekt (formerly Kirovsky prospekt) and ulitsa Bolshaya Morskaya (formerly ulitsa Gertsena), we'll put the old name in parenthesis next to the new, as most Petersburgers just can't seem to take those changes to heart.

St Petersburg has two streets called Bolshoy prospekt: one on Petrograd Side, one on Vasilevsky Island. The two sides of some Vasilevsky Island streets are known as lines *(linii)* and opposite sides of these streets have different names – thus 4-ya linia (4th line) and 5-ya linia (5th line) are the east and west sides of the same street – which collectively is called 4-ya i 5-ya linii (4th and 5th lines).

Name Changes in St Petersburg
Streets

New Name	Old Name
Admiralteysky Kanala naberezhnaya	naberezhnaya Kanala Krushteyna
Atamanskaya ulitsa	ulitsa Krasnogo Elektrika
Bolshaya Konyushennaya ulitsa	ulitsa Zhelyabova
Bolshaya Monetnaya ulitsa	ulitsa Skorokhodova
Bolshoy Sampsonevsky prospekt	prospekt Karla Marxa
Furshtadtskaya ulitsa	ulitsa Petra Lavrova
Galernaya ulitsa	Krasnaya ulitsa
Gorokhovaya ulitsa	ulitsa Dzerzhinskogo
Grafsky pereulok	ulitsa Marii Ulyanovoy
Italyanskaya ulitsa	ulitsa Rakova
Kamennoostrovsky prospekt	Kirovsky prospekt
Karavannaya ulitsa	ulitsa Tolmacheva
Kavalergardskaya ulitsa	ulitsa Krasnoy Konnitsy
Kazanskaya ulitsa	ulitsa Plekhanova *
Konnogvardeysky bulvar	bulvar Profsoyuzov
Kronverksky prospekt	prospekt Maxim Gorkogo
Lanskoye shosse	prospekt N I Smirnova
Malaya Konyushennaya ulitsa	ulitsa Sofie Perovskoy
Malaya Morskaya ulitsa	ulitsa Gogolya
Malaya Posadskaya ulitsa	Bratev Vasilevykh ulitsa
Maly prospekt (Petrogradskoy storony)	prospekt Shchorsa
Maly Sampsonievsky prospekt	ulitsa Bratstva
Millionnaya ulitsa	ulitsa Khalturina
Moshkov pereulok	Zaporozhsky pereulok
Nikolskaya ploshchad	ploshchad Kommunarov
Novocherkassky prospekt	Krasnogvardeysky prospekt
Panteleymonovskaya ulitsa	ulitsa Pestelya
Pochtamtskaya ulitsa	ulitsa Soyuza Svyazy
Pochtamtsky pereulok	pereulok Podbelskogo
Polozova ulitsa	ulitsa Anny Ulyanovoy
Preobrazhenskaya ploshchad	Radishcheva ploshchad
Pribrezhnaya ulitsa	Kodatskogo ulitsa and Pogranichikov prospekt
Rizhsky prospekt	prospekt Ogorodnikova
Sennaya ploshchad	ploshchad Mira
Shpalernaya ulitsa	ulitsa Voynova
Sirenevy bulvar	Pelshe ulitsa
Staro-Petergofsky prospekt	prospekt Gaza
Troitskaya ploshchad	ploshchad Revolutsii
ulitsa Bolshaya Morskaya	ulitsa Gertsena
ulitsa Mikhailovskaya	ulitsa Brodskogo
Vitebskaya ulitsa	ulitsa Voytika
Voznesensky prospekt	prospekt Mayorova
Vvedenskaya ulitsa	ulitsa Olega Koshevogo
naberezhnaya Kanala Yekatarinski	naberezhnaya Kanala Griboedova **
Yeletskaya ulitsa	ulitsa Fotevoy
Yenotaevskaya ulitsa	ulitsa Fofanovoy
Zakharevskaya ulitsa	ulitsa Kalyaeva

* This street-name change had been suspended (there was already another Kazanskaya ulitsa).

** This street is still generally referred to only by its Soviet-era name; in this book we bow to general usage and use the old name.

Bridges

New Name	Old Name
Kharlamov most	Komsomolsky most
Panteleymonovsky most	most Pestelya
Sampsonevsky most	most Svobody
Silin most	Pionersky most
Troitsky most	Kirovsky most

Parks

New Name	Old Name
Alexandrovsky Sad	Sad imeni A M Gorkogo
Lopukhinsky Sad	Sad imeni F E Dzerzhinskogo
Udelny Park	Chelyuskintsev Park

Metro Stations

New Name	Old Name
Devyatkino	Komsomolskaya
Novocherkasskaya	Krasnogvardeyskaya
Sennaya Ploshchad	Ploshchad Mira

CLIMATE & WHEN TO GO

St Petersburg's climate is maritime, and much milder than its extreme northern latitude would suggest. January temperatures average -8°C ; a really cold day will get down to -15°C. It's a windy city though, and in some areas (near the Pribaltiskaya Hotel pops to mind) the wind chill is quite fierce, so bring a good warm hat and scarf.

Summer is cool and takes a while to get going: snow in late April is not uncommon, and the warm weather doesn't really get going until the period between June and August, when temperatures usually reach 20°C. Winter usually sees the Neva freeze over, though the past few years have been unusually mild. Despite its Baltic location and profusion of canals, rivers and waterways, humidity is not a problem.

That northern latitude means long days in summer and long nights in winter. During the summer White Nights festival, around the time of the summer solstice, night is reduced to a brief dimming of the lights at around 1 am, only to turn to dawn a couple of hours later. And in winter, the city would seem to be in a constant state of dusk.

When to go depends on what you're here for; the city is a year-round destination, so see the Things to See & Do chapter. In winter, hotels and tourist attractions are less crowded, and while some describe the winter weather

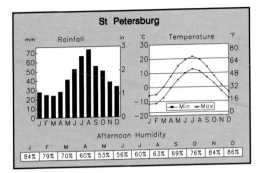

St Petersburg

merely as 'dark', there's a twinkling magic about the winter sky that others find very romantic. And while white nights are undeniably beautiful, some will find it rather disconcerting to look out a hotel window and think it's about 8 pm when it's really 3 am! Practically speaking, most attractions other than the statuary in the Summer Garden and the like are open year round. If you do go in winter, remember that it gets very slushy, so bring along good waterproof boots or rubbers. And in summer, dive-bombing mosquitoes are rife (St Petersburg was built on a swamp); bring mosquito repellent (see the Dangers & Annoyances section in Facts for the Visitor chapter).

Pollution

Air Thanks to St Petersburg's wide streets and prevalent winds, the place is relatively smog free, but that's not for lack of trying. Cars roam free without the encumbrance of catalytic converters or pollution control devices and trucks and buses emit unbelievable clouds of soot-filled exhaust, and that is only part of the story. St Petersburg's industrial plant is a major air and water polluter, and the situation is not getting any better, despite attempts at clean-up by Scandinavian and other Western observers and firms. But at the end of the day, the air quality here is about on a par with that of other developing cities.

Radiation St Petersburg's semi-infamous Sosnovy Bor nuclear power plant, about 70 km west of the city, threatened to blow its stack in 1992 (it didn't). It's an RBMK-style reactor, the same model as the doomed

Chernobyl reactor, except this one's older. It's also highly maintained and continually prodded by foreign experts (it's close enough to Scandinavian countries to make them take active interest). Radiation levels in the city are said to be at international norms.

POPULATION & PEOPLE

The number of residents in the city of St Petersburg in 1995 was estimated to be 4,829,000, or just over 5.5 million if the outer suburbs were included. As in much of the Russian Federation, the make-up of St Petersburg's population is almost entirely ethnic Russian. Minorities include Jews (still considered to be a nationality in Russia), Ukrainians, Belarusians and other nationalities from within the former Soviet Union. The expatriate community of Western businesspeople and students is continually growing; in 1994 there were an estimated 10,000 such residents, among them almost 3,500 Americans and an almost equal number of Germans. There are also significant numbers of students from African nations studying in the city.

ARTS

Architecture

Unrestricted by winding old streets or buildings from the past, the early European and European-trained designers of St Petersburg created a unique waterside city of straight avenues, wide plazas and grand edifices in the Baroque, Rococo and classical styles of the 18th and early 19th centuries.

Few major buildings had reached their final form by Peter the Great's death in 1725, though his version of Petergof Palace was complete and the SS Peter & Paul Cathedral and the Twelve Colleges were well under way. Empress Elizabeth (1741-61) commissioned the first grand wave of buildings, from Bartolomeo Rastrelli, an Italian who engraved her love of fun on the city's profile. His inspired creations like the Winter Palace, Smolny Cathedral and the Great Palace at Pushkin, playful in their Rococo detail yet majestic in form, mirrored her glittering court, which drew European diplomats, artists and travellers.

Catherine the Great and Alexander I launched fleets of projects to make St Petersburg Europe's most imposing capital, employing an international array of designers to beat the West at its own architectural games. Both monarchs rode the new wave of classical taste, whose increasing severity can be traced through some of their chief buildings. The Academy of Arts by J B M Vallin de la Mothe (France), Pavlovsk Palace by Charles Cameron (England) and the Hermitage Theatre by Giacomo Quarenghi (Italy) display the simpler, earlier classicism of Catherine's reign. Quarenghi's Smolny Institute for Alexander was halfway towards the later, heavier works of another Italian, Carlo Rossi, who created the Mikhail Palace (now the Russian Museum), the General Staff building and ploshchad Ostrovskogo.

The more grandiose branch of later classicism known as Russian Empire style is typified by the Kazan Cathedral and the Admiralty, both built by Russians for Alexander. The huge-domed St Isaac's Cathedral by Ricard de Montferrand (France), mostly built under Nicholas I (1825-55), was the city's last major classical building.

Painting & Sculpture

Icons Icons – images intended to aid the veneration of the holy subjects they depict, sometimes believed able to grant luck, wishes or even miracles – were the key art form up to the time of Peter the Great, though only in the 20th century did they really come to be seen as 'works of art'. They're most commonly found on the iconostasis of a church, the large screen in front of the east end sanctuary.

Icons were originally painted by monks as a spiritual exercise, and Byzantine rules decreed that only Christ, the Virgin, the angels, saints and scriptural events could be painted, all of which were supposed to be copies of a limited number of approved prototype images. Christ images include the Pantokrator (All-Ruler) and the Mandilion, called 'not made by hand' because it was supposedly developed from the imprint of Christ's face on St Veronica's handkerchief.

Icons were traditionally painted in tempera (inorganic pigment mixed with a binder like egg yolk) on wood. When they faded they were often touched up, obscuring the original work.

Peredvizhniki In the 18th century, when Peter the Great encouraged Western trends in Russian art, Dmitry Levitsky's portraits were the outstanding achievement. The major artistic force of the 19th century was the Peredvizhniki (Wanderers) movement, which saw art as a force for national awareness and social change. The movement gained its name from the touring exhibitions which helped it gather a wide audience. The Peredvizhniki artists were patronised by the industrialists

NICK SELBY

ROGER HAYNE

Top: School excursion to Palace Square
Bottom: Photographs for tourists, Kazan Cathedral

NICK SELBY

ROGER HAYNE

Top: Help is never far away
Bottom: 'Time of the Tsars' musician

Savva Mamontov, whose Abramtsevo estate near Moscow became an artists' colony, and Pavel Tretyakov. They included Vasily Surikov, who painted vivid Russian historical scenes, Nikolai Ge (biblical and historical scenes), and Ilya Repin, perhaps the best loved of all Russian artists, who ranged from social criticism *(Barge Haulers on the Volga)* through history *(Zaporozhie Cossacks Writing a Letter to the Turkish Sultan)* to portraits of the famous.

Isaak Levitan, who revealed the beauty of the Russian landscape, was one of many others associated with the Peredvizhniki. The end-of-century genius Mikhail Vrubel, inspired by sparkling Byzantine and Venetian mosaics, showed early traces of Western influence.

Futurism Around the turn of the century the World of Art (Mir Iskusstva) movement in St Petersburg, led by Alexandr Benois and Sergey Diaghilev under the motto 'Art pure and unfettered', opened Russia up to Western innovations like Impressionism, Art Nouveau and Symbolism. From about 1905 Russian art became a maelstrom of groups, styles and -isms as it absorbed decades of European change in a few years before giving birth to its own avant-garde Futurist movements, which in turn helped Western art go head over heels.

Mikhail Larionov and Natalia Goncharova were the centre of the Cézanne-influenced Knave of Diamonds group (with which Vasily Kandinsky was associated) before developing neo-Primitivism, based on popular arts and primitive icons.

In 1915 Kazimir Malevich announced the arrival of Suprematism, declaring that his utterly abstract geometrical shapes with the black square representing the ultimate 'zero form' finally freed art from having to depict the material world and made it a doorway to higher realities. Another famed Futurist, who managed to escape subordinate -isms, was Vladimir Mayakovsky, who was also an acclaimed poet.

The Soviet Era Futurists turned to the needs of the revolution – education, posters, banners – with enthusiasm. They had a chance to act on their theories of how art shapes society. But at the end of the 1920s, Formalist (abstract) art fell out of favour. The Party wanted Socialist Realism. Striving workers, heroic soldiers and inspiring leaders took over; 2 million sculptures of Lenin and Stalin dotted the country; Malevich ended up painting portraits (penetrating ones) and doing designs for Red Square parades; Mayakovsky committed suicide.

After Stalin, an avant-garde 'Conceptualist' underground was allowed to surface. Ilya Kabakov painted or
sometimes just arranged the debris of everyday life to
show the gap between the promises and realities of
Soviet existence. Erik Bulatov's 'Sotsart' pointed to the
devaluation of language by ironically reproducing
Soviet slogans or depicting words disappearing over the
horizon. In 1962 the authorities set up a show of such
'unofficial' art at the Moscow Manezh; Khrushchev
called it 'dog shit' and sent it back underground. In the
mid-1970s it resurfaced in the Moscow suburbs only to
be literally bulldozed back down.

Eventually a thaw set in and the avant-garde became
international big business. In 1988, *A Fundamental
Lexicon* by Grisha Bruskin, a multipanelled iconostasis-
like work satirising both Soviet propaganda and the
Church, sold for £242,000 at a Sotheby's sale in Moscow.

The avant-garde of the 1990s is a disparate cluster of
artists of varying ability, with Malevich, Kabakov and
Bulatov among its gurus and Andrey Roiter, Vadim
Zakharov, Kostia Shchvedeshchotov, Andrey Monastyrsky
and Ivan Chuikov among its leading lights. Like all avant-
gardes, this one is largely ignored by the general public. To
see its work you must usually find your way to the few
specialist galleries.

The most popular painter in Russia is the religious artist
Ilya Glazunov – a staunch defender of the Russian Orthodox cultural tradition. Hundreds of thousands of people
visit exhibitions of his work. Moscow's Tretyakov Gallery
and St Petersburg's Russian Museum have the country's
chief collections of Russian art, while the Hermitage (St
Petersburg) and the Pushkin Fine Arts Museum (Moscow)
have world-famous West European collections. Both cities
also stage dozens of temporary exhibitions.

Literature

St Petersburg's status as cultural centre of Russia has a
lot to do with the writers and poets associated with it.
The list is a veritable 'Who's Who' of literary figures:
Pushkin, Dostoevsky, Lermontov (whose *Death of a Poet*
accused the government of plotting Pushkin's death),
Blok, Akhmatova ...

Pushkin, Russia's best-loved poet, was born in 1799.
After his graduation in 1817, Pushkin started living it up
in St Petersburg, and committed many of his liberal
ideas to paper. These papers eventually made their way
to the police, who were not amused; Pushkin was exiled
from St Petersburg in 1820, which probably is the only

reason he wasn't standing with the Decembrists in 1825 (he said so himself, later, to Nicholas I).

In the 1830s, Pushkin had lost popularity with the general Russian reading public, and had married Natalya Goncharova, with whom, some say, he was obsessed. He set up *The Contemporary*, a literary magazine, which was doomed to failure from the start despite Pushkin's tireless efforts to see it through. On 27 January 1837, Pushkin challenged Baron Georges D'Anthès, a French noble who had been openly courting Natalya, to a duel. Pushkin was shot and died two days later. His last flat is now a museum (see the Things to See & Do chapter).

ROGER HAYNE

Memorial to Nikolai Gogal, playwright and novelist

Pushkin's most famous work, published posthumously in 1841, is *The Bronze Horseman*, depicting the great flood of 1824. In it, the hopes and wishes of the people – represented here by the lowly clerk Yevgeni, who has lost his beloved in the flood – take on the conquering, empire building spirit of Peter the Great, represented by the animation of the bronze statue of him installed by Catherine the Great.

Dostoevsky's descriptions of St Petersburg's slums are legendary; and he was the first major writer to show fully the seedy, dangerous and filthy side of life in the grand Russian capital. For a walk through his *Crime and Punishment* and information on his last flat, now a museum, see the section on Sennaya ploshchad in the Things to See & Do chapter.

Alexandr Blok (1880-1921) took over where Dostoevsky left off, writing of prostitutes, drunks, Gypsies and other assorted rabble. Blok's sympathies to the revolutions of 1905 and 1917 were held up by the Bolsheviks – as was the work of Mayakovsky – as an example of an established writer who had come and seen the light; Blok's *The Twelve*, published in 1918 is pretty much a love-letter to Lenin. The flat where Blok spent the last eight years of his life is now a museum, see the section on Teatralnaya ploshchad in the Things to See & Do chapter.

No literary figure, though, is as inextricably linked to the fate of St Petersburg-Petrograd-Leningrad as Anna Akhmatova, the long suffering poet whose work contains bittersweet depictions of the city she so loved. Akhmatova's life was filled with sorrow and loss – her family imprisoned and killed, her friends exiled, tortured and arrested, her colleagues constantly hounded – but she refused to leave the city she loved, except for brief periods, and died here in 1966. Her work depicts the city with both realism and monumentalism, painted with Russian as well as personal history. While the characterisation of her as a mixture of 'a nun and a whore' may not have been fair, her love for her city was unconditional but unblinking: 'The capital on the Neva, Having forgotten its greatness, Like a drunken whore, Did not know who was taking her'.

Akhmatova's flat is now a quiet little museum, where you can see English translations of her work and hear recordings of her voice, see South of the Summer Garden section in the Things to See & Do chapter.

Theatre

Theatre in Russia has its roots in religious battling between Western Christian and Russian Orthodox churches vying for members as early as the 16th century: as Jesuits used dramatic scenes to propagandise and spread its message, the Russian Orthodox church found it had to do likewise to stop an exodus to Catholicism. Over the next few centuries, drama was almost exclusively used in a similar fashion by schools and the Church, until Tsars and nobility began importing tragedy and comedy from the West.

The galvanising force in Russian theatre was the defeat of Napoleon in 1812, after which nationalistic sentiment lead writers to shun French as the language of drama in favour of Russian, and a return to real Russian values in theatre led to the ousting of French theatre companies from the country. Vaudeville – biting, satirical one-act comedies poking fun at the rich and powerful that had been created on the streets of Paris – had found its way into Russia, and the practice of using theatre to put forth the party or church line on social issues came under attack by playwrights like Pushkin and Lermontov. Other writers, such as Gogol, Griboedov and Ostrovsky, wrote plays that attacked not just the aristocracy, but the bourgeoisie as well.

Anton Chekhov's earlier one-act works were true to vaudeville, but his full-length plays, especially *Uncle Vanya* and *The Seagull* are his legacy – though they took a while to catch on: the opening night of *The Seagull* at the Alexandrinsky Theatre was a total bomb. Towards the end of the 19th century, Maxim Gorky's *The Stormy Petrel*, which raised workers to a level superior to that of the intellectual, earned him reverence by the Soviets as the beginning of Social Realism.

Nicholas I had set up an incredibly complex system to manage the theatre, going so far as putting the secret police in charge of repertory (and often himself as casting director) to protect the 'message' being put forth through drama, and the Soviets always were good at picking up on good ways of managing information. The Soviet period saw drama used almost exclusively as a propaganda tool, and when foreign plays were performed it was usually for a reason – hence the popularity in Russia of *Death of a Salesman*, which showed just what Western (US) greed and decadence will lead to.

Cinema

While producing greats like Eisenstein (*The Battleship Potyomkin*) and Tarkovsky (*Solaris, Andrey Rublev*), the Soviet film industry struggled to find a role for itself from the moment it was nationalised in August 1919 to the collapse of the country. The battle between ideology and box office success, between art and the need to provide inexpensive entertainment for the seething masses, resulted in a system that alternately produced touching human drama, blatant propaganda and sensationalist crap.

Some Soviet film makers, limited in their scope, range and budget by the powers that were, managed to create memorable films, pushing – often at great personal risk – the limits of the censorship to which they were subjected. The interesting feature of the ones that are memorable is that, while pushing the boundaries of the socio-political norms, they tackled issues that by today's standards are, well, milktoast – the crowds that queued for hours in 1985 to see the then shocking *Kindergarten* (they came to see the scene of a naked blonde in a post-sauna roll in the snow) would probably have fainted at the sight of the interrogation scene in *Basic Instinct* (I certainly did). Soviet comedies were amusing, but not outstanding, and, let's face it, a chase scene featuring two Ladas doesn't exactly hold up against the offerings of the West – even against stinkers like *To Live and Die in LA*.

The themes of many of the Soviet Union's films in the 1960s and 1970s were less overtly political than one would imagine – it wasn't a bunch of happy workers holding wheat, but rather a time of cautious introspection. And, of course, cheap thrills: along with the favourite topics of the period like WW II, there was a lot of CIA/KGB intrigue ('Freeze, KGB!!') and 'hit-em-over-the-head' propaganda such as *The Nineteenth Committee*, which forecast the imminent use of bacteriological weapons by the West against the USSR.

The box-office life of the more introspective films tended to be shortest: one of the most controversial films of the 1970s, Tarkovsky's *Solaris*, tackled the subject of whether Man was entitled to head for space before cleaning up the mess he'd made here on earth; not surprisingly, the government decided that, yes, Man should, and after a short run it disappeared from the cinemas.

Since the fall of the Soviet Union, Russian film making, or more specifically, the Russian film-making infrastructure, has been sent into a tailspin. A brain drain is in progress, with many talented Russians heading to more artistically generous countries, like Italy, Norway, Sweden and the UK. Russian production is down, from its height of over 400 films in 1991, to fewer than 100 in 1992, many of which never saw the light of a projector.

St Petersburg's Lenfilm studios on Kamennoostrovsky prospekt, once one of the largest and most powerful studios in the country, has been reduced to job lot duties, selling parcels of services like lighting, costuming and small technical packages to Western studios looking to save lots of money on European productions as opposed to actual film production.

Many of the big-budget films in production today are being made with, at the least, foreign money, and usually lots of foreign intervention. Generally speaking, many productions of note today consist of Russian story, director, tech crew and cast ... and English, French or Italian producers. But Lenfilm is desperately struggling to flog its services on the international market. In 1994, a Canadian-English-Russian production of Len Deighton's *Bullet To Beijing*, starring Michael Caine, was shot in town (it was interesting and sometimes very funny watching St Petersburg's fledgling service industry trying to accommodate big-budget picture types – 'Don't you *like* uncooked pig fat, Ms Sara?'); the 1995 shooting of a James Bond thriller starring Pierce Brosnan, *GoldenEye*, saw T-72 tanks shooting up the streets and police cars flying into canals while locals pressed against barricades to get a peek at the action.

But entirely Russian-made product is still being churned out, and perhaps the need to compete can only help the situation. The most notable Russian film to have emerged since the fall of the Soviet Union is clearly Nikita Mikhalkov's *Burnt By The Sun*, which won the 1994 Academy Award for Best Foreign-Language Film at the 1994 Oscars. The film, set in Stalin-era Russia, tells the story of Sergey Kotov, a war veteran living in the quiet Russian countryside until the appearance of his wife's former lover, now a member of the Secret Police.

But there's no denying that at the end of the day, Russians would rather sit down and watch some good old Western-made schlock than any high-fallutin' Russian intellectual stuff. Necrophilia, sex, mysticism and violence fare far better, and make a lot more money here. Yuri Gladilshchikov, writing in *Nezavisimaya Gazeta*, summed things up quite accurately: 'The most important of the arts for us continues to be movies ... bloody and immoral ones'.

Music

Classical The roots of Russian music lie in folk song and dance and Orthodox Church chants. Epic folk songs of Russia's peasantry, *byliny*, preserved folk culture and lore through celebration of particular events such as great battles or harvests. More formal music slowly reached acceptance into Russian society; first as religious aid, followed by military and other ceremonial use, and eventually for entertainment.

When Peter the Great began throwing Western culture at his fledgling capital, the music of Western European composers was one of the chief weapons in his arsenal. He held weekly concerts of music by composers from the West – Vivaldi was a favourite. Catherine the Great further encouraged this, and Western music gained popularity. St Petersburg was the birthplace of Russian opera, when Mikhail Glinka's opera *A Life For The Tsar*, which merged traditional and Western influence, was performed on 9 December 1836.

The defining period of Russian music was from the 1860s to 1900. As Russian composers (and painters and writers) struggled to find a national identity, several influential schools formed from which some of Russia's most famous composers and finest music emerged. The Group of Five – Mussorgsky, Rimsky-Korsakov, Borodin, Kui and Balakirev – believed that a radical departure was necessary, and they looked to byliny and folk music for themes. Their main opponent was the Russian Musical Society, and especially Anton 'go, go-status-quo' Rubenshteyn, who felt that Russian classical music should be firmly based in the traditions of masters like Schubert, Mendelssohn and Chopin.

The middle ground was, it seems, discovered by Peter Tchaikovsky, a student of the St Petersburg Conservatory, who embraced both Russian folklore and music as well as the disciplines of the Western European composers. Tchaikovsky is widely regarded as the father of Russian national composers.

Rock Russian rock was born in the 1960s, when the 'bourgeois' Beatles filtered through despite official disapproval. Rock developed underground, starved of decent equipment and the chance to record or perform to big audiences, but gathered a huge following among the disaffected, distrustful youth of the 1970s (the Soviet hippie era) and 1980s.

Bands in the 1970s started by imitating Western counterparts, but eventually a home-grown music emerged, whose lyrics often reflected real social issues. Some artists, like Boris Grebenshikov and his band Akvarium (Aquarium), became household names but still needed other jobs to get by. Music was circulated by illegal tapes known as *magizdat*, the musical equivalent of samizdat; concerts were held, if at all, in remote halls in city suburbs, and even to attend them could be risky.

Punk and heavy metal came into fashion in the early 1980s. Under glasnost, the authorities eventually allowed the true voices of youth to sound out: rock festivals were held in outlying Soviet republics such as

Georgia and Estonia, big concerts took place in major cities, and the state record company, Melodia, started to produce albums by previously unacceptable groups.

Come glasnost, rock initially flowered, with New Wave music, fashionable from about the mid-1980s, appealing to a Russian taste for theatricality. The tone of many of the more 'serious' groups of the 1980s was one of protest about, or a gloomy resignation to, the frustration and alienation of Soviet life – messages that still find a big response in 1990s Russia, where many of the same groups remain popular. The tortured droning of Viktor Tsoy and the chunky riffs of his band Kino were archetypal. Tsoy died in 1990 but other 1980s bands are still leaders in the field today, among them Akvarium; Va Bank from Moscow and DDT from St Petersburg, both punk-influenced; Orkestr Populyarnaya Mekhanika (Popular Mechanics Orchestra), a St Petersburg 'performance rock' outfit; and Nautilus Pompilius, an electronic New Wave band from Yekaterinburg.

Rock groups now play openly in music clubs and nightclubs and there's little that's 'underground' about them any more, though the Russian rock scene remains homely and amateurish by Western standards. The loss of the underground/protest niche perhaps explains the shortage of major new bands to come to the fore since the early 1990s. The two top newcomers are Dva Samolyota (Two Aeroplanes), good-time ska messengers from St Petersburg, and Nogu Svelo (Cramp in the Leg) from Moscow, which plays a mixture of styles from pop to reggae, post-punk and German beer-hall music.

Russian pop is as popular as ever. Two top acts to look out for are Bravo, a Moscow band playing polished bebop/rockabilly, and the everlasting Alla Pugachyova, a female solo singer who puts tons of energy into her shows.

Dance

The Russian Ballet evolved as an offshoot of French dance combined with Russian folk and peasant dance techniques, which stunned Western Europeans when first brought on tour in the 19th century. At the turn of the 20th century, the heyday of Russian Ballet, the St Petersburg's Imperial School of Ballet rose to world prominence cranking out superstar after superstar, including Nijinsky, Anna Pavlova and Olga Spessivtzeva – the *Ballets Russes* took Europe by storm. An attraction in its own right, the décor was unlike anything seen before. Painted by artists (like Alexander Benois) and not stagehands, it suspended disbelief and shattered the audience's sense of illusion.

Ballet under the Soviets was treated as a natural resource – a nose-thumbing at the West – and enjoyed highly privileged status, which allowed schools like the Vaganova School of Ballet and companies like the Kirov to maintain this level of lavish production and no-expense-spared star-searches. And despite collapse of the economy, defections (political and financial) by stars to the West and other hardships, the Russian ballet and the Kirov company remain world renowned.

SOCIETY & CONDUCT

The key to harmonious interaction with Russians depends not just on your behaving inoffensively, but also in your reaction to what you may consider to be highly offensive behaviour. Blowing your top in reaction to a surly waiter, irascible ticket clerk or cheeky coat-check babushka is (a) unlikely to remedy the situation, (b) asking for further trouble and (c) offensive to those around you, who will look upon you as being 'uncultured'. Patience, here more than anywhere, is a virtue and a smile goes further than everything up to and perhaps including a revolver.

In Russian Orthodox religious services, hands in pockets attract frowns. Women visitors can often get away without covering their heads, but mini skirts are most unwelcome and even trousers sometimes attract disapproval. Men in shorts are also frowned upon. Photography at services is generally not welcome, though you might get a yes if you ask. Always feel out the situation first, and ask if in doubt.

In everyday life, the role of men and women is still rather old-worldly by Western standards; men are expected to be gentlemanly by holding open doors, lighting cigarettes, pulling out chairs etc for women.

When visiting someone's house, always remove your shoes before entering – you'll be given slippers *(tapochki)* to wear inside.

Avoid nationalistic sentiment ('Boy, you Russians sure got whupped in the Cold War!') in conversation. Swearing is frowned upon and considered vulgar.

Superstition plays a large part in many customs, sometimes overtly (like never shaking hands across the threshold of a doorway) and sometimes covertly (like never shaking hands with gloves on). Big no-nos are returning home to get something you forgot, leaving empty bottles on the table during dinner parties and stepping on someone's foot without giving them the chance to do the same to you.

RELIGION

Russian Orthodox Church

After decades of closures and confiscations of property, and victimisation, deportations and executions of believers, under the Soviet regime, the Russian Orthodox Church (Russkaya Pravoslavnaya Tserkov) is enjoying a big revival. By 1991 it already had an estimated 50 million members. Numbers have grown thanks not only to the new religious freedom initiated by Mikhail Gorbachev and enshrined in Russia's 1993 constitution, but also because of the growth of Russian nationalism, for the Church is an intimate part of many Russians' notions of Russia and 'Russianness', despite recriminations over the Church's infiltration by the KGB during the Soviet era (three metropolitans – senior bishops – were accused in 1992 of having been KGB agents).

History & Hierarchy Prince Vladimir of Kiev effectively founded the Russian Orthodox Church in 988 by adopting Christianity from Constantinople. The Church's headquarters stayed at Kiev till 1300 when it moved north to Vladimir, and then in the 1320s to Moscow.

Patriarch Alexy of Moscow & All Russia is head of the Church. The Patriarch's residence is the Danilov Monastery, Moscow, though some Church business is still conducted at the Trinity Monastery of St Sergius at Sergiev Posad, his residence until the late 1980s. The Church's senior bishops bear the title Metropolitan. The Russian Orthodox Church is one of the main fellowship of 15 autocephalous ('self-headed') Orthodox churches, in which Constantinople is a kind of first among equals.

Beliefs & Practice Russian Orthodoxy is highly traditional, and the atmosphere inside a church is formal and solemn. Priests dress imposingly, the smell of candles and incense permeates the air, old women bustle about sweeping and polishing. Churches have no seats, no music (only chanting), and no statues – but many icons (see the earlier Arts section in this chapter) with people often praying, even kissing the ground before them. Men bare their heads and women usually cover theirs.

As a rule, working churches are open to one and all, but as a visitor take care not to disturb any devotions or offend sensibilities (see Society & Conduct).

The Virgin Mary (Bogomater, Mother of God) is greatly honoured. The language of the liturgy is 'Church

Facts about St Petersburg

NICK SELBY

ROGER HAYNE

Top: St Isaac's Cathedral
Bottom: St Isaac's interior, main dome

Slavonic', the old Bulgarian dialect into which the Bible
was first translated for Slavs. Easter *(Paskha)* is the focus
of the Church year, with festive midnight services to
launch Easter Day. Christmas *(Rozhdestvo)* falls on 7
January because the Church still uses the Julian calendar
that the Soviet state abandoned in 1918.

In most churches, Divine Liturgy *(Bozhestvennaya
Liturgia)*, lasting about two hours, is at 8, 9 or 10 am
Monday to Saturday, and usually at 7 and 10 am on Sunday
and festival days. Most churches also hold services at 5 or

6 pm daily. Some of these include an akathistos *(akafist)*, a series of chants to the Virgin or saints.

Church Names In Russian, *sobor* means cathedral; *tserkov* and *khram* mean church. Common church names include:

Blagoveshchenskaya (Annunciation)
Borisoglebskaya (SS Boris & Gleb)
Nikolskaya (St Nicholas)
Petropavlovskaya (SS Peter & Paul)
Pokrovskaya (Intercession of the Virgin)
Preobrazhenskaya (Transfiguration)
Rizopolozhenskaya (Deposition of the Holy Robe)
Rozhdestvenskaya (Nativity)
Troitskaya (Trinity)
Uspenskaya (Assumption or Dormition)
Vladimirskaya (St Vladimir)
Voskresenskaya (Resurrection)
Voznesenskaya (Ascension)
Znamenskaya (Holy Sign)

Old Believers The Russian Church was split in 1653 by the reforms of Patriarch Nikon, who thought it had departed from its roots. He insisted, among other things, that the translation of the Bible be altered to conform with the Greek original, and that the sign of the cross be made with three fingers, not two. Those who couldn't accept these changes became known as Old Believers *(Starovery)* and came in for persecution. Some fled to the Siberian forests or remote parts of Central Asia, where one group who had never heard of Lenin, electricity or the revolution was found in the 1980s. Only in 1771-1827, 1905-18 and again recently have Old Believers had real freedom of worship. They probably number over a million but in 1917 there were as many as 20 million.

Other Christian Churches

Russia has small numbers of Roman Catholics, and Lutheran and Baptist Protestants, mostly among the German and other non-Russian ethnic groups. Other groups such as the Mormons, Seventh Day Adventists, and the Salvation Army are sending missionaries into the potentially fertile ground of a country where God officially didn't exist for 70 years.

Islam

Islam has, like Christianity, enjoyed growth since the mid-1980s. Though it has been some Muslim peoples –

notably the Chechens and Tatars – who have been the most resistant of Russia's minorities to being brought within the Russian national fold since the fall of the Soviet Union in 1991, nationalism has played at least as big a part as religion in this, and militant Islam has as yet barely raised its head in Russia.

Islam in Russia is fairly secularised – eg women are not veiled, the Friday sabbath is not a commercial holiday.

Working mosques are closed to women and often to non-Muslim men, though men may occasionally be invited in. If you are asked in, you'll have to take your shoes off (and hope your socks are clean! – dirty socks, like dirty feet, may be an insult to the mosque).

Judaism

Many of Russia's 700,000 or so Jews are assimilated to Russian culture and do not seriously practise Judaism. However there were approximately 30 synagogues in Russia by 1991. Jews have long been the target of prejudice and even pogroms – ethnic cleansing – in Russia. Since glasnost, hundreds of thousands of Jews have emigrated to Israel and other countries to escape the state-sponsored anti-Semitism that existed under the former government.

Unlike the country's other religious groups Jews have no central coordinating body, though a *yeshiva*, or rabbinical academy, opened in Moscow in 1956.

Buddhism

The members of St Petersburg's Buddhist *datsan* (monastery) are members of the Gelugpa or 'Yellow-Hat' sect of Tibetan Buddhism, whose spiritual leader is the Dalai Lama. Buddhism was tolerated by the Soviet state until Stalin nearly wiped it out in the 1930s.

Religious Services

There are a number of English and other Western-language services in town; check the *St Petersburg Press* for current information during your stay. Some services in English (E), German (G), Hebrew (H), Russian (R) and Latin (L), and places of worship, follow:

Anglican/Episcopalian Open Christianity Centre (☎ 277 87 50), Chernoretsky Pereulok 4/6, metro Ploshchad Alexandra Nevskogo – services first Sunday of month at 10 am (E)

Armenian Church of St Catherine (☎ 311 57 95), Nevsky prospekt 40/42

Church of Jesus Christ of Latter Day Saints (☎ 119 61 48), Dom Aktyor, Nevsky prospekt 86 – services daily at 9.30 am and 1 pm, Sunday school etc (E, R)

Christ Church (☎ 110 18 70), Professora Popova ulitsa 47 – services Wednesday and Sunday (E, R)

Chabad-Lubavitch (☎ 113 62 09), Lermontovsky prospekt 2 – Shabbas services Friday at sundown, daily services at 9.30 am etc (H)

Evangelical Lutheran Church (☎ 311 24 23), St Anne's Church (Spartak Cinema), Saltikova-Shchedrina ulitsa 8, metro Cherneshevskaya – service at 10.30 am Sunday (G)

Mosque of the Congregation of Muslims (☎ 233 98 19), Kronverksky prospekt 7 – open daily from 10 am to 7 pm

Buddhist Temple (☎ 239 13 41), Primorsky prospekt 91, metro Chyornaya Rechka

Nondenominational Services (☎ 292 06 05), Oranienbaum-skaya ulitsa 5, room 50, 3rd floor, – bible classes, services etc (E, R)

Our Lady of Lourdes (Roman Catholic; ☎ 272 50 02), Kovensky pereulok 7 (near ulitsa Mayakovskaya) – Sunday Mass 11.30 am (L, R), 1.30 pm (E), 5 pm (G)

Russian Orthodox services are available at several locations throughout the city. Check the *St Petersburg Press*, *The Traveller's Yellow Pages* or *Where in St Petersburg* for listings.

LANGUAGE

Just about everyone in Russia speaks Russian, though there are also dozens of other languages spoken by ethnic minorities. Russian and most of the other languages are written in variants of the Cyrillic alphabet. It's easy to find English-speakers in the big cities but not so easy in small towns (sometimes not even in tourist hotels).

Russian grammar may be daunting, but your travels will be far more interesting if you at least take the time to learn the Cyrillic alphabet, so that you can read maps and street signs.

Since most of what's in this section is aimed at spoken situations, Cyrillic forms are mostly accompanied with phonetic translations rather than direct transliterations.

Books

A good teach-yourself set (a book and two tapes) is the BBC's *Get By in Russian*. Another good book & cassette set for beginners is *Colloquial Russian* by Svetlana le Fleming & Susan E Kay. The paperback *Penguin Russian Course* is good for more devoted learners. When you go, take along Lonely Planet's detailed and useful *Russian Phrasebook* and a small dictionary such as the *Pocket Oxford Russian Dictionary*.

Two recent books are worthy of mention. The four-kg *Random House Russian-English Dictionary of Idioms* by Sophia Lubensky is a must for any serious student of Russian. Developed over 12 years, originally to help spooks speak (it was undertaken by the US National Cryptologic School, Department of Defence), it contains over 7500 idioms and set expressions not found in traditional Russian-English dictionaries. It's not much fun for beginners – all the Russian listings are in Cyrillic, and no direct (only idiomatic) translations are given. Also note that the meanings and spellings are in American English. *Russian Proverbs* by Chris Skillen & Vladimir Lubarov is a lovely little hardcover with a selection of the most charming Russian proverbs – from 'it's madness to bring a samovar to Tula' to 'a bad peace is better than a good fight'. It lists both Russian and English and has very nice illustrations (though a couple are in the wrong place!) throughout.

Cyrillic Alphabet

The Cyrillic alphabet resembles Greek with some extra characters. Each language that uses Cyrillic has a slight variant. The alphabet chart in the Appendix at the back of the book shows the letters used in Russian, Ukrainian and Belarusian with their Roman-letter equivalents and common pronunciations.

Pronunciation The sounds of a, o, e and я are 'weaker' when the stress in the word does not fall on them – eg in вода (*voda*, water) the stress falls on the second syllable, so it's pronounced '*vo-DA*', with the unstressed pronunciation for o and the stressed pronunciation for a. The vowel й only follows other vowels in so-called diphthongs (vowel combinations), eg ой '*oy*', ей '*ey, yey*'. Russians usually print ё without the dots, a source of confusion in pronunciation.

The 'voiced' (when the vocal cords vibrate) consonants б, в, г, д, ж and з are not voiced at the end of words (eg хлеб, bread, is pronounced '*khlyep*') or before voiceless consonants. The г in the common adjective endings -его and -ого is pronounced '*v*'.

Two letters have no sound but only modify others. A consonant followed by the 'soft sign' ь is spoken with the tongue flat against the palate, as if followed by the faint beginnings of a '*y*'. The rare 'hard sign' ъ after a consonant indicates a slight pause before the next vowel.

Transliteration There's no ideal system for going from Cyrillic to Roman letters; the more faithfully a system indicates pronunciation, the more complicated it is. This book uses the simple US Library of Congress System I, good for deciphering printed words and rendering proper names in familiar form.

In this system Cyrillic e (pronounced *'ye'*) is written as Roman *e* except at the start of words where it's *ye* (eg Yeltsin). The combination кс becomes *x*. At the end of words certain pairs get special forms: -ия is written *-ia*, -ье *-ie*, -ьи *-yi*. Russian names are simplified by making final -ый and -ий into plain *-y*.

In a few cases exceptions are made for common usage. The names of 18th to 19th-century Russian rulers are anglicised – eg Peter the Great not Pyotr, Tsar Nicholas not Nikolay. For names ending in -чёв we write *-chev* not *-chyov* (eg Gorbachev); similarly for -шёв and -щёв. Other familiar exceptions – which would all be spelled differently if we stuck adamantly to the system – are *rouble*, *nyet*, *soviet*, *perestroika*, Baikal, Tchaikovsky, even Intourist.

Capital letters in the transliterations indicate where the stress is put in a word.

Useful Words & Phrases

Two words you're sure to use are Здравствуйте (*'ZDRAST-vooy-tyeh'*), the universal 'hello' (but if you say it a second time in one day to the same person, they'll think you forgot you already saw them!), and Пожалуйста (*'pa-ZHAHL-stuh'*), the multipurpose word for 'please' (commonly included in all polite requests), 'you're welcome', 'pardon me', 'after you' and more.

Yes.	
da	да
No.	
nyet	нет
Thank you (very much).	
spuh-SEE-ba (bal-	
SHOY-uh)	Спасибо (большое).
Pardon me.	
pra-STEE-tyeh, pa-ZHAHL-	Простите,
stuh	пожалуйста.
Can you help me?	
pa-ma-GEET-yeh mnyeh?	Помогите мне?
No problem/Never mind.	
ni-che-VOH	Ничего.
(lit: nothing)	
Good/OK.	
kha-ra-SHOH	хорошо

Greetings

Good morning.
DOH-bra-yuh OO-tra   Доброе утро.
Good afternoon.
DOH-bri dyen   Добрый день.
Good evening.
DOH-bri VYEH-chir   Добрый вечер.
Goodbye.
das-fi-DA-nya   До свидания.
Goodbye. (casual)
pah-KAH   Пока.

Meeting People

When introducing yourself use your first name, or first
and last. Russians often address each other by first name
plus patronymic, a middle name based on their father's
first name – eg Natalya Borisovna (Natalya, daughter of
Boris), Pavel Nikolaevich (Pavel, son of Nikolay).

What's your name?
kahk vahs za-VOOT?   Как вас зовут?
My name is ...
min-YA za-VOOT ...   Меня зовут ...
Pleased to meet you.
OH-chin pree-YAHT-na   Очень приятно.
How are you?
kak dyi-LAH?   Как дела?
Where are you from?
aht-KUH-dah vi?   Откуда вы?
I am from ...
ya iz ...   Я из ...

Australia
uf-STRAH-li-uh   Австралия
Canada
ka-NA-duh   Канада
France
FRAHN-tsi-yuh   Франция
Germany
gehr-MAH-ni-yuh   Германия
Great Britain
vi-LEE-ka-bri-TA-ni-uh   Великобритания
Ireland
eer-LAHN-di-yuh   Ирландия
New Zealand
NOH-vuh-yuh zyeh-
LAHN-di-yuh   Новая Зеландия

USA, America
  seh sheh ah, uh-MYEH-ri-kuh   США, Америка

Language Problems

I don't speak Russian.
  ya nye ga-var-YU pa-RU-ski   Я не говорю по-
                                                      русски.
I don't understand.
  ya nye pah-ni-MAH-yu   Я не понимаю.
Do you speak English?
  vih ga-var-EE-tyeh pa-an-GLEE-ski?   Вы говорите по-
                                                      английски?
Will you write it down, please?
  zuh-pi-SHEE-tyeh, pa-ZHAHL-stuh?   Запишите,
                                                      пожалуйста.

Signs
MEN'S
  MOOZH-skoy tu-al YET   МУЖСКОЙ (М)
WOMEN'S
  ZHEN-ski tu-al-YET   ЖЕНСКИЙ (Ж)
ENTRANCE
  fkhot   ВХОД
EXIT
  VIH-khut   ВЫХОД
OPEN
  aht-KRIT   ОТКРЫТ
CLOSED
  zuh-KRIT   ЗАКРЫТ
NO SMOKING
  nyi ku-REET   НЕ КУРИТЬ
NO VACANCY
  myest nyet   МЕСТ НЕТ

Getting Around

How do I get to ...?
  kak mnye paPAST' v ...?   Как мне попасть в ...?
Where is ...?
  gdye ...?   Где ...?

When does it leave?
kug-DA aht-li-TA-yit? Когда отлетает?
Are you getting off?
vih-KHA-di-tyeh Выходите?

CASHIER/TICKET OFFICE
KAH-suh КАССА
transport map
SKHEM-uh trahns-POR-tuh схема транспорта
ticket(s)
bee-LYET(-i) билет(ы)
metro token(s)
zhi-TOHN, zhi-TOHN (-i) жетон(ы)
one-way
vah-DYIN ka-NYETS, ye-DYIN-i в один конец, единый
return
tu-DA ee a-BRAHT-na туда и обратно
bus
uf-TOH-boos автобус
trolleybus
trahl-YEY-boos троллейбус
tram
trum-VAI трамвай
bus stop
ah-sta-NOV-kuh остановка
train
PO-yest поезд
railway station
zhi-LYEZ-nuh da-ROHZH-ni vahg-ZAHL железно дорожный (ж. д.) вокзал
taxi
tahk-SEE такси

Accommodation
How much is a room?
SKOL-ka STO-eet NOHM-yer? Сколько стоит номер?
Do you have a cheaper room?
u vahs dye-SHYEV-lye NOHM-yer? У вас дешевле номер?

hotel
gus-TEE-nit-suh гостиница
room
NOHM-yer номер

key
  klyooch   ключ
blanket
  ah-di-YAH-la   одеяло

The...isn't working.
  ...ni ruh-BOH-tuh-yit   ...не работает.

tap/faucet
  krahn   кран
heating
  a-ta-PLEN-i-yeh   отопление
light
  sfyet   свет
electricity
  eh-lik-TREE-chist-va   электричество

Around Town

House numbers are not always in step on opposite sides
of the street. Russian addresses are written back-to-
front; see Post & Telecommunications in the Facts for the
Visitor chapter.

Where is...?
  gdyeh...?   Где...?
I'm lost.
  ya zuh-blu-DEEL-suh (m)/   Я заблудился/
  ya zuh-blu-DEE-lus (f)   я заблудилась.
May I take a photo?
  fa-ta-gruh-FEE-ra-vut   Фотографировать
    MOZH-na?   можно?

avenue
  pra-SPYEKT   проспект (просп.)
boulevard
  bool-VAHR   бульвар
building
  KOR-poos   корпус
church
  TSER-kuf   церковь
circus
  tsirk   цирк
highway
  sha-SEH   шоссе
lane
  pi-ri-OO-lahk   переулок (пер.)

museum
  mu-ZYEY   музей
square/plaza
  PLOH-shchut   площадь (пл.)
street
  OO-leet-suh   улица (ул.)
theatre
  ti-ATR   театр

Directions

north
  SYEH-vir   север
south
  yook   юг
east
  va-STOK   восток
west
  ZAH-puht   запад
to/on the left
  nuh-LYEH-va   налево
to/on the right
  nuh-PRAH-va   направо
straight on
  PRYAH-ma   прямо
here
  toot   тут
there
  tahm   там

Bank, Post Office & Telephone

bank
  bahnk   банк
currency exchange
  ahb-MYEHN vahl-YU-tuh обмен валюты
small change
  ruz-MYEN   размен
travellers' cheques
  da-ROHZH-nih-yeh CHEH-ki дорожные чеки

post office
  pahch-TAHMT   почтамт
postcard
  aht-KRIT-kuh   открытка

stamp
  MAR-kuh   марка

telephone
  ti-li-FOHN   телефон
intercity/international
  telephone office
  mizh-du-gahr-OHD-ni/   международный/
    mizh-du-nah-ROHD-ni   международный
    ti-li-FOHN-i punkt   телефонный
                                     пункт

fax
  fahx   факс or телефакс

Food

For a longer list of words and phrases related to ordering
meals, and specific foods, dishes and drinks, see Places
to Eat.

What is this?
  shto E-ta?   Что зто?
I'd like ...
  ya vaz-MU ...   Я возму ...

breakfast
  ZAHF-truk   завтрак
lunch
  a-BYET   обед
dinner/ supper
  OO-zhin   ужин
restaurant
  ri-sta-RAHN   ресторан
café
  ka-FYEH   кафе
canteen
  sta-LO-vuh-yuh   столовая
snack bar
  bu-FYET   буфет

Shopping

Do you have ...?
  u VAHS ...?   У вас ...?
How much is it?
  SKOL-ka STO-eet?   Сколько стоит?

bookshop
  KNEEZH-ni muh-guh-ZYIN   книжный магазин

department store	*u-ni-vir-SAHL-ni muh-guh-ZYIN*	универсальный магазин
market	*RIH-nuk*	рынок
newsstand	*sa-YOOZ-pi-chat, gazetnyi kiosk*	союзпечать, газетный киоск
pharmacy	*up-TYEK-a*	аптека
souvenirs	*su-vin-EER-i*	сувениры

Numbers

How many?
SKOL-ka   Сколько?

0	*nohl*	ноль
1	*ah-DYIN*	один
2	*dva*	два
3	*tree*	три
4	*chi-TIR-yeh*	четыре
5	*pyaht*	пять
6	*shest*	шесть
7	*syem*	семь
8	*VO-syim*	восемь
9	*DYEV-yut*	девять
10	*DYES-yut*	десять
11	*ah-DYIN-ut-sut*	одиннадцать
12	*dvi-NAHT-sut*	двенадцать
13	*tri-NAHT-sut*	тринадцать
20	*DVAHT-sut*	двадцать
21	*DVAHT-sut ah-DYIN*	двадцать один
100	*stoh*	сто
1000	*TIH-suh-chuh*	тысяча
one million	*ah-DYIN mi-li-OHN*	один миллион

Time & Dates

Round hours are fairly easy, except that there are three different ways of saying the Russian equivalent of 'o'clock', depending on the hour. Thus one o'clock is *'ah-DYIN chahs'* (or simply *'chahs'*), two o'clock is *'dva chuh-SAH'* (and similarly for three and four o'clock) and five o'clock is *'pyaht chuh-SOF'* (and similarly up to 20). For in-between times the standard formula gives brain-twisters like 'without-25-five' for 4.35. You'll be understood if you say the hour followed by the minutes: eg 9.20 is девять-двадцать (*'DYEV-yut DVAHD-sut'*). For minutes under 10 insert zero, ноль *('nohl')*: eg 2.08 is два-ноль-восемь *('dva nohl VOH-sem')*. Timetables use a 24-hour clock: eg 3 pm is пятнадцать часов *('pyit-NAHT-sut chuh-SOF')*.

What time is it?
  ka-TOR-i chahs?   Который час?
At what time?
  fka-TOR-um chuh-SOO?   В котором часу?

hour
  chahs   час
minute
  mi-NOOT-uh   минута
am/in the morning
  oo-TRA   утра
pm/in the afternoon
  dnya   дня
in the evening
  VYEH-chi-ruh   вечера
local time
  MYEST-na-yuh VREM-yuh   местное время
Moscow time
  muh-SKOF-skuh-yeh
    VREM-yuh   московское время

Dates are given day-month-year, with the month usually in Roman numerals. Days of the week are often represented by numbers in timetables; Monday is 1.

When?
  kahg-DA?   когда?
today
  si-VOHD-nyuh   сегодня
yesterday
  fchi-RA   вчера
tomorrow
  ZAHF-truh   завтра
day after tomorrow
  pa-sli-ZAHF-truh   послезавтра

Days of the Week
Monday
  pa-ni-DEL-nik   понедельник
Tuesday
  FTOR-nik   вторник
Wednesday
  sri-DA   среда

Thursday
  chit-VERK   четверг
Friday
  PYAT-nit-suh   пятница
Saturday
  su-BOHT-uh   суббота
Sunday
  vas-kri-SEN-yuh   воскресенье

Museum Dates Centuries are represented with Roman numerals.

century(ies)	в(в).
year(s)	г (г).
beginning, middle, end	начало, середина, конец
AD (lit: our era)	н.э.
BC (lit: before our era)	до н.э.
10th century AD	X в. н.э.
7th century BC	VII в. до н.э.

Emergencies

I need a doctor.
  mnyeh NU-zhin vrahch   Мне нужен врач.
hospital
  BOHL-nit-suh   больница
Fire!
  pa-ZHAR!   Пожар!
Help!
  na POH-mushch! or *pa-ma-GEET-yeh!*   На помощь! or Помог ите!
Thief!
  vor!   Вор!
police
  mi-LEET-si-yuh   милиция

Facts for the Visitor

Regulations and exchange rates change in any country – as anyone who took a bath buying British pounds in 1992, Mexican pesos in 1994 or US dollars in 1995 can attest. But due to the sweeping and radical changes in the fabric of post-Soviet life, the information contained in this chapter is subject to change at any second. It's a volatile climate, say, about as volatile as a nitroglycerin cocktail on a long-distance bus in Sumatra. In the course of writing this chapter, certain visa regulations changed substantially, and the rouble devalued almost 150% against the US dollar, or a total 60% devaluation of the currency The guidelines, regulations and exchange rates listed herein were the case at the time of writing, but expect further valuation shifts and minor (or even major) changes in the visa regulations. As often as possible we've listed sources for further information; check them for regulation changes before your visit.

VISAS

All foreigners visiting Russia need visas. To get one you must technically have confirmed accommodation for every night you'll be in the country, though in practice, there are countless ways around this.

At the time of writing, a Russian visa is a passport-sized paper document; nothing goes into your passport. There is, however, talk of changing over to stamps in your passport. A visa lists entry/exit dates, your passport number, any children travelling with you, and visa type (see Types of Visa later).

It's an exit permit too, so if you lose it (or overstay), leaving the country can be harder than getting in.

The following sections give general information about visa procedures before you go to Russia and once you're there. Despite changes in details here and there, these guidelines have remained essentially static since the fall of the Soviet Union.

Registration

When you check in to a hotel, camping ground or hostel, you surrender your passport and visa so the hotel can register you with OVIR *(Otdel Viz i Registratsii)*, the

Department of Visas & Registration. You'll get your documents back the next morning if you ask (though nobody seems to remember them for you at check-out time).

If you're travelling on your own, you must remember that *all* Russian visas must be registered with OVIR within three business days of your arrival in Russia. No ifs or buts about it. Many companies, including some Finnish travel agencies in Helsinki, will claim that their 'visas needn't be registered'. This is not true: *all* Russian visas whether issued by the HI St Petersburg Hostel or the office of the Russian President need to be registered with the nearest office of OVIR within three working days of arrival in the country. Be highly suspicious of any company that tells you otherwise. Sometimes you have to pay a registration fee of US$5 to US$10.

Extending a visa that's not registered can be impossible, and getting out of the country with an unregistered visa could be a very expensive proposition. On the other hand, you may waltz out with just a lecture or even unhindered. But travellers have reported that fines of up to US$500 have been levied at the Finnish and Norwegian borders, and St Petersburg and Moscow airport officials aren't about to let a juicy penalty walk past them. It's not worth the risk.

Visa Registration Offices

OVIR offices in the city are:

Main Office
Saltykova-Shchedrina ulitsa 4
(☎ 278 24 81, 273 90 38),
open Monday to Friday
from 9.30 am to 5.30 pm

Dzerzhinsky District
Chekhova ulitsa 15
(☎ 272 55 56)

Frunzensky District
Obvodnogo Kanala
naberezhnaya 48
(☎ 166 14 68)

Kalininsky District
Mineralnaya ulitsa 3
(☎ 540 39 87)

Kirovsky District
Stachek prospekt 18
(☎ 252 77 14)

Krasnoselsky District
Avangardnaya ulitsa 35
(☎ 136 89 06)

Kuybyshevsky District
Krylova pereulok 3
(☎ 310 41 17)

Leninsky District
Sovietsky pereulok 9
(☎ 292 43 56)

Moskovsky District
Moskovsky prospekt 95
(☎ 294 81 55; 298 18 27)

Novocherkassky District
Krasnodonskaya ulitsa 14
(☎ 224 01 96)

Oktyabrsky District
Bolshaya Podyacheskaya ulitsa
26 (☎ 314 49 01)

Petrogradsky District
Bolshaya Monetnaya ulitsa 20
(☎ 232 11 19)

Primorsky District
Generalnaya Khruleva ulitsa 15
(☎ 394 72 13)

Smolninsky District
Mytninskaya ulitsa 3
(☎ 274 57 10)

Vyborgsky District
Lesnoy prospekt 20
(☎ 542 21 72)

Vasileostrovsky District
19-ya liniya 10 (☎ 355 75 24)

Registration Problems

The company or organisation that invited you to Russia is responsible for your registration, and no other company can support your visa. You can't take a visa that was issued on the invitation of, say, the HI Hostel in St Petersburg and have it registered in Moscow by the Travellers Guest House.

If you're not sure which organisation invited you (if the sponsorship line – on tourist visas this begins with the words *V uchrezhdenie* – has a name you've never heard of), one option is to spend a night at one of the major (expensive) hotels, which will register your visa for you for varying fees.

The other way is a bit time-consuming, but a lot cheaper if you already have a place to stay. Your embassy may be able to help you find the organisation's address. If not, prepare for a trip to Moscow, where you can get assistance in finding the sponsor at The Association of Joint Ventures, International Unions & Organisations (AJVIUO), Gorbachev Foundation Building, Leningradsky prospekt 55, Moscow. They will charge US$10 for a search that finds your sponsor, US$30 for a fruitless search (you work it out). The search takes one day.

If you've found your sponsor's address, you must go there and ask someone to help you register. If they welcome you with open arms, you're set! They'll take in your visa and register it for you. If they refuse to do anything for you, have them write a letter to OVIR stating that they are refusing to take responsibility for you (you can use this at OVIR to help your case for a new visa).

If the search for your sponsor turned up the fact that your sponsor is not a registered company (in other words, your visa was obtained using a fraudulent sponsorship letter), you'll need that in writing from the AJVIUO. Armed with that letter, head to OVIR.

In both of these situations where Things Go Wrong, the best place to head to for assistance in St Petersburg is the HI St Petersburg Hostel (and in Moscow the Travellers Guest House), where the staff are well versed in the dramas inherent in a visa situation gone bad.

Another important thing to remember is that different offices of OVIR handle things differently; one office may be able to perform a service that another office can't (as with UVIR, the national head visa office in Moscow, which can extend transit visas, while OVIR in St Petersburg can (will?) not).

Stop Press: New Visa Requirements in the Pipeline

Midway through 1995, at least two Moscow newspapers published stories regarding plans by the Russian Ministry of Foreign Affairs (MID) to change significantly the procedure for obtaining a visa invitation. The proposal would require the Russian entity issuing the invitation – whether an individual or a business, for a tourist or a business visa – to obtain from the Office of Visas & Registration (UVIR) a pre-printed invitation and mail this to the foreign visa applicant. Facsimiles of this form would not be acceptable.

The stated reason for this was that the visa situation had grown uncontrollable, and that many organisations were issuing visa invitations in exchange for money (true), which was leading to security problems (probably not true, but in any case exaggerated).

The potential ramifications of such an act are manifold. At the very least it would result either in significant delays in transmission of these invitations by post or in a substantial addition to the cost of delivery as senders resorted to the use of Western express-mail companies. But should the ministry prove to be cracking down on the quality, rather than the quantity, of visa invitations issued, many requests for business or other long-term, non-specific visas might be rejected out of hand. Such a move could severely impede independent travellers.

According to an article in the *Moscow Times*, MID said that the new measures would come into effect in September or October 1995. The forms, the article continued, would be 'introduced gradually, first in Moscow and then in St Petersburg and other cities'.

More current information on Russian visa requirements may be available on Lonely Planet's World Wide Web site. ■

HIV/AIDS Testing

The Russian government has gone back and forth on this issue. At the time of writing, HIV/AIDS testing is required for foreigners staying in the Russian Federation longer than three months. By definition, this does *not* affect tourist visas, which are only issued for shorter term stays. Details on enforcement and procedures are sketchy. The Russian Embassy in Washington, DC, said that a certificate from your doctor at home would be required before issuance of long-term visas, but that leaves questions about testing once inside Russia, and about the situation for people who were issued visas without such a certificate.

Types of Visa

Six types of visas are available to foreign visitors and are listed below.

For all visas you'll need:

- a passport valid for at least a month beyond your return date plus photocopies of the passport validity and personal data pages. A UK Visitor's passport or other temporary papers won't do. You may be able to get away with giving the embassy or consulate just the photocopies of the front pages of your passport instead of the whole passport, though some consulates, notably Munich, charge you for the privilege;
- three passport-size (4 by 4.5 cm), full-face photos, not more than a year old. Vending-machine photos with white background are fine if they're essentially identical. It's probably wise not to make radical changes in your appearance between photo time and your arrival in Russia;
- a completed application form, including entry/exit dates;
- a handling fee of amounts that vary from country to country and sometimes depending on your citizenship.

Tourist Visa A tourist visa is issued to, well, tourists: those who have booked hotel or hostel space and are in Russia for purposes other than business. As far as the visa game goes, these are the most straightforward and inflexible available. In theory you're supposed to have booked accommodation for every night you'll be in the country, but in practice you can often get away with only booking a few, even just one – ask the travel agent, hotel or hostel you're booking through.

Extending a tourist visa is not easy, and the extension, if granted, will usually be only for a short time. Tourist visas are best for trips when you know exactly what you're doing, when and where and for how long you'll be doing it. To obtain a tourist visa, you will need, in addition to the above:

- confirmation of hotel reservations, which can be a faxed copy on hotel letterhead signed and stamped by the hotel; or confirmation of bookings from Intourist or a travel agent; or a visa-support letter from a youth hostel/guesthouse. (See the business visa section for tourist-visa-support fees charged by some hostels and guesthouses in Russia.)

Business Visa Far more flexible and desirable to the independent traveller is a business, or commercial, visa supported by a Russian company. The invitation eliminates the need for prearranged hotel confirmations, because the company inviting you ostensibly puts you up for the duration of your stay. While a visa to Russia supposedly allows you to travel anywhere, holders of tourist visas may have a harder time getting accommodation in smaller regional cities that are not listed on their visas than will holders of business visas doing the same thing.

To obtain a business visa you must have:

• a letter of invitation from a registered Russian company guaranteeing to provide accommodation during the entire length of your stay. The letter *must* be signed by a Russian director of that company (a Western friend's signature, even the Western director or partner in a Russian joint-stock company, will probably be turned down).

There are many organisations that will send you a business invitation for a fee, usually not an outrageous one. The fastest and most reliable way to get a business invitation is through hostels: the HI St Petersburg Hostel and the Travellers Guest House in Moscow issue business invitations. You will need to send them a fax or e-mail containing your name as it appears in your passport, date and place of birth, nationality, passport number and expiry date, dates of entry to and exit from Russia (these can be approximate) and the consulate at which you intend to apply for your visa. Listed below are some sample fees for visa-support services which include an invitation and registration services upon arrival:

HI St Petersburg Hostel (☎ (812) 329 80 18; fax (812) 329 80 19; e-mail ryh@ryh.spb.su for hostel information, bookings @ryh.spb.su to book) – Tourist visa: (with reservation; for accommodation booked plus two weeks of added time in country) US$10; (without reservation) US$25. Business visa: three months single-entry US$40; three months dual-entry US$60; six months multiple-entry (eight weeks advance notice required for MID (Ministry of Foreign Affairs) approval) US$150. Need credit card (Visa/MasterCard) or other payment in advance.

Peter TIPS, St Petersburg (☎ (812) 279 00 37) – Tourist visa-support letter: three months single-entry US$10; three months extendable US$20. Conversion from single to multiple-entry US$200. Registration US$15.

Russian Youth Hostels & Tourism (RYHT), Redondo Beach, USA (☎ (310) 618 2014; fax (310) 618 1140; e-mail 71573.2010@compuserve.com) – Tourist visa (with reservation at HI St Petersburg or Moscow hostels or Travellers Guest House in Moscow) US$40; (without reservation) US$55; Business visa: three months single-entry US$60; three months dual-entry US$90; six months multiple-entry (eight weeks advance notice required for MID approval) US$175. Need credit card or other payment in advance. Includes guaranteed processing by Russian embassy/consulate.

Travellers Guest House/IRO Travel, Moscow (☎ (095) 971 40 59; fax (095) 280 76 86; e-mail tgh@glas.apc.org) – All with reservation. Tourist visa: one month's single-entry US$30. Business visa: three months single-entry US$45; three months multiple-entry US$150; six months multiple-entry US$175; one year's multiple-entry $250.

There are scores of other companies willing to issue commercial visa invitations, some cheaper, some more expensive. We are listing the above because we know them to be reliable and experienced, and because they follow through with registration.

Student Visa Student visas can be wonderful things; flexible, extendible and they even entitle you to pay Russian prices for airfares, train fares, and other items affected under the country's dual-pricing system (see Costs later in this chapter). Problem here is that you pretty much have to be legit: you'll need proof of enrolment at an accredited Russian school or university, which usually requires a lot of prepayment.

'Private' Visa This is what you get for a visit by personal invitation, and it's also referred to as an 'ordinary' visa by some authorities. The visa itself is as easy to get as a tourist visa but getting the invitation is complex.

The person who is to invite you must go to their local office of OVIR (or to the police in smaller towns) and fill out an invitation form for approval of the invitation. Approval, which takes several weeks, comes in the form of a notice of permission (*izveshchenie*), good for one year, which the person inviting must send to you. With this and with the standard application form you apply for the visa, which is valid for as many as 60 days in your host's town.

'On-the-Spot' Visa These are basically fast-track business visas, freed from the requirement for advance invitations. Individuals arriving from overseas at Moscow's Sheremetevo-2 or St Petersburg's Pulkovo-2 airports can get short-term visas at a special Intourist office before passport control. To get one of these, you'll have to arrange to be met at the airport by a representative of a Russian company, who will 'invite' you to Russia.

This kind of visa is good for up to a month, and attracts a fee of about US$150 to US$250. Though expensive and problematic, it may be one way around the paperchase.

Transit Visa This is for 'passing through', which is loosely interpreted. For transit by air it's usually good for 48 hours. For a nonstop Trans-Siberian Railway journey it's valid for 10 days, giving westbound passengers a few days in Moscow without the obligatory hotel prebooking (eastbounders can't linger in Moscow). Under certain circumstances, travellers transiting through Russia, holding valid entry/exit visas to Armenia, Belarus, Kazakstan, Kyrgyzstan, Tajikistan or Uzbekistan need not apply for a Russian transit visa. The requirements on this are sketchy, and while a Russian consulate may say it's unnecessary, the odds of being allowed into or out of Russia on the premise that you're holding a Tajik visa are slim. Many border guards are not familiar with the latest regulations handed down in Moscow, so it's always best to play it safe, especially when travelling to border crossings in remote areas.

Visa-Free Travel

Prebooked cruise passengers can visit Russian ports for up to four days without a visa if they sleep aboard the ship. In 1994, the Russian government added a curfew of 2 am to that restriction, but this may change in the future. This won't work for round-trip passengers on ordinary scheduled sailings. Visa-free cruises are available to several cities, see Getting There & Away for more information.

When to Apply

Apply as soon as you have all the documents you need (but not more than two months ahead). Business, tourist, private and student visas all take the same amount of time to process once you have the paper – be it invitation, confirmation or izveshchenie. This ought to be 10 working days, but at busy embassies such as London's it may be longer. You can pay a higher fee for quicker service at most embassies. Transit visas normally take seven working days, but may take as little as a few hours at the Russian Embassy in Beijing.

How to Apply

Russian visa procedures are straight out of Kafka. Individuals can arrange their own visas, though long queues at embassies and consulates are common in the high season and Russian consular officials are sometimes somewhat less than bright and perky – and they rarely answer the telephone. If you're booking your flight or accommodation through a travel agency, they'll get your visa too for an extra fee, usually between US$5 and US$30 (agencies in Hong Kong, which must go to Bangkok for visas, nail you for more). For group tours, the agency does the work.

Visa Agencies Certain agencies specialise in getting visas: eg in the USA, Visa Services (☎ (202) 387 0300), 1519 Connecticut Ave NW, Washington, DC 20036; in the UK, Worldwide Visas (☎ (0171) 379 0419), 9 Adelaide St, Charing Cross, London WC2 N4HZ. Unless you're really pressed for time or especially badly affected by impersonal bureaucracies, it seems a bit lavish, really. An agency will put your paperwork together and forward it to the embassy for you – for a fee of up to US$65.

In Person To do it yourself, go to the nearest Russian embassy or consulate (if you're not near one, see the following By Mail section). Bring your passport or photocopies of the pages covering your personal information and passport validity, your photographs and your hotel confirmation, hostel or business invitation, proof of enrolment, izveshchenie or through tickets. Ask for, and complete, the visa application, and then wait.

How long you wait depends on how much you're willing to pay. Rush fees vary not just by country but by individual consulate, but, as an example, the Russian Consulate in Seattle charges US$20 for service in 10 working days, US$40 for five-day service, US$60 for three-day service and US$100 for same or next-day service. A visa issued within half an hour and for a multi-entry visa costs US$120.

While Russian consular officials in some locations are friendly and even smile once in a while, those at others are often not. Unfortunately, there's not much you can do except be very polite and get out of there as quickly as you can. You *do* have the right to shop around: nothing is stopping you from taking care of your visa by mail at a known friendly consular office (in our experience) such as Helsinki, Warsaw or San Francisco.

By Mail It's possible to do it all by mail, with stamped, self-addressed envelopes or, if you have them, Federal Express, Airborne, DHL or TNT airbills, complete with your account number for all requested forms and completed documents. When you get the visa check it carefully, including expiry, entry and exit dates and any restrictions on entry or exit points.

Fax-Back Service In the USA (or if you use a US telephone carrier to get '1-800' service from overseas) you can obtain current visa requirements and application forms by fax by calling the Russian Fax-Back Service (embassy's consular section in London offers an interactive recorded message about visas (☎ 1-800 634 4296). A voice and touch-tone-driven menu will offer you choices of available documents. You may select up to four. The fax-back service will send within 10 minutes all the documents you select to any fax machine in the world (for international calls enter the code 011 plus your country and city code). The service is free.

London Interactive Telephone Service For callers in the UK, the Russian Embassy's consular section in London offers an interactive recorded message about visas (☎ (0891) 171 271). This is a premium-rate number which costs £0.49 per minute peak, £0.38 per minute cheap, but it tells you most of what you'll need to know in five to 10 minutes. Choose from six messages dealing with different types of visa. You then have to visit or write to the consulate to get the relevant forms. Even if (by some administrative oversight) you were so lucky as to get through on the main consulate number, you'd be referred to this recording anyway.

World Wide Web Information Those crazy, hacking diplomats at the Seattle, USA Russian Consulate have come up with a World Wide Web site (http://www.seanet.com/RussianPage/RussianPage.html) featuring reasonably accurate and relatively up-to-date visa information and requirements for several types of visas including tourist, business and transit. If you have further questions you can try to e-mail at consul@consul.seanet.com, though after receiving replies from this address I was more confused than when I began ...

Visa Extensions & Changes

Extensions have become time-consuming, if not down-right difficult. A tourist visa can now only be extended through official hotels (not hostels) and with a great deal of advance notice and perhaps of money.

Visitors on ordinary visas have succeeded in extending them by going to the local OVIR or police office and presenting telegrams from friends elsewhere in Russia inviting them to visit.

Where Can You Go?

Some cities in Russia are still off-limits to foreigners but these are few and far between. Technically any visa is valid for all of Russia except these closed cities. Practically speaking, no-one cares where you go.

You may have trouble with a tourist visa in a hotel in a strange city, not listed on the visa, though this can usually be talked around. If you will be venturing off the beaten path, it's best to play it safe and get a business visa, whose authoritative appearance effectively grants you the run of the country.

Lost or Stolen Documents

In order to facilitate replacement of your documents, it is imperative that you make and carry photocopies of them, especially your Russian visa. Without this photocopy, replacing a lost or stolen visa can be a nightmare, sometimes even requiring you to contact the issuing embassy and ask them to track down your visa number.

Your embassy or consulate in Russia can replace a lost or stolen passport, but if you lose your visa you must go to the local visa office, OVIR. A Russian travel agent, Intourist, your hotel service bureau, or the youth hostels can help with this, including reporting the loss to the police. Again, both procedures are much easier if you've stashed a few passport-size photos, your visa number and photocopies of your visa and your passport's personal information and validity pages.

EMBASSIES

Russian Embassies Abroad

Unless otherwise specified, the details listed below are for embassies.

Facts for the Visitor

Australia
78 Canberra Ave, Griffith,
Canberra, ACT 2603
(☎ (06) 295 9033, 295 9474;
fax (06) 295 1847)
Consulate: 7-9 Fullerton St,
Woollahra, NSW 2025
(☎ (02) 327 5065)

Austria
Reisnerstr 45-47, A-1030 Vienna
(☎ (0222) 712 1229, 712 3233, 713
1215; fax (0222) 712 3388)
Consulate: Bürgelsteinstr 2,
A-5020 Salzburg (☎ (0662) 62 41
84; fax (0662) 621 7434)

Azerbaijan
Hotel Azerbaijan, 370133 Baku
(☎ (8922) 98 60 16;
fax (9822) 98 60 83)

Belarus
vulitsa Staravilenskaja 48,
220002 Minsk (☎ (0172) 345 497;
fax (0172) 503 664)

Belgium
66 Avenue de Fre, B-1180
Brussels (☎ (02) 374 3406, 374
6886, 374 3106; fax (02) 374 2613,
346 2453)

Canada
285 Charlotte St, Ottawa,
Ontario K1N 8L5
(☎ (613) 235 4341, 235 5376, 236
1413;
fax (613) 236 6342)
Consular Section: 52 Range Rd,
Ottawa, Ontario K1N 8J5
(☎ (613) 236 6215, 236 7220;
fax (613) 238 6158)
Consulate: 3655 Avenue du
Musée, Montreal, Quebec H3G
2E1 (☎ (514) 843 5901, 842 5343;
fax (514) 842 2012)

China
4 Baizhongjie, Beijing 100600
(☎ (10) 532 2051, visa section 532
1267)
Consulate: 20 Huangpu Lu,
Shanghai 200080
(☎ (21) 324 2682)

Croatia
Bosanska 44, HR-41000 Zagreb
(☎ (041) 57 54 44, 57 54 35;
fax (041) 57 22 60)

Czech Republic
Podkaštany 1, Prague 6
(☎ (02) 38 19 43, 38 19 40;
fax (02) 37 38 00)

Consulate: Hlinky 1462, CZ-
60300 Brno (☎ (05) 33 44 27;
fax (05) 33 44 29);
Petra Velikého 18, CZ-36001
Karlovy Vary (☎ (017) 2 26 09;
fax (017) 2 62 61)

Denmark
Kristianiagade 5, DK-2100
Copenhagen (☎ 31 38 23 70,
31 42 55 85; fax 31 42 37 41)

Egypt
95 Giza St, Cairo
(☎ (2) 348 9353/4/5;
fax (2) 360 9074)

Estonia
Pikk 19, EE-0200 Tallinn
(☎ (22) 44 30 14; fax (22) 44 37 73)
Consulate: Vilde 8, EE-2020
Narva (☎ & fax (235) 3 13 67)

Finland
Tehtaankatu 1B, FIN-00140
Helsinki (☎ (90) 66 14 49, 66 18
76/7, 60 70 50; fax (90) 66 10 06)
Consulate: Vartiovuorenkatu 2,
20700 Turku (☎ (21) 233 64 41;
fax (21) 231 97 79)

France
40-50 Boulevard Lannes,
F-75116 Paris (☎ (1) 45 04 05 50,
45 04 71 71; fax (1) 45 04 17 65)
Consulate: 8 Rue Ambroise Pare,
F-13008 Marseille (☎ 91 77 15 25;
fax 91 77 34 54)

Germany
PO Box 200908, Waldstr 42,
D-53177 Bonn
(☎ (0228) 31 20 85/6/7, 31 25
29/32, 31 20 74;
fax (0228) 31 15 63)
Consulate: (☎ (0228) 31 20 75;
fax (0228) 38 45 61)
Consulate Berlin: Unter den
Linden 63-65, D-10117 Berlin
(☎ (030) 2 29 14 20;
fax (030) 2 29 93 97)
Consulate Hamburg: Am
Feenteich 20, D-22085 Hamburg
(☎ (040) 2 29 52 01;
fax (040) 2 29 77 27)
Consulate Leipzig:
Kickerlingsberg 18, D-04105
Leipzig (☎ (0341) 5 18 76;
fax (0341) 5 85 24 04)
Consulate Munich: Seidelstrasse
8, D-80355 Munich
(☎ (089) 59 25 03;
fax (089) 5 50 38 28)

Consulate Rostock:
Tuhnenstrasse 3, D-18057
Rostock (☎ (0381) 2 26 42;
fax (0381) 2 27 43)

Greece
Paleo Psikhico, 28 Nikiforou
Litra St, GR-15452 Athens
(☎ (01) 672 5235, 672 6130,
671 4504; fax (01) 647 9708)

Hungary
Bajza utea 35,
H-1062 Budapest V1
(☎ (1) 132 0911, 112 1013;
fax (1) 252 5077)

Ireland
186 Orwell Rd, Rathgar, Dublin
(☎ (01) 492 3525, 492 2048;
fax (01) 492 3525)

Israel
120 Rehov Hayarkon,
Tel Aviv 63573 (☎ (3) 522 6744,
522 6733/6; fax (3) 522 6713)

Italy
Via Gaeta 5, I-00186 Rome
(☎ (06) 494 1680/1, 494 1649;
fax (06) 49 10 31)
Consulate: Via St Aquilino 3,
I-20148 Milan
(☎ (02) 48 70 59 12, 48 70 60 41)

Japan
2-1-1 Azabudai, Minato-ku,
Tokyo 106 (☎ (3) 3583 5982, 3858
4297; fax (3) 3505 0593)
Consulate: (☎ (3) 3586 0707;
fax (3) 3505 0593)
Consulate Osaka-Fu: Toyonaka-
Shi, Nishimidorigaoka 1-2-2,
Osaka-Fu (☎ (6) 848 3452;
fax (6) 848 3453)
Consulate Sapporo: 826 Nishi,
12-chome, Minami 14 Jo,
Chuo-ku, Sapporo 064
(☎ (11) 561 3171/2;
fax (11) 561 8897)

Kazakstan
ulitsa Dzhandosova 4, Almaty
(☎ (3272) 44 83 32, visa enquiries
44 66 44)

Kyrgyzstan
ulitsa Pervomayskaya 17,
Bishkek (☎ (3312) 22 16 91;
fax (3312) 22 18 23, 22 17 10)

Latvia
Paeglesiela 2,
LV-1397 Riga
(☎ (2) 33 21 51, 22 06 93;
fax (2) 21 25 79)

Lithuania
Juozapaviciaus gatve 11, LT-2000
Vilnius (☎ (22) 35 17 63;
fax (22) 35 38 77)

Moldova
bulvar Stefan del Mare 151,
277019 Chisinau
(☎ & fax (2) 23 26 00)

Mongolia
Friendship St A 6,
Ulan Bator (☎ (1) 7 28 51, 2 68 36,
2 75 06)

Netherlands
Andries Bickerweg 2, NL-2517 JP
The Hague (☎ (070) 345 13 00/1,
346 88 88, 34 10 75 06;
fax (070) 361 7960)
Consulate: (☎ (070) 346 7940)

New Zealand
57 Messines Rd, Wellington
(☎ (04) 476 6113;
fax (04) 476 3843)

North Korea
Choson Minjujuii inmin,
Chuji Soryong Tesagwan,
Conghwaguck, Pyongyang
(☎ (2) 81 31 01/2)

Norway
Drammensveen 74,
0271 Oslo (☎ 22 55 32 78/9;
fax 22 55 00 70)

Poland
ulitsa Belwederska 49,
PL-00-761 Warsaw
(☎ (022) 21 34 53, 21 59 54;
fax (02) 625 3016)
Consulate: ulitsa Batorego 15,
PL-80-251 Gdansk-Wrzeszcz
(☎ (058) 41 42 00, 41 96 39)
Consulate Kracow: ulitsa
Westerplatte 11,
PL-31-033 Kracow
(☎ (012) 22 26 47, 22 92 33,
22 83 88)
Consulate Poznan: ulitsa
Dukowska 53A, PL-60-567
Poznan (☎ (061) 41 75 23,
41 77 40)
Consulate Szezecin: ulitsa P
Skargi 14, PL-71-422 Szezecin
(☎ (091) 22 22 45, 22 48 77, 22 21
19, 22 03 33)

Portugal
Rua Visconde de Santarem 59,
P-1000 Lisbon (☎ (01) 8462424,
8462524, 8462623;
fax (01) 8463008)

Romania
Sioseaua Kiseleff 6, Bucharest
(☎ (1) 617 0120/8/9, 617 23 22,
617 0129; fax (1) 617 7659, 312
8405)
Consulate: Str Mihai Viteazul 5,
Constantina
(☎ (41) 61 51 68, 61 11 06)

Slovakia
Godrova 4, SK-81106 Bratislava
(☎ (7) 31 34 68; fax (7) 33 49 10)

Slovenia
Cesta II.st 7,
SLO-61000 Ljubljana
(☎ (061) 26 11 89;
fax (061) 125 4141)

South Africa
PO Box 6743 Pretoria 0001,
Butano Building,
316 Brooks St, Menlo Park
0081
(☎ (12) 43 27 31/2;
fax (12) 43 28 42)
Consular Section:
135 Bourke St, Sunnyside 0002
(☎ (12) 344 4820, 344 4812;
fax (12) 343 8636)
Consulate: 8 Riebeeck St,
Cape Town 8001
(☎ (21) 418 3656/7, 419 2651;
fax (21) 419 2651)

South Korea
10001-13/14/15 Dacchi-Dng,
Kangnam-Ku, Seoul
(☎ (2) 554 9674, 555 8051;
fax (2) 558 5608, 563 3589)

Spain
Velázquez 155, E-28002 Madrid
(☎ (91) 411 0807, 562 2264;
fax (91) 562 9712)
Consulate: Avenida Pearson
40-42, E-08034 Barcelona
(☎ (93) 204 0246;
fax (93) 280 5541)

Sweden
Gjoerwellsgatan 31, S-11260
Stockholm
(☎ (08) 13 04 41/2/0, 53 37 32;
fax (08) 618 2703)

Switzerland
Brunnadernrain 37,
CH-3006 Bern (☎ (031) 352 05
66, 352 64 65; fax (031) 352 55 95)
Consulate: Brunnadernrain 53,
CH-30006 Bern
(☎ (031) 352 05 67, 352 64 25;
fax (031) 352 64 60)

Consulate Geneva: 24 Rue Jean
Schaub CH-1202 Geneva
(☎ (022) 734 79 55, 734 90 83)

Turkey
Karyagdi Sok 5, Cankaya TR-
06692 Ankara (☎ (312) 440 8217,
439 2122/3; fax (312) 438 3952)

Turkmenistan
11 Turkmenbashy Shaely,
744004 Ashkhabad
(☎ (3632) 25 39 57, 29 84 66;
fax (3632) 29 84 66)

Ukraine
vulitsya Kutuzova 8, UKR-
252000 Kiev (☎ (044) 294 79 36;
fax (044) 292 66 31)

UK
13 Kensington Palace Gardens,
London W8 4QX
(☎ (0171) 229 3628/9;
fax (0171) 727 8624/5, 299 5804)
Consular Section: 5 Kensington
Palace Gardens, London W8
4QS (☎ (0171) 229 8027, visa
message (0891) 171271);
fax (0171) 229 3215)
Consulate: 9 Coates Cres,
Edinburgh E 113 7RL
(☎ (0131) 225 7098;
fax (0131) 225 9587)

USA
2650 Wisconsin Ave NW,
Washington, DC 20007
(☎ (202) 298 5700, 298 5772;
fax (202) 298 5749)
Visa Department: 1825 Phelps
Pl NW, Washington, DC 20008
(☎ (202) 939 8907;
fax (202) 939 8909)
Consulate Seattle: 2323 Westin
Bldg, 2001 Sixth Ave, Seattle,
WA 98121-2617
(☎ (206) 728 1910;
fax (206) 728 1871; e-mail
consul@consul. seanet.com;
Internet
http://www.seanet.com/
RussianPage/RussianPage.html)
Consulate San Francisco:
2790 Green St,
San Francisco, CA 94123-4609
(☎ (415) 928 6878;
fax (415) 929 0306)
Consulate New York:
9 East 91st St,
New York, NY 10128
(☎ (212) 348 0926, 348 0955;
fax (212) 831 9162)

Uzbekistan
ulitsa Nukusskaya (formerly
ulitsa Poltoratskaya) 83, 750015
Tashkent (☎ (3712) 54 36 41,
55 92 18, 55 91 57;
fax (3712) 55 87 74)

Vietnam
58 Tran Phu, Hanoi
(☎ (4) 25 46 31/2; fax (4) 25 61 77)

Yugoslavia
Deligradska 32, YU-11000 Bel-
grade (☎ (11) 65 67 24, 64 53 45)

Foreign Consulates in St Petersburg

Consulates in St Petersburg include:

Bulgaria
Ryleeva ulitsa 27 (☎ 273 73 47;
fax 272 57 18)

Canada
Malodetskoselsky prospekt 32
(☎ 119 84 48; fax 119 83 93)

China
naberezhnaya Kanala
Griboedova 134 (☎ 114 62 30)

Cuba
Ryleeva ulitsa 37 (☎ 272 53 03)

Czech and Slovak Republics
ulitsa Tverskaya 5 (☎ 271 04 59,
271 61 01; fax 271 46 15)

Denmark
Bolshaya alleya 13, Kamenny
Ostrov (☎ 234 37 55)

Estonia
Bolshaya Monetnaya ulitsa 14
(☎ 233 55 48)

Finland
ulitsa Chaykovskogo 71
(☎ 273 73 21, emergency
116 06 52)
Commercial Department: 4-ya
Krasnoarmeyskaya ulitsa 4a
(☎ 316 16 41)

France
naberezhnaya reki Moyki 15
(☎ 314 14 43)

Germany
ulitsa Furshtadtskaya 39
(☎ 273 55 98, 279 32 07)

Hungary
ulitsa Marata 15
(☎ 312 67 53, 312 64 58)

India
Ryleeva ulitsa 35 (☎ 272 19 88)

Italy
Teatralnaya ploshchad 10
(☎ 312 32 17, 312 31 06)

Japan
naberezhnaya reki Moyki 29
(☎ 314 14 18, 314 14 34)

Latvia
Galernaya ulitsa 69 (☎ 315 17 74)

Netherlands
prospekt Morisa Toreza
(☎ 554 48 90, 554 49 00)

Poland
5-ya Sovietskaya ulitsa 12
(☎ 274 43 18, 274 41 70)

South Africa
naberezhnaya reki Moyki 11
(☎ 119 63 63)

Sweden
10-ya linia No 11, Vasilevsky
Island (☎ 213 41 91)

UK
ploshchad Proletarskoy
Diktatury 5 (☎ 119 60 36)
Visa Department: (☎ 119 61 66)

USA
ulitsa Furshtadtskaya 15 (metro:
Chernyshevskaya; ☎ 274 86 89,
274 85 68, 275 17 01). It's open
for routine business for US
citizens from 9 am to 5.30 pm
Monday to Friday, Notarial
services until noon Monday to
Friday. There's a 24-hour duty
officer for emergencies.

Australian and New Zealand citizens must apply to
their embassy in Moscow, though in emergencies you
can seek help at the British, Canadian and US consulates.

CUSTOMS

Customs agents seem as little interested in extra hassle as travellers are, and rarely seem to make wilful trouble. Bags on trains are rifled through (usually cursorily); bags on planes are x-rayed for security as well as customs purposes.

On arrival, fill out a customs declaration (*deklaratsia*), listing all your money and valuables, including jewellery, cameras, portable electronics etc. There is no Green line through customs – everyone's checked except diplomats.

You may be waved right through but don't count on it. The deklaratsia is duly written on, stamped with a smart bang and returned to you. When you leave Russia you give it to customs, as well as another declaration of what you're taking out.

What You Can Bring In

You may bring in modest amounts of anything for personal use except illegal drugs (even today several foreigners are serving stiff jail terms in Russia), weapons and roubles. Cameras, notebook computers, video cameras, radios and Walkmans, and video and audio tapes are OK. If you're bringing in hypodermic needles, make sure you bring in a prescription for them.

A few pairs of jeans and up to 250 cigarettes are fine but large amounts of anything sellable are suspect. Food is allowed (except for some fresh fruit and vegetables) and a litre of hard liquor or wine.

You can get a receipt (*kvitantsia*) for any confiscated item and you might succeed in reclaiming it when you leave.

What You Can Take Out

Anything bought from a *beryozka* or Western-style shop or department store can go out, but save your receipts. You technically can't take Russian currency with you, though they won't usually check your pockets or wallet. The money statement on your declaration is designed to prevent you from taking more money out of the country than you brought in. If you're bringing in a large amount, declare it; when you bring in amounts over US$1000 in cash you will probably be asked to show the customs agent the cash when you arrive – this is to prevent you from inflating your claim on the way in to cover an amount you plan to take out.

Anything vaguely 'arty', like manuscripts, instruments, coins, jewellery, antiques or antiquarian books (meaning those published before 1975) must be assessed by the Ministry of Culture in St Petersburg (☎ (812) 314 82 34) at naberezhnaya Kanala Griboedova 107. There, bean-counting bureaucrats will issue a receipt for tax paid (usually 100% of the purchase price – bring your sales receipt) which you show to customs on your way out of the country. If you buy something large, a photograph will usually be fine for assessment purposes.

If you're counting on a benevolent customs agent on the way out, we've got some primo beachfront property in Chernobyl to sell you; uncleared art commands punitive taxation in excess of 600% at customs, when you're trying to get on that plane and you're in a hurry ...

A painting bought at tourist art markets, or in a department store or a commercial gallery, is probably not a cultural treasure, though it should be declared and receipts should be kept. Generally speaking, customs in airports is much more strict and thorough than any other border crossing. Drug dealers routinely carry their cargo on trains, and thorough car searches are a rare thing indeed but they do happen occasionally, so beware.

Since 1990, the removal from the country of certain consumer goods – including furs, caviar, tea, fabrics, some clothing, carpets, leather, photo equipment, electrical appliances and precious metal and stones (but not fine art) has been prohibited. Customs agents at Pulkovo-2 airport seem to have magic noses capable of sniffing caviar at 100 metres. They'll happily rip through bags to find it, and when they do they'll confiscate it.

MONEY

The Russian currency unit is the rouble *(ROO-bl)*, whose name is its most consistent property. Under the Soviets, the rouble's value was fixed at a preposterous parity with the British pound (perhaps the cause of the collapse of the pound?) but since 1991 the value has been given more or less freedom to float. As one would imagine, it floated right into a sink-hole and is now one of the world's most worthless currencies. But prices do stay relatively stable when looked at in US$ equivalents, which is what we use in this book. We also round up to the nearest US$0.10 or US$1, depending on the value of the particular listing.

Free market exchange has pressured the currency so greatly that its present value of about US$1 = R4500 has resulted in the discontinuation of the rouble's incremental unit, the kopek, and the last couple of years have seen mass redesign of the currency and introduction of ever-increasing note denominations, and each note has a distinct colour and many have different sizes.

Currently there are R100 (blue), R200 (pink), R500 (green), R1000 (green), R5000 (red), R10,000 (lighter green), R50,000 (beige-orange) and R100,000 (yellowish) notes available. Just before we went to press, new notes were in the process of being introduced, which would circulate side-by-side with existing currency. These new notes feature scenes of Moscow (R100,000), St Petersburg (R50,000) and Krasnoyarsk (R10,000).

Currency reform has made all notes issued before 1993 worthless. Don't accept any blue R5000 or red R10,000 notes or any note bearing a picture of Lenin, unless you're looking for souvenirs. A further result of the reform is that all transactions made within the

ROGER HAYNE

Imperial soldiers (extras for a movie)

Russian Republic must be made in roubles – hard-currency bars or shops are no more. There are only a couple of exceptions to this (eg international air tickets), and credit cards (see later) are accepted, though you'll see that the amount you pay has been converted from roubles at the exchange rate set by the central bank on the day of the transaction as it is everywhere else.

Foreign Currency

US dollars are the most widely accepted foreign currency, followed by Deutschmarks and Finnish markka. It's best to carry one of these because other currencies, no matter what they're worth on the international marketplace, are difficult to change into roubles.

Whatever currency you're taking into Russia, make certain that all the notes are in pristine condition. Worn, damaged, faded or written on notes will be refused. Larger notes are more readily accepted than smaller notes, but you should always also have at least US$100 in small denomination notes for times when you're stuck changing money at an awful rate.

If you're taking US dollars, make sure all your US$20, US$50 and US$100 notes were minted after 1991. As an anti-counterfeit device, these newer notes have an embedded thread (microprinted with the currency face value) running from top to bottom approximately beneath the words 'This Note Is Legal Tender ...' (to the left of the portrait). The thread is visible when the note is held up to light and Russian moneychangers always check for it.

Rules & Regulations

The currency statement on entry to the country is designed to thwart those taking *out* more money than they brought *in*. If you write that you're bringing in, say, US$5000, customs agents will ask you to show them the money, to prove that you're not padding to cover an amount that you're coming to Russia to pick up, or plan on earning while in the country.

Exchange Rates

Australia	A$1 =	R3423
Canada	C$1 =	R3387
Germany	DM1 =	R3165
France	Ffr1 =	R903
UK	UK£1 =	R7133
USA	US$1 =	R4507
Japan	¥100 =	R4469

Banks & Exchange Offices

There are legal exchange offices practically everywhere in St Petersburg in hotels, restaurants, boutiques, back alleys, vegetable shops etc.

Here are some of the more prominent exchange offices and banks in the city:

Promstroy (Industry & Construction) Bank
> Head office: Nevsky prospekt 38, entrance in Mikhailovskaya ulitsa across from the Grand Hotel Europe (though it has small offices all over town) – offers cash advances on Visa/MasterCard/Eurocard

Saint Petersburg Savings Bank
> Head office: Nevsky prospekt 38, entrance in Mikhailovskaya ulitsa across from the Grand Hotel Europe – offers cash advances on Visa/MasterCard/Eurocard, buys and sells travellers' cheques

Astrobank
> Nevsky prospekt 58 is a moneychanging office

Hotels: Astoria, Grand Hotel Europe, Nevskij Palace, Oktyabrskaya, Moskva, Saint Petersburg, Prebaltiyskaya, Hotelship Peterhof, Helen, Pulkovskaya and others – many offer cash advances on Visa/MasterCard/Eurocard; the Grand Hotel Europe and Nevskij Palace Hotel can organise travellers' cheques as well

Banks and exchange offices are competitive; representative rates are printed in the *Moscow Times* and the *St Petersburg Press*, so comparison shopping is quite easy. Generally speaking, private exchange offices are a few points higher than the central bank rate, but as competition increases, we will see greater spreads between buy and sell rates and more gouging of the rates at and around popular tourist spots, such as the Hermitage.

Whether you change in a bank or an exchange office, they will fill out an official receipt showing your name, the date and the currency and exchange rate. This is for your records only; practically speaking, you don't need this receipt to reconvert roubles, and you needn't show it to customs on the way out to justify expenditure of money along the way.

A 1995 rule designed (if you can believe this) to keep track of the money supply requires that you show your passport whenever you change money in the Russian Federation whether at a private exchange office or a bank. This rule was widely ignored in Moscow, but taken to heart in St Petersburg, and may or may not be current practice when you visit.

Whenever you change money, your cash will be subjected to some of the most ridiculous counterfeit detection methods you'll ever see. Try not to get insulted, and if there is a question about your note, point out watermarks and other counterfeit prevention features. If you're turned away, hit the next exchange office.

The Black Market

Russia's famous black marketeers are as quaint as the dictatorship of the proletariat, but those *fartsovshchiky* are indeed a resilient lot. Despite the fact that legal, privately owned exchange booths are as plentiful in St Petersburg as they are in Amsterdam, the question 'Change money?' will still ring in the ears of foreigners as they walk the city's streets.

Tourist hotels and markets and state-run exchange offices are the favourite haunts of the people who make at least a part-time living by wheeling and dealing with foreigners.

When you have a legal alternative, and in St Petersburg you almost always do, it's best to avoid the black marketeers completely. Their rates are not much (or at all) better than the official rate. Furthermore, they have been at this game for a long time and given a great deal of thought as to how to separate you from your money, and practice does make perfect.

If you decide to change money on the street, take every precaution and use common sense.

Travellers' Cheques, Cash or Credit Cards?

Yes. Take all three if you can. Cash is always the preferred method of payment, though credit cards are making big inroads, at least in the city itself, where Visa, MasterCard/Eurocard and American Express are widely accepted.

The fact that travellers' cheques are refundable makes them the safest way to carry your money, and you can also use them to pay direct for many goods and services. But outside St Petersburg and Moscow, cheques can be more difficult to cash, and as difficult as cash to replace.

US dollar travellers' cheques are probably your best bet. Take both small denominations (for buying roubles when the rate is awful) and big ones (to minimise commission, which is charged per cheque, for when you need to cash a lot of money). American Express is the most widely recognised brand in Russia, and their full service office (☎ 119 60 09) is at the Grand Hotel Europe, Mikhailovskaya ulitsa 1/7, open 9 am to 5 pm daily except Sunday. The exchange office there (and the one across the street) will usually encash US dollar travellers' cheques directly into US dollars for a 1% commission, though if they're short on cash they give preference to American Express brand cheques.

Thomas Cook is another widely recognised international brand, though they are much cagier about refund procedures than American Express. If your cheques are lost or stolen, you are required to call their world headquarters in the UK (☎ (44 1733) 502 995), which will assess your claim and, if they're very happy about everything and you don't sound dodgy, they'll authorise a refund through their Moscow offices at ulitsa Kuznetsky Most 15 (☎ (095) 924 17 34).

Visa travellers' cheques can be cashed in St Petersburg and Moscow relatively easily. Westpac travellers' cheques, though, are very difficult to cash in Russia – they may be big down under but not here.

Credit cards are accepted at many of the better restaurants, hotels and shops, and cash advances against Visa and MasterCard are a simple matter in St Petersburg. Generally, there's a 3% to 5% commission tacked onto the amount of the cash advance. The US Consulate in St Petersburg recommends that you use a bank, as opposed to an exchange office, for cash advances of large sums; if you're really rich and want to get sums of US$10,000 or more, one day's notice is usually required.

It's harder to get cash advances in smaller towns and cities, but credit cards are being accepted in more and more places. Visa, MasterCard/Eurocard, and American Express/Optima are the most widely accepted cards, while some places also accept Diners Club and JCB. The Discover card is not accepted in Russia.

Be very careful when paying by credit card that you see how many slips are being made of your card, that you destroy all carbons, and that as few people as possible get hold of your card number and expiry date. You're usually safe in Western-owned establishments, but one major hotel had problems with its staff making multiple copies of cards. The stolen credit card market in Russia is booming, so protect you card as much as possible.

Also note that sometimes a Visa sign is just a decoration. Russians love colourful Western stickers, and Visa signs are 'pretty'. Even if you see the sign, ask if the card is accepted before you go and order the pheasant under glass.

Wire Transfers

Wire-transferring money to Russia is far easier than it used to be, though the price is high. The fastest way to transfer money from the US, Canada, UK, New Zealand,

Australia, Germany, France and Finland, as well as the most expensive, is through Western Union, which has branch offices in St Petersburg at the following banks:

Inkombank, Nevsky prospekt 57 (☎ 113 19 70), and other branches
Moskovsky Bank, Kamennoostrovsky prospekt (Kirovsky prospekt) 40 (☎ 234 44 79)
Mezhekonombank, Blagodatnaya 6 (☎ 296 01 81)
Promstroybank, Galernaya ulitsa 24 (☎ 312 43 42)
St Peterburgbank, ploshchad Ostrovskogo 7 (☎ 119 61 87)

Western Union charges US$40 for a US$500 transfer, US$15 for a US$100 transfer.

Direct bank-to-bank wire transfer is also possible. You'll probably need to open an account at a local bank, and pay fees and a percentage of the money wired into that account. Depending on the bank, service takes one to five days. Ask at the hotels or the hostels or check *The Traveller's Yellow Pages* or *Where In St Petersburg* for a listing of banks in the city.

Emergency Cheque Cashing

If you're an American Express or Optima card-holder, you can use your personal cheque to buy travellers' cheques from the American Express full-service office at the Grand Hotel Europe, Mikhailovskaya ulitsa 1/7. If you don't have a personal cheque, you can still get some travellers' cheques, but the limits are much lower. Laws on this, at the time of writing, were iffy; if the American Express office can't perform this service for some reason, they'll refer you to a bank that will perform it, usually nearby. Limits depend on your card type and/or credit limit. Every 21 days you can get up to US$1000 on a green card, US$5000 on a gold card and US$10,000 on a platinum card (on Optima cards you're also limited by the amount of available credit).

Costs

St Petersburg is not as cheap as other Eastern European cities, nor even as the rest of Russia (outside Moscow). A major cost is accommodation: unless you're staying at one of the hostels or at a homestay, it's hard to get accommodation for less than US$20 to US$30 a day, even if a hotel's rack (standard, walk-in) rate is listed here as less. The reason is a serious demand-versus-supply situation and what amounts to one of the world's great seller's markets.

If you're careful, that is you stay in a cheap homestay or hostel, stick to self-catering and inexpensive restaurants/cafés and don't drink much beer, other alcohol or Western soft drinks, you may be able to squeak through on about US$20 to US$25 per day in summer (high season). Staying at a higher-end B&B or inexpensive hotel and eating in inexpensive restaurants will cost US$35 to US$50, and a double room in a hotel with a private bath, a television and a telephone will average US$60 with advance reservations or through a travel agent, much more without.

It's still a worthwhile effort to check out package tours as an option. While Lonely Planet readers need no introduction to the benefits of individual travel, Russia's tourism infrastructure, which was for so many years geared to moving in herds of tourists and shepherding them from site to site, still rewards group travellers with some pretty hard-to-beat bargains.

Public transportation may as well be free; in 1995, a ride on a bus or the metro cost US$0.06. Taxis are slightly more expensive (and slightly complicated; see the Getting Around chapter for more information) but are still priced less than their Western equivalents.

Here are a few sample prices just to give you an idea:

- lunch or dinner with drinks (per person) in a hotel, state-run or inexpensive restaurant US$5 to US$15; in a good restaurant US$30 to US$100)
- bus, tram, trolleybus or metro ride about US$0.10
- taxi from the Admiralty to the airport US$10 to US$15; taxi from the airport to the HI St Petersburg Hostel US$20 to US$25 unless your Russian's great; taxi from Petrogradskaya metro to the HI St Petersburg Hostel US$2
- excursion from St Petersburg to Petrodvorets US$15 per person in a group; US$100 for up to six people in St Petersburg Travel Company car with guide; US$5 unguided using public hydrofoil
- admission to the Hermitage US$9 for foreigners, US$0.20 for Russians
- litre of milk US$0.55
- loaf of bread US$0.40
- copy of *Time* US$4
- 6" Subway roast beef sandwich US$3.85
- bottle of Russian/imported beer in a kiosk or shop US$0.30/1

Value Added Tax

The usurious 23% Value Added Tax (VAT, in Russian NDS) is usually included in the price listed for purchases, but make sure.

Tipping

A lasting bequest of Communism in this place is that
tipping is not as widespread as it could be. It's standard in
the better restaurants; count on a straight 10% there,
whereas elsewhere 5% to 10% will be fine. Tipping your
guide, if you have one, is an accepted practice. This is
totally discretionary: we tend to tip more to guides from
smaller companies than larger ones, but generally about
US$5 to US$10 for a day would be a nice tip. Small gifts,
like a bottle of skin cream, a box of imported chocolates or
a cassette or CD, are appropriate if the service was great,
but remember that the gifts of yore (packets of Marlboro,
badges and pins etc) are no longer of value here.

Dual-Pricing System

You can call it an outrage, you can call it unfair, but at the
end of the day, you'll call it 1000% more for foreigners than
for Russians on most entry fees to museums and cultural
events. Foreigners will have to pay about twice the Russian
rate for many hotels, about a third more for train fares and
several times more for airfares. Ask a Russian why this is
true and they'll give you a variety of justifications: 'it is not
so much for you, I think', 'you have more money than us',
and 'this museum is here for Russians, not for foreigners'
top the list of frequently heard responses (that last one
coming from the head curator of St Petersburg's Hermitage, who was justifying a US$9 entry fee for foreigners and
US$0.20 for Russians).

There's nothing you can do but try as often as you can
to get the Russian rate. Speak Russian as best you can,
don't show your passport until the last possible second,
proffer the correct amount that Russians would pay to
cash desk clerks (never volunteer the foreigner rate
unless you're feeling overly philanthropic), and have
Russian friends buy train, bus and theatre tickets for you
wherever possible (for more information see the Getting
Around chapter). Use student and senior citizen discount cards (see the following section) as often as
possible and fight for the discount. Note that it's difficult
to get a Russian price on the train between St Petersburg
and Moscow unless your Russian is quite good.

Youth, Student & Senior-Citizen Discounts

These do exist, though they're rarely advertised. Full-
time students and people aged under 26 or over 59 tend
to get a substantial discount on admissions, transport

and perhaps even hotels. Always try flashing your ID
before paying.

Full-time students can get an International Student
Identification Card (ISIC) from student agencies worldwide; if you're not a student but you are under 26, ask
your student agency for information. ISIC cards are
available through the HI St Petersburg Hostel, which
also has an up-to-date list of where it's good for discounts in St Petersburg. The price is about US$10, and
the ISIC is good throughout the world.

British Railways and the American Association for
Retired People issue identification cards for seniors, and
similar organisations exist in other Western countries.

TOURIST OFFICES & INFORMATION

The pioneering, nonprofit Tourist Information Centre
(TIC), in the lobby of the Hotel Astoria, was closed in the
spring of 1995, but several organisations now fill the gap
left by the TIC's demise.

Peter TIPS

The first fully fledged tourist information centre to
operate entirely independently from the organs of state
tourism opened in 1995 at Nevsky prospekt 86, in Dom
Aktyor, the House of Actors. It's a subsidiary of Ost-West
Contact Service, a German-owned travel services
company. Peter TIPS (☎ 279 00 37) is a very friendly place
that hands out free city maps, city information, pamphlets and brochures, and practical information about
transportation in and around St Petersburg. It offers free
hotel-booking services and its staff are generally good
eggs.

For a fee, city and regional tours and excursions can
be arranged – eg a one-hour bus tour of St Petersburg is
US$15, a German-language tour to Novgorod including
transport and lunch is US$140 for one person, then
US$25 for each additional person. Tickets to all the city's
cultural outlets are sold at the Russian price plus a 10%
mark-up; Kirov ballet tickets from them in May 1995
would therefore cost US$3.75. Other services include the
issuing and support of tourist, business and cultural
exchange visas – a three-month invitation costs US$10,
though they charge US$15 for visa registration. Contact
Ost-West at ☎ 279 36 35 for more information.

HI St Petersburg Hostel

The registration desk at the HI St Petersburg Hostel
(☎ 329 80 18) is staffed by very helpful English-speaking
staff who are experienced in getting around the city
cheaply. They'll book most of the things that can be
booked by other agencies and hotels, but they'll give you
more of an idea of what's really available. There's also a
budget travel agency, downstairs (see the Travel Agencies section in Getting There & Away), and they sell
domestically and internationally published guidebooks
(including Lonely Planet).

St Petersburg Travel Company

The St Petersburg Travel Company (formerly Intourist)
(☎ 315 51 29) has a desk in the Astoria, where it arranges
city tours and a wide range of other (albeit for profit)
services, including car rentals, theatre and Kirov tickets
etc. Its main office is directly across the street at
Isaakievsky ploshchad 11 (the sign on the building says
'Dresdner Bank'), room 101, to the left as you enter.

Hotels

The concierge desks in the Grand Hotel Europe and the
Nevskij Palace Hotel have extremely knowledgeable
and helpful staff, and they'll usually help you even if you
don't look like a millionaire, but it's best to dress neatly.
They can also arrange everything that you'd expect a city
travel desk to arrange: tours, excursions, car rentals,
theatre tickets etc. These services cost a lot in the form of
marked-up prices, though they'll dish out a good deal
of advice free for the asking.

Other Information Sources

Newspapers The *St Petersburg Press* is a reliable and
readable weekly English-language newspaper with an
ever-growing classified advertising section. It's also available on line through the Internet, on its World Wide Web
home page (http://www.spb.su/) that also features other
services like photos of the city, room-by-room tours of the
Hermitage etc. Well worth checking out.

Pulse is a slick colour monthly with tons of club, pub,
nightlife and other information about the city at large,
written with a very young and fresh outlook. It's available free in outlets all over the city.

The city's other English-language offering, the *Neva
News*, is pathetic and sometimes laughably incoherent.

The *Moscow Times* is available at the two youth hostels and in some hotels and so far it's free.

Expatriate Organisations If you're staying in town for business, you may want to attend a meeting of the American International Business Association, a group comprised of Western businesspeople (not just Americans) which addresses problems and concerns of expatriate residents. For more information contact the association's executive administrator Luke Angell (☎ 110 60 42; fax 311 07 94), ulitsa Bolshaya Morskaya (ulitsa Gertsena) 57.

Notice Boards There's a notice board at the US Consulate, inside the room used for visas and citizen services, that sometimes has notices for accommodation, translators, language tutors etc. There's also a board at the HI St Petersburg Hostel where travellers post notices and restaurant reviews, tips etc but it's under used.

CULTURAL CENTRES

There's a whole lot o' culture going on at naberezhnaya reki Fontanki 46. On the 3rd floor sits the British Council St Petersburg (☎ 119 60 74), part of the organisation that 'represents Britain in the areas of culture ... in over 100 countries'. Now, just hold on a second; it's more than just upper-middle-aged rock bands and Monty Python stars being shamelessly junketed by the old-boy-network; this is serious stuff. The council sponsors classical concerts, theatre and other performances and arranges for exchanges of students, professionals and (frighteningly) economists between the two countries, and has a great resource centre for foreign teachers of English.

Down one flight of stairs, the Prince George Vladimirovich Golitsyna Memorial Library (☎ 311 13 33) is a lovely reading room containing books in English and Russian pertaining to Russian culture and British-Russian links. They also have encyclopaedias and other reference books, and they allow you to photocopy sections free.

The Goethe Institute St Petersburg (☎ 219 49 75)) is in the same building but is hard to find: walk into the lobby, straight to the back, turn right, follow the narrow hallway and take the flight of stairs up to find the German cultural centre. It works on similar lines to the British Council, but offers less fodder for jokes.

The American Center (☎ 311 89 05) at the Marble Palace disseminates American culture (snigger). It's open from 9 am to 5.30 pm at ulitsa Millionnaya 5.

BUSINESS HOURS

Government offices open Monday to Friday from 9 or 10 am to 5 or 6 pm. Foreign exchange banks usually open from 9 am to noon; those in major cities also open from 1 to 8.30 pm.

Most shops are open Monday to Saturday. Food shops tend to open from 8 am to 8 pm except for a break *(pereryv)* from 1 to 2 pm or 2 to 3 pm; some close later, some open Sunday until 5 pm. Other shops operate from 10 or 11 am to 7 or 8 pm with a 2 to 3 pm break. Department stores may open from 8 am to 8 or 9 pm without a break. A few shops stay open through the weekend and close Monday.

Restaurants typically open from noon to midnight except for a break between afternoon and evening meals (yes, for lunch). Cafés may open and close earlier.

Museum hours change like quicksilver, as do their weekly days off. Most shut entrance doors 30 minutes or an hour before closing time and may have shorter hours on the day before their day off. Some just seem to close without reason and a few stay that way for years.

Beware the *sanitarnyy den* (sanitary day). Once a month, usually near the end of the month (the last Tuesday, for example), nearly all establishments – shops, museums, restaurants, hotel dining rooms – shut down for cleaning, each on its own day and not always with much publicity.

PUBLIC HOLIDAYS

After more than seven decades of official atheism, religious holidays are once again kosher in Russia.

The main public holidays are:

1 January
  New Year's Day
7 January
  Russian Orthodox Christmas Day
23 February
  Defenders of the Motherland Day – a new holiday from 1996 to celebrate the anniversary of the founding of the Red Army
8 March
  International Women's Day
1 & 2 May
  International Labour Day/Spring Festival
9 May
  Victory (1945) Day
12 June
  Russian Independence Day
7 November
  Great October Socialist Revolution Anniversary

FESTIVALS & EVENTS

During the white nights of the last 10 days of June, when night never falls, many St Petersburgers stay out celebrating White Nights quietly or otherwise all night, particularly at weekends. There's a tourist-oriented White Nights Dance Festival with events ranging from folk to ballet, but the main Kirov company doesn't always take part – more often its students do. The Russian Winter (25 December to 5 January) and Goodbye Russian Winter (late February to early March) festivities centre outside the city, with troyka rides, folk shows and performing bears.

NICK SELBY

Fireworks over Peter & Paul Fortress during Victory Day
(WW II) celebrations

Less tourist-oriented are the Christmas Musical Meetings in Northern Palmyra, a classical music festival held, since 1991, during the week before Christmas. The locations change; check the *St Petersburg Press* for details. The St Petersburg Music Spring, an international classical music festival held in April or May, and the mid-November International Jazz Festival, Osenie Ritmy (Autumn Rhythms), is built around St Petersburg's jazz club.

Russian festivals have shaken off the joyous-workers'-march-past image. A miscellany:

7 January
  Russian Orthodox Christmas (Rozhdestvo) – begins with midnight church services.
Late February, Early March
  Goodbye Russian Winter – festivities centre outside the city, with troyka rides, folk shows etc.
March-April
  Easter (Paskha) – main festival of Orthodox Church year. Easter Day begins with celebratory midnight services, after which people eat special dome-shaped cakes called *kulichy* and curd-cakes called *paskha*, and may exchange painted wooden Easter eggs. The devout deny themselves meat, milk, alcohol and sex in the 40-day pre-Easter fasting period of Lent. Palm Sunday in Russia is Pussy Willow Sunday, as palms don't exist this far north (seriously).
April-May
  St Petersburg Music Spring – international classical music festival.
Last 10 days of June
  St Petersburg White Nights – general merrymaking and staying out late, plus dance festival.
Second Sunday in July
  Fishermen's Day (Den Rybaka) – games, stalls, evening music and dance in fishing ports.
7 November
  Great October Socialist Revolution Anniversary – see the generals on TV staying heroically upright as they salute the tribal roars of their troops from open limos bouncing over the Red Square cobbles. Just kidding; it's actually not celebrated as such, though it is still a holiday.
Mid-November
  Osenie Ritmy (Autumn Rhythms) – jazz festival, St Petersburg.
20 December to 8 January
  Christmas Musical Meetings in Northern Palmyra – a classical music festival held since 1991 in St Petersburg. Runs for three weeks, from the week before Western Christmas to Orthodox Christmas; hence exact dates may vary slightly.

25 December to 5 January
> *Russian Winter Festival* – tourist-oriented troyka rides, folklore shows, games, vodka. Still celebrated in St Petersburg (Olgino).

31 December & 1 January
> *Sylvestr and New Year* – the main winter and gift-giving festival. Gifts are put under the traditional fir tree *(yolka)*. See out the old year with vodka and welcome the new one with champagne while listening to the Kremlin chimes on radio and TV.

COMMUNICATIONS

Post

St Petersburg's main international and domestic post and telegraph office *(glavpochtamt)* is at ulitsa Pochtamptskaya 9, two blocks south-west of St Isaac's Cathedral. There are also over 400 branch offices in the city. The services provided by branches are usually in proportion to their size – most can cope with international letters and postcards, some can even send international telegrams.

Outward post is slow but fairly reliable. Air-mail letters take two to three weeks from St Petersburg to the UK, and three to four weeks to the USA or Australasia. Inward post is decidedly unreliable, with delivery times ranging from three weeks to never.

An air-mail letter (up to 20 grams) or postcard to any foreign address costs US$0.30. Registration *(zakaznoe)* – a good idea for anything of value – is another US$0.60.

Books and printed matter are cheaper to send by surface mail at small-packet *(melkiy paket)* rates; eg about US$5.70 (unregistered) as opposed to US$14.60 by air. An international parcel must go from the city's designated international post office; go to any window marked *posylki* (parcels).

In addition to selling stamps, envelopes and postcards, a few hotel post offices also do registration and express services, and will wrap and post books and printed matter (only). They usually register these and do the required customs forms, too (they must be filled out in Russian).

Some 'postcards' on sale in souvenir kiosks are not meant to be posted as such. They have a message on the back like ОТПРАВЛЯТЬ ПО ПОЧТЕ ТОЛЬКО В КОНВЕРТЕ ('to be sent through the post only in an envelope'). If you send these like postcards they may not make it.

Visitors can usually find what they need – postcards, envelopes and stamps – at the small postal desks in tourist hotels. You can also post books and printed matter abroad from these desks. They tend to open from about 10 am to 3 pm.

Non-book parcels, such as clothing, must go from the main post office. For the moment, Window 26 is for international mail, though it keeps being shuffled so just walk to the far left side of the counter at the opposite end of where you enter the hall and look for a sign; window 38 is for fax, photocopying, and domestic and international telegrams.

Express Services The term Express Mail Service (EMS), provided by EMS Garantpost (☎ 311 96 71, 311 78 21), is a relative one: packages take about a week to get where they're going, though they generally do get there. The packages must be taken to Garantpost, bulvar Konnogvardeysky 6, Dom 4.

Westpost (☎ 275 07 84; e-mail wp@sas.spb.su) is a privately run, US-managed international mail service at Dom Aktyor, Nevsky prospekt 86, for monthly and one-time clients. Mail is trucked daily from St Petersburg to Lappeenranta, Finland (which seems to be the Switzerland of matters postal around here), and mailed from there. One-time users pay a fee – US$1 for a letter or postcard or US$4 per kg – plus Finnish postage. Westpost is located through the main entrance and through the first door on the right hand side.

A similar, though less flashy, Russian-run post service, Post International (☎ 219 44 72), sends letters 'several times a week', dropping them into the US or British postal system. For letters to the USA and Europe, the cost is US$2.00 for the first ounce (28.5 grams), US$1 for each additional ounce; express mail to the USA for nonmembers is US$23. It's at Nevsky prospekt 20: go through the door with the 'Fuji' sign, straight back through a second door, turn left, and left again, past the staircase, then go right and into the office. Whoo.

The three main Western express mail services in town offer two-day delivery to Europe and the USA/Canada, and three-day delivery to Australia/New Zealand.

TNT Express Worldwide, at Liteyny prospekt 50 (☎ 122 96 70, 104 36 84), is the cheapest of the Western-run firms; a 500-gram package to the UK/Europe costs US$38.50; to the USA/Canada, US$43; to Australia/NZ, US$47.50.

DHL has been here the longest and has two locations: the main office is at Kanala Griboedova 5 kv 325 (☎ 311 26 49; e-mail dhlled@ru.dhl.com); the other office is at the Nevskij Palace Hotel (☎ 119 61 00, 119 61 17). It offers overnight service between St Petersburg and Moscow. A 500-gram package to the USA/Canada costs US$54.12; to the UK/Europe, US$55.35; to Australia/NZ US$77.49.

Federal Express, at ulitsa Mayokovskogo 2, (☎ 279 12 87), offers more limited services because the reshuffling of FedEx offices worldwide ended intra-European service. It's also the most expensive of the Western services. A 500-gram letter from Russia to the USA/Canada (three days) costs US$65; to Australia/NZ (five days) it's US$73.

Sending Mail You can address outgoing international mail as you would from any country, in your own language, though it might help to *precede* it with the country name in Cyrillic. Some Cyrillic country names are:

America (USA) – Америка (СЩА)
Australia – Австралия
Canada – Канада
France – Франция
Germany – Германия
Great Britain – Великобритания
New Zealand – Новая Зиландия

Russian addresses are written opposite to Western ones, starting with the country and ending with the addressee's name – eg Россия 103123, г. Москва, улица Островског о, д. 32 кв. 14, ИВАНОВ А. В. (Rossia 103123, g Moskva, ulitsa Ostrovskogo, d 32 kv. 14, Ivanov A V). The return address is written below the main address.

The six-digit number is the postal index. Before the place-name may be written *gorod* or *g* (town), *posyolok* (settlement), *derevnya* (village) or, in some remote addresses, *kolkhoz* (collective farm), *sovkhoz* (state farm) or *selsoviet* (rural council).

Receiving Mail Incoming state mail service is so flaky that it's rare for anyone on the move to find anything, but you can try. The most reliable option for those not staying in luxury hotels (which all provide mail service via Finland or other Scandinavian countries) is limited to American Express and Optima card-holders. The wonderful folk at American Express (☎ 119 60 09) will hold mail (letters only, no packages) and messages for card-holders and holders of travellers' cheques for up to 30 days at the company's office in the Grand Hotel Europe; the mailing address is American Express, PO Box 87, SF-53501 Lappeenranta, Finland – mail is brought from Lappeenranta down to the American Express Office daily, at no charge. You'll need to bring your card or travellers' cheques with you, along with your passport or other ID, to get your mail. From the USA, Canada and Western Europe, mail takes about a week to arrive.

Westpost (☎ 275 07 84; e-mail WP@sas.spb.su), at
Dom Aktyor, Nevsky prospekt 86, offers post boxes in
Lappeenranta, with daily pick up and delivery to their
offices, or, for corporate clients, to their address in St
Petersburg. You can become a basic Westpost client for
US$20 per month, and they also offer a US-magazine
subscription service. Nonclient visitors can have mail
delivered for a US$1 fee to PL 8, SF-53501 Lappeenranta,
Finland; you can pick it up at the Westpost office.

For US$50 a month, Post International (see the earlier
Express Services section for directions) offers a post box
in the USA from which mail is forwarded to you in St
Petersburg.

Poste restante *(do vostrebovania)* is notoriously useless
but if you want to try, the St Petersburg address is:

Rossia 190400
St Petersburg
Nevsky prospekt 6
Do Vostrebovania

Россия 190400
С.-Петербург
Невский проспект 6
до Востребования

followed by your name (surname first).

When sending mail from abroad to Russia, it's best,
as in the above example, to put Latin characters on top
to get it to Russia, and Cyrillic on the bottom to get it to
it's ultimate destination.

At St Petersburg's official post restante address there's
no obvious office at all. Bring along your passport to get
your mail. Forget about sending parcels through poste
restante. Embassies and consulates won't hold mail for
transient visitors.

Telephone

The world of international, and even domestic, telecommunications has changed immensely since 1991; it's
now possible to do all sorts of magical things like dial a
number in another country and have it connect. But with
the improvement in services, there's been an explosion
of providers that can get confusing and, if you're not
careful, expensive.

Private Telephones From a private phone in St
Petersburg, dialling outside Russia is very simple, but

the prices keep rising and are now even higher than equivalent calls from the West to Russia. To dial internationally dial 8, wait for the second tone, then dial 10 plus the country and city codes, then the number. Omit any noughts (zeroes) from the city code (eg to Sydney the code would be 8 (tone) 10 61 2 number).

At the time of writing, daytime telephone prices per minute were:

US$2.95 to the USA, Canada, Australasia;
US$1.25 to Continental Europe and the UK.

Some useful country codes are: USA and Canada 1, UK 44, Australia 61, New Zealand 64, France 33, Denmark 45, Sweden 46, Norway 47, Poland 48, Germany 49, Finland 358, Lithuania 370, Latvia 371, Estonia 372

Payphones Pay phones Таксофн *(taksofon)* are located throughout the city and are generally in working order. They accept metro tokens *(zhetony)* as payment. Place the token in the slot on top of the phone, dial the number; when the party answers, the token should drop. A series of beeps means place another token in the slot or risk disconnection.

Domestic (which means within Russia or to any former Soviet republic) long-distance calls may be made from payphones marked междугородный *(mezhdugorodny)*; using different, wrinkled-metal tokens, they work on a similar principle, but you need to push the Ответ *(otvet)* button on the phone's face when your party answers. Dial 8, wait for the second tone, and dial the city code (including noughts) and the number. New card-operated payphones are all over the city; you can buy cards at the central telephone office, Peter TIPS, and the major hotels. These phones can be used for local, long-distance and international calls.

BCL (☎ 311 14 88) has card-operated payphones all over town at a surprising number of locations. You can buy cards from anywhere that has a BCL payphone. Their prices are somewhat steep. BCL phonecard rates per minute are: Russia, US$1.50; Europe, US$3.50; North America, US$6.50; rest of the world, US$8.

Peterstar (☎ 119 60 60) operates credit-card-operated payphones around town at similar rates.

State/Central Telephone Office The State-run long-distance telephone office is at ulitsa Bolshaya Morskaya (ulitsa Gertsena) 3/5. Generally speaking, you can make telephone calls from here with no waiting;

the international card-operated phones are straight to the back of the office and to the left – you can buy cards from the kiosk in the centre of the hall. Alternatively, you can make a left as soon as you enter the hall and head for the hexagonal kiosk on the right, where you can pre-pay and the operator connects you immediately. Prices are identical to those of home (private) phones.

Country Direct   This service allows you to dial a toll-free number in St Petersburg (or in Moscow) and be connected with an operator from the USA, who can put through collect or calling-card calls to the USA and, in some cases, other countries. AT&T USA Direct is the only company at the time of writing that allows access to some toll-free (800) telephone numbers in the USA at no charge to the caller; it all depends on whether the (800) number you're dialling will accept international connections, so call AT&T to check. MCI is the only company at the time of writing to offer country direct service from St Petersburg (dial 8, wait for the tone, dial 10 800 497 7222). Other companies at the time of writing must be accessed through Moscow: AT&T (☎ (095) 155 50 42 (for an English-speaking operator), 155 55 55 (for a Russian-speaking operator); and Sprint (☎ (095) 155 61 33 (English), 938 61 33 (Russian). At the moment, neither BT nor Australia Telecom offer this service.

Calling from a Hotel   The Grand Hotel Europe, Nevskij Palace, Okhtinskaya, Astoria, Pribaltiyskaya and other hotels, as well as the HI St Petersburg Hostel, have satellite-linked, international direct-dial telephones with no waiting for varying outrageous fees. Of these, the HI St Petersburg Hostel has the lowest rates (US$4/minute to USA/Canada/Australia/NZ, US$2 to UK/Europe).

If you're staying at a hotel that doesn't offer satellite service, international and domestic long-distance calls may be booked with hotel reception.

Most hotel-room telephones have a direct-dial number (on a card in the room, or ask reception) for incoming calls which saves you having to be connected through the switchboard.

Local calls can usually be made free from your room (sometimes directly, sometimes with a prefix number).

Cellular Service   Cellular telephone service has been available in and around St Petersburg since 1991. Cell phone service is unbeatable outside the cities, where the state telephone system is effectively non-existent. It allows immediate access to international, as well as domestic, phone lines.

Most of Russia's cellular service operates on the 450 mHz Scandinavian standard; if you have a Scandinavian cell phone you can 'roam' in Russian cities for varying fees; service is transferred to local cellular providers automatically. You can rent cell phones in Helsinki and other Finnish cities that work in Russia. Rentals are also available in St Petersburg, but the price is sky-high.

There are currently three cellular service providers in town, and roaming is available on all. It ain't cheap by any means.

North West at the Hotel Moskva, ploshchad Alexandra Nevskogo 2 (☎ 528 47 47), operates on the GSM system and has rates comparable to private telephone charges.

SPT Motorola at ploshchad Ostrovskogo 5 (☎ 311 55 93), rents phones that work on the NAMPS system for US$23 to US$27 a day plus air-time.

Delta Telecom at ulitsa Bolshaya Morskaya (ulitsa Gertsena) 22 (☎ 314 61 26), was the first company to offer cellular service in St Petersburg. Delta's other claim to fame is as the world's most expensive cell service provider. Delta operates on the NMT system (Scandinavian standard).

Fax

Faxes can be sent and received at the Central Telephone Office: incoming fax number (☎ (7 812) 314 33 60). Generally speaking, faxes are sent out within 48 hours of your dropping them off, but you can request *srochny* (express) and have it sent out immediately for twice the price. Faxes can also be sent and received at all major hotels and at the two youth hostels (see listings for incoming fax numbers), at varying prices. You can also send and receive faxes at the American Business Center (see Business Services later). Faxes can also be sent via electronic mail (see below).

Fax Prices At the time of writing, the cost per page to send or receive a fax from the American Business Center was:

US$3.60 to the USA and Canada
US$2.70 to Europe
US$1.50 to Finland and the Baltic Countries
US$4.50 to the rest of the world
US$0.25 for incoming faxes

At the time of writing, the cost per page to send or receive a fax from the Central Telephone Office was:

US$3.95 to the USA, Canada, Australasia
US$1.70 to continental Europe and the UK
US$0.60 for incoming faxes

Other companies charge different prices, generally more, and average about US$5 per page.

Electronic Mail

Electronic mail (e-mail) is probably the most reliable and inexpensive method of communication between Russia and the rest of the world. The vast majority of foreign residents in Russia use e-mail as one of their primary international communications methods, so service is readily available.

To use e-mail, you'll need a computer with a modem and the software to run it, a telephone line, and an account with an e-mail provider. Generally speaking, e-mail service providers give a local access number, through which you access the service and your e-mail account. Depending on the service to which you subscribe, e-mail messages reach their destination from 15 minutes to three days after you post them through the service (the bigger companies like Glasnet, Relcom, Sovam and SprintNet usually take no longer than an hour to send your message).

Many e-mail providers also allow access to the Internet, an international computer network. At its most basic application, this allows you to send e-mail between providers, for example between CompuServe and MCIMail or, more practically, between a Russian e-mail provider and your e-mail provider back home. An Internet e-mail address looks like this: 74442.3034@compuserve.com or talk2us@lonelyplanet.com.au.

There is a staggering range of other features of the Internet like the World Wide Web that can be explained by your service provider.

A drawback is that you can only send e-mail to other people with e-mail service. But even if the person you're trying to contact doesn't have e-mail, you can send an e-mail message by fax (by having your e-mail server leave the computer network and dial the phone, sending the message by fax) and the cost is still usually cheaper than it would be by using a traditional fax machine, as e-mail providers usually get (and pass on) bulk rate long-distance service.

If you're currently a subscriber to CompuServe, SprintNet, MCIMail or SFMT, you can access your account in Russia (see below for access numbers and how to subscribe before you arrive) but surcharges will apply (with CompuServe this can get expensive at US$49 per hour!).

Signing on in Russia to a service such as Glasnet, Sovam, Relcom or Demos/+, generally entails a one-time fee plus a flat monthly charge in addition to 'air-time' charges. Note that because of Russia's notoriously poor local telephone lines, you'll need a modem with 'built in error correction', or 'MNP' – software error correction is not enough.

If you're just trying to get word home, you can use the e-mail at the HI St Petersburg Hostel for a small fee. Sovam Teleport's office in St Petersburg (☎ 311 84 12, Nevsky prospekt 30) sometimes allows visitors to use the in-house e-mail to send a message for a small fee, but no longer officially sets up temporary accounts.

Below are contact numbers and information for some of the e-mail providers operating in Russia, and their voice telephone numbers for contact before you arrive in Russia. The home page addresses are for people with World Wide Web browsers.

Sovam Teleport
　☎ (095) 229 72 95; fax (095) 229 41 21; e-mail spbsales@sovam.com; St Petersburg access number ☎ (812) 311 03 65 (2400 baud); Moscow access number ☎ (095) 932 67 65, 932 69 65 (2400 baud); home page http://www.sovam.com/
Glasnet
　☎ (812) 168 55 89; fax (095) 207 08 89; e-mail support@glas.apc.org; St Petersburg access number ☎ (812) 168 54 74; home page http://www.glas.apc.org/ or http://www.glasnet .ru/, whichever works best for you
A/O Relcom
　☎ (095) 194 25 40; fax (095) 194 33 28; home page http://www.spb.su/
Demos/+
　☎ (812) 233 00 34; fax (812) 233 50 16; e-mail info@demos.su
CompuServe
　Usenet news group alt.onlineservice.compu serve; Moscow access number ☎ (095) 110 77 92 NTW = SPR (2400 baud); international subscription numbers (Australia) ☎ 1 800 025 240, (UK) ☎ 0800 289 458, (USA) ☎ 1 800 848 8990
Sprint Network
　☎ (095) 201 68 90; fax (095) 923 23 44; St Petersburg access number ☎ (812) 110 77 92 (2400 baud); international subscription numbers (Australia) ☎ (02) 218 4825, (UK) ☎ 0800 289 751, (USA) ☎ 1 800 877 1997
MCIMail
　e-mail mcihelp@mcimail.com; Moscow access number ☎ (095) 971 51 01 (2400 baud); international subscription numbers (USA) ☎ 800 444 6245, (US number for rest of world) ☎ (1 202) 833 8484

Surfing to Russia ... On the Internet

Getting information, other than the bare basics, out of Russian government sources can be a frustrating and fruitless task. So it's good to know that it's easy to get heaps of practical local information from Russia via the Internet and the World Wide Web. You don't even need a pocket protector or a degree in computer engineering: just a computer, a modem capable of transmitting and receiving at least 9600 bits per second, a telephone connection and an Internet service provider.

The advent of graphical browsing software, like Netscape and Mosaic, has made jumping from site to site on the World Wide Web as easy as operating a Macintosh computer or a PC running Windows. Point-and-click 'surfing', or moving from point to point within the Web, has brought millions of new users in touch with electronic resources stored on computers all over the world.

In Russia, use of the Internet has spread like wildfire. As you would imagine, in a country where long-distance telephones hardly work at all, any technology that allows people to communicate reliably and inexpensively draws significant interest. There are Internet service providers and World Wide Web sites in almost every large Russian city, offering information on hundreds of subjects.

The upshot of all this is that getting information out of Russia is easier than ever. Russian sites offer loads of information, with Internet links back and forth around the globe to universities and Russian studies centres. But this is not all educational and dry, academic stuff being tossed about in the ether. It's club dates and KGB documents, media information and guided photo tours of the Hermitage, gay and lesbian resources and the nitty-gritty on registering a Russian company.

You can find out more about the Internet and the World Wide Web in books such as *The Whole Internet User's Guide* (O'Reilly & Associates), or even the embarrassing-to-buy but helpful *The Internet for Dummies* (IDG Books) available at good bookshops or computer shops everywhere. Once you choose a provider and get wired, drop in to Lonely Planet's home page (http://www. lonelyplanet.com), where you'll find travel news, information, the best travel health resource centre in the business, reader's letters, 'On The Road' features (destination profiles from LP authors, including one on Russia and St Petersburg) and much more.

The addresses below will get you connected enough to surf freely on the Russian Web. For the non-English sections you run into, you'll need to get KOI8 or other Cyrillic fonts and install them, though if you don't speak Russian it won't matter if you go without.

http://www.spb.su/ – St Petersburg Relcom home page, one of the cooler places to hang out; includes the *St Petersburg Press* (see next listing), *Severo Zapad*, *St Petersburg Business Journal, St Petersburg Picture Gallery, The Other St Petersburg, Eco-Chronicle.*

http://www.spb.su/sppress/index.html – *St Petersburg Press* home page; weekly newspaper packed with practical information, listings, cultural information, exchange rates etc.

http://www.glas.apc.org – Glasnet, including a mirror site of Econet, with connections to ecological resources and information from all over the world, Al-Anon, Judaism and Jewish life in Russia and other helpful and educational resources.

http://www.sovam.com/ – Sovam Teleport home page, with connections to everywhere: software, Russian Web mailing-list archive, FSUMedia mailing-list archive, search engines, FAQ lists etc.

http://sunsite.unc.edu/pjones/russian/outline.html – Exhibition of formerly secret documents from the Soviet Union, including a 1979 KGB report detailing serious design flaws at the Chernobyl nuclear reactor. Reports are available in facsimile of original documents or in translated form.

http://www.mplik.ru/ – Ural Relcom home page, Yekaterinburg. Mostly Russian-language information (KOI8 fonts required), but a very comprehensive list of Russian Web servers, and a clickable map to help locate them.

http://www.kiae.su/www.wtr/kremlin/begin.html – A virtual walking tour of the Moscow Kremlin, complete with scary but unenforceable copyright infringement threats.

http://www.sunsite.oit.unc.edu/sergei/Grandsons.html – Dazhdbog's Grandchildren, a quirky but interesting site run by a guy at the University of North Carolina Chapel Hill. Also links to other Russian servers.

http://www.ic.gov/94fact/country/200.html – Pop quiz: Russia is a member of all of the following organisations *except* UNESCO, UNIDO, UNIKOM, UNOMOZ, UNICORN. Find out which on (we swear, it's true) the CIA's home page, which has lists and lists of mind-numbing facts about Russia and the FSU.

http://www.elvis.msk.su/ – Elvis server. No, it's not info on a dead, bloated old pop star, but a site that has a couple of useful features, like an interactive Russian-English dictionary (KOI8 fonts required)

Off the Internet, on-line services such as The CompuServe Travel Forum and America On Line offer travel forums (Go: travsig or Keyword: Traveler, respectively) and US State Department Travel Advisories for foreign countries (Go: state or Keyword: Travel Advisories, respectively). These services also offer bulletin-board-type listings and discussion groups on Eastern Europe, Russia and Russian cities.

Nick Selby, 74442.3034@compuserve.com

Telegram

Telegrams are another easy, cheap and reliable way to reach the outside world. International telegrams can be sent from many of the larger post offices, as well as from Window 38 at the main post office. If you can get an English-speaking operator you can also arrange telegrams from a private telephone (☎ 066). Telegrams can take from three to five days to arrive at their destination. Ask for a *blank mezhdunarodyy telegramma* (international telegram form). A message in English is no problem if it's clearly printed. At the time of writing, approximate telegram rates per word were:

To Europe US$0.22
To Asia US$0.26
To USA/Canada US$0.28
To Australasia US$0.30

Emergency Contact

In an emergency the most straightforward way for someone to reach you from outside Russia is by telephone to your hotel or hostel – language problems, bad connections, slack service and changeable numbers notwithstanding.

International calls to major cities in Russia can be dialled directly, and operators can assist in reaching many of even the smallest towns. Next best is a fax or telegram, care of your hotel, though the staff won't always chase you up if one arrives. A telegram takes one to two days to arrive.

As a last resort, most foreign affairs ministries maintain 24-hour emergency operators – eg the British Foreign Office (☎ (0171) 270 3000), the US State Department (☎ (202) 647 5225; 647 4000 outside business hours), and the Australian Department of Foreign Affairs & Trade (☎ (06) 261 3331) – who can call your embassy in Russia. Embassies prefer that other means have been exhausted before they're contacted. Your itinerary will be of help in the hunt for you, so leave a copy with someone at home.

BUSINESS SERVICES

The best deal for foreign business people, specifically US citizens or those working with a US-owned company, looking for a temporary business address is the American Business Center, St Petersburg, (local ☎ 110 60 42; local fax 311 07 94; international ☎ (7 812) 850 19 00;

international fax (7 812) 850 19 01), a project of the US Department of Commerce and the Foreign Commercial Service. What all this bureaucracy boils down to is a slick business centre at very reasonable rates: you can rent PC terminals (US$20 for four hours), offices and conference rooms (both US$35 for four hours). The centre has photocopiers, word processing services, e-mail, telex and telephone service and a gaggle of other options including guides and translators/interpreters at similarly reasonable prices. There is also a slew of useful free services, including instructions on how to register businesses in Russia, a list of business contacts and synopses of business climates in cities all over the Russian Federation. The centre is open from Monday to Friday 9 am to 5 pm, at ulitsa Bolshaya Morskaya (ulitsa Gertsena) 57, near St Isaac's and the central post office.

Each of the major luxury hotels (and some of the cheesy ones) has a full-service business centre, each quite expensive for anything other than a one-time fax or photocopy, with rates at about US$0.50 per page for copies and outrageous international telephone and fax charges. In the Nevskij Palace Hotel, aside from their 2nd floor offering, an American Business Centre charges slightly less – it's on the ground floor, at the back of the atrium lobby.

At Shvedsky Pereulok 2 is Ipris (☎ 210 76 69, a very friendly copy centre with brand new Xerox brand copiers, doing photocopies for about US$0.11 each.

TIME

Russians use a 24-hour clock; 1 pm is 1300, 6 pm is 1800, midnight is 0000. From the early hours of the last Sunday in September to the early hours of the last Sunday in March, St Petersburg time is GMT/UTC plus three hours. From the last Sunday in March to the last Sunday in September, 'summer time' is in force and it's GMT/UTC plus four hours.

When it's noon in St Petersburg it's ...

1 am in San Francisco;
4 am in New York and Toronto;
9 am in London;
10 am in Warsaw, Prague and Budapest;
11 am in Helsinki, Bucharest and Ankara;
5 pm in Ulan Bator and Beijing, 4 pm in summer Beijing;
8 pm in summer Sydney, 6 pm in winter Sydney;
10 pm in summer Auckland, 8 pm in winter Auckland.

ELECTRICITY

Electricity is 220 volts, 50 Hz AC, and very reliable in St Petersburg. Sockets require a Continental or European plug adaptor with two round pins. American/Japanese appliances need a 220V to 110V/100V converter.

WEIGHTS & MEASURES

The metric system is in use. Drinks are served in measures of 50 or 100 grams, about 1.75 or 3.5 ounces (whoo). Russian restaurant menus list food and drink servings by weight; a tea glass is about 200 grams. The unit of items sold by the piece, such as eggs, is *shtuka* or *sht.* which literally means thing or piece. Numbers are written with the comma and decimal point reversed relative to US, Canadian, Australian and English standards, so 1000 roubles would be written 1.000,-.

LAUNDRY

Unless you're staying at a hotel, the laundrette is as close as your bathroom. The HI St Petersburg Hostel has a washing machine for the use of hostel guests for US$2. Hotels (even cheap ones) offer laundry services for various prices that take between one and three days, but as yet there's no public laundry facilities to speak of in town.

TOILETS

Free or inexpensive toilets are scattered around town, marked with the Latin characters 'WC' or the Russian Платный туалет *(platny tualet)* (pay toilet). There are also free or inexpensive toilets available at the bus and railway stations. It is hard to believe that toilets can be uniformly this disgusting, but there it is. In any toilet, Ж stands for *zhenskiy*, women's, and М *muzhkoy*, men's. Walking into restaurants or hotels and asking usually results in permission to use the, er, facilities.

BOOKS & MAPS

Background Reading

If you're planning any trips to the former gulag camps in the north, *The Gulag Archipelago* by Alexandr Solzhenitsyn is required reading. Through interviews with and testimony from hundreds of gulag prisoners, the writer brings to light some of the most heinous prison conditions the world has ever known in a style so familiar you're enveloped in the stories before you're quite aware of it. Much of *USSR: From an Original Idea by Karl Marx* by Marc Polonsky & Russell Taylor is still all too relevant. It's a 1980s street-wise look at the headaches of travel by authors who ran a company specialising in 'real life' Soviet tours. It's funny enough to keep you up when the trip gets you down. It's hard to find, but worth looking for.

Guidebooks

If you're travelling outside of St Petersburg, Lonely Planet's *Russia, Ukraine & Belarus* is simply the most comprehensive practical guide available on those countries. Lonely Planet also has guides to many neighbouring countries including Finland, the Baltic States & Kaliningrad, Poland, the Czech & Slovak Republics, Hungary and Central Asia.

Ian Watson's terrific *The Baltics and Russia Through The Back Door* is a short and sweet, bare-bones practical guide that covers major sights in St Petersburg and Moscow. It's published annually in a form that's a cross between a magazine and a paperback. Great practical info and very up-to-date prices, though it makes no attempt to cover history or background.

While hopelessly dated on practicalities, the *Blue Guide Moscow and Leningrad* by Evan and Margaret Mawdsley does a toothcomb-thorough job on architecture and history of both cities, dense with detail about every doorway you pass – an excellent reference guide.

Fresh Air Publications, Russia, produced *The Visitor's Guide to the New Saint Petersburg* in 1992, and later *The Fresh Guide to St Petersburg*. It's published periodically (they skipped 1995, but say they'll be back in 1996) by a local publisher and available in local bookshops and at the HI St Petersburg Hostel. Their 'Other Things To See & Do' section is filled with interesting activities like bungee jumping, and Ben Lehrer's language section is a scream, with all sorts of useful questions like 'Why are you driving on the sidewalk?' and 'Do you charge by the hour?'!

Insight Guides St Petersburg is a nice read, though not at all good on practicalities.

St Petersburg History, Art and Architecture by Kathleen Berton Murrell is a lovely book of just what it says it is complete with colour photographs. It's published by the Russian Troika Publishing house, and it's available in many shops in St Petersburg and Moscow.

Robert Greenall's *An Explorer's Guide to Russia* (1994) has a lot of good info for independent travellers but, despite its title, only covers central and northern European Russia and is decidedly shaky on practical information. It's particularly good for those with the time and inclination to explore small, off-the-beaten-track places around Moscow.

Louis Motorist's Guide to the Soviet Union (1987) by Victor & Jennifer Louis, covers most places that were open to Westerners in the mid-1980s, by the Soviet method of piling fact upon fact, but is studded with gaps and distortions, and its maps are almost useless. However it has an enormous phrase list covering everything that could go wrong with your car eg 'Oil is leaking from the reduction gear of the rear axle' and some things that you'd pray won't, like 'The engine fails at all rpm'.

History

For a quick and dirty coverage, *A Traveller's History of The USSR and Russia* by Peter Neville is quite a good read, and good on pre-Gorbachev Russia, though it's offensive that the book wasn't really updated (it constantly refers to the USSR in the present tense), but rather a hastily drawn chapter was thrown in at the end.

Imperium by Ryszard Kapuscinski is a 1994 collection of essays, journalism and recollections of the Soviet empire by the Polish correspondent and travel writer. Kapuscinski's boyhood town, Pinsk, was in the part of Poland taken over by the USSR in 1939 (it's in Belarus today). His teacher and some classmates were deported then, and the experience left him with a loathing of the Soviet system which comes across strongly.

Robert Kaiser's *Russia: The People and The Power* is a wonderful account of Soviet life in the 1970s that gives terrific detail while escaping the trap of judging the place on Western standards. *The New Russians* by Hedrick Smith is this former *New York Times* correspondent's overview of Russian life – a 1990 update of the original version but still useful. The USSR, incidentally, produced its own equivalent of Hedrick Smith back in the 1960s in the shape of *Those Americans* by N Mikhailov & Z Kossenko, published in English by Henry Regnery (1962). Normal American men-on-the-street the authors encounter make remarks like 'Capitalism has degraded America to the point that ... the individual is on the verge of decay ...'

Women's Glasnost vs Naglost by Tatyana Mamonova (1994) combines essays by this Russian women's movement leader with interviews of a cross-section of women in a country where wife-beating and abortion reach horrific levels.

Reference

The Traveller's Yellow Pages St Petersburg is a comprehens-ive, and mostly accurate, pocket-sized yellow-page telephone book. It also has seating plans to major thea-tres, opera houses and stadiums, and is indexed in English, Russian, German and French.

Where In St Petersburg and the *Russia Survival Guide* from Russian Information Services (Montpelier VT, USA) are all selective and business oriented, but their *Russian Travel Monthly* update magazine is good on prac-tical info, visa regulation changes etc.

Bookshops

So far there are no Western-style bookshops here, but the Russian-run bookshops are getting better all the time. Start at Dom Knigi, the biggest bookshop in town, which has some books in Western languages plus books on Russian-language courses, science and engineering, school texts and, upstairs, maps and postcards. It's on the corner of naberezhnaya Kanala Griboedova and Nevsky prospekt in the pre-Revolutionary St Petersburg headquarters of the Singer Sewing Machine company; walk in, go to the back past the stairs, then turn left and left again.

Grouped near the corner of Nevsky prospekt and ulitsa Bolshaya Morskaya (ulitsa Gertsena) you'll find four bookshops facing each other. Iskusstv, on the south-west corner, is tiny but has a good collection of real art books. Of the four, the one next door to Iskusstv is the cheapest, and features some Western-language books, Euro-Cart maps and some stationery. It's also got a tacky souvenir shop and a Baltiysky Bank cash exchange desk that says it gives cash advances for Visa and MasterCard. Across Nevsky and west of the corner, the art bookshop is pretty much a rip-off, while on the east side, Staraya Knigi has a good collection of old books (including, perhaps, some second-hand novels in English) and other ... er ... old stuff.

Nevsky prospekt is lined from top to bottom with smaller book and map shops (there's another good one at Nevsky prospekt 141), and there are various others around the city. Pedestrian subways are rife with book stalls.

The HI St Petersburg Hostel sells internationally and locally produced travel guides, including Lonely Planet guides.

Maps

It's no longer a big deal finding maps for walking around; hotels and restaurants hand them out as a matter of routine, and city, regional and even country maps are readily available at bookshops and kiosks. The Russian-made regional topographical maps that are available at larger bookshops are generally quite good, though they're cumbersome as they can take up to 25 large pages.

The most readily available commercial map of St Petersburg is the US-published *New St Petersburg City Map & Guide*, available in English and Russian. *The Traveller's Yellow Pages City Map*, published in the USA by InfoServices Russia and printed by an Estonian firm, is good but the scale is somewhat erratic and the maps have little pictures of major sights which can be distracting. It does, however, have a unique and extremely useful English/Russian street index that pushes it ahead of the crowd. In St Petersburg you can find them in some hotels, shops and bookshops, and at the Airport Duty Free. The *New St Petersburg City Map & Guide* is also available from Russian Information Services (☎ 254 92 75).

The *Marshruty Gorodskogo Transporta (Municipal Transit Routes)* map published by St Petersburg's Culture & Tourism Office is very useful and is available at kiosks along Nevsky prospekt. The *Turistskaya Skhema (Tourist Map)* is also now readily available at bookshops along Nevsky prospekt (try Art Books at Nevsky prospekt 20; Dom Knigi at No 28; or Knigi at No 141) and at kiosks on the busier streets. It's available in Russian, English and German.

Interesting for the central areas – and useful now that many streets are reverting to precommunist names – is *Peterburg Leningrad Starye i Novye Grodskie Nazvania (Peterburg Leningrad Old and New City Names)*, which gives the 1989 and 1878 names of most streets. We found it on sale at the Russian Museum and you could also try in antiquarian bookshops on Nevsky prospekt and Liteyny prospekt.

MEDIA

The Russian media are now as free as one would expect; the mass privatisation of Ostankino and other television and radio outlets, and almost all print media, has seen to that. There are still over 8000 newspapers and periodicals in print in Russia, despite paper shortages and economic realities. And while Western involvement in radio and television is growing, Russian-owned outlets are developing a distinctive style that's a hybrid of slick 'But wait ... there's more!' shucksterism and Russian sensationalism.

Russian-Language Print Media

Russian print media has come an awfully long way; scandals are sought and exposed, sometimes to the detriment of the reporter (several have been killed over the past years while investigating corruption and mismanagement of the military and intelligence organs). But the free press in Russia has produced some truly surprising scoops, and hard-hitting investigative stories in papers such as *Izvestya* and *Moskovky Komsomolets* have brought to light scandals (including those that led to the killing of MK reporter Dmitry Kholodov, as well as the multibillion-rouble MMM pyramid scheme scam and collapse).

Most of the dozens of Russian-language newspapers in St Petersburg are mouthpieces for various political parties, or involved in sensationalism in one way or another; the monthly *Sovershenno Sekreto (Top Secret)* claims that all its articles are based on info culled from secret Soviet archives: who knows?

The weekly *Argumenty I Fakty* does politics, economics, and the occasional movie star interview. *Express Gazetta* claims the dubious distinction of being 'Russia's first tabloid', and *Chas Pik (Rush Hour)* is a daily rag that's as serious as you'd want. There are several information and listings papers, like *Vsyo Dla Vas (Everything for You)* which is a free classified advert paper; *To Du Syo (This and That)* is a what's on listings paper, and *Chto Pochyom (What Costs What)* has listings of prices around town for everything from construction materials to tanning salons and everything in between. *SPID Info (AIDS Info)* is a highly deceptive title: it claims to be a 'popular scientific' paper, but perhaps its popularity is due to the fact that it contains nothing but smut: 'I never thought I'd be writing to you, but last week ...'.

Finally, pick up a copy of one of the city's lunatic fringe rags; *Novy Svet (New Light)* is an occasionally published anarchist paper ('Free the Chechens! Bash the Government!'), and *Trudovaya Rossi (Labour Russia)*, espouses the usual about the noble workers, yadda yadda yadda.

English-Language Print Media

The undisputed king of the hill in locally published English-language news is the *Moscow Times*, a first-rate daily staffed by top-notch journalists and editors covering Russian and international issues. It's available free (for the time being) at hotels, business centres, restaurants, and also by subscription. The *Times* also publishes a weekly international edition, which sums up Russian news only. It's available by subscription (see Subscriptions below) worldwide. Another Moscow daily, the *Moscow Tribune*, is available as well.

The *St Petersburg Press*, once an upstart with lofty ideas, is now an integral part of life in the city. Though a decidedly lower budget affair than either the *Times* or the *Tribune*, the Kiwi-led team puts together a reliable weekly, especially its 'Prospekts' section packed with practical information and listings of clubs, pubs, restaurants, museums, theatre etc. It's available at bookshops, hotels, restaurants and youth hostels.

Pulse is a slick colour monthly with tons of club, pub, nightlife and other information about the city at large, written with a very young and fresh outlook. It's available free in outlets all over the city.

Newsstands in the bigger hotels usually have a few good Western newspapers of the *International Herald-Tribune*, *Times*, *Guardian* etc variety, four or more days old. They cost about one-and-a-half times more than back home.

Subscriptions The *St Petersburg Press* is available by international subscription (US$135/year) by writing to Akadeemia 21G, EE-0026 Tallinn Estonia (☎ (372) 2 531 171). *Moscow News* subscriptions are US$99/year (US$50/year for students) in the USA, and are available through East View Publications (☎ (1 612) 550 0961), 3020 Harbor Lane North, Plymouth, MN 55447, or e-mail to admin@eastview.com.

Russian Information Services (☎ in the USA (1 802) 223 4955) handles US and Canadian subscriptions (US$155/6 months) to the weekly edition of *The Moscow Times*; Europe (US$130/6 months) and the rest of the world is handled by MT's Dutch partners, Van Eeghenstraat (☎ (31 20) 676 0701).

Russian-Language Radio

From the little *radio tochka* box in your hotel room you can usually get Radio Rossii, it's annoying programmes and it's offensive hourly rendition of *Moscow Nights* played on the boing-a-phone. The switch on that box will be set either to 'Off' or 'Loud'.

Radio in Russia is broken into three bands, AM, UKV (the lower band of FM from 66-77 mHz) and FM (100-107 mHz). A Western-made FM radio usually won't go lower than 85 mHz.

The Yanks are here, and in droves; Westwood One, Harris Corporation and Story First Communications are all here and making (generally album-oriented rock) noise. Private Russian-language radio has come a long way, and it's worth listening to, though it's rare to hear any Russian bands other than oldies-but-goodies like Akvarium, Kino and Time Machine. Check the *Moscow Times* or the *St Petersburg Press* for radio listings. Some stations are:

- Yevropa Plus, with one of the most annoying jingles on earth, plays a lot of Western disco and rock. You'll hear a fair bit of ABBA and Donna Summer. It's constantly expanding to more cities – check locally for listings as they jump on all bands;
- Radio 7, a US-Russian joint venture, does a Morning Zoo (in English), comedic morning show and AC format music at 104.7 FM and 73.8 UKV;
- Radio Maximum is the slickest of the lot, with US money and equipment and a compressed, tight h-h-hot sound at 102.8 FM.

English-Language Radio

The clearest BBC World Service short-wave (SW) frequencies in the morning, late evening and at night are near 9410, 12,095 (the most reliable) and 15,070 mHz. You can get the BBC:

from midnight to 2 am GMT/UTC, at 6180 and 7325 mHz
from 2 to 4 am, at 6195 mHz
from 2 to 7 am, at 9410 mHz
from 4 am to 8.30 pm, at 12,095 mHz
from 1 to 8 pm, at 13,070 mHz
and from 8 pm to midnight, at 5930, 6180 and 7325 mHz.

Radio Maximum serves Moscow and St Petersburg on 102.8 FM. They do an hour-long jazz show in English on Monday at midnight and Kasey Kasem's Top 40 Countdown is on Sunday from 9 am to 1 pm but we're not *that* desperate, are we? Voice of America is on at 6866 mHz 24 hours a day. St Petersburg English-language radio also includes Radio Modern, 104 FM Saturday at 11.15 am and Tuesday at 6.15 pm; and the BBC World Service every day on 1260 AM.

Russian-Language TV

In St Petersburg you can see the two national channels plus two local ones; St Petersburg Television, with some pithy, unconventional current-affairs programmes that have gained a wide audience, and Channel 4, evening educational TV.

English-Language TV

Most large hotels have satellite television, showing a wide variety of Western programming from CNN, CNBC, The Discovery Channel, MTV (of course), BBC, TV 5 and Pro7.

FILM & PHOTOGRAPHY

Kodak Express has nine drop-off locations and two full-service shops in town, doing fast developing and selling a range of film at European prices. Main branches are at ulitsa Bolshaya Morskaya (ulitsa Gertsena) 32 (☎ 110 64 03) and ulitsa Malaya Konyushennaya 7 (☎ 110 64 97). Agfa (☎ 311 99 74) does fast (if not one-hour) developing, and sells film and camera supplies on the 3rd floor of Nevsky prospekt 20. Fuji's shop near the Anichkov Bridge (☎ 314 49 36) does about the same; it's at naberezhnaya reki Fontanki 23.

A great deal on Russian photo equipment can be had at the Photo Shop No 76 (☎ 232 19 02), Bolshoy prospekt (Petrograd Side) 63; it's open from 10 am to 7 pm. Specials at the time of writing included a Zenit body with 50 mm lens for US$50 and a top-of-the-line FC 122 with a huge lens for US$155.

For cheap passport photographs (US$0.50 for four) head for the machine inside the shop at Nevsky prospekt 128, which also has an exchange booth.

HEALTH

Water

Don't drink the tap water in St Petersburg. It contains *Giardia lamblia*, a parasite that causes stomach cramps, nausea, bloated stomach, watery and foul-smelling diarrhoea and frequent gas. There is no preventative drug. Metronidazole (brand name Flagyl) is the recommended treatment but should only be taken under medical supervision. Antibiotics are of no use. Symptoms may not appear for up to several weeks after infection.

To be absolutely safe, only drink water that has been boiled for 10 minutes or filtered through an antimicrobial water filter (Pur brand makes a good portable one; check with a sporting goods store before you come). Avoid fruits and vegetables that may have been washed in the water – vegetables that peel are safest.

But even if you boil or filter away the Giardia, there're still very high levels of pollution and lead present in the water here; it's best to stick to bottled water, even for brushing your teeth. Bathing, showering and shaving, though, should cause no problems.

Medical Services

Unless you're an uninsured US or South African resident and citizen, medical treatment in St Petersburg will be beneath the standards you're used to receiving at home. Nonetheless, St Petersburg is second only to Moscow and offers adequate routine, and some emergency, treatment. More serious medical emergencies are best treated outside Russia; Finland is the best option.

The best bet for Western-quality treatment in St Petersburg is the American Medical Center (AMC) (☎ 119 61 01; fax 119 61 20), a US-run facility offering a range of medical services including prenatal, gynaecological and paediatric care, dentistry, 24-hour emergency care, on-site urgent care facilities, private ambulance services, house calls and 24-hour coordination of medical evacuations from the CIS. They also have a complete Western pharmacy. Of course, it's gonna cost ya: prices are stellar, with a basic check-up clocking in at a robust US$135 for members and US$185 nonmembers and it's all uphill from there. HIV screens cost US$35, but you'll also need a counselling session: the total package price for a visa AIDS test is US$75.

But for routine matters, a Russian *poliklinika* is often able to provide perfectly adequate care. We asked AMC doctors where they'd send their family members if the AMC weren't an option: they all said Poliklinika No 2 (☎ 292 62 72), the former clinic of choice for diplomatic staff, at Moskovsky prospekt 22; or Gastello Hospital (☎ 291 79 60, 293 70 10) at ulitsa Gastello 20. For more listings, check *The Traveller's Yellow Pages*.

Ambulance

The state-run ambulance service is still free; Russian speakers can get help by dialling ☎ 03. Saying it's for a foreigner may help get faster and better service. Private ambulance service is available through the AMC, and house calls are available 24 hours a day.

Pharmacies

Pharmacies (singular *apteka*, which is what you should ask for) are located all over the city. Generally, pharmacies in St Petersburg are almost, but not really, well stocked, and many have Western medications. The higher quality ones have everything you may need.

Apteka Petrofarm is an all-night pharmacy that's packed with Western everything. The entrance is at the corner of Nevsky and Bolshaya Konyushennaya from 8 am to 9 pm; the night entrance (for use from 9 pm to 8 am) is around the corner at Bolshaya Konyushennaya 14, through the archway, turn to the right and it's at the top of the small staircase. Apteka No 4 at Nevsky prospekt 5 is a good pharmacy with a large range of Western stuff and tampons. There's also a full Western pharmacy at the AMC.

Sexually Transmitted Diseases

Treatment of gonorrhoea or syphilis is by antibiotics, available at the AMC, and at Skin & Venereal Dispensaries (*Kozhno-venerichskie Dispansery*) throughout the city, which offer diagnosis and treatment of sexually transmitted diseases (check *The Traveller's Yellow Pages St Petersburg* for listings of these clinics). The incidence of AIDS is on the rise in Russia, and there is no cure for this disease. Researchers say that condoms afford the best protection outside of abstinence.

WOMEN TRAVELLERS

In general you're unlikely to experience sexual harassment on the streets, but sexual stereotyping remains strong and revealing clothing will probably attract unwanted attention. With lawlessness and crime on the rise, you need to be wary; a woman alone should certainly avoid private taxis at night.

Any young or youngish woman alone in or near flashy foreigner-haunt bars risks being mistaken for a prostitute.

Russian women dress up and wear lots of make-up on nights out. If you wear casual gear, you might feel uncomfortable at dinner in a restaurant, or at a theatre or ballet. So consider packing something 'smart' to change into at the end of a day's travel or sightseeing.

You might be treated rudely or ignored by female service bureau staff while a man standing next to you is getting smiles and answers to his questions. Persevere to get the help you need. Even if your Russian isn't up to much you can get by.

GAY & LESBIAN TRAVELLERS

Article 121.1 of the Russian Criminal Code, which punished homosexual sex with up to three years imprisonment, was repealed in May 1993. There is an active gay and lesbian scene in St Petersburg, but it's still in its infancy. To date there are only three gay/lesbian clubs (see the Entertainment chapter). Organisations are cagey about contact details (understandably so, given the volatile political climate in the country), and there's not anything approaching the kind of community support infrastructure common in the West.

Key reading is *The Rights of Lesbians & Gay Men in the Russian Federation*, a 130-page, US$15 book in Russian and English published by the International Gay & Lesbian Human Rights Commission (☎ (415) 255 8680; fax (415) 255 8662), 1360 Mission St, Suite 200, San Francisco, CA 94103.

The *Spartacus guide* (readily available in the West) lists several organisations, clubs, cruising areas and health services, though its listings tend to be dated – some gay travellers have reported problems when relying on a dated listing, so be sure to confirm listings.

In St Petersburg, The Chaykovsky Fund (☎ 311 09 37) is a gay resource centre with strong connections to German and American centres that holds Gay Pride Day parades, demonstrations and distributes safe sex and other information. Krilya (☎ 312 31 80) is a political and social action group which organises AIDS awareness drives, and lobbies for gay and lesbian rights. Olga Krauze's Independent Women's Club is a lesbian information centre (☎ 511 91 16).

In Moscow, contact the *AESOP Center* (☎ & fax (7 095) 141 8315; satellite (7 502) 224 3118; e-mail aesop@glas.apc.org), PO Box 27, Moscow 121552, which is a gay and lesbian resource centre that also does awareness and AIDS support group work, or the Moscow Union of Lesbians (☎ (095) 152 16 57).

DISABLED TRAVELLERS

Inaccessible transport, lack of ramps and lifts and no centralised policy for people with physical limitations make St Petersburg a challenging destination for wheelchair-bound visitors. More mobile travellers will have a relatively easier time, but keep in mind that there are obstacles along the way. Toilets are frequently accessed from stairs in restaurants and museums; distances are great and public transport highly crowded. While disabled people are treated with respect and people do go out of their way to be helpful, the experience may be frustrating.

There are exceptions. The Grand Hotel Europe and the Nevskij Palace Hotel are wheelchair accessible, as are their restaurants. While the HI St Petersburg Hostel has no lift, it has a good amount of experience with wheelchair-bound visitors. And other major hotels will all provide assistance and information.

What is required is patience and planning to know what to expect.

Organisations

There are a number of organisations and tour providers around the world that specialise in the needs of disabled travellers:

Australia

Independent Travellers, 167 Gilles St, Adelaide SA 5000; (☎ (08) 232 2555, toll-free (008) 811 355; fax (08) 232 6877) is a travel agent that provides specialised advice for disabled travellers to a number of destinations.

Russia

The All-Union Association for the Rehabilitation of the Disabled is at 1 Kuibyahera ploshchad, Moscow (☎ 298 87 37; fax 230 24 07).

UK

RADAR, 250 City Rd, London (☎ (0171) 250 3222), is a good resource centre.

USA

Twin Peaks Press publishes several useful handbooks for disabled travellers, including *Travel for the Disabled* and the *Directory of Travel Agencies for the Disabled* and can be contacted at PO Box 129, Vancouver, WA 98666 (☎ (202) 694 2462, or toll free in the USA and Canada ☎ (800) 637 2256).

Access, the Foundation for Accessibility by the Disabled, can be contacted at PO Box 356, Malverne, NY 11565 (☎ (516) 887 5798).

Information Center for Individuals with Disabilities. Call or write for their free listings and travel advice. Fort Point Place, 1st Floor, 27-43 Wormwood Street, Boston, MA 02210 (☎ (617) 727 5540, TTY 345 9743 or (800) 248 3737).

Mobility International USA, PO Box 3551, Eugene, OR 97403, (☎ & TDD (503) 343 1284; fax (503) 343 6812; e-mail miusa@igc.apc.org), advises disabled travellers on mobility issues. It also runs an exchange programme, and has run several programmes in Russia.

Moss Rehabilitation Hospital's Travel Information Service is at 1200 W Tabor Road, Philadelphia, PA 19141-3099 (☎ (215) 456 9600; TTY 456 9602).

SATH, Society for the Advancement of Travel for the Handicapped is at 347 Fifth Ave No 610, New York, NY 10016 (☎ (212) 447 7284).

Handicapped Travel Newsletter is a nonprofit, bimonthly publication with good information on travelling around the world and US government legislation. Subscriptions are US$10 annually. Its address is PO Drawer 269, Athens, TX 75751 (☎ & fax (903) 677 1260).

Electronic Resources

As you would imagine, the World Wide Web is brimming with information on the subject of physical disabilities. These will get you started:

Disabled Peoples' International Home Page, a nonprofit and well-done home page with absolutely tons of listings and great links; they're based in Canada and seem to think truly globally.
http://wpg-01.escape.ca/dpi/
The Disability Directory, a long but sometimes tricky-to-navigate gopher list of resources.
gopher://gopher.inforM.umd.edu:70/11/EdRes/Topic/Disability
EKA (Evan Kemp Associates), a company selling products for the disabled, runs a good site with lots of links.
http://disability.com

DANGERS & ANNOYANCES

Street Crime

St Petersburg's streets are about as safe or dangerous as New York's, Mexico City's, London's or Amsterdam's. There's petty theft, pickpocketing, purse-snatching and other such crimes that are endemic in big-city life anywhere in the world. Travellers have reported muggings in broad daylight along Nevsky prospekt. Many travellers have reported problems with groups of Gypsies (Romanies or Travellers), who surround foreigners ostensibly to panhandle but end up closing in, with dozens of hands probing your pockets.

The key here is to be neither paranoid nor insouciant. Common sense must be applied, and you'll need to be aware that it's pretty obvious you're a Westerner. Here are some anti-crime tips:

- Bum bags (fanny packs) are out; they're easily cut with a razor and hey, wasn't that your wallet? If you're going to use a pouch, use a strong leather one or, better yet, an under-the-clothes model so your money is next to your skin. Carry around enough cash so you won't have to pull your pants down to buy a Pepsi.
- An exciting way to meet Russian photo enthusiasts is to walk down Nevsky prospekt with your Nikon slung carelessly over your shoulder. Bag it.
- Don't do anything you wouldn't normally do at home. Flashing jewellery, cash, or speaking on your cellular phone while walking down the street is inviting trouble.

- Keep your wallet in your front pants pocket, never in back or outside pockets, such as in your coat or jacket.
- Watch out when in crowds and on public transport. Assume any displays of anger or altercations in crowds to be diversionary tactics and act accordingly.
- Don't change money on the street unless it's absolutely necessary, and then take as much control as you can of the situation and stay alert. Keep your Western and Russian currencies in different pockets. Always pocket the roubles before handing over your Western currency. Isolate yourself, and never let yourself be the center of a group – even a group of three including yourself. And just go to a bank, for God's sake.

The 'Mafia'

The Western media has had a field day talking about the dangers of the Russian Mafia, painting a portrait of a country inundated with Al Capone types who race through the streets indiscriminately firing Kalashnikov rifles at tourists. In fact, the organised crime problem in Russia is far more complex, and far less of a threat to visitors than one would guess after reading an issue of *Newsweek*.

In general, when people discuss the Mafia they're speaking of the black marketeers and criminal gangs that blossomed with glasnost's removal of the state's channels of fear. It's a loosely applied term, ranging from any group making a few pay-offs to hold down a little corner of the black market, to vicious gangsters who do indeed occasionally settle scores with Kalashnikovs.

Mafia fingers are in all sorts of pies, including currency speculation, extortion from businesses (that's why so many joint-venture restaurant managers have a haunted look), drugs, transportation, staple goods distribution, bootlegging, gunrunning and prostitution.

Crime against foreigners has grown as well, but the Western press has completely gone over the top, making it sound as if the moment you leave the airport you're going to get shot by the 'Mafia'.

Assume for a moment that you're a Mafiosa. You have at your disposal the criminal might to extort, say, a percentage of the profits of a multinational food and beverage corporation with a nationwide distribution network, *or*, alternatively, the contents of the handbag of Mrs J Whistlethwaite of Staines. What would you do? The same as Mafiaosi do in Russia: unless you're involved in high-flying currency speculation, organised criminals aren't really going to waste their time with you. What you have to watch for is the very real threat of street crime carried out by drunken or angry punks and hoods.

Burglary

Break-ins to flats and cars are epidemic so don't leave anything of value – this includes sunglasses, cassette tapes, windscreen wipers and cigarettes – in a car. Valuables lying around hotel rooms are also tempting providence. At camping grounds watch for things being stolen from clotheslines or even cabins. If you'll be living in a flat, invest in a steel door (see *The Traveller's Yellow Pages* or *Where in St Petersburg* for suppliers).

Reporting Theft & Loss

If you're here in a group, your tour guide or service bureau should be your first resort if you want to report a theft or loss. If not, speak to your hotel or hostel administrator for help. You may end up talking to the police *(militsia)*, whose telephone number is ☎ 02, and if you don't speak Russian you'll need a translator. *Vorovstvo* and *krazha* both mean theft in Russian. For lost passports or visas, see the Visa section earlier in this chapter.

Racism

Overt hostility is almost unheard of, though a high level of entrenched racism, or at least racist attitudes, exists in St Petersburg and indeed in Russia. What is most surprising is that racist attitudes or statements can come from otherwise highly educated Russians. The word 'nigger' is not generally seen here as anything other than racially descriptive, and the word is liberally used when speaking about (not to) anyone with dark skin including Georgians or Chechens. Jews, targets of state-sponsored anti-Semitism during the Communist reign, are more distrusted than hated, though the hatred certainly exists. Gypsies, also known as Romanies or Travellers, however, are openly reviled.

KGB

The *Komitet Gosudarstvennoy Bezopastnosti*, Committee for State Security, is on the scrap-heap of Soviet history. Its successor, the Federal Counter-Intelligence Service (Federalnaya Sluzhba Kontrrazvedki; ☎ (095) 924 31 58) has far better things to do with its time than run around following a bunch of tourists.

Arrest

If you are arrested, the Russian authorities are obliged to inform your embassy or consulate immediately and allow you to communicate with it without delay. You can insist on seeing an official from your embassy or consulate straight away. Be polite and respectful and things will go far more smoothly for you. *'Pazhalsta, ya khatelbi pozvanit v posoltstvo moyay stroni'* means 'I'd like to call my embassy'.

Mosquitoes

St Petersburg's prime swamp-front location means that in summer, mossies are rife. Malaria isn't a problem, it's just that the damn things are so completely annoying you may wish to leap from the very window that let the bastards in in the first place. In St Petersburg or any point north (where they get huge and become *screaming* dive bombers), you will want to bring along industrial-strength mosquito repellent, such as REI Jungle Juice (available by mail through Recreational Equipment Incorporated in Sumner, Washington, USA (☎ (206) 891 2500 or, within the US, (800) 426 4840)) or other repellent that's at least 95% DEET. This or mosquito coils or a net is essential. You can also bring along some of the plug-in gizmos, commonly available throughout Europe, that slowly heat cardboard pads that have been saturated with repellent.

Holes

There are uncovered manholes and other subterranean access ports throughout the city: there are no signs, flags or other markers (except the occasional reverberating 'aaaaahhhhh' emanating from the deep). Watch your step.

General Annoyances

One thing you can't do anything about is the tangle of opening hours whereby every shop, museum and café seems to be having its lunch or afternoon break, or day off, or is *remont* (closed for repairs), or is simply closed full stop, just when you want to visit.

Other things you might find annoying are alcoholic late-night comings, goings and door banging in hotel corridors; engine-revving, car-alarm testing, tyre-screeching and more door-banging outside hotels after the restaurant finishes; the brain-numbing volume of restaurant bands; the redolent clouds of cigarette smoke that billow from most gatherings of Russian citizens;

and fartsovshchiky (black marketeers) and prostitutes
who sometimes still walk into your hotel room offering
caviar, sex, currency deals or Soviet military watches.

Not so annoying are the lesser fartsovshchiky who
approach you gently outside hotels to ask 'Where you
from?'. They soon accept the message if you quietly
repeat that you're not interested in any 'business'.

WORK

There are relatively few people who come to Russia to
get rich (those who do tend to be less like you and me
and more like, say, Duane Andreas, chairman of the
high-rolling, US Government-subsidised, commodity
broking agro-giant Archer Daniels Midland Corporation). But working your way through Russia, especially
if you've got some Russian language and a sophisticated
sense of humour, is a great way to really get to know the
country and its people.

While regulations on foreigners working in Russia are
arcane and visa procedures Byzantine, getting permission to work here is, practically speaking, more a
question of lining up your gig than fumbling with
paperwork. Once you have an employer, all the red tape
seems to magically disappear, and a multiple-entry business visa will be yours once your new company's
facilitators are on the job. There are taxes and duties and
residence problems to be coped with, but these change
so quickly and so regularly that committing them to ink
is folly (though we're a follyful lot; see the earlier Visas
section for some key regulations).

The question any applicant will face is whether to
work for a Western or a Russian company. There are
advantages and disadvantages to both, and it's really a
question of what you're in it for that will influence your
decision. Generally speaking, a Western company will
provide you with a level of financial security that will be
unmatched by many Russian companies. This means
that you will probably be paid.

Be especially careful if you're considering working for
a large formerly Soviet Russian company that has been
doing business for years: that type of firm generally
takes the longest to switch over to the idea that employees are people the company hires to do a job in exchange
for money. Late payments, perhaps accompanied by
colourful tales of corporate penury, are frequent, and
non-payment is not uncommon. And should you com-
plain too much, you'll no doubt be reminded of those
poor bastards slaving away in Kamchatkan tractor combines who haven't been paid for seven months, or were

last paid in tampons or spark plugs; and how much did those lovely Nike running shoes cost you back home in the decadent West where you live with your rich family?

If you can hold out financially, though, working for a Russian company can be rewarding in other ways, such as working on your language, learning the ropes from a truly Russian perspective, and possibilities of pleasure and business trips with co-workers that will gain you entry to activities and places that would probably be closed to foreigners under normal circumstances. If you're looking to live like a Russian, you should probably start by being paid like one.

Getting a job at a Western firm isn't as easy as it was in the early days, when your CV was your Western passport and your willingness to stay in the country. Today there's stiff competition for positions in Russia, which are seen as side-door entry ports to multinational corporations, or if you're already in the front door, a hardship post to be followed by a cushy assignment at the end of your Russian tenure.

Along with the competition, there's also the fact that foreign companies consider your on-the-ground presence to be a profound plus; setting up the gig beforehand is much more difficult when you're competing with someone already established in Russia. Unless you've already got Russian contacts to assist you, the best strategy is to simply show up and establish yourself, and count on the job coming through sometime after you've got a flat and you know the city. A huge percentage of long-term resident expatriates did things just that way.

Use resources overseas to get your search started. Operate on the theory that you won't get anything till you get there but you can make things much easier by making as many connections as you can beforehand – a good rule of thumb is if you can't get someone to meet you at the airport, you don't yet have enough connections to make the trip. Check the *St Petersburg Press* and the *Moscow Times* classified sections for jobs postings as well as employment services (headhunters). Check the *Russian Life* adverts also. Use Internet connections to get in Russian business circles and establish a presence before you arrive. Check *The Traveller's Yellow Pages* and *Where In St Petersburg* for companies in your field and contact their overseas offices.

The Expat Community

The expatriate community in Russia is a close-knit one; the feeling of being ground-breakers in a hostile territory is, though diminished over the last couple of years, still a major factor. Foreign business associations are well established in St Petersburg. The network of expatriates looks after its own, and once you're accepted as a serious resident, it's as chummy as any old-boy network the West has to offer. The American International Business Association (see Information, earlier) is a good place to start. You can also contact the International Small Business Association on (☎ 275 07 84) at Nevsky prospekt 86.

Getting There & Away

AIR

Pulkovo-1 and 2, respectively the domestic and international airports that serve St Petersburg, are 17 km south of the city centre, about a half-hour taxi ride and an hour to an hour and a half by public transport.

There's daily service to St Petersburg from many European capitals. Carriers that offer daily service include British Airways, Lufthansa, Finnair, Delta and SAS. Other carriers, notably ČSA, LOT Polish, and Malév, offer service to St Petersburg several times a week. Many major airlines have offices in St Petersburg (see Leaving St Petersburg by Air).

Carriers regularly serving European Russian airports include Aeroflot, Air China (CAAC), Air France, Air India, Air Mongol, Alaska Airlines, Alitalia, ANA (All Nippon Airways), Balkan, British Airways, ČSA, Delta, Deutsche BA, Finnair, JAL, KLM, Korean Air, LOT Polish, Lufthansa, Malév, PIA, Sabena, SAS, Swissair and THY (Turkish Airlines).

Bargain Tickets & Flights

Airlines are not the people to buy cheap tickets from, but their best deals, usually advance-purchase tickets, will give you a reference point. Cheaper and more convenient are agencies who specialise in finding low fares, like STA Travel and Trailfinders in the UK, Kilroy Travel in Finland, Travel Overland in Germany, Council Travel in the USA, Travel Cuts in Canada and the UK and STA Travel in Australia and New Zealand. See the To/From sections below for more information.

Apex (Advance-Purchase Excursion) Fares You get sizeable discounts from some carriers by booking well ahead (eg a 28-day advance booking knocks 25% off the London-St Petersburg return fare). But Apex fares come with big penalties for changes or cancellations.

Charter Flights Group-tour charters can be as much as a third cheaper than scheduled flights in the low season. You may be able to arrange this in advance but normally it's a last minute affair.

Discount Flights Some airlines drop prices as the departure date nears. In many large cities, 'bucket shops' – discount clearing houses – offer some of the best bargains in the Western hemisphere, but of course none will hand over a ticket until the last minute and many are just crooks in disguise. Check that they're licensed by the International Air Transport Association (IATA) or an equivalent national body and get the tickets before you pay.

In London, bucket shops advertise in Sunday-paper travel sections, the 'What's On' section of *Time Out* (the weekly entertainment guide) and in the free weekly *The News & Travel* (TNT) magazine. In the USA, major city newspapers often have classified ads in their Sunday travel sections. Bucket shops advertise in papers like the *Village Voice* (New York), the *San Jose* (California) *Mercury News* and the *New Times* (Miami). In Germany, try *In (München)*, a free biweekly available in cafés and bars.

In Australia, the *Sydney Morning Herald* and the Melbourne *Age* weekend travel sections have advertisements for bucket shops and bargains. Good Asian bucket-shop cities are Bangkok, Hong Kong, Singapore and Delhi.

Nowadays, virtually any travel agent in the world can assist you getting bookings, confirmations and many domestic travel tickets for many areas of Russia. You needn't go through a Russia specialist or Intourist to book trips into Russia, though if you're booking land packages in addition to air the more experience your agent has the better off you'll probably be. The exception to this is if you're just looking for a cheap ticket to the country, in which case you should go with whatever agency has the best deal at the time you're flying.

The following include travel agencies specialising in Russian or discount travel from abroad. See also Tours later in this chapter.

To/From Moscow

In May 1995 the Russian Department of Air Transport granted Transaero, a high-quality Russian airline offering Western-standard service aboard mostly Western-made aircraft (mainly Boeing 737s and 757s), the right to compete with Pulkovo Airlines, the 'baby-flot' that previously had the route monopoly. Pulkovo had held exclusive rights to the route since Soviet times, when it was the Leningrad division of Aeroflot. The result of the new arrangement is better service and – dare we say it – choice. Prices between the two carriers are competitive, with Transaero coming in a bit cheaper in economy class; return airfare between the cities is US$170 (economy class) and US$350 (business class) on Transaero and US$178 (economy) and US$230 (business) on Pulkovo. Tickets for both Pulkovo and Transaero can be purchased at Aeroflot offices, travel agencies such as Sindbad Travel and IRO Travel in Moscow, and through Transaero agents in both cities.

To/From the UK

Zwemmer Tours (☎ (0171) 374 6249; fax (0171) 379 6383), 28 Denmark St, London WC2 H8NJ, does discount booking for Aeroflot flights from Heathrow and Manchester to Moscow and from Heathrow to St Petersburg. It can also arrange a number of services, such as transfers.

Intourist UK (☎ (0171) 538 8600; fax 538 5967) may be the best Intourist offices around; too bad its office is way out at the Docklands at 219 Marsh Wall, Isle of Dogs, London E14 9FJ. It does cut rate Moscow-St Petersburg trips in the £400 to £600 range.

To/From Continental Europe

NBBS Travels (☎ (020) 638 17 38), the Dutch Student Travel Service, is a reliable source of bargain air tickets from Amsterdam, though as a bargain ticket hub, Amsterdam's not what it used to be. NBBS has offices throughout the Netherlands.

Because of restrictions, travel from Germany to Russia is quite expensive, with a Frankfurt-St Petersburg ticket costing about DM1000, or about DM600 from a discount travel agency. The best deal at the time of writing was from Munich and Frankfurt via Budapest, on Malév; the round-trip ticket, valid for three months and including a stopover in Budapest was under DM550. Travel Overland (☎ (089) 272 760), at Barerstrasse 73, is Munich's premiere budget travel agency; it also has an office in Bremen (☎ (0421) 320 477). In Berlin, try Die Neue Reisewelle (☎ (030) 323 1078);

From Warsaw, the terrific folks at LOT Polish Airlines and other carriers offer a round trip to St Petersburg for under US$250. Expect similar fares from Prague and Budapest.

To/From North America

A heavily restricted discount flight from New York to St Petersburg at the time of writing was about US$600, slightly more from Los Angeles.

Russian Youth Hostels & Tourism (☎ (310) 618 2014; fax (310) 618 1140; e-mail 71573.2010@compuserve.com), at 409 North Pacific Highway, Building 106, Suite 390, Redondo Beach, CA 90277, is the US partner and handling agent for all three St Petersburg hostels, as well as the hostel in Novgorod and the Travellers Guest House in Moscow. It can arrange Trans-Siberian Rail journeys and other independent Russian trips, as well as visa processing and support (they take your visa into the Russian Consulate and deal with it) if you're in the USA, or invitations and visa support worldwide. This is one of the most reliable companies in the USA to deal with in visa matters.

STA Travel (☎ (212) 627 3111), at 10 Downing St, New York, NY 10014, is the US incarnation of the Australian student travel specialist. It doesn't offer tours, but does offer cheap-as-possible bookings on all major airlines. It also has offices in San Francisco (☎ (415) 391 8407), Boston (☎ (617) 266 6014), Cambridge (☎ (617) 576 4623), Philadelphia (☎ (215) 382 2928), Washington DC (☎ (202) 887 0912), Berkeley (☎ (510) 642 3000), Melrose (☎ (213) 934 8722), Westwood (☎ (310) 824 1574), Santa Monica (☎ (310) 394 5126), with offices in Chicago and Seattle opening in 1995; elsewhere in the USA and Canada call ☎ (800) 777 0112.

CCTE Council Travel (☎ (212) 661 1450, or from the USA and Canada (800) 226 8624), at 205 East 42nd St, 16th Floor, is the head office of a national chain of student travel offices, doing essentially the same thing as STA on a larger scale.

To/From Australasia

Flight Centres International and STA Travel are major dealers in cheap airfares, each with offices throughout Australia and New Zealand. Flight Centre's main offices are at 19 Bourke St, Melbourne 3000 (☎ (03) 9650 2899), and 317 Swanston St, Melbourne 3000 (☎ (03) 9663 1304); and 82 Elizabeth St, Sydney 2000 (☎ (02) 235 3522). STA's are at 224 Faraday St, Carlton, Victoria 3053 (☎ 03) 9347 6911), and 732 Harris St, Ultimo, NSW 2007 (☎ (02) 281 9866; and, in New Zealand, at 10 High St, Auckland (☎ (09) 309 9995).

The best place to arrange a visa with an invitation and no prepaid accommodation is Passport Travel (☎ (03) 9824 7183, toll-free (008) 337 031; fax (03) 9822 3956), 320B Glenferrie Rd, Malvern, Victoria 3144. It is also the agent for Red Bear Tours (see Tours later in this chapter).

To/From Hong Kong & Beijing

Monkey Business (☎ Hong Kong (852) 723 1376; Beijing (861) 329 2244, extension 406; e-mail (both offices) 100267.2570@compuserve.com) is a well-established trans-Siberian specialist, which does trans-Siberian bookings, flights, and bookings for the Moscow Travellers Guest House and the HI St Petersburg Hostel. There were several complaints about Monkey Business in 1994 from travellers who felt they had been overcharged for some services and given inaccurate accounts of on-the-ground costs. But the company has been around a while and handles lots of people, and should not be ruled out on the strength of a few complaints. It's at Chung King Mansions, Nathan Rd, 36-44 E-Block, 4th Floor, Flat 6, Kowloon, Hong Kong; or Beijing Commercial Business Complex, No 1 Building Yu Lin Yi Office, Room 406, 4th floor, You An Men Wai district, 100054 Beijing, China.

Arriving in St Petersburg by Air

The arrivals hall in Pulkovo-2 has a currency exchange office that has ... let's call them ... 'odd' hours of operation. There are also a couple of unfathomably expensive car rental agencies. See the Getting Around chapter for information on transport to/from the city.

Leaving St Petersburg by Air

All airlines charge US dollars for international tickets purchased in St Petersburg, one of the few remaining services still permitted to charge in that currency. All airlines accept credit cards and almost all offer same-day ticketing. Most offices are open from 9 am to 5 pm.

Aeroflot
   Nevsky prospekt 7 on the corner of ulitsa Gogolya (☎ 104 38 22)
Air France
   at Pulkovo-2 (☎ 104 34 33)
Austrian Airlines
   Nevskij Palace Hotel (☎ 104 38 22)
Balkan Bulgarian Airlines
   ulitsa Bolshaya Morskaya (ulitsa Gertsena) 36 (☎ 315 50 30)
British Airways
   ulitsa Bolshaya Morskaya (ulitsa Gertsena) 36 (☎ 311 58 20)
ČSA Czech Airlines
   ulitsa Bolshaya Morskaya (ulitsa Gertsena) 36 (☎ 315 52 59)

Delta Airlines (USA)
   ulitsa Bolshaya Morskaya (ulitsa Gertsena) 36 (☎ 311 58 20)
Finnair
   Gogolya ulitsa 19 (☎ 315 97 36)
KLM
   at Pulkovo-2 (☎ 104 34 40)
LOT Polish Airlines
   Karavannaya ulitsa 1 at ploshchad Manezhnaya (☎ 273 57 21)
Lufthansa
   Vosnesensky prospekt 7 (☎ 314 49 79, 314 59 17)
Malév Hungarian Airlines
   Vosnesensky prospekt 7 (☎ 314 63 80, 315 54 55)
Scandinavian Airlines System (SAS)
   Nevskij Palace Hotel (☎ 314 50 86)
Swissair
   Nevskij Palace Hotel (☎ 314 50 86)

BUS

St Petersburg's two long-distance bus stations are Avtovokzal 1, at naberezhnaya Obvodnogo Kanala 118 (near Baltiyskaya metro), which serves northern destinations such as Vyborg, Karelia etc; and Avtovokzal 2, at naberezhnaya Obvodnogo Kanala 36 (10 minutes from metro Ligovsky Prospekt), which serves Baltic countries (Estonia included), and destinations to the south and east such as Novgorod, Pskov, Vologda, Moscow and beyond.

To/From Finland

There are three bus companies offering shuttle services between Helsinki's autobus station and St Petersburg. St Petersburg Express is the cheapest of the bus services; at the time of writing it charged US$43.50 for the St Petersburg-Helsinki trip. Buses leave from the Hotel Astoria at 12.30 pm and arrive in Helsinki at 7.35 pm.

Finnord (☎ 314 89 51) runs buses to/from Helsinki via Vyborg and Lahti from its office at ulitsa Italyanskaya 37, and from the Hotel Astoria. At the time of writing the cost of a one-way ticket to Helsinki was US$46. Buses leave the Astoria at 3.10 pm and arrive in Helsinki at 10.15 pm.

Sovtransavto Express Bus (☎ 264 51 25) has daily coaches to/from Helsinki and Lapeenranta, as well as a Vyborg-Lapeenranta service. As a way of saving money and costing time take the electric train from St Petersburg to Vyborg and then the bus to Lapeenranta. In St Petersburg buses leave from the Hotel Pulkovskaya, Hotel Astoria, Grand Hotel Europe and St Petersburg Hotel. The bus for Helsinki costs US$46, and leaves from the Grand Hotel Europe at 8.45 am, arriving at 3.45 pm. See the service desk or concierge at these hotels for more information, or call Sovtransavto.

From Helsinki, buses leave the bus station for St Petersburg at 7.15 am (St Petersburg Express), 9 am (Finnord and Sovtransavto).

TRAIN

The main international rail gateways to St Petersburg are Helsinki, Tallinn, Warsaw and Berlin. Trains leave daily from St Petersburg to those and, by connections, to many European capitals. You can also use Moscow as a gateway, opening up the possibility of more connections. Rail passes are not valid in Russia.

To/From Moscow

Most of the 12 or more daily Moscow trains take seven to 8½ hours. Several are overnight sleepers, which save time and a night's hotel costs. To Moscow the best overnight trains are Nos 1 (11.55 pm), 3 (11.59 pm) and 5 (11.38 pm). From Moscow, Nos 2 (11.55 pm), 4 (11.59 pm) and 6 (11.10 pm) are the best. All of these trains cost approximately US$20/35 for 2nd/1st class.

For the same price, there's also the once-weekly, high-speed ER200, which covers the 650 km in less than five hours – it leaves St Petersburg on Thursday at 12.15 pm, and Moscow on Friday at 12.20 pm.

In St Petersburg, tickets to Moscow can be purchased at the Central Train Ticket Office, the Intourist counter in Moscow Station, Sindbad Travel and, at a huge mark-up, from any luxury hotel (the Grand Hotel Europe charges US$65 for tickets; see also the Leaving St Petersburg by Train section). Foreigners are required to pay the foreigner rate for tickets between Moscow and St Petersburg; many (non-Russian-speaking) foreigners trying to use the cheaper tickets for Russians are told they must pay the conductor the difference between the Russian and foreigner tickets or they cannot board the train (this is essentially a bribe to the conductor). If your Russian is good, give it a shot, but if you're caught the bribe to the conductor can be higher than the face value of the foreigner tickets.

To/From the Czech Republic

Prague to St Petersburg trains connect through Warsaw's Central Station (Warszawa Centralna); the night train from Prague arrives in Warsaw at 6.50 am, and connects with the 9 am Warsaw-Moscow train (24 hours). You can stick around for the day (check out the Stare Miasto) and catch the night train at about 12.44 am from Warsaw's Gdansk station to St Petersburg (29 to 39 hours).

UK, US and Western European passport holders need no visa to enter the Czech Republic; those with Canadian, Australian and NZ passports need one.

To/From Estonia

There are two daily sleepers to St Petersburg leaving Tallinn at 8.10 and 11 pm, and arriving in St Petersburg at 7.15 and 9.45 am.

To/From Finland

On the heavily travelled Helsinki-Vyborg-St Petersburg corridor the rail crossing is at Vainikkala (Luzhayka on the Russian side). There are two daily trains between St Petersburg and Helsinki. The *Repin*, a Russian-run train that's cleaner than most Russian trains, departs from St Petersburg's Finland Station (Finlandsky vokzal) at 8.05 am and arrives in Helsinki at 2.03 pm. The return train leaves Helsinki at 3.32 pm and arrives in St Petersburg at 11.20 pm. The *Repin* costs single/return US$63/126 in 2nd class, US$116/232 for 1st class.

The *Sibelius*, a quite civilised Finnish Railways-run train that's more convenient, more pleasant, faster and, if you're travelling in 1st class, cheaper, leaves St Petersburg at 3.55 pm, arriving in Helsinki at 9.34 pm. It leaves Helsinki at 6.30 am and arrives in St Petersburg at 1.55 pm. At the time of writing, 2nd-class tickets are the same price as for the *Repin*, while 1st-class tickets are US$102.25/204.50 for a single/return.

On the way back, you can save yourself about US$15 by costing yourself a lot of time: from Finland Station, take any elektrichka (suburban train) to Vyborg Station, where you can meet the Helsinki-bound *Repin* at 10.16 am, and the *Sibelius* at 6.15 pm. The trip to Vyborg takes about 2½ hours and costs less than US$0.50. From Vyborg to Helsinki a 2nd-class ticket on either train is US$46.25

In St Petersburg's Finland Station, tickets can be purchased at Window 46 *(Repino)* or 53 *(Sibelius)*; the ticket booth is open Monday to Saturday from 8 am to 1 pm and from 2 to 7 pm, and on Sunday from 8 am to 1 pm and from 2 to 4 pm. In Helsinki's main station, tickets are sold in the long-distance-tickets room at the international counter; take a number from the middle number generator near the door and walk straight to the back of the hall. Sindbad Travel at the HI St Petersburg Hostel sells tickets from St Petersburg to Helsinki at US$15 off the retail price.

No visa is needed for entry to Finland by US, Canadian, UK, Australian or NZ passport holders for up to three months stay.

To/From Poland

There's a daily service between Warsaw and St Petersburg (29 to 39 hours). These trains cross at Kuznica, which is near Hrodna (Grodno) in Belarus. You'll change wheels just outside the Bialystock station, which takes about three hours.

No visa is needed for entry for citizens of the USA, Germany or the Netherlands, but UK, Canadian, Australian, French and New Zealand citizens need a visa. Transiting through Belarus from Europe, your Russian visa will act as a Belarusian transit visa as long as you don't leave the train. On the return trip, you should be issued a transit visa at the Russia-Belarus border at no charge (scream bloody murder if a border guard tries to charge you).

Arriving in St Petersburg by Train

St Petersburg has four chief main-line stations, all south of the river, except Finland Station which is at ploshchad Lenina, Vyborg Side, and serves trains on the Helsinki line. Moscow Station, at ploshchad Vosstania on Nevsky prospekt, handles trains to/from Moscow, the far north, Crimea, the Caucasus, Georgia and Central Asia; Vitebsk Station (Vitebsky vokzal), at Zagorodny prospekt 52, deals with Smolensk, Belorussia, Kiev, Odessa and Moldova; and Warsaw Station (Varshavsky vokzal), at naberezhnaya Obvodnogo Kanala 118, covers the Baltic republics, Pskov, Lvir (Lvov) and Eastern Europe. Baltic Station (Baltiysky vokzal), just along the road from the Warsaw Station, is mainly for suburban trains.

Leaving St Petersburg by Train

Domestic and international train information is available from the Intourist counter (13) at the Central Train Ticket Office, naberezhnaya Kanala Griboedova 24 between the Kazan Cathedral and the Bankovy Bridge (open Monday to Saturday from 8 am to 4 pm; Sunday from 9 am to 4 pm). The problem here is one of definition: Intourist has apparently confused 'capitalism' with 'extortion'; it charges US$0.15 *per question* about train times and prices (though it always has the most up-to-date information on prices). You can also get information about domestic trains from the Intourist counter at Moscow Station (Moskovsky vokzal), which is inside the main hall – the first small door on the right after passing the schedules if you enter from ploshchad Vosstania.

The reception desk at the HI St Petersburg Hostel will help get you where you need to get, and also has a ticket-buying service for those who just can't cope with the folks at the station, for which it tacks a straight US$5 charge onto the ticket price.

Train Rip-Offs

Reports of robberies on the overnight trains between St Petersburg and Moscow have been increasing. Try to get a bottom bunk and place your belongings in the bin beneath your bed when you go to sleep. Make sure that the lock on your door is operational, and flip up the steel latch – about two-thirds of the way up on the left hand side of the door – to prevent entry by thieves who may have a skeleton key to carriages. Jam a piece of paper or cork underneath the latch to prevent it being flipped down again by the more keen thieves who use bent coat-hangers for that purpose. To go slightly over the top (but not much), Nick always carries a couple of metres of climbing rope and a couple of carrabiners (available at any good sporting goods store for under US$6) in case the lock or latch doesn't work. Slip the 'beeners over the lock switch (thus placing steel, as opposed to rope, in any opening of the door if it's forced) and tie them off to one of the steel handles that are secured to the wall.

CAR & MOTORBIKE

See the Getting Around chapter for specific driving tips for the city.

Foreigners can now legally drive almost all of Russia's highways, and can even ride motorcycles. On the debit side, driving in Russia, while truly an unfiltered Russian experience, is *truly* an unfiltered Russian experience. Poor roads, maddeningly inadequate signposting (except in St Petersburg's centre), low quality petrol (76 octane usually, though higher octane grades are becoming more readily available) and keen highway patrolmen can lead to frustration and dismay.

Motorcycles, while legal, undergo vigorous scrutiny by border officials and highway police, especially if you're driving anything vaguely Ninja-ish. But one traveller said that while riding his hand-built motorcycle across the entire former Soviet Union, the only attention he attracted from the police consisted of admiring questions and comments.

Motorcycles are definitely not wise in St Petersburg, where crime is high and traffic police are widespread. Finally, while foreign automobile companies now have an established presence in Moscow, St Petersburg and other cities, motorcycles in the former Soviet Union are almost exclusively Russian or East German-made – it is to be doubted that a Ural-brand carb will fit your Hog.

Most of the Russian border is lined on the inside with a strip, 25 km deep, within which access is controlled even for Russian citizens who live there. In these zones photos are frowned on and individuals are unlikely to get away with genuinely independent movement – you may be sent out of the area by police or border patrols unless you have a business visa and a letter from a Russian company stating why you need to be in the area.

The Basics

To be allowed to drive your own car/motorcycle in Russia you'll need your driving licence and either an International Driving Permit with a Russian translation of your licence's information or a certified Russian translation of your full licence (you can certify translations at a Russian embassy or consulate).

You will also need your vehicle's registration papers and proof of insurance. Be sure your insurance covers you in Russia. Russian insurance should be available at the border through Ingosstrakh (head office (☎ (095) 233 17 59, 233 05 50, 233 20 70; fax (095) 230 25 18), Pyatnitskaya ulitsa 12, Moscow). Your insurance agent at home or one in Finland may also be able to get you a policy covering driving in Russia.

Finally a customs declaration promising to take your vehicle with you when you leave is also required.

Speed limits are generally 60 km/h in cities and between 80 and 100 km/h on highways. Russians drive on the right, and traffic coming from the right has the right of way. Filling stations are located throughout the city. The most common fuel is 76 octane but higher octane petrol, like 92 and sometimes even 98, is available as well.

Technically it is legal to have a blood-alcohol level of up to 0.04%, but in practice it's illegal to drive after you have consumed *any* alcohol at all. This is a rule that is strictly enforced. Safety belt use is mandatory.

Motorcyclists (and passengers) must wear a crash helmet.

Crossing In

You'll first pass the neighbouring country's border point, where you'll need to show your auto registration and insurance papers (including Finnish or Scandinavian proof of coverage if you're coming from Finland or Norway), your driving licence, passport and visa. Scandinavian formalities are usually minimal for Western citizens.

On the Russian side, chances are your vehicle will be subjected to a cursory inspection by border guards (your life will be made much easier if you open all doors and the boot yourself, and shine a torch (flashlight) for the guards at night). You pass through customs separately from your car, walking through a metal detector and possibly having hand luggage X-rayed.

You no longer need to file an itinerary, or state in which direction you're heading.

To/From Finland

Highways cross at the Finnish border posts of Nuijamaa (Brusnichnoe on the Russian side) and Vaalimaa (Torfyanovka on the Russian side). From there to St Petersburg the road is said by everyone to be infested with modern-day highwaymen (though we've driven it literally dozens of times and never had any difficulties). Don't stop for anybody, fill up with petrol on the Finnish side (preferably before you get to the border filling station, which is more expensive than others and closes early). There's a radar speed-trap just outside the St Petersburg city line, where the limit is 60 km/h (hint: radar detectors are legal in Russia). Be sure and watch for all road signs; a few involve tricky curves and sign posting is not all it should be. It's best to make this drive for the first time during daylight hours.

There's only one car rental outfit in Helsinki that rents cars that can be taken into Russia, and that's Transvell (☎ (90) 351 33 00) at Ormuspellontie 5. There is a branch outlet in St Petersburg. These cars are not cheap; see the Getting Around chapter for more information.

To/From Estonia

The nearest border crossing from Tallinn is at Narva and the road from there is uneventful, if not particularly fast.

To/From Ukraine & Belarus

The road border crossings into Russia are open to foreign drivers.

BOAT

The Baltic Shipping Company's *Konstantin Simonov*, *Anna Karenina* and *Ilich* sail from Helsinki, Kiel and Stockholm to St Petersburg You can use the ships for straight transport (one way or return) or book a cruise. A huge advantage of the cruise option is that it's visa free – as long as you sleep on the ship, you don't need a visa.

High season runs from mid-May to mid-September, and mid-December to the second week in January. Sailing schedules change from year to year, but expect the *Konstantin Simonov* to sail to/from Helsinki twice a week (currently Monday and Thursday) from May to November. A bed in a quad room for a one-way trip is US$70/65 for the high/low season. The cheapest four-day cruises including return passage start at US$150/135 (high/low season) in a four-person inside cabin.

The *Anna Karenina* sails from Kiel, Germany, on Saturday, and Nynashamn (45 minutes from Stockholm) on Sunday, and arrives in St Petersburg on Tuesday at 9 am. The cheapest one-way fare from Kiel is US$285/245 (high/low season), and the cheapest visa-free cruise is US$370/320; from Nynashamn it's US$110/100, US$205/175.

The *Ilich* sails between Stockholm and Riga, and Stockholm and St Petersburg; schedules and prices are very complicated. Contact the Baltic Shipping Company for more information at:

St Petersburg (☎ 355 16 16, 355 61 40)
Helsinki (☎ (358 9) 66 57 55)
Stockholm (☎ (46 0) 20 00 29)
Kiel (☎ (49 431) 982 0000)
US Agent (EuroCruises) (☎ (800) 688 3876 or (212) 366 4747, (212) 691 2099)

Passenger ships dock at the Sea Terminal (Morskoy vokzal) at the west end of Bolshoy prospekt on Vasilevsky Island (take bus No 128 from Vasileostrovskaya metro or trolleybus No 10 from Nevsky Prospekt or Primorskaya metro).

River Cruises To/From Moscow

In summer, passenger boats ply the rivers and canals between Moscow and St Petersburg. The route follows the Neva River to Lake Ladoga, to the Svir River and Lake Onega, the Volga-Baltic canal to the Rybinskoe

Reservoir and through some of the Golden Ring along
the Volga to Moscow.

River cruises to Moscow leave from the St Petersburg
River Station at prospekt Obukhovskoy oborony 195
near metro Proletarskaya (turn right on exit and take any
tram one stop) and sometimes from the Passenger Sea
Terminal on Vasilevsky Island (Metro Primorskaya then
trolleybus No 10 or 23). Cruises to Moscow range from
US$392 to US$630. The St Petersburg Travel Company
can also arrange cruises and tours. See the Excursions
for information about cruises to Valaam and Kizhi
Island.

The Moscow terminus for these sailings is the Northern River Station (Severny Rechnoy vokzal (☎ (095) 459
74 76; fax (095) 459 70 16) at Leningradskoe shosse 51
(Rechnoy Vokzal metro).

If you thought the break-up of Aeroflot was something, wait till you see what has happened to state-run
ship services. The state services are being pared down
further and further, handing over their boats to private
enterprises, but at the time of writing sailings between
Moscow and St Petersburg leave each city for the other
every two weeks.

Sindbad Travel, at the HI St Petersburg Hostel and
Latti (☎ 262 04 07), at the River Station, offer standard
two-day cruises to Valaam (see Excursions) from May to
August for US$88 to US$126 including meals, and
US$129 to US$189 if you tack on an extra day or two and
Kizhi Island as well.

TRAVEL AGENTS

This is a fledgling field, and dozens of agencies are
popping out of the woodwork. Be careful, and check
with the airlines to see if the agent is actually getting you
a better deal before you use one. Concierges at the better
hotels can perform some standard booking services,
though at a price.

Sindbad Travel (☎ 327 83 84; fax 329 80 19; e-mail
sindbad@ryh.spb.su), owned by the HI St Petersburg
Hostel, is a genuine Western-style student and discount
air ticket office, specialising in one-way and short or
no-advance-purchase tickets. It operates as a full service
ticketing centre for Kilroy Travel and STA, and can
forward-book youth hostel accommodation through the
IBN system. Basically it offers all the same services of the
big guys it represents, and has friendly service from
people who understand what they're booking. It's at the
HI St Petersburg Hostel, 3-ya Sovietskaya ulitsa 28, on
the ground floor.

American Express, at the Grand Hotel Europe, does discounted return tickets to European and American destinations on Deutsche BA and other airlines. Check their specials, sometimes advertised in the *St Petersburg Press*. Other travel agencies are popping up all the time, check the *St Petersburg Press* for adverts.

TOURS

From the UK

Travel For The Arts (☎ (0171) 483 4466; fax (0171) 586 0639) does luxury 'culture' based tours to St Petersburg and other Eastern and Western European cities; it's at 117 Regent's Park Rd, London NW1 8UR.

Exodus Adventure (☎ (0181) 675 5550; fax (0181) 673 0779) does heaps of adventure stuff in the former Soviet Union; it can also arrange walking trips around Lake Baikal and trips to Moscow, St Petersburg and Karelia, including Valaam. It's at 9 Weir Rd, London SW12 0LT. Goodwill Holidays (☎ (043871) 6421) at Manor Chambers, The Green, School Lane, Weleyn, Herts AL6 9EB, offers tours of cities in Russia and the former Soviet Union including St Petersburg.

From North America

REI Adventures, PO Box 1938, Sumner, Washington 98389-0880 (☎ (206) 395 8111, 395 8119, toll-free (800) 622 2236; fax (206) 395 4744), offers a huge array of adventure tourism packages for Russia and the former Soviet Union.

General Tours (☎ (617) 621 0977 or (800) 221 2216), at 139 Main St, Cambridge, MA 02142, is a well-established company offering 'to your right is the Kremlin'-style packages to Moscow, St Petersburg and the Golden Ring for a wide range of prices. Prices in the high season start at about US$1500 per person for eight days Moscow/St Petersburg including airfare, transfers, transport, tours, excursions and two meals a day (usually the guide arranges for lunch, which is paid for separately). Pioneer Tours (☎ (617 547 1127), at 203 Allston St, Cambridge, MA 02142, specialises in independent travel packages which can consist of à la carte hotel bookings or homestays and airfare.

EuroCruises (☎ (800) 688 3876) is the US agent for Baltic Shipping Company, the Russian company that organises visa-free cruises from Scandinavian cities to St Petersburg and the Golden Ring. The address is 303 W 13th St, New York, NY 10032.

Inside Russia Sojourns (☎ (704) 265 4060), RR 2 Box 324; Boone, NC 28607, does bicycle trips together with its partner, the St Petersburg Bicycle Club.

From Australia

Eastern Europe Travel Bureau (☎ (01)262 1144; fax (02) 262 4479), 75 King St, Sydney 2000, does budget tours (airfares not included): Moscow, four days A$270; Moscow and St Petersburg, six days A$525; Moscow to St Petersburg cruise by river and canal, 15 days from A$1075. Homestays (language tuition optional) in Moscow or St Petersburg can also be arranged from A$485.

Passport Travel, the representative of Red Bear Tours (☎ (03) 9824 7183), toll-free (008) 337 031; fax (03) 9822 3956), 320B Glenferrie Rd, Malvern, Victoria 3144, can arrange skiing tours, language courses, far east rail and port tours, and Trans-Siberian Railway tours from A$1175.

The prolific leaflet-writers at GateWay Travel (☎ (02) 745 3333; fax (02) 745 3237), 48 The Boulevarde, Strathfield, NSW 2135, arrange homestays, B&Bs, youth hostels, apartments and hotels from A$40 to A$215, and say they can also arrange tours and cruises.

From Finland

The very helpful and friendly Eurohostel (☎ (90) 66 44 52; fax (90) 65 50 44) works closely with the Russian Youth Hostel Association, and can help with paperwork, visa support, bus reservations and car rentals. It's also said to be getting ready to offer discounted train tickets from Helsinki to St Petersburg, and is part of the 'Hostel The Baltic Triangle' group, which arranges hostelling stays between Helsinki, St Petersburg and Tallinn. It is just off the Silja Lines port in Helsinki at Linnankatu 9, and is a key source in Helsinki for Russia-related travel information.

Finnsov Tours (☎ (90) 694 20 11), formerly privately owned but now owned by Intourist Moscow Ltd, offers short but expensive package tours from Helsinki to St Petersburg and dozens of other Russian cities by train, bus and ship. It has a five-day St Petersburg-Tallinn tour by train at US$805. If you're game, so are they: you'll find them at Eerikinkatu 3, Helsinki.

From Estonia

Karol (☎ (2) 454 900, 446 240; fax (6) 313 918) was a major player in the establishment of a St Petersburg-Helsinki-

Tallinn youth hostel network, and specialises in cheap independent travel to Russia, including full visa support. It's at Lembitu 4, Tallinn EE0001.

Virone (☎ (2) 448 960) does simple packages from Tallinn to St Petersburg including hotel and city tours with driver. It's at Pronski 11, Tallinn 200010.

WARNING

The information in this chapter is particularly vulnerable to change: prices for international travel are volatile, routes are introduced and cancelled, schedules change, special deals come and go, and rules and visa requirements are amended. Airlines and governments seem to take a perverse pleasure in making price structures and regulations as complicated as possible. You should check directly with the airline or a travel agent to make sure you understand how a fare (and ticket you may buy) works. In addition, the travel industry is highly competitive and there are many lurks and perks.

The upshot of this is that you should get opinions, quotes and advice from as many airlines and travel agents as possible before you part with your hard-earned cash. The details given in this chapter should be regarded as pointers and are not a substitute for your own careful, up-to-date research.

Getting Around

St Petersburg's excellent public transport system makes getting around the centre very simple and inexpensive. Outlying areas are served, though less efficiently, and if you're staying out at the end of any metro line in a 'microregion', your journey to the centre will probably be a combination of bus and metro. The centre, especially Nevsky prospekt, is best seen on foot.

TO/FROM THE AIRPORT

St Petersburg's airport is at Pulkovo, about 17 km south of the centre. The cheapest do-it-yourself transport is bus-plus-metro. From Moskovskaya metro (not Moskovskie vorota), bus No 39 runs to Pulkovo-1, the domestic terminal, and bus No 13 runs to Pulkovo-2, the international terminal, stopping at the Hotel Pulkovskaya en route. They go whenever they feel like it, take 15 minutes and cost less than US$0.50. This is a difficult airport to reach by bus alone. From the airport, take bus No 13 to Moskovskaya metro and the metro from there into the city.

There is a US$1 express bus that takes 45 minutes to the domestic terminal only, from a small Aeroflot office at ulitsa Bolshaya Morskaya (ulitsa Gertsena) 13, one block off Nevsky prospekt. It goes about every half-hour throughout the day, and every hour and a half at night; there's a timetable in the office window. The bus is labelled Городской Аэровокзал Аэропорт Пулково ('Gorodskoy Aerovokzal Aeroport Pulkovo'). Shuttles run between the domestic and international terminals, but you'll probably have to pay about US$2 to US$5.

Regular city buses accept tickets called *talony*, which you can buy in strips of 10 from drivers for US$1.50, and which are useful on all city buses, trolleybuses and trams.

It's cheaper to get a taxi to the airport (about US$6 to US$10) than from it (at least US$20 unless your Russian's great, then at least US$10). One good way to reduce the bill is metro-plus-taxi; from Moskovskaya metro a taxi will only cost about US$3 to US$5.

The drivers that hang out at the airport are your introduction to what everyone calls the 'Mafia' and what is actually just a bunch of thugs who control who can park their car there and wait for fares.

A not-stupid way to do it is to arrange to be met at the airport by faxing one of the more reliable (read expensive) taxi services before you get on the plane. When you arrive, they'll be waiting with your name on a sign. Expect to pay US$25 to US$35 for a ride to the centre using these services (see Taxis, below, for contact numbers), but for this price you won't have to hassle and haggle after your arrival and possible ordeal with customs. Could be worth it.

If you're staying at any of the luxury hotels in town, or if your hotel package includes transfers, you'll be met by bus or minivan

TO/FROM STATIONS & SEAPORTS

The Vasilevsky Island seaport is on the bus No 7 and trolleybus No 10 routes leaving from near the Hermitage. The St Petersburg Travel Company, as well as the more expensive taxi services like SVIT, offer transfers to/from railway stations, hotels and the seaport for about US$35 per car load. Every railway terminus has a metro station next door, and taxis are easy to get if you walk a block or two away from the station before trying.

PUBLIC TRANSPORT

Metro

Though less majestic than Moscow's, the St Petersburg metro leaves most of the world's other 'undergrounds' in the dust. You'll rarely wait more than three minutes for a train (even at 6 am on a Sunday), and the clock at the end of the platform shows elapsed time since the last train departed.

It's the quickest way around the wider city and in 1995 tokens *(zhetony)* cost less than US$0.10! Buy your tokens at the booths in the stations, place them in the entry gates, wait for the coins to drop and walk through (memo to potential fare-beaters: spring-mounted gates slam shut once you pass the beam of an electric eye – this at the very least makes a lot of noise and gate-activation will certainly earn you the wrath of several screaming babushki and possibly a policeman). If you're staying in town more than a week, you may want to get a monthly or half-monthly pass, sold at stations and in kiosks. Show the pass to the person watching the open gate at the end of the entry gate row.

Since 1993, the lines have been numbered, which has simplified only the typing of this paragraph. Colours vary depending on the map you're looking at, but looking at the southernmost part of any map, Line 1 is always at the left; Line 4 at the right. The grandest looking stations seem to be on Line 1. Stations open at 5.30 am and close at 1 am, and the metro begins closing down at about 12.30 am.

St Petersburg's metro is not as extensive as Moscow's, nor as user-friendly. Many station platforms (eg on Line 3 to Vasilevsky Island, and many stations on Line 2 north of Nevsky prospekt) have outer safety doors, so you can't see the station from an arriving train; also, you can't rely on spotting the signs on the platforms as you pull in. Furthermore, the announcements in the carriages are confusing: just before a departing train's doors close, a recorded voice, full of the optimism of Socialist progress, announces *'Ostorozhno! Dveri zakryvayutsya. Sleduyushchaya stantsia* (name of next station)'. This means 'Caution! The doors are closing. Next station (name of next station)'. Just before the train stops at the next station, it announces its name. In case you don't catch these, or they come confusingly close together, as they often do in St Petersburg, the surest way of getting off at the right station is to count the stops. Another small annoyance (actually it's quite funny) is when the tape-playback units wow and flutter, making the voice sound like either Mickey Mouse or Louis Armstrong

You're expected to give your seat to the elderly – stand up, point to your seat and say *'pazhalsta'*. On crowded (this means all) public transport people also usually give up seats to women with children or a lot of baggage. People manoeuvre their way out by confronting anyone in the way with *'Vy vykhodite seychas?'* (*'vih vih-KHO-dee-tyeh sih-SHASS?'*, meaning 'Are you getting off now?'), or just *'Vykhodite?'* ('Getting off?'). If you're asked this, and aren't getting off, step aside but quick.

Stations are mostly identified from outside by big 'M' signs. To exit to the street, follow signs saying 'Выюд в город' *'Vykhod v gorod'*, meaning 'Exit to the city'. If there's more than one exit, each sign names the street you come out on. If you need to change to another line, the process is much the same whether it passes through the same station or through a nearby one linked by underground walkways. The word to look for is 'Переод' *'perekhod'*, meaning 'change', often with a blue-background man-on-stairs sign, followed by 'На станси' *'na stantsiyu...'* (to ... station) or 'на лини.' *'na ... liniyu'* (to ... line), then usually 'к поездам до стаисий' *'ke poezdam do stantsiy ...'* (to trains to ... stations).

Bus, Trolleybus & Tram

A US$0.07 ticket is used on all buses, trolleybuses (electric buses) and trams. They're sold in kiosks at major

interchanges, by hawkers at the railway stations, and
often in strips of 10 by drivers. Punch the ticket in the
ticket-punch boxes; failure to do so results in on-the-spot
fines should you be so unlucky as to run into one of the
plain-clothes ticket inspectors.

Bus stops are marked by 'A' signs (for avtobus), trolleybus stops by 'T' or ⊓ signs by the roadside, tram
stops by a 'T' sign over the roadway, all usually indicat-
ing the line numbers too. Stops may also have roadside
signs with little pictures of a bus, trolleybus or tram.
Most transport runs from 6 am to 1 am.

The following are some important long routes across
the city:

Along Nevsky prospekt between the Admiralty and Moscow
    Station: bus Nos 7, 44; trolleybus Nos 1, 7, 10, 22. Trolley-
    bus Nos 1 and 22 continue out to Hotel Moskva and
    Alexandr Nevsky Monastery.
Around the Sadovaya ulitsa ring road south of Nevsky pro-
    spekt: tram Nos 3, 13, 14. Tram No 3 continues north of
    Nevsky prospekt and crosses the Kirovsky Bridge into
    Petrograd Side.
From the Hermitage to the Pribaltiyskaya Hotel on Vasilevsky
    Island: bus Nos 7, 30, 44; trolleybus No 12.
From the Hermitage to Krestovsky Island (Petrograd Side):
    bus No 45 terminates at the bridge to Yelagin Island. From
    metro Gostiny Dvor via Liteyny Bridge to the same termi-
    nus: tram No 12.
From the Hermitage via prospekt Kronverksky to
    Kamennoostrovsky prospekt (Petrograd Side): tram No
    63.

ROGER HAYNE

You guessed it – a bus stop

Along Kamennoostrovsky prospekt (Petrograd Side): bus Nos 46, 65. These cross the Neva on the Troitsky Bridge.
Along Lesnoy prospekt (Vyborg Side): trolleybus No 23; tram Nos 20, 32. These all cross the Neva on the Liteyny Bridge.

Bridges

Most transport shuts down between 1 and 6 am, and, when the river isn't frozen, the following Neva bridges (mosty) are raised at night to let seagoing ships through. Most St Petersburgers (and many visitors) have stories of being marooned, and the fun of paying triple price to have a taxi race at break-neck speed to try to beat a bridge opening wears thin quickly – don't get caught on the wrong side! Below are times when the bridges are up:

- Alexandra Nevskogo, 2.35 to 4.50 am
- Bolshoy Okhtinsky, closed for repairs until 1997; normally up from 2.45 to 4.45 am
- Liteyny, 2.10 to 4.40 am
- Troitsky, 2 to 4.40 am
- Dvortsovy, 1.35 to 3.05 and 3.15 to 4.45 am
- Leytenanta Shmidta, 1.55 to 4.50 am
- Birzhevoy, 2.25 to 3.20 and 3.40 to 4.40 am
- Tuchkov, 2.20 to 3.10 and 3.40 to 4.40 am

Exceptions to the schedule are only made during all-night festivals such as White Nights.

TAXI

There are two main types: the official ones (four-door Volga sedans with a chequerboard strip down the side and a green light in the front window) and 'private' taxis (any other vehicle you may see).

Official taxis have a meter that they use more often than not, though you can almost always negotiate a meter-off price. There's a flag-fall charge and the number on the meter must be multiplied by the multiplier listed on the sign that should be on the dashboard or somewhere visible. Extra charges are incurred for radio calls and some night hour calls.

Unofficial taxis are anything you can stop. They're probably used more often than official taxis and are a legitimate form of transport in Russia. Stand at the side of the road, extend your arm and wait until something stops – it could be an ambulance, an off-duty city or tour bus, army Jeep or just a passenger car (Nick once stopped an off-duty *tram*).

When something stops for you, it's common to negotiate destination and by speaking to the driver through either the passenger-side window or a partially open door. State your destination, and if the driver's game, one of a couple of things will happen. If the driver asks you to *sadites* (sit down), just get in and when you reach the destination you pay what you feel the ride was worth. If the driver states a price, you can negotiate – your offer has been rejected if the driver drives off in a huff.

Lastly, the driver may just ask you how much it's worth to you. For this you'll need to speak with locals to determine the average taxi fare at the time of your visit. Practise saying your destination and the amount you want to pay so it comes out properly; the smoother you speak, the lower the fare.

Prices

In 1995 the standard official taxi rates were US$0.30 flagfall, US$0.30 per km; US$1 fee for reservation, and US$3 an hour waiting time. The multiplier was 7.5 times the meter.

A short trip through the centre of St Petersburg was about US$2; from Pulkovo-2 to the HI St Petersburg Hostel was US$20 to US$25; from metro Petrogradskaya to Pulkovo-2 was US$10 to US$15, from Finlandsky voksal to the HI St Petersburg Hostel was US$3. If you can, have a Russian friend negotiate for you: they'll do better than you will.

Risks & Precautions

Now and then tales crop up of rip-offs or robberies in taxis. Russian citizens rather than foreigners seem to be the chief victims. The sort of things reported are robberies of VCRs, personal computers and so on, brought back from abroad – but there are also sudden demands for a fare rise along the way, and robberies, sometimes violent, of foreign passengers have occured. The following tips refer to both official and unofficial taxis, though the former are generally safer than the latter.

Avoid taxis lurking outside foreign-run establishments, luxury hotels etc – they charge far too much and get uppity when you try to talk them down. Know your route, be familiar with how to get there and how long it should take. Never get into a taxi with more than one person in it, especially after dark. Keep your fare money in a separate pocket to avoid flashing large wads of cash. Have the taxi stop at the corner nearest your destination, not the specific address if you're staying at a private residence. Trust your instinct: if a driver looks creepy, take the next car. Check the back seat of the car for hidden friends before you get in.

Calling to order a taxi is a reliable way to get one. If you're a Russian speaker or you know one, the city-run taxis are the easiest. Call only when you need the taxi, as calling far in advance just makes the dispatcher cranky.

City Taxi Service (☎ 265 13 33)
SVIT (☎ 356 93 29; fax 356 00 94, 356 38 45) will arrange to meet you at the airport if you fax them a day in advance.
Interavto (☎ 277 40 32) will do airport pick-ups if you call them a day in advance, but they're harder to reach.

CAR

It's true: the best way of getting around the city by car is by bus. St Petersburg's roads are gnarled, its laws are strange, and the *semper vigilans* eyes of the GAI guys (traffic cops), who are empowered to stop you and fine you on the spot, are always on you. Oh, yeah, they can also *shoot* at your vehicle if you don't heed their command to pull over, which is a wave of their striped (sometimes lighted) stick towards your car. While shooting is not common, neither is it uncommon: one trouble-making American expatriot resident had 18 bullet holes put in his car after he refused to stop! OK, maybe they're lousy shots (he lived), but it's probably best to pull over. The GAI claim to shoot at about 15 cars a month.

GAI officers are stationed all over the city, and during major events they can literally be on every street corner in the centre.

Driving Tips

See the Getting There & Away chapter for information on national driving regulations and crossing in with your car. Left turns are illegal except where posted; you'll have to make three rights or a short U-turn (this is safer?). Street signs, except in the centre, where they have been sponsored by advertisers, are woefully inadequate, street lights almost nonexistent, and Russian drivers make Italian drivers seem downright cuddly! Watch out for drivers overtaking on the inside, which would appear to be the national sport. There are potholes everywhere – straddle them.

A Day with One of Russia's Most Hated Public Servants

In the United States, it's the IRS. In the Soviet Union, it was the KGB. In England it's Manchester United fans, but in the new Russia, motorists and passengers alike loathe, fear and despise the ubiquitous members of the Gosavtoinspektsia: GAI.

GAI ('gah-yee') are traffic officers who stand at inter-sections throughout the country looking for signs of vehicular misbehaviour. Actually, they can pull you over for anything they want. And they do. But what makes them really annoying is that they're entitled to impose on-the-spot fines. Oh, yeah, one more thing: if you don't stop when they wave you over, they can shoot at your vehicle.

On my last trip I got pulled over twice in one day, while riding in two separate vehicles. I thought, 'What makes these guys tick? How do they decide whom to pull over? And is it

NICK SELBY

'But officer ...'

exciting to be an armed traffic cop?'. I mean, their New York City counterparts would give a limb for the opportunity. In the interests of fair play, I spent a rainy Monday morning with some of the guys at St Petersburg GAI Central.

[7 am. Roll Call] No big surprise, kinda like Hill Street Blues with shabbier uniforms. Hot sheet covered, accidents discussed, criminal element lamented. I learn that GAI guys work two days on, two days off, and they have regular beats.

[9 am. Upstairs Office] Meeting with Sergei (not his real name), a captain. Yes, we can shoot at your car. No, I can't tell you how many officers we have, but there are enough to keep control of the situation. I asked him what a foreigner can do if he should disagree with an officer's charges against him. 'Well, his documents will be confiscated and then he can go to the address on the ticket the officer gives him and get them back...' Oh.

[10 am. Parking Lot] Sergei leads the way to his spanking new Ford Escort GAImobile. We're off to check out the boys on patrol. Obeying the seat-belt law, I fasten mine. Sergei ignores his, peels out of the parking space, turns on the revolving blue light and, in blatant violation of every St Petersburg traffic law, does 120 km/h (80 mph) through narrow city streets; he runs all red traffic lights, honks and shoots truly terrifying looks at motorists he passes – which is all of them.

[10.30 am. Checkpoint on the St Petersburg-Murmansk Highway] There are GAI checkpoints at all major roads leading out of the city. We arrive in time to see one incoming and one outgoing car being tossed by Kalashnikov-wielding officers. They salute Sergei, who leads me into the checkpoint station house where he proudly shows off the station sauna (it's a four-seater). Has another officer demonstrate the state-of-the-art computer system (it's a 386 running MTEZ). They dial in to the GAI Server and the officer stumbles through the log-in and after five minutes he gives up and instead proffers the hand-written hot-sheet.

[11.15 am. Through the City] Screeching through residential neighbourhoods, Sergei is explaining how the officers we're whizzing by are trained professionals – they spend six months in the GAI academy after their army service. We pass about half a dozen stopped cars, and Sergei is saying, 'He's checking documents...This one's checking insurance...that one's investigating a stolen car...' He can tell all that by passing them at speed. Amazing. Sergei says he's been in 'many' high-speed car chases and I believe him totally. Not out of idle curiosity, I ask him how long it takes to fill in an accident report. He says a minimum of one hour.

[11.40 am. Checkpoint on the St Petersburg-Vyborg Highway] This is exactly the same as the first checkpoint, except this one is on the road leading to Finland and there's no sauna. There's an enormous pile of cash on the desk. The checkpoint officer tells me that their radar gun is 'out for repair', but helpfully points out one of the other pieces of crime-fighting equipment present: the telephone. Sergei says that radar detectors are 'unfortunately not prohibited here'. That's Russian cop lingo for: 'They're legal'.

[12.10 pm. Petrograd Side] As we careen home, Sergei spots a stalled pick-up truck at an intersection. His face a mask of pure anger, he screeches to a halt, tickets the hapless driver, radios his number plates (to ensure follow-up action) and we drive away. As we tear back to the station house, Sergei suddenly stops for a dump truck, for whom the signal is green, pass through an intersection, and (I swear) says solemnly, 'You know, even though I have this siren on, I still have a responsibility to maintain safety on the roads'.

And people say these guys aren't dedicated public servants. ∎

Rental

Renting a car here is now a pretty simple thing, though as with most simple things in Russia, it can be inordinately expensive; below are some agencies offering self and chauffeur-driven vehicles:

Astoria Rent A Car (☎ 210 58 58), Hotel Astoria, rents Nissans with or without drivers for about US$75 per day.

Avis, Pulkovo-2 International airport (☎ 235 64 44), with a second office at Remeslennaya ulitsa 13 (same ☎), has *got* to be kidding; Renault Lagunas are US$165 per day, with 100 km free and US$1.10 per km for each additional km. It also has less expensive cars, but they rent out very, very quickly in summer.

Hertz's office in St Petersburg, at Nekrasova ulitsa 40, was temporarily closed in 1995. Even when it's open it only rents chauffeur-driven cars (you must pay for the rental plus your chauffeur).

Svit (☎ 356 93 29), Prebaltiyskaya Hotel, rents Fords with drivers; they cost US$15 per hour, US$12 an hour for long-term rentals.

Transvell (☎ 113 72 53, 113 72 28) rents self and chauffer-driven cars. It also has an office in Helsinki, and you can drive its cars between Finland and Russia. Phone the Helsinki office (☎ (358 0) 351 33 00) or Harri's mobile phone (☎ (949) 728 793). In St Petersburg, its cars start at US$71 a day (US$65 for each additional day) plus VAT and insurance (US$30 to US$50 per day), but from Finland when VAT and insurance are added on the cost can total US$200 a day or more.

Fuel

In addition to state-run filling stations, Neste, a Finnish firm, currently operates five full-service filling stations that charge more for petrol but offer faster service and accept major credit cards. At the time of writing, you could get leaded and unleaded fuel at the following places in St Petersburg:

- Teatralnaya ploshchad
- Aleksandrovsky park
- reki fontanki naberezhnaya 156
- Maly prospekt (Vasilevsky Island) 68 (Neste)
- Pulkovskoe shosse 44 (Neste)
- Moskovsky prospekt 100 (Neste)
- Avangardnaya ulitsa 36 (Neste)
- Savushkina ulitsa 87 (Neste)

Parking

There are guarded lots outside the Astoria, Pribaltiyskaya and some other hotels – use them when you can. Never leave anything of value, including sunglasses, cassette tapes and cigarettes, in a car. Remove your windscreen wipers or they will be gone the moment you turn your back (old habits die hard). Street parking is pretty much legal wherever it seems to be; it's illegal anywhere on Nevsky prospekt. Use common sense, avoid dark side streets and isolated areas.

Emergencies

The law says that when you have an accident you're supposed to remain at the scene unti the GAI arrive, but in practice, if the damage isn't major, most people would rather leave than add insult (a fine) to injury. There's a joint-venture towing company in town called Spas 001 dial (☎ 001) and they'll come and get you 24 hours a day. They may speak German better than English, but Russian's your best bet. There are a number of foreign car service centres in town (check the *Traveller's Yellow Pages St Petersburg*; a miscellany:

Chrysler (☎ 237 75 33)
Inavtoservice (Volvo) (☎ 298 39 10)
Innis (Nissan) (☎ 238 37 09)
Sovinteravto service (all makes) (☎ 290 15 10, 292 77 18)

NICK SELBY

Typically clear parking regulations

BICYCLE

It's not really a good place to do it – bumpy, pothole-filled roads and lunatic drivers not accustomed to seeing bicyclists make it a dangerous proposition. It could be nice to have a bike in areas outside the centre, or through the parks, but as a method of transport it's not recommended. That said, the number of bicycles on St Petersburg's streets has been increasing as of late. Lock it before you leave it, preferably with a Kryptonite or other 'U'-type lock and not just a chain and padlock.

BOAT

In this 'Venice of the North' there is surprisingly no waterborne public transport other than river tour ships (see the following entry) and hydrofoil and ferry services to Petrodvorets, Kronshtadt and Lomonosov.

TOURS

City

See the Tourist Offices & Information section of the Facts for the Visitor chapter for addresses of the tour companies. The St Petersburg Travel Company has the most concretely set tour schedule – tours leave its offices at Isaakievskaya ploshchad at the following times, and tickets are available from its main office or through the branch office in the Hotel Astoria:

Monday
> 10 am city tour (US$10), 2.30 pm Peter & Paul Fortress and St Isaac's Cathedral (US$16)

Tuesday
> 9.30 am Pavlovsk (US$16); 2.30 pm Hermitage (with Tsar's Jewellery collection) (US$25)

Wednesday
> 10 am city tour (US$10), 2.30 pm Pushkin (US$16)

Thursday
> 10 am city tour (US$10), 2.30 pm Hermitage (US$15)

Friday
> 9.30 am Petrodvorets (US$16), 10 am city tour (US$10), 2.45 pm Yusupov Palace (US$14)

Saturday
> 9.30 am Pushkin (US$16), 10 am city tour (US$16), 2.30 pm Hermitage (US$15)

Sunday
> 9.30 am Petrodvorets (US$16), 10 am city tour (US$10), 2.15 pm Hermitage (US$15)

Peter TIPS offers coach tours of the city for about US$15 They also offer specialised tours (museums, churches, rivers etc). All the city's luxury hotels' concierge desks or service bureaux offer tours ranging from standard coach affairs to absoutely lavish treats, like chartered river-boat soirees etc.

The HI St Petersburg Hostel has a minivan and is offering city orientation tours and special events.

There are so many other agencies offering tours of the city that there's no point in trying to list them all; check the *St Petersburg Press*, or *The Traveller's Yellow Pages* for tour agencies.

River & Canal

In summer – roughly May to September – excursion boats leave the Anichkov Bridge landing on the Fontanka River, just off Nevsky prospekt, every 15 minutes from 10.45 am to 8 pm for a 75-minute, US$2.50 tootle round the canals and smaller rivers, sometimes with commentary in Russian.

There are also 80-minute City on the Neva cruises, up the river and back from Hermitage No 2 landing, every 40 minutes or so for US$0.75. Also 40-minute trips sometimes go from Letny sad (Summer Garden). You'll generally putter into the Neva, headed east, around the horn and south to Smolny, where you turn back and head for home. The boats' cafés sell snacks, beer and champagne – bring an ice bucket *and* ice.

Queues for these public boats can be long but, should you be of the wealthy persuasion or in a group of four, you can hire a water taxi (motorboat) at various landings throughout the city, particularly just north of Nevsky prospekt at the Griboedova Canal, and further south, at the landing just north of the Bankovsky Bridge. You can also catch water taxis on the Moyka at Nevsky prospekt, and one landing south of there, near ulitsa Gorokhavaya. The benefit of this (other than the obvious lack of screaming children and sometimes belligerent and/or vomiting co-passengers) is that you can choose the canals you want to see and take them at a pace you set.

The price for trips on a water taxi is as much as you're willing to pay, with a rock bottom starting price of about US$30; expect to pay at least US$35 unless you're a good negotiator.

Helicopter

Now that aviation restrictions have loosened, helicopter tours are much more common. You still can't fly directly over the centre, but you can fly over the Neva, between the Admiralty and the Peter & Paul Fortress and over to Smolny. Air Len (☎ 104 16 76, 350 07 60), though hard to reach by phone, is probably the most reliable company in town (it won the contract for aerial shots of the Goodwill Games), and its flights leave from the SKK Sports Complex, near metro Park Pobedy, many times a day during summer.

You can show up and wait to join a tour (about US$15 for 20 minutes) or you can charter the chopper by the hour for US$500 to US$700 depending on the destination. You can fit up to 20 people in the Mi8 helicopters, so this is not a bad deal for groups especially for the 10-minute jaunt down to Pushkin! They'll also do charters to Kizhi Island, Staraya Russa, Novgorod, Pskov and Petrozavodsk.

Things to See & Do

THE TOP 10

Things you'll kick yourself for missing:

- The Hermitage & Dvortsovaya Ploshchad
- St Isaac's Cathedral
- The Peter & Paul Fortress
- The Smolny Cathedral
- The Admiralty
- The Alexandr Nevsky Monastery
- The Summer Garden & Palace
- The Church of the Resurrection of Christ
- The Kazan Cathedral
- Gostiny Dvor and Passazh

THE HISTORIC HEART

For two centuries the Russian government was centred on the half-km strip of territory that stretches from the Winter Palace to ploshchad Dekabristov. Today its great buildings are devoid of political muscle but stand as monuments to the extravagant splendours of tsardom.

Dvortsovaya Ploshchad

From Nevsky Prospekt or Gostiny Dvor metro, a 15-minute walk along Nevsky prospekt, or a quick bus or trolleybus ride, brings you to Dvortsovaya ploshchad (Palace Square) where the stunning green, white and gold **Winter Palace** (Zimny dvorets) appears like a mirage, its Rococo profusion of columns, windows and recesses topped by rows of larger-than-life statues. A residence of tsars from 1762 to 1917, it's now the biggest part of the Hermitage art museum.

On Bloody Sunday (9 January 1905), Tsarist troops fired on workers who had peaceably gathered in the square, thus sparking the 1905 revolution. And it was across Dvortsovaya ploshchad that the much-exaggerated storming of the Winter Palace took place during the 1917 October Revolution. There *was* gunfire before the Provisional government surrendered to the revolutionaries, but the famous charge across the square was largely invented by film maker Sergei Eisenstein.

ROGER HAYNE

NICK SELBY

Top: Winter Palace, residence of tsars from 1762 to 1911
Bottom: General Staff Building, on Dvortsovaya ploshchad

The 47.5-metre Alexander Column in the square com-
memorates the 1812 victory over Napoleon and is
named after Alexander I. On windy days, contemplate
that the pillar is said to be held on its pedestal by gravity
alone!

The former **General Staff building** of the Russian
army (1819-29) curve around the south of the square in
two great blocks joined by arches over ulitsa Bolshaya
Morskaya. The arches are topped by a chariot of victory,
another monument to the Napoleonic wars.

Admiralty

The gilded spire of the old Admiralty across the road
from Dvortsovaya ploshchad is an unmistakable St
Petersburg landmark. It's visible along most of
Gorokhovaya ulitsa, Voznesensky prospekt and Nevsky
prospekt, the three streets that originate practically at the
Admiralty's front door. This spot was the headquarters
of the Russian navy from 1711 to 1917.

The present building houses a naval college. It was
constructed in 1806-23 to the designs of Andreyan
Zakharov, and with its rows of white columns and plentiful reliefs and statuary it is a foremost example of the
Russian Empire style of classical architecture. One
feature you can get a close look at is the nymphs holding
giant globes flanking the main gate. Its gardens and
fountains are particularly lovely in summer – it's worth
walking three or four blocks out of your way to or from
the Hermitage to see these.

Ploshchad Dekabristov

West of the Admiralty, ploshchad Dekabristov
(Decembrists' Square) is named after the first feeble
attempt at a Russian revolution – the Decembrists'
Uprising of 14 December 1825. Inspired by radical ideas
from France during the Napoleonic campaigns, young
officers tried to depose the new Tsar Nicholas I by
drawing up troops in the square. But they allowed their
opponents to argue with them and were finally dis-
persed with grapeshot. Most of the leaders ended up on
the gallows or in Siberia.

The most famous statue of Peter the Great, the **Bronze
Horseman**, with his mount rearing above the snake of
treason, stands at the river end of the square. This statue
was cast for Catherine the Great by the Frenchman
Etienne Falconet. Its inscription reads 'To Peter I from
Catherine II – 1782'. The statue, along with the view of
the SS Peter & Paul Fortress against raised drawbridges

during summer white nights, has become the trademark image of the new spirit of St Petersburg.

Most of the west side of the square is occupied by the Central State Historical Archives in the former Senate and Synod buildings, built in 1829-34. These institutions were set up by Peter the Great to run the civil administration and the Orthodox Church.

The **Manege Central Exhibition Hall** (☎ 314 82 53) across the street used to be the Horse Guards' Riding School (constructed 1804-07 from a design by Quarenghi). It now has rotating exhibitions and is open daily except Thursday, from 11 am to 7 pm. Admission for foreigners is US$0.40.

St Isaac's Cathedral

The golden dome of bulky St Isaac's Cathedral (Isaakievsky sobor), looming just south of ploshchad Dekabristov, dominates the St Petersburg skyline. The Frenchman Ricard de Montferrand won a competition organised by Alexander I to design the cathedral in 1818. It took so long to build (until 1858) that Alexander's successor Nicholas I was able to insist on a more grandiose structure than Montferrand had planned. Special ships and a railway had to be built to carry the granite from Finland for the huge pillars. There's a statue of Montferrand holding a model of the cathedral on the west façade.

Inside, St Isaac's is open as a museum from 11 am to 6 pm Thursday to Monday, 11 am to 5 pm Tuesday, and is closed Wednesday and the last Monday of the month. It's obscenely lavish. Since 1990, after a 62-year gap, services have been held here on major religious holidays and St Isaac's may return to full Church control before long. Admission is about US$8.50 (US$4.25 for ISIC holders), photos (no tripods or flashes) cost another US$8.50 and video cameras command a whopping US$21.

Don't miss the sublime city views from the colonnade (kolonnada) around the drum of the dome, which is open from 11 am to 5 pm Thursday to Monday, 11 am to 4 pm Tuesday, closed Wednesday. You need separate tickets for the colonnade, and there are often long queues to pay the US$2.80 (US$1 for ISIC holders), another US$3.10 for photos and US$10.50 for video. You could avoid the crowds by joining any tour from the usual suspects – try St Petersburg Travel Company across the street (St Isaac's is often combined with the Peter & Paul Fortress). Note that it's several hundred steps up the spiral staircase to the colonnade, and there are no escalators. Every

ROGER HAYNE

NICK SELBY

Top: Admiralty, home of the Naval College
Bottom: Bronze Horseman (Peter the Great)

NICK SELBY

View from St Isaac's Cathedral

printed resource on this matter seems to come up with a different number; I got bored after counting 180, though 262 seems reasonable, but a couple of guides put the number at 562; send *your* totals to Lonely Planet Steps Contest, c/o the Federal Counter-Intelligence Service, Lubyanka ulitsa 1/3, Moscow.

New Holland

About a five-minute walk west alongside the Moyka River, where it meets the Kryukov and Admiralteysky canals, is the island of **Novaya Gollandiya**, or New Holland. The buildings on this sweet and serene (but closed) little island were used to store wood.

St Petersburg History Museum

About 600 metres west of ploshchad Dekabristov, at Angliyskaya naberezhnaya 44, this museum focuses on St Petersburg since the 1917 revolution. Though there's no material in English, it's good on the 1941-44 siege; it's open from 11 am to 5 or 6 pm, closed Wednesday.

THE HERMITAGE

Set in a magnificent palace from which tsars ruled Russia for one-and-a-half centuries, the State Hermitage (Gosudarstvenny ermitazh) fully lives up to its reputation as one of the world's great art museums. You can be absorbed for days by its treasures and still come out wishing for more.

The enormous collection amounts almost to a history of Western European art, displaying the full range of artists such as Rembrandt, Rubens and Picasso, and schools including the Florentine and Venetian Renaissance, Impressionism and postimpressionism. There are also Prehistoric, Egyptian, Russian and Oriental sections plus excellent temporary exhibitions.

The vastness of the place – five main buildings, of which the Winter Palace alone has 1057 rooms and 117 staircases – and its huge numbers of visitors demand a little planning. It may be useful to make a reconnaissance tour first, then return another day to enjoy your favourite bits.

The State Hermitage consists of five linked buildings along riverside Dvortsovaya naberezhnaya – from west to east they are the **Winter Palace**, the **Little Hermitage**, the **Old** and **New Hermitages** (sometimes grouped together and called the Large Hermitage) and the **Hermitage Theatre**. The art collection is on all three floors of the Winter Palace and the main two floors of the Little and Large Hermitages. The Hermitage Theatre isn't generally open.

History

The present Baroque/Rococo Winter Palace was commissioned from Rastrelli in 1754 by Empress Elizabeth. Catherine the Great and her successors had most of the interior remodelled in classical style by 1837. That year a fire destroyed most of the interior, but it was restored virtually identically. It remained an imperial home until 1917, though the last two tsars spent more time in other St Petersburg palaces.

The classical Little Hermitage was built for Catherine the Great as a retreat that would also house the art collection started by Peter the Great, which she expanded. At the river end of the Large Hermitage is the Old Hermitage, which also dates from her time. At its south end, facing ulitsa Millionnaya, is the New Hermitage, which was built for Nicholas II to hold the still-growing art collection and was opened to the public for the first time in 1852. The Hermitage Theatre was built in the 1780s by the classicist Quarenghi, who thought it one of his finest works.

The art collection benefited when the state took over aristocrats' collections after the revolution, but Stalin sold some treasures, including about 15 Rembrandts, for foreign currency. The famous Impressionist and postimpressionist collections of the pre-Revolutionary Moscow industrialists Sergey Shchukin and Ivan Morozov were moved to the Hermitage in 1948.

In 1995 the Hermitage ran a highly controversial temporary display, called 'Hidden Treasures Revealed', composed entirely of art captured by the Red Army in 1945. The exhibit contained 74 paintings, among them notably works by Monet, Degas, Renoir, Cézanne, Picasso and Matisse, almost all never before publicly displayed. Originally slated to run to October, 1995, the exhibition was extended to at least the end of 1995, and at the time of writing it was reported that the collection was to be returned to storage after January 1996, though a huge political debate raged as to whether the paintings belonged back in Germany, where they might see the light of exhibition once again. Stay tuned.

Admission

The Hermitage (☎ 311 34 65) is open from 10.30 am to 5.30 or 6 pm Tuesday to Saturday, 10.30 am to 5.00 pm Sunday and closed Monday. The main ticket hall is inside the main entrance on the river side of the Winter Palace. In summer there are also ticket kiosks outside a second entrance at the west end of the Winter Palace, but neither kiosks nor entrance are always open.

The dual pricing system (whereby Westerners pay the rouble equivalent of about US$8 to US$9 while Russians pay less than US$0.20) infuriates many visitors, but it is not about to change. Still photographs, but not tripods or flashes, are permitted, though you'll have to pay a US$3 charge; to bring in a video camera costs US$7. Unless your Russian's good, forget about getting in for the Russian price – these babushki have an eagle eye for Western

ROGER HAYNE

ROGER HAYNE

Top: The giant foot of Atlas, New Hermitage
Bottom: Malachite vase, Winter Palace

ROGER HAYNE

ROGER HAYNE

Top: Hermitage Pavilion Hall
Bottom: Streetlamp outside Winter Palace

running shoes, bum bags, University of Whatever sweatshirts etc.

Tickets entitle you to wander freely (crowds permitting), and the last are sold an hour before closing time. At busy times the queues can be horrendous and you might wait well over an hour to get in. On a wet November Tuesday, there'll hardly be a queue at all.

To avoid queues altogether, you can join a standard tour, which whizzes round the main parts in about an hour and a half but at least provides an introduction to the place in English. It's easy enough to 'lose' the group and stay on till closing time. The tours take place most afternoons and can be arranged at hotels, the St Petersburg Travel Company, other travel agents, or with the Hermitage itself; the tours' office is down the corridor to the right as you enter, up the stairs and the last door on the left.

The café, just off the Jordan Staircase, is hardly worth queuing for. The hot dogs and hamburgers are highly overpriced at US$1; if you plan a long visit, take your own snacks and, buy a Coke (US$0.30) and sit at the café's tables.

Orientation

The rooms are numbered. The river is on the north side and Dvortsovaya ploshchad is south. There's only space to show 15% to 20% of the collection, so the works on view are changed from time to time and sometimes rooms are closed. Only a few sections have any English labelling.

From the main ticket hall, the Rastrelli Gallery (which has a few book and card stalls usually selling small Hermitage plans in Russian) leads to the white marble Jordan Staircase, with windows and mirrors on all sides, which takes you up to floor 2 of the Winter Palace. The staircase is one of the few parts of the interior to maintain its original Rastrelli appearance.

See the list under The Hermitage Collection for a more thorough run-down on what's in all the rooms at the time of writing. If your time is limited, the following route takes in the major highlights (room numbers are in bold type):

Winter Palace, floor 2: 189 Malachite Hall; **190-198** great state rooms.

Little Hermitage, floor 2: 204 Pavilion Hall, with its view onto the 'Hanging Garden' .

Large Hermitage, floor 2: 207-215 Florentine art 13th to 16th centuries; **217-222 & 237** Venetian art 16th century;

229-236 more Italian art 16th century; 238 Italian art of the 17th and 18th centuries; 239-240 (temporarily located in 143-146) Spanish art 16th to 18th centuries; 245-247 Flemish art 17th century; 249-252 & 254 Dutch art 17th century.

Winter Palace, floor 3: 315-320 Impressionists and post-impressionists; 344-348 Picasso and Matisse.

The Hermitage Collection
This is a list of many of the items within the Hermitage, verified in May 1995. While changes do occur, the head curator has said that things should remain static for the next few years at least. That said, consider these words of wisdom: 'Everything will remain exactly where it is except for those things which do not.'

Winter Palace, ground floor
1-33 Russian Prehistoric artefacts: **11** Palaeolithic and Mesolithic, 300th to 6th millennia BC; **12** Neolithic and Bronze Ages 5th to 1st millennia BC, including petroglyphs from the second half of the third millennia BC taken from the north-eastern shores of Lake Ozero; **13** Bronze Age, western steppes 4th to 2nd millennia BC; **14** Bronze Age, southern Siberia and Kazakstan 2nd millennium to 9th century BC, fine bronze animals; **15-18** Scythian culture 7th to 3rd centuries BC – but the best Scythian material is in the Special Collection; **19 & 20** forest steppes 7th to 4th centuries BC; **21-23 & 26** material from Altai Mountains' burial mounds, including **26** human and horse corpses preserved for over 2000 years complete with hair and teeth; **24** Iron Age, Eastern Europe, including Finno-Ugrians and Balts, 8th century BC to 12th century AD; **33** southern steppes tribes 3rd century BC to 10th century AD – some fine Sarmatian gold.
34-69 The Russian East: **34-39** Central Asia, 4th century BC to 13th century AD; **55-66** Caucasus and Transcaucasia 10th century BC to 16th century AD, including **56** Urartu 9th to 7th century BC, **59** Dagestan 6th to 11th centuries AD, **66** 14th-century Italian colonies in Crimea; **67-69** Golden Horde 13th to 14th centuries.
100 Ancient Egypt: a fine collection, much of it found by Russian archaeologists; sadly no labelling in English, except the signs saying 'Please Do Not Touch'.

Little Hermitage, ground floor
101 & 102 Roman marble.

New Hermitage, ground floor
Ancient Classical culture: **106-09 & 127** Roman sculpture 1st century BC to 4th century AD; **111-14** Ancient Greece 8th to 2nd centuries BC, mostly ceramics and sculpture; **115-17 & 121** Greek colonies around northern Black Sea, 7th century BC to 3rd century AD; **128** the huge 19th-century jasper Kolyvanskaya Vase from Siberia; **130 & 131** Ancient Italy 7th to 2nd centuries BC, including Etruscan vases and bronze mirrors.

MAP 2

Hermitage - Ground Floor
Эрмитаж - первый этаж

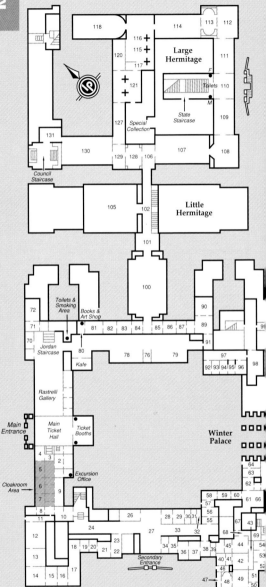

Winter Palace – floor 2

143-146 Spanish Art from the 16th to 19th centuries; **147-89** Russian culture and art: **147-50** 10th to 15th centuries; **151** 15th to 17th centuries; **152** icons, ceramics, jewellery etc from 'Moscow Baroque' period, first half 17th century; **153** items relating to Peter the Great; **155-66** late 17th, early 18th century, including **155** Moorish Dining Room, and **156** Rotunda with a bust of Peter the Great and a brass Triumphal Pillar, topped by a Rastrelli-created statue of Peter; **157-first half of 161** Petrovskaya Gallereya, including lathing machinery used by Peter, and **160** mosaic of Peter by Lomonosov, **161** a chandelier partly built by the Great Guy; **167-73** mid to end 18th century – spot the bizarre 1772 tapestry image of Australia (**167**); **175-87** (start at **187** and work your way back) Rooms occupied by the last imperial family, now displaying 19th-century interior design, including **178** Nicholas II's Gothic library; **188** Small Dining Room (Malaya stolovaya), where the Provisional Government was arrested by the Bolsheviks on 26 October 1917; **189** Malachite Hall (Malakhitovy zal) with two tonnes of gorgeous green malachite columns, boxes, bowls and urns.

190-92 Neva Enfilade, one of two sets of state rooms for ceremonies and balls: **190** Concert Hall (Kontsertny zal) for small balls, with an 18th-century silver coffin for the remains of Alexandr Nevsky; **191** Great or Nicholas Hall (Bolshoy zal), scene of great winter balls now used, like **192**, the Fore Hall, for temporary exhibitions.

193-98 Great Enfilade, the second series of state rooms: **193** Field Marshals' Hall; **194** Peter the Great's Hall (Petrovsky zal), with his throne; **195** Armorial Hall, bright and gilt encrusted, displaying 16th to 19th-century west European silver.

197 The 1812 Gallery: hung with portraits of Russian and allied Napoleonic war leaders.

198 Hall of St George or Great Throne Room: once a state room, now used for temporary exhibitions.

200-02 West European tapestry 16th to 19th centuries.

263-68 German art 15th to 18th centuries, including Dürer and Lucas Cranach the Elder.

269-71 West European 18th-century porcelain (**271** was the tsars' cathedral).

272-89 French art 15th to 18th centuries, including: **272-73** tapestries, ceramics, metalwork; **279** Poussin; **280** Lorrain; **284** Watteau.

298-302 British art 16th to 19th centuries, including: **299** Reynolds; **300** Gainsborough's *Lady in Blue*.

303 'Dark Corridor': West European tapestry 16th to 18th centuries, mainly Flanders. Follow the confusing trail through **167** and **308** to get to **304**, a wonderful collection of Western European stone engravings from the 13th to the 19th centuries; **305** the Burgundy Hall, containing English and French Porcelain; **306** Maria Alexandrovna's bedroom; and **307** the Blue Bedroom, French, Austrian and German porcelain.

Little Hermitage – floor 2

204 Pavilion Hall (Pavilonny zal): a sparkling white-and-gold room with lovely chandeliers, tables, galleries, and columns. The south windows look on to Catherine the Great's hanging garden; the floor mosaic in front of them is copied from a

Roman bath. Roman and Florentine mosaics from the 18th and 19th centuries, and the amazing *Peacock Clock* – a revolving dial in one of the toadstools tells the time, and on the hour (when it's working) the peacock, toadstools, owl and cock come to life.
258 Flemish art 17th century.
259 West European applied art 11th to 15th centuries.
261-62 Dutch art 15th and 16th centuries.

Large Hermitage – floor 2
206 next to the Council (Soviet) Staircase with its marble, Malachite and glass triumphal arch; **207-215** Florentine art 13th to 16th centuries: **209** 15th century, including Fra Angelico; **213** 15th and early 16th centuries, including two small Botticellis, Filippino Lippi, Perugino; **214** Russia's only two Leonardo da Vincis – the *Benois Madonna* and the strikingly different *Madonna Litta*, both named after their last owners; **215** Leonardo's pupils, including Correggio and Andrea del Sarto.
216 Italian Mannerist art 16th century – and a view over the little Winter Canal to the Hermitage Theatre.
217-22 Venetian art, mainly 16th century: **217** Giorgione's *Judith (Yudif)*; **219** Titian's *Portrait of a Young Woman (Portret molodoy zhenshchinu)* and *Flight into Egypt (Begstvo v Egipet)*, and more by Giorgione; **221** more Titian, including *Danaë* and *St Sebastian*; **222** Paolo Veronese's *Mourning of Christ (Oplakivanie Khrista)*.
226-27 Loggia of Raphael: Quarenghi's 1780s copy of a gallery in the Vatican with murals by Raphael.
228-38 Italian art 16th to 18th centuries: **228** 16th-century ceramics; **229** Raphael and disciples, including his *Madonna Conestabile* and *Holy Family (Svyatoe Semeystvo)*, plus wonderful ceramics and decorations AND Russia's only Michelangelo, a marble statue of a Crouching Boy; **230-236** always seem closed, but they should contain, **232** Caravaggio and Bernini; **237** 16th-century paintings, including Paolo Veronese and Tintoretto; **238** 17th and 18th-century painters, including Canaletto and Tiepolo, also two huge 19th-century Russian malachite vases. **237 & 238** have lovely ceilings.
239-40 (temporarily in 143-46) Spanish art 16th to 18th centuries: **239** Goya's *Portrait of the Actress Antonia Zarate (Antonii Sarate)*, Murillo's *Boy with a Dog*, Diego Velazquez' *Breakfast*; **240** El Greco's marvellous *St Peter and St Paul*.
241 Marble sculptures, Antonio Canova and Albert Thorwaldsen; **243** The Giddyap Room; Western European armour and weaponry from the 15th to 17th centuries, featuring four 16th-century German suits of armour atop armoured (and, thankfully, stuffed) horses.
244-47 (closed at the time of writing for renovation, allegedly until 1997) Flemish art 17th century: **245** savage hunting and market scenes by Snyders; **246** Van Dyck portraits; **247** a large room displaying the amazing range of Rubens, including *Descent from the Cross (Snyatie c kresta)*, *Bacchus (Bakkh)*, *The Union of Earth and Water (Soyuz zemli i vody)*, *Portrait of a Curly-Haired Old Man (Golova starika)*, and *Roman Charity (Ottselyubie rimlyanki)*.
248-52 & 254 Dutch art 17th century: **249** landscapes and portraits by Ruisdael, Hals, Bol and others; **250** 18th-century Delft ceramics; **254** more than 20 Rembrandts ranging from lighter, more detailed early canvases like *Abraham's Sacrifice*

of Isaac (Zhertvoprinoshenie Avraama) and Danaë through *The Holy Family (Svyatoe semeystvo)* of 1645 to darker, penetrating late works like *The Return of the Prodigal Son* and two canvases entitled *Portrait of an Old Man (Portret starika)*, plus work by Rembrandt's pupils, including Bol.

Winter Palace, floor 3

An approximately chronological order in which to view the French art collection is **314**, **332-28** in descending order, **325-15** in descending order and **343-50** in ascending order. The staircase beside room **269** on floor 2 brings you out by room **314**.

314-20, 321-25, 328-32 French art 19th century: **321-25, 328, 329** mostly Barbizon School, including Corot, Courbet, Millet; **331** Delacroix.

315 Impressionists and Postimpressionists: **315** Rodin sculptures; **316** Gauguin, Tahitian works; **317** Van Gogh, Rousseau, Forain, Latour; **318** Cézanne, Pissarro; **319** Pissarro, Monet, Sisley; **320** Renoir, Degas.

334 20th-century European and American art.

334-42 European art 19th century, including landscapes by Caspar David Friedrich.

343, 349-50 French art 19th to 20th centuries: Bonnard, Vlaminck, Marquet, Leger and others.

344 & 345 Picasso: **344** mainly blue and Cubist periods; **345** Cubist and later periods.

346-48 Matisse.

351-71, 381-96 Oriental culture and art: **351-57, 359-64** China and Tibet, an excellent collection; **358** Indonesia; **365-67** Mongolia; **368-71** India; **381-87** Byzantium, Near and Middle East.

398 & 400 Coins.

Special Collection

To get into this mind-bending display of crafted gold, silver and jewels off **121** you must either book in with a group at hotel concierge desks or at the St Petersburg Travel Company, or hire a guide from the deep thinkers in the Hermitage's excursion office. Even at these prices places are scarce, so try to book it as soon as you reach St Petersburg. The excursion office at the museum is to the right as you enter, up the small staircase and towards the back, and it's the last door on the left-hand side.

The focus is a hoard of fabulously worked Scythian and Greek gold and silver from the Caucasus, Crimea and Ukraine, dating from the 7th to 2nd centuries BC when the Scythians, who dominated the region, and the Greeks, in colonies around the northern Black Sea, crafted the pieces to accompany the dead into the afterlife. The treasure was unearthed from graves in the late 19th century. The rest of the collection is European jewellery, precious metals and stones of the 16th to 19th centuries, amassed by tsars from Peter the Great onwards. ∎

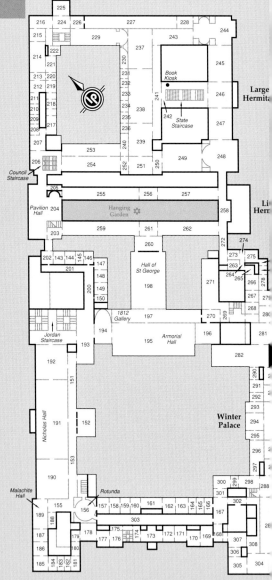

MAP 3

Hermitage - Floor 2
Эрмитаж - второй этаж

225
216 224 226 227 228 244
215 229 243
214 222 237 245
221 230
213 220 231 Book 246
212 219 232 Kiosk
211 218 233 241 247
210 217 238 242 State
209 234 Staircase
208 235 239 248
207 236 240
253 249
Large
Hermita
206 254 252 251 250
Council
Staircase
205
255 256 257
Pavilion 204 258 Li
Hall Hanging Her
Garden
203
259 261 262
260 274
202 143 144 145 146 272 275
201 147 Hall of 273
148 St George 263 278
200 149 198 264 265 266 279
150 271 267
1812 196 268 280
194 Gallery 197 270 269
193 195 Armorial 281
192 Hall
282
151 290
291
191 292
Nicholas Hall 152 293
Winter 294
Palace 295
153 296
297
190
300 299 298
Malachite 301 288
Hall 155 156 Rotunda 157 158 159 160 161 162 163 164 165 166 167 302 28
189 188 303 307 308
187 178 175 306
186 179 177 176 174 173 172 171 170 169 168 305 304
185 184 183 182 181 180

Hermitage - Floor 3
Эрмитаж - третий этаж

ROGER HAYNE

Atlas statues, New Hermitage

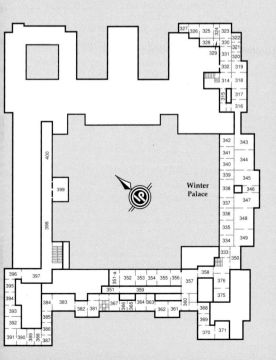

MAP 4

NEVSKY PROSPEKT

Russia's most famous street runs four km from the Admiralty to the Alexandr Nevsky Monastery, from which it takes its name. The inner 2½ km to Moscow Station is St Petersburg's seething main avenue, the city's shopping centre and focus of its entertainment and street life. Pushing through its shopping-bag-clutching crowds is an essential St Petersburg experience.

Today a walk down Nevsky is a walk into the heart of the new Russia: a buzzing, swirling mishmash of new and colourful shop fronts, restaurants, bars, toy shops, art galleries, banks and perfumeries that's packed to overflowing with tourists and natives, workers and beggars, scamrunners, pickpockets, purse snatchers, yahoos and religious fanatics, Russians and expats – and all of them are shoving past on their way to the action.

Nevsky prospekt was laid out in the early years of St Petersburg as the start of the main road to Novgorod and soon became dotted with fine buildings, squares and bridges. Today five metro stations – Nevsky Prospekt, Gostiny Dvor, Mayakovskaya, Ploshchad Vosstania and Ploshchad Alexandra Nevskogo – are scattered along its length, and buses and trolleybuses hunt in packs: see the Getting Around chapter for useful routes.

The 1994 Goodwill Games brought fresh coats of paint for all Nevsky's treasures, and a new layer of asphalt for St Petersburg's moonscape-like streets. Nevsky's brightly coloured buildings – including the newly renovated Nevskij Palace Hotel, the Beloselsky-Belozersky Palace, the House of Journalists, Yeliseevsky Food Shop (back to private ownership after 74 years), the Grand Hotel Europe, Dom Knigi and the Kazan Cathedral – have not looked this good since St Petersburg's heyday at the turn of the 20th century.

Admiralty End

Inner Nevsky, ulitsa Gogolya (now Malaya Morskaya ulitsa) and ulitsa Gertsena (now ulitsa Bolshaya Morskaya) were the heart of the pre-Revolutionary financial district, and if Credit Lyonnais Russie (back in Russia after the 'late unpleasantness'), The Russian Bank of Trade and Industry, and Baltiysky Bank get their way, it will be again; all of these institutions have headquarters or offices in this area today.

Tchaikovsky died at ulitsa Gogolya 13. The wall of Nevsky prospekt 14, a school, bears a blue-and-white stencilled sign maintained since WW II. Starting Граждане! *('Grazhdane!')*, it translates: 'Citizens! At

times of artillery bombardment this side of the street is
most dangerous!'

Close to the Moyka River, the **Kafe Literaturnoe** is,
despite its repugnant food, one of St Petersburg's most
interesting eateries, for its Pushkin associations and
ambience. Across the Moyka, Rastrelli's green
Stroganov Palace (1752-54) has kept most of its original
Baroque appearance. If you absolutely must know *yes*,
their chef did create a certain beef dish.

Kazan Cathedral Area

A block east of the Moyka, the great colonnaded arms of the
Kazan Cathedral (Kazansky sobor) reach out towards the
avenue. Its design, by Andrey Voronikhin, a former serf, was
influenced by St Peter's in Rome. Built in 1801-11, it's named
after the supposedly miraculous Kazan icon which it once
housed. The square in front of it has been a site for political
demonstrations since before the revolution.

The cathedral houses the **Museum of the History of
Religion** (☎ 311 04 95); the museum genuinely covers
the history as well as the infamies of many religions. In
the north transept is the grave of Field Marshal Kutuzov,
the Russian commander against Napoleon in 1812.
There's no explanatory material in English, so if you're
particularly interested, go with a group. The museum is
open Monday, Tuesday, Thursday and Friday from 11
am to 5.30 pm, Saturday and Sunday from 12.30 to 5 pm.
Entrance fees for foreigners are US$3 (US$1.50 for ISIC
holders, children and pensioners), and the Russian rate
is about US$0.25. It's easy to get the Russian rate.

Opposite, St Petersburg's biggest bookshop, **Dom
Knigi**, is topped by the globe emblem of the Singer
sewing machine company, which constructed the building in 1902-04. Just behind the Kazan Cathedral, a bit
south of the Train Ticket Centre, sits the **Bankovsky
Bridge**, one of St Petersburg's loveliest bridges. Suspended by cables emerging from the mouths of
golden-winged griffins, the wooden bridge affords a
splendid view north up the Griboedova Canal past
Nevsky prospekt to the Church of the Resurrection of
Christ. In the next block of Nevsky prospekt, pavement
artists cluster in front of the **Central Art Salon**
(Tsentralny khudozhestvenny salon).

Griboedova Canal to the Fontanka
River

The area around this section of Nevsky is perhaps the
busiest; a whirlwind of activity and colour of which the

Grand Hotel Europe (the Yevropeyska under the Soviets) is the epicentre. The unbelievably lavish hotel was completely renovated from 1989-91, and is again one of the city's architectural gems, boasting shameless splendour: marble and gilt, sweeping staircases, antique furnishings, casino, four restaurants with imported food, a caviar bar and billiards room, and modern touches like a shopping arcade, health club and satellite TV. If you're feeling wicked enough to visit, you can lounge about in the atrium – you don't even have to buy one of their US$3 cups of coffee.

Diagonally across Nevsky, the arcades of the **Gostiny Dvor** department store stand across ulitsa Dumskaya from the clock tower of the former **Town Duma**, seat of the pre-Revolutionary city government. One of the

NICK SELBY

NICK SELBY

Top: View from Grand Hotel Europe
Bottom: Grand Hotel Europe

NICK SELBY

NICK SELBY

Top: Clock Tower of Town Duma
Bottom: Backgammon players at ploshchad
        Ostrovskogo

world's first indoor shopping malls, this 'Merchant Yard' dates from 1757-85, and is another Rastrelli creation. The St Petersburg equivalent of Moscow's GUM, Gostiny Dvor housed hundreds of small shops, counters and stalls. Under the Sovs, of course, it became one giant place in which to find the same nothing stretched out over a large area that was freezing in winter, broiling in summer and inconvenient year-round. In recent years, though, it's been progressively improving, and if they ever finish the renovation of the façade, it will probably look good as well.

The area in front of Gostiny Dvor along Nevsky prospekt has become a kind of Day-Glo Hyde Park Speaker's Corner, attracting representatives of the most reprehensible lunatic-fringe political groups, religious proselytisers, and purveyors of posters featuring a range of subjects from smut to 1970s vintage Erik Estrada and Fonzy.

On the other side of Nevsky, in the arcade at No 48, the **Passazh** department store was the first St Petersburg shop to move to self-financing, independent of the state supply network. Today, Passazh is everything that Gostiny Dvor wants to be: stylish, packed with desirable goods and, more important, shoppers with cash to spend. Downstairs in the basement, there's a fully fledged and well-stocked Western supermarket (see Self-Catering in Places to Eat).

Tucked in a recess between the banks and the café near ulitsa Mikhailovskaya, the **Armenian Church** (1771-80), one of two in St Petersburg, is open though under extensive renovation. The Soviets deemed it reasonable to bash the place to bits, and install a 2nd floor, which blocked the view of the cupola. The renovation, performed by members of the congregation, has included removal of the 2nd floor, and restoration of the cupola and several icons, but there is still a long way to go. They're in the process of creating a new iconostasis as well.

The **Vorontsov Palace** on Sadovaya ulitsa, opposite the south-east side of Gostiny Dvor, is another noble town house by Rastrelli. It's now a military school.

Ploshchad Ostrovskogo

An enormous statue of **Catherine the Great** stands amidst the chess, backgammon and sometimes even mahjong players that crowd the benches here. The statue depicts, according to the *Blue Guide*, 'The towering figure of the Empress [standing] above her close associates ...' Well, among those 'close associates' are at least three known lovers of Cathy's – Orlov, Potyomkin and Suvorov – it would be safe to assume that the rest were, too.

Formerly the home of a 'Tourist Art Market', this airy square was created by Carlo Rossi in the 1820s and 1830s and its west side is taken up by the **Saltykov-Shchedrin Public Library**, St Petersburg's biggest – it's even got an English-language section. Rossi's **Pushkin Theatre** (formerly the Alexandrinsky) at the south end is one of Russia's most important. In 1896 the opening night of Chekhov's *The Seagull* was so badly received here that the playwright fled to wander anonymously among the crowds on Nevsky prospekt. Behind the theatre, on ulitsa Zodchego Rossi, is a continuation of Rossi's ensemble. It is proportion deified: 22 metres wide and high and 220 metres long. The **Vaganova School of Choreography** situated here is the Kirov Ballet's training school, where Pavlova, Nijinsky, Nureyev and others learned their art.

The **Anichkov Palace**, between Ploshchad Ostrovskogo and the Fontanka River (its main façade faces the river), was home to several imperial favourites, including Catherine the Great's lover Grigory Potyomkin.

Anichkov Bridge & Beyond

Nevsky prospekt crosses the Fontanka on the **Anichkov Bridge**, with famous 1840s statues of rearing horses at its four corners. A photogenic Baroque backdrop is provided by the red 1840s **Beloselsky-Belozersky Palace**, formerly a home of Communist Party officials. Between the Fontanka and Moscow Station, Nevsky prospekt has fewer historic buildings but heaps more shops and cinemas. This is one of the most concentrated areas of chi-chi shops and restaurants, and in the centre of the strip, **Nevskij Palace Hotel**, in the former Baltiyskaya Hotel Building. Another spectacular renovation (actually a gut rehab), the Nevskij Palace has fine restaurants, bars and nightclubs, and a very flash atrium lobby. Across the street, in the Dom Aktyor (House Of Actors) building, is **Peter TIPS**, a very helpful tourist information office. Behind the Afrodite restaurant is one of St Petersburg's most popular summer beer gardens, and just up the road, towards the Fontanka, is Domenico's, one of the city's most popular nightclubs.

Marking the division of Nevsky prospekt and Stary Nevsky prospekt is **ploshchad Vosstania** (Uprising Square), whose landmarks are the giant granite pillar with the Commie star, Moscow Station and the huge colour animation screen atop the building next to the station.

Stary Nevsky juts off the square at a 45° angle and heads south-east, to the Alexandra Nevskogo bridge. Its charm lies in its relative desolation; despite the appearance of Benetton, some tourist-oriented art galleries and a Len West shoe shop, the mood on Stary Nevsky is far more laid back.

Alexandr Nevsky Monastery

The working Alexandr Nevsky Monastery, with the graves of some of Russia's most famous artistic figures, is entered from ploshchad Alexandra Nevskogo opposite the Hotel Moskva. It was founded in 1713 by Peter the Great, who wrongly thought this was where Alexandr of Novgorod had beaten the Swedes in 1240. In 1797 it became a lavra (superior monastery). Today it is open to the public and, sadly, the courtyard is filled with homeless beggars.

You can wander freely around most of the grounds, but to tour the two most important graveyards you're supposed to join a group tour in Russian. Tickets for foreigners cost US$0.75 or US$0.35 for ISIC holders and US$0.25 for Russians; photographs are an additional US$0.25. They are sold outside the main gate (to your right as you enter) and in summer you may have to book an hour or two ahead. Opening hours are from 11 am to 6 pm, except Thursday and the first Tuesday of the month. Alternatively, travellers have been known to act dumb and just wander past the elderly babushka who guards the gate and on to the graveyards from the path inside the main gate.

The **Tikhvin Cemetery** (Tikhvinskoe kladbishche), on the right as you enter, contains the most famous graves. In the far right-hand corner from its gate, a bust of Tchaikovsky marks his grave. Nearby are Rubinshteyn, Borodin, Mussorgsky, Rimsky-Korsakov and Glinka. Following the wall back towards the gate you reach the tomb of Dostoevsky. The **Lazarus Cemetery** (Lazarevskoe kladbishche), facing the Tikhvin across the entrance path, contains several late great St Petersburg architects – among them Starov, Voronikhin, Quarenghi, Zakharov and Rossi.

Across the canal in the main lavra complex, the first main building on the left is the 1717-22 Baroque **Annunciation Church** (Blagoveshchenskaya tserkov), now the City Sculpture Museum (Muzey gorodskoy skulptury) and closed for renovation. About 100 metres further on is the monastery's 1776-90 classical **Trinity Cathedral** (Troitsky sobor). It is open for worship Saturday, Sunday and holidays from 6 am to the end of evening services (closed for cleaning between 2 and 5 pm); early liturgy from 7 am, late liturgy from 10 am and all-night vigils begin at 6 pm. Hundreds crowd in on 12 September to celebrate the feast of Alexandr Nevsky, now a saint.

Opposite the cathedral is the St Petersburg **Metropolitan's House**. On the far right of the grounds facing the canal is St Petersburg's **Orthodox Academy**, one of only a handful in Russia (the main one is at Zagorsk, near Moscow).

BETWEEN NEVSKY & THE NEVA

It's a pleasure to stroll in the gardens, waterways and squares of the old area north of Nevsky prospekt and west of the Fontanka River. Here are some of St Petersburg's best museums.

Ploshchad Iskusstv

Just a block north of Nevsky Prospekt metro, quiet ploshchad Iskusstv (Arts Square) is named after its cluster of museums and concert halls: the **Russian Museum**, one of St Petersburg's best; the **Museum of Ethnography**; the **Large Hall** (Bolshoy zal) of the St Petersburg Philharmonia, venue for top classical concerts; and the **Maly Theatre**, the city's second fiddle to the Mariinsky for opera and ballet. Two of our walks pass through here (see Walks, later in this chapter).

The **Brodsky House-Museum** at No 3 is a former home of Isaak Brodsky, one of the favoured artists of the revolution. It has works by top 19th-century painters like Repin, Levitan and Kramskoy, but the Russian Museum has better collections by the same artists. A statue of Pushkin stands in the middle of ploshchad Iskusstv. The square, and ulitsa Mikhailovskaya which joins it to Nevsky prospekt, were designed as a unit by Rossi in the 1820s and 1830s.

Russian Museum The former Mikhail Palace, now the Russian Museum (Gosudarstvenny Russky muzey), houses one of the country's two finest collections of Russian art (the other is in Moscow's Tretyakov Gallery). It's open daily, except Tuesday, from 10 am to 6 pm. There's a decent little café inside on the same basement level as the *kassa* (cashier). Admission is US$1.90 for foreigners, US$1 for students.

The palace was built in 1819-29 for Grand Duke Mikhail, brother of Alexander I and Nicholas I. The Museum was founded in 1898, under Alexander II. The Benois building, now connected to the original palace and accessible

The Russian Museum
A Room-by-Room Tour

Rooms 1-4: 12th to 15th-century icons – We liked the *Siege of Novgorod by the Suzdalians* (2) and *Apostle Peter* and *Apostle Paul* by Andrey Rublyov and others (3).

5-9: 17th to 18th-century sculpture, portraits and tapestries.

10, 12, 14: late 18th-century, early 19th-century paintings and sculpture – interesting old St Petersburg townscapes in **14.**

11: the White Hall, the finest in the palace, with period furniture by Rossi.

15: big 19th-century canvasses mainly by graduates of the official Academy – Aivazovsky's Crimea seascapes stand out.

18-22: first half of the 19th century focusing (**19**) on the beginnings of the socially aware 'Critical Realist' tradition.

23-38: Peredvizhniki and associated artists including (**24, 27, 28**) landscapes; (**25**) Kramskoy; and (**26**) Nikolai Ge, including his fearsome *Peter I interrogating Tsarevich Alexey at Peterhof.*

32: Polenov, including his *Christ and the Singer;* Antakolsky sculptures.

33-35, 54: a permanent exhibition of the work of Repin, probably Russia's best-loved artist; **33** has portraits and *Barge Haulers on the Volga* (when its not out on loan or at the Tretyakov), an indictment of Russian 'social justice'; **34** has *Zaporozhie Cossacks Writing a Letter to the Turkish Sultan* (officially entitled *Zaprozhtse*); and **54** contains the massive *Meeting of the State Council,* Repin's rendering of the meeting at the Mariinsky Palace on 7 May 1901 (it's full of tsarist hot shots; there's a scheme in the room to help you tell who's who).

36: Russian history, portraits by Surikov, a national revivalist.

37, 38: landscapes by Kuingi.

39: popular 19th-century painter Malyavin's depictions of stereotypical Russian mothers and maidens.

40: Ryabushkin on pre-Peter the Great 17th-century Russian history, includes the very telling and humorous *Yedut,* or *They Are Coming,* depicting the perturbed-looking reception committee for the first foreigners allowed in Russia.

41: Vasnetsov, including *Russian Knight at the Crossroads* and other 'sketches' for his mosaics.

42-47: currently under renovation and will be used to permanently exhibit Levitan and other late 19th-century painters.

48: Antakolski sculptures. (Exits to the right lead to the 10 halls of Russian folk art exhibition, including handicrafts, wood work, carvings, pottery, toys etc.)

49: actually a long corridor; it houses panels prepared by Korovin for the 1900 Paris Exhibition depicting northern Russian scenes; white nights, northern Russian nature etc.

66: the Vrubel room featuring his epic *Russian Hero* (it's a fat man on a fat horse and, when compared with *Russian Knight at the Crossroads,* points out the fascinating contrast between the two sides of the Russian nature), *The Demon* and *The Six-Winged Seraph.* It's through the windowed corridor leading to the Benois building and up the stairs.

67: Nesterov's religious paintings of the history of the Orthodox Church; Konenkov sculptures.

68: work from the Fellowship of the World of Fine Arts: Benois, Somov, Dobuzhinsky, Bakst and others (we liked the portrait of SP Diaghilev).

69: Borisov-Musatov, considered by many to be the father of Russian modern art; Meteev's sculpture.

70, 71: Serov, portraits of Russian aristocracy and other high-rollers; Trubitskoy sculptures of same.

72: Impressionists Korovin, Grabar and Serebryakova; and Trubitskoy's sculptures of Lev Tolstoy and *Unknown Woman*.

73: Kustodiev's paintings of 'stereotypical' Russians.

74: Rerikh fans unite, it's The Rerikh Room, cocktails free to those who can name the street on which he used to live (just kidding).

75-79: Russian avant-garde, symbolism, neoclassical works of artists, including Saryan Kuznetsov, Petrov-Vodkin, Grigoriev, Shukhaev, Altman, Lenturov etc; note that **79** will be the home of the museum's Chagall and Malevich collection as soon as it returns from revenue-producing exhibitions abroad (in other words, don't hold your breath).

83-113: rotating exhibition halls.

through an entrance on naberezhnaya Kanala Griboedova, was constructed in 1916.

The museum has been under constant renovation for years, and it is not possible to get a firm date on when it will finally be finished; there have been major changes in exhibition layouts, though the curator tells us that the layout has been finalised pending only the return of a small portion of the museum's collection (albeit an important one, including the museum's entire Chagall collection, currently on world tour).

Room numbering in the museum is not always chronological, and the room to room tour (see box) is essentially a straightforward walk through the rooms open to the public. Rooms 1-15 are on the 2nd floor (upstairs from the State Vestibule, originally the main entrance), and rooms 18-38 are on the ground floor, of the Mikhail Palace. Rooms 39-54 are on the ground floor and rooms 66-113 are on the 2nd floor of the Benois Building.

Ethnography Museum The State Museum of Ethnography (☎ 219 11 74) displays the traditional crafts, customs and beliefs of many of the peoples who make up Russia's impossibly fragile ethnic mosaic – you know, the mosaic whose members are currently throwing bombs at one another. There's a lot of blatant propaganda going on here, but there are some notable exceptions: the sections on Transcaucasia and Central Asia, upstairs, are fascinating, with wonderful rugs and two full-size *yurts* (nomad's portable tent-house). Throughout the museum, a guide makes a lot of difference to how much you understand.

It's open daily from 10 am to 6 pm except Monday and the last Friday of the month. Admission for foreigners is

Russian Museum

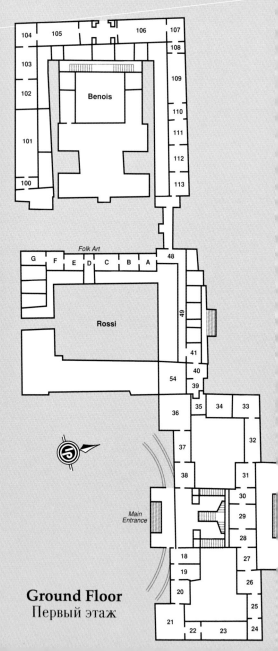

104 105 106 107

108

103

Benois

109

102

110

101 111

112

100 113

Folk Art

G F E D C B A 48

49

Rossi

41

40

54 39

36 35 34 33

32

37

31

38 30

29

Main Entrance 28

18 27

19 26

20 25

21 24

22 23

Ground Floor
Первый этаж

Russian Museum

MAP 5

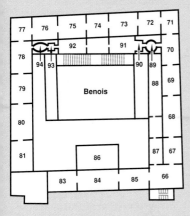

| 77 | 76 | 75 | 74 | 73 | 72 | 71 |

| 78 | 92 | 91 | 70 |
| 94 | 93 | 90 | 89 | 69 |

Benois

88 | 68

79

80

81

86

87 | 67

83 | 84 | 85 | 66

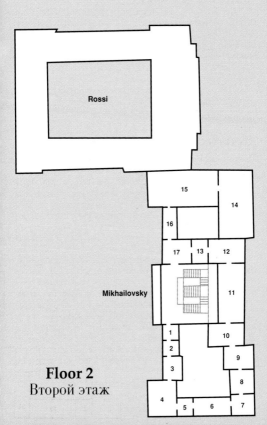

Rossi

15

14

16

17 | 13 | 12

Mikhailovsky

11

1

10

2

3

9

8

4

5 | 6 | 7

Floor 2
Второй этаж

US$1.60 (US$0.05 for Russians, ISIC holders, children and pensioners). In 1995 a permanent exhibition of gold and other jewellery began, for which there was a separate admission of US$3.25 for foreigners, US$1.60 for Russians.

Winter Stadium

East of the Ethnography Museum, the **Winter Stadium** (Zimny stadion) is a place to bring the kids when they need their video game fix (it's mainly vile crap like Streetfighter II, Beast Busters and the like though they do have some pinball machines). All the machines operate on metro tokens. It's a strange atmosphere, as this bleeping-squawking noise is in the entrance to an unseen world-class stadium.

The Olympic-class arena, with an indoor track and a terrific scoreboard in both Cyrillic and English courtesy of the 1994 Goodwill Games, is through the back room, to the left and then straight back through the double doors. Events such as karate, wrestling, races etc are held regularly. The hall is used for exhibitions of perfume, rare stones (and also, probably, blenders, cars, video cassette recorders ...). Admission for events that charge it (many don't) is about US$1 per person at the door.

Resurrection Church

The multi-domed **Church of the Resurrection of Christ** (Khram Voskresenia Khristova) on the Griboedova Canal just off ploshchad Iskusstv was built in 1887-1907 on the spot where Alexander II, despite his reforms, was blown up by the People's Will terrorist group in 1881. Because of its site it's also known as the Church of the Saviour of the Spilled Blood (Khram Spasa na Krovi), and because various translations of *that* term float around you may hear it called several other names by tour guides and hotel concierges, such as 'Church of the Spilled Blood', 'Church of the Bleeding Saviour' etc. It can get confusing.

It's partly modelled on St Basil's in Moscow, in an effort to revive earlier Russian architecture. The scaffolding that had marred the exterior for as long as anyone can remember was finally removed in 1992, and it is a gift that today the exterior can be enjoyed. While there are some fine mosaics inside, until the job of turning it into a museum of mosaics is completed you won't be able to see the interior.

Pushkin Flat-Museum

Pushkin's last home (he only lived here for a year), at naberezhnaya reki Moyki 12, is beside one of the prettiest curves of the Moyka River – between two small bridges and almost opposite the little Winter Canal, which branches off to join the Neva beneath the Hermitage arches. This is where the poet died after his duel in 1837.

His killer was a French soldier of fortune, D'Anthès, who had been paying public and insulting court to Pushkin's beautiful wife, Natalia. The affair was widely seen as a put-up job on behalf of the tsar, who found the famed poet's radical politics inconvenient and who, gossip said, may have been the one stalking Natalia.

The little house is now the Pushkin Flat-Museum (☎ 312 19 62), open daily from 11 am to 6 pm, except Tuesday and the last Friday of the month; admission for foreigners is about US$1.40 (US$0.45 for ISIC holders, children and pensioners) including a Russian-language tour (English tours can be arranged on advance notice).

Mars Field

The Mars Field (Marsovo pole) is the open space south of the Troitsky Bridge. Don't take a short cut across the grass – you may be walking on graves from the 1917 revolution, the civil war, or of later communist luminaries also buried here. There's a monument to the luminaries in the middle. The field is so named because it was the scene of 19th-century military parades.

Across ulitsa Millionnaya, in the courtyard of the Marble Palace, there's a pedestal which once displayed the armoured car from which Vlad Lenin uttered his rallying call 'Da zdrastvuet sotsialisticheskaya revolyutsia' ('Long live socialist revolution') at the Finland Station on 3 April 1917. Now it's sort of a rotating-exhibition pedestal: in summer 1994, it sported a full-sized, marbelised Ford Mondeo.

The **Marble Palace**, built for Catherine the Great's lover Grigory Orlov in 1768-85, formerly housed a Lenin Museum; currently it is a branch of the Russian Museum (☎ 312 91 96), featuring rotating exhibitions. A three-year exhibition of 18th to 20th-century handicrafts and portraits was scheduled to begin in late 1995. It's open daily except Tuesday from 10 am to 6 pm; admission for foreigners is US$5.40 (US$2.25 for ISIC holders, children and pensioners), photo and video cameras are US$2.25. Also in the Marble Palace are the cranky guys and busy gals at the **American Culture Center**.

ROGER HAYNE

ROGER HAYNE

Church of the Resurrection of Christ

Summer Garden

Perhaps St Petersburg's loveliest park, the Summer Garden (Letny sad) is between the Mars Field and the Fontanka River. You can enter at the north or south ends. It opens at 8 am daily, except in April when it's shut, and closes at 10 pm from May to August, 8 pm in September and 7 pm from October to March.

Laid out for Peter the Great with fountains, pavilions and a geometrical plan to resemble the park at Versailles, the garden became a strolling place for St Petersburg's 19th-century leisured classes. Though changed, it maintains a formal elegance, with thousands of lime trees shading its straight paths and lines of statues. In winter individual wooden huts are placed over the statues to protect them from the cold.

The modest, two-storey **Summer Palace** in the northeast corner was St Petersburg's first palace, built for Peter in 1704-14, and is pretty well intact. Little reliefs around the walls depict Russian naval victories. Today it's open as a museum (Muzey Letny Dvorets Petra I; ☎ 314 03 74) from early May to early November daily from 11 am to 6 pm, except Tuesday and the last Monday of the month. Many rooms are stocked with early 18th-century furnishings. Tickets are sold in the nearby **Tea House** (Chayny domik) for Russian-language group tours, usually from 11 am to late afternoon. Admission for foreigners is US$1.60, US$0.80 for children and students.

Neither the Tea House nor the Coffee House (Kofeyny domik) behind it offers tea, coffee or anything else to eat or drink. Nor does anywhere else in the garden. Surprise, surprise. But they do hold various small exhibitions – art

ROGER HAYNE

Statue in Summer Garden

openings and the like. Buy tickets from the Tea House, or the little kiosk near the palace. Admission for foreigners is US$1.60, US$0.80 for children/ISIC holders.

South of the Summer Garden

A much greater Summer Palace used to stand across the canal from the south end of the Summer Garden. But Rastrelli's almost fairy-tale, wooden creation for Empress Elizabeth was knocked down in the 1790s to make way for the bulky, brick **Engineers' Castle** of Paul I, an insanely cruel tsar who lived in fear of assassination and was indeed suffocated in his bed a month after moving into the castle. Later it became a military engineering school (hence the name). The pleasant **Mikhail Gardens** are over the road, while the yellow **Sheremetev Palace** across the Fontanka, built in 1750-55, houses a recently opened museum to the great, long-persecuted poet Anna Akhmatova (1889-1960). It's open Tuesday to Sunday from 11 am to 5.30 pm, closed Monday and last Wednesday of the month.

SMOLNY REGION

Tauride Gardens

The Tauride Gardens, encompassing the **City Children's Park** (Gorodskoy detsky park), are worth a stop on the way to Smolny. It's a great place for children under 10; the kiddie rides are among the best in Russia. Even though the beauty of this lovely park's canals and little bridges has been somewhat marred, you can watch Russians enjoying themselves and have a look across the lake at the fine **Tauride Palace** (Tavrichesky dvorets), built in 1783-89 for Catherine the Great's lover Potyomkin.

The palace takes its name from the region of Crimea (once called Tavria), which Potyomkin was responsible for conquering. Between 1905 and 1917 the State Duma, the Provisional Government and the Petrograd Soviet all met here. Today it's home to the Parliamentary Assembly of the Member States of the CIS and you can't go in. The gardens are a block-and-a-half east of Chernyshevskaya metro. Bus Nos 5, 46, 58 and 134 to Smolny pass alongside.

Flowers Exhibition Hall

One of the finest ways to escape momentarily from a St Petersburg winter is to head for the Flowers Exhibition Hall, an indoor tropical paradise just north-west of the City Children's Park at the corner of Potyomkinskaya ulitsa and Shpalernaya ulitsa. Dig the 'monster' tree to the right of the entrance. It also has a wishing well, and there's a flower-selling stall at the front. It's open year-round, daily from 11 am to 7 pm, except Monday and Thursday. There's a florist next door, and one diagonally across the street as well.

Smolny

The **cathedral** at Smolny, three km east of the Summer Garden, is one of the most fabulous of all Rastrelli's buildings, and the Smolny Institute next door was the hub of the October Revolution. Buses here include No 6 from the Admiralty via much of Nevsky prospekt, and trolleybus No 5 or 7 from ploshchad Vosstania.

The cathedral is the centrepiece of a convent mostly built, to Rastrelli's designs, in 1748-57. His inspiration was to combine Baroque details with the forests of towers and onion domes typical of an old Russian monastery. There's special genius in the proportions of the cathedral, to which the convent buildings are a perfect foil. Rastrelli also planned a gigantic bell tower needling up at the west end of the convent, facing down Shpalernaya ulitsa, but funds ran out. Today the convent houses the city administration's offices while the cathedral is a concert hall, usually open only for performances.

The **Smolny Institute**, built by Quarenghi in 1806-08 as a school for aristocratic girls, had fame thrust upon it in 1917 when Trotsky and Lenin directed the October Revolution from the headquarters of the Bolshevik Central Committee and the Petrograd Soviet, both of which had been set up here. In its Hall of Acts (Aktovy zal) on 25 October, the All-Russian Congress of Soviets conferred power on a Bolshevik government led by Lenin, which ran the country from here until March 1918.

About 100 metres west of the Smolny Cathedral, on Shpalernaya ulitsa, the former home of one General Kikhin is today **Music School No 2**. Kikhin, who built this house about the same time as the Menshikov Palace was being constructed across town, fell from Peter's graces and dropped from the pages of St Petersburg history. The house was formerly a branch of the Kunstkammer (see Museum of Anthropology & Ethnography, later), as well as a Soviet sports school.

Further west, near the corner of Tavricheskaya ulitsa, stands one of the last remaining statues of **Felix Dzerzhinsky**, founder of the infamous Cheka, predecessor to the KGB. You can, by the way, buy eggs just one block away at the little shop on the corner of ulitsas Tavricheskaya and Tverskaya.

NICK SELBY

ROGER HAYNE

ROGER HAYNE

Top: Smolny Cathedral
Middle: Smolny Institute Spires
Bottom: Entrance to Smolny Cathedral

The Big House

Speaking of the KGB, their headquarters were a bit west of here in the enormous **Bolshoy dom** (the vicious-looking granite cube festooned with radio antennae) at Liteyny prospekt 4. These days it's still packed with spooks, though now they prefer to be referred to as 'Interior Ministry' and 'Counter Espionage' personnel.

SOUTH & WEST OF NEVSKY PROSPEKT

Sennaya Ploshchad Area

This teeming square, dominated by what seems to be a permanent exhibition of construction equipment, is the gateway to Dostoevskyville. The peripatetic writer, who occupied around 20 residences in his 28-year stay in the city, once spent a couple of days in debtors' prison in what is now called the Senior Officers' Barracks, just across the square from the Sennaya Ploshchad metro station. Dostoevsky had been thrown in there by his publisher, for missing a deadline ('Had we but thought of it ...' – T Wheeler). At the site of the metro station there was once a large cathedral that dominated the square.

Just west of the square and across the river, at ulitsa Kaznacheyskaya 7, is the flat where Dostoevsky wrote *Crime and Punishment*; Raskolnikov's route to the murder passed directly under the author's window (see St Petersburg Walks later in this chapter).

NICK SELBY

Sennaya Ploshchad

Vladimirskaya Ploshchad Area

Around Vladimirskaya ploshchad are the indoor **Kuznechny market**, St Petersburg's biggest and best stocked (open daily), plus a clutch of entertainment venues, a bitchin' Irish pub, small museums and a smattering of eateries and shops. The onion-domed working **Vladimir Church** (1761-83) dominates the square.

Dostoevsky wrote most of *The Brothers Karamazov* in a flat at Kuznechny pereulok 5, just past the market, and died there in 1881. It's now a small **Dostoevsky Museum** (☎ 311 18 04), open from 11 am to 5 pm daily except Monday and the last Wednesday of the month. Admission for foreigners is US$2, US$1 for students.

The **Arctic & Antarctic Museum** (☎ 113 19 98) on ulitsa Marata focuses on Soviet polar exploration and ratty taxidermy exhibitions. Admission is US$0.15. It's open Wednesday to Sunday from 10 am to 6 pm. There's a small **Rimsky-Korsakov Flat-Museum** at Zagorodny prospekt 28, open from 9 am to 8 pm Wednesday to Saturday, 11 am to 6 pm Sunday. Zagorodny prospekt continues past Pionerskaya ploshchad, where in 1849 Dostoevsky and 20 others, sentenced to death for socialist leanings, were lined up to be shot – only to be told at the last moment that their sentences had been commuted. No, it wasn't altogether a spook show, and most were shipped off to Siberia.

Teatralnaya Ploshchad Area

Known throughout the world during the Soviet reign as the Kirov, the **Mariinsky Theatre** resumed its original name in 1992, though the ballet company still uses the name Kirov. Its home, at Teatralnaya ploshchad, is an area of quiet, old canal-side streets (and a nice Irish pub). Teatralnaya ploshchad has been a St Petersburg entertainment centre since fairs were held here in the mid-18th century.

A good way to get to Teatralnaya ploshchad is to walk along the Moyka River from Isaakievskaya ploshchad. On the way, you'll pass the old **Yusupov Palace** (☎ 311 53 53) at naberezhnaya Reki Moyki 94. It was here in 1916 that Grigory Rasputin, invited to dinner by Prince Felix Yusupov and friends to meet Yusupov's wife (to whom the priest was allegedly attracted), was filled with poisoned food, cakes, cookies and drink. After he ate and drank all this and was happily (and healthily) licking his fingers, the Yusupov gang did what they probably should have done in the first place: shot ol' Raspy repeatedly.

But like a Tsarist-era Terminator, the mystic refused to die and when Yusupov knelt over him, Rasputin grabbed him by the throat! At that point, Yusupov did what any sane man would do: he ran away. When he returned with reinforcements, they found the mystic had dragged himself outside. They shot him a few more times, beat him with sticks for good measure, and finally stuffed him through the ice of the frozen river. Legend has it that the mystic did not die until he was submerged – water was found in his lungs.

The palace's ground floor and 2nd floor are open to visitors (US$1.60) but to see the basement chamber in which Raspy ate the poisoned puffy-stuff, you'll need to arrange a 'Rasputin Tour' with the museum administrator, who generally wants US$8 per person in a group of at least three. Consolation: you'll see wax figures of the priest and Felix.

A route no less fraught with bloody historical associations is along Griboedova Canal from the Kazan Cathedral, passing close to Sennaya ploshchad and the scene of the murder of the old pawn broker in *Crime and Punishment*.

North east of Teatralnaya ploshchad, before it twists south-west, the canal runs under yet another beautiful beast-supported suspension bridge, the **Lviny Bridge**, with chains emerging from the mouths of lions.

Bus Nos 3, 22 and 27 from Nevsky prospekt, Nos 2 and 100 from Ploshchad Lenina via the Mars Field and Nevsky prospekt, and tram No 31 from Kronverksky prospekt on the Petrograd side via the Admiralty, all serve Teatralnaya Ploshchad.

Outside performance times you can usually wander into the Mariinsky Theatre's (☎ 114 12 11, 314 90 83) foyer, and maybe peep into its lovely auditorium. Built in 1860, the Mariinsky has played a pivotal role in Russian ballet and opera ever since. The St Petersburg Conservatory faces it.

Tickets can be a problem, as Westerners are charged as much as they possibly can be, and official tickets are rationed out to the larger hotels and tour companies well in advance. You can try at the box office, where the face price of tickets is about US$4. Go as early as you can (the booking office is open from 11 am to 7 pm; performances start at 7 pm). Should you get turned away from there you have several choices, including the *Teatralnaya kassi* (theatre ticket booths) around town, Peter TIPS, tourist agencies like the St Petersburg Travel Company, concierge desks at the larger hotels and, if it comes down to it, touts in front of the theatre itself (see Tickets in the Entertainment chapter for more information).

The Baroque spires and domes of **St Nicholas' Cathedral** (1753-62), rising among the trees at the bottom of ulitsa Glinki, shelter many 18th-century icons and a fine carved wooden iconostasis. A graceful bell tower overlooks the Kryukov Canal, crossed by the Staro-Nikolsky bridge. South along this canal and across a footbridge over the Fontanka is blue-domed **Trinity Cathedral** on

NICK SELBY

Lviny Bridge

Izmaylovsky prospekt, an impressive 1828-35 classical edifice; sadly, it was boarded up at the time of writing.

The flat where Alexandr Blok spent the last eight years of his life, at Dekabristov ulitsa 57, is now a museum (☎ 113 86 33) open Thursday to Tuesday from 11 am to 5 pm, closed Wednesday and the last Tuesday of the month.

Moskovsky Prospekt

This long avenue south from Sennaya ploshchad is the start of the main road to Moscow. The iron **Moscow Triumphal Arch** 3½ km out, looking very like Berlin's Brandenburg Gate, was built in 1838 to mark victories over Turks, Persians and Poles. It was demolished in 1936 then rebuilt in 1959-60. Local legend has it that the gate is built on the spot where travellers entering the city in the early days had to show that they had brought with them bricks or stones to be used in the construction of buildings.

A couple of km further south, east off Moskovsky prospekt on ulitsa Gastello, is the **Chesma Palace**. Built for Catherine the Great to rest en route to the city of Tsarskoe Selo (now Pushkin) it has a ground plan like a radiation warning sign. More interesting is the red-and-white 18th-century Gothic **Chesma Church**, behind the Hotel Mir at No 17. The church, built in honour of the Battle of Çesme (1770) when the Russian fleet sailed from the Baltic to the Aegean to beat the Turks, houses the curious Chesma Victory Museum, currently under renovation and scheduled to reopen in 1997; it has a lurid diorama of the battle.

Wide Moskovskaya ploshchad, a little way south of ulitsa Gastello, was intended under a 1930s plan to become the centre of St Petersburg, replacing the old tsarist centre. It is a testament to the stubbornness of St

Petersburgers that during the time of Stalin's terror, this plan was universally ignored. Moskovsky prospekt ends a few hundred metres further on at ploshchad Pobedy, where the **Monument to the Heroic Defenders of Leningrad,** commemorating the siege of WW II, makes a striking first impression on entering St Petersburg.

VASILEVSKY ISLAND

The interesting parts of Vasilevsky Island are its eastern 'nose', the Strelka (Tongue of Land), where Peter the Great first wanted his new city's administrative and intellectual centre, and the embankment facing the Admiralty.

In fact, the Strelka became the focus of St Petersburg's maritime trade, symbolised by the white colonnaded **Stock Exchange**. The two **Rostral Columns** on the point,

NICK SELBY

Rostral Column, early navigational beacon

studded with ships' prows, were oil-fired navigation
beacons in the 1800s (on some holidays gas torches are
still lit on them). The area remains an intellectual centre,
with the St Petersburg State University, the Academy of
Arts and a veritable 'museum ghetto'.

The Strelka also has one of the best views in the city:
you look left to the Peter & Paul Fortress and right to the
Hermitage, the Admiralty and St Isaac's Cathedral.

At the inner end of the island many north-south
streets have separate names and independent numbering for each side or 'line' (linia). Thus the street beside
Menshikov Palace is Sezdovskaya linia on the east side
and 1-ya (*pervaya*, first) linia on the west, the next street
is 2-ya linia on the east and 3-ya on the west, and so on.

Museums near the Strelka

The Stock Exchange is now the **Central Naval Museum**
(Tsentralny Voenno-Morskoy muzey; ☎ 218 25 02), full
of maps, excellent model-ships, flags and photos of and
about the Russian navy right up to the present. Also on
display is the *Botik*, Peter's first boat (the granddaddy of
them all), a pre-turn-of-the-century submarine (it's a
two-seater) and some big oars. It's open from 10.30 am
to 5.30 pm (last entry at 4.45 pm), closed Monday,
Tuesday and the last Thursday of the month. Admission
for foreigners is US$1, US$2 for a Russian-language
excursion and US$1 for photos or video cameras.

To the right (north) of the Exchange is a former maritime
warehouse and former Museum of Agriculture. Beyond
this the old Customs House, topped with statues and a
dome, is now called Pushkin House (Pushkinsky dom),
and is home to the **Institute of Russian Literature**, and a
Literary Museum with exhibits on Tolstoy, Gogol,
Lermontov, Turgenev, Gorky and others. It's open from 11
am to 5.30 pm, closed Monday and Tuesday.

To the left (south) of the Exchange in another former
warehouse is the **Museum of Zoology** (Zoologichesky
muzey; ☎ 218 01 12), said to be one of the biggest and best
in the world, with more stuffed animals than you can shake
a stick at, plus insects and fish from all over the world.
Among the dioramas and the tens of thousands of
mounted beasties is a complete woolly mammoth (!)
thawed out of the Siberian ice in 1902. The museum is open
from 11 am to 6 pm (last entry 5 pm), closed Friday. And
it's a bargain: admission for foreigners is US$0.20 (US$0.05
for ISIC holders, children and pensioners). Guided tours
for groups of up to 30 people can be had for US$14.25
(US$11.50 for ISIC holders, children and pensioners). On
Thursday, the administrator said, admission is free

except for tours. You pay at the microscopic cash window just west of the main entrance.

Museum of Anthropology & Ethnography

The blue-and-white building with the steeple was the city's first museum, founded in 1714 by Peter himself. In contrast to the State Museum of Ethnography, this museum (Muzey Antropologii i Etnografii; ☎ 218 01 18) is about peoples outside the former USSR, with wonderfully campy dioramas and displays on the cultures of Asia, Oceania, Africa and the Americas. The old anatomy theatre is the big draw, with selections from Peter's original *Kunstkammer*. While this translates from German to 'art chamber', the bloodthirsty crowds are really here to see Peter's collection of 'curiosities': bugs and snakes, gold ornaments from Siberian tombs and a truly ghoulish collection of preserved freaks, foetuses and body parts. It's fun for the whole family.

The museum is open from 11 am to 6 pm (last entry 4.45 pm), closed Thursday. Admission for all is US$1.70. The entrance is around the corner in Tamozhyonny pereulok.

Menshikov Palace

Alexandr Menshikov was a close friend (many now say lover) of Peter the Great. For helping the tsar defeat the Swedes he was made Governor General of St Petersburg and given Vasilevsky Island. Peter later took the island back, but in 1707 Menshikov put up one of the city's first buildings, a riverside palace (Dvorets Menshikova) just west of the Twelve Colleges. He effectively ran Russia from here for three years between Peter's death and his own exile.

Later the palace was a military academy and then it went to seed until Lenin suggested it be saved. Now its lavish interiors are again filled with period art and furniture as a museum of 'Russian Culture of the First Third of the 18th century' (☎ 213 11 22). It's open from 10.30 am to 4.30 pm, closed Monday; admission for foreigners is US$4.50 (US$3.40 for ISIC holders and children), photos are US$2.85, video cameras US$7.60. Russian-language tours, which start every 10 minutes, are included in the price.

Academy of Arts Museum

Two blocks west of the Menshikov Palace, at Universitetskaya naberezhnaya 17, is the Russian Academy of

Arts' Research Museum (Muzey Akademii Khudozhestv; ☎ 213 64 96; tour desk 213 35 78), guarded by two imported Egyptian sphinxes said to be about 3500 years old. Inside are works by Academy students and faculty since its founding, plus changing exhibitions, sometimes by foreign artists. The classical entrance hall with its dusty statues is itself a sight. It's open from 11 am to 7 pm (last entry 5 pm), closed Monday and Tuesday. Admission for foreigners is US$3 (US$1.40 for ISIC holders, children and pensioners), US$0.50 for photos and video cameras. A Russian-language tour is about US$12.

Churches

Four untended, mostly unused classical churches are in the blocks just west of the university. The handsomest is the former Lutheran **Church of St Catherine** (Tserkov Yekateriny, 1771) at Bolshoy prospekt 1, now a Melodia sound studio.

More intriguing is what looks like a homage to Istanbul's Sancta Sofia, behind high walls at the west end of Bolshoy prospekt. This Byzantine mystery is now a naval training school so there's no way in. Take bus No 7 or trolleybus No 10 from the Hermitage.

Twelve Colleges

West of the Anthropology Museum and marked by a statue of the scientist-poet Mikhail Lomonosov is Mendeleevskaya linia and the skinny, 400-metre-long Twelve Colleges building. Meant originally for Peter's government ministries, it's now part of the university, which stretches out behind it.

PETROGRAD SIDE

Petrograd Side (Petrogradskaya storona) is a cluster of delta islands between the Malaya Neva and Bolshaya Nevka channels. On little Zayachy Island, Peter the Great first broke ground for St Petersburg and built the Peter & Paul Fortress. Most of Petrograd Side's other sights are near the fortress, though the Kirovsky Islands feature some vast parklands and old dacha-palaces which are currently the stomping ground of government big-wigs, large gentlemen of indeterminate occupation who drive Mercedes Benzes, rich foreign businessmen and the occasional Danish diplomat.

Peter & Paul Fortress

Founded in 1703, the Peter & Paul Fortress (Petropavlovskaya krepost) is the oldest building in St Petersburg. Peter planned it as a defence against the Swedes but defeated them before it was finished. Its main use up to 1917 was as a political prison; one of its first inmates was Peter's own son Alexey, whose torture Peter is said to have overseen personally. Other famous residents were Dostoevsky, Gorky, Trotsky and Lenin's older brother, Alexandr. Most worth seeing are the **Cathedral of SS Peter & Paul**, with its landmark needle-thin spire, and the **Trubetskoy Bastion**.

The cathedral, though plain on the outside, was radically different from traditional Orthodox churches. If you haven't overdosed on churches, don't miss its magnificent Baroque interior. All of Russia's pre-Revolutionary rulers from Peter the Great onwards, except Peter II, Ivan VI and Nicholas II, are buried here. Peter I's grave is at front right, and people still leave fresh flowers on it. Individuals might avoid queues by discreetly moving upstream through the crowds exiting, into the adjoining **Grand-Ducal Mausoleum**. The mausoleum, built at the turn of this century, has a free exhibit on the reconstruction of the fortress. Between the Cathedral and the **Senior Officers' Barracks** is a new statue of a seated Peter the Great, with somewhat interestingly proportioned head and hands. The joint Russian-USA production was unveiled in 1991.

In the fort's south-west corner are reconstructions of the grim cells of the **Trubetskoy Bastion**, where Peter supervised the torture to death of his son. The cells were used by later tsars to keep a lid on original thinking in the empire.

In the south wall is **Nevsky Gate**, a later addition, where prisoners were loaded on boats for execution elsewhere. Notice the plaques showing water levels of famous floods. Outside are fine views of the whole central waterfront. Around to the left in summer is a fascinating collection of anglers, joggers and standing sunbathers (standing's said to give you a *proper* tan), and in winter you might see people swimming in holes cut through the ice (an activity that's said to be 'good for the health'). Above this, on the artillery platform, is a summer café serving chicken, sandwiches, beer and soft drinks.

At noon every day a cannon is fired from **Naryshkin Bastion**, scaring the daylights out of tourists.

The **Commandant's House** is a Museum of the History of St Petersburg up to the 1917 revolution, and includes a room restored to its 1820s appearance. It's been under renovation for quite some time. The **Engineers' Building** has a museum on the city's architecture.

Entry to the fort is free but for most buildings inside you'll need to either obtain a ticket from the kiosk at the east end, or make a payment at the door.

The fort is open from 11 am to 6 pm (to 4 pm Tuesday), closed Wednesday and the last Tuesday of the month. The closest you can get by bus from near the Hermitage is on a No 10 or 45 to the zoo, but it's a very pleasant walk along Dvortsovaya naberezhnaya, and across the Troitsky Bridge to Kamennoostrovsky prospekt and the entrance. Gorkovskaya metro is in Lenin Park, a three-minute walk from the fortress.

Behind the Fortress

Across the moat, in the fort's original arsenal, is the **Artillery Museum** (Artilleriysky muzey, ☎ 232 02 96), open from 11 am to 6 pm, closed Monday and Tuesday. It's a great place if you like weapons: it seems to have one of everything right back to the Stone Age. They've also got Lenin's armoured car parked in their driveway. Admission for foreigners is US$2.40.

West of that is the **St Petersburg Zoo** (☎ 232 28 39), which, though it's not as bad as it was, is still pretty gruesome and full of miserable animals and happy kids. The zoo suffers from a lack of funds and it's a sad sight indeed; it's open 10 am to 6 pm daily, admission is about US$0.60 for adults and US$0.20 for children.

Preventing Animal Cruelty

While the animal-rights situation in Russia has shown some improvement over the past few years, it's still light years behind that in Western countries. Zoo and circus animals are mistreated to an extent that would be criminal in other countries, and there is not yet a national network of animal shelters; strays are routinely rounded up and drowned.

Some animal trainers and zoo workers defend the standard practices – chaining elephants by a back leg to the ground on a one-metre lead; placing horses, lions, bears, tigers and other large animals in tiny cages – by saying that the country has enough trouble providing its pensioners with food and shelter, and that it can't be worried about animals.

Others see absolutely nothing wrong with any of it. Janice Cox of the World Society for the Protection of Animals (WSPA, pronounced 'wispa') says that she's spoken with circus trainers in Moscow who defend the use of ice-skating polar bears with the explanation, 'It's their natural habitat ... they're on the ice'.

Things to See & Do

Though the treatment of zoo and circus animals has improved tremendously in St Petersburg and Moscow, where the money and attention brought by tourism have led to better conditions, more food and cleaner cages, the problem is still enormous. And the situation in the rest of the country is still heartbreaking, as any visitor to a regional zoo or circus can attest.

If you should see inhumane treatment of animals in zoos or circuses during your trip, you can help to do something about it. Take photographs if you can, or take notes of the animals' condition and exact location, and report it to Janice Cox, Central and Eastern European Department, WSPA (☎ (0171) 793 0540, fax (0171) 793 0208), 2 Langley Lane, London SW8 ITJ, or to Zoo Check (☎ (0306) 71 2091), an international organisation that monitors and investigates the conditions in which animals are housed in zoos and seeks widespread reforms. It's part of the Born Free Foundation, at Coldharbour, Dorking, Surrey RH5 6HA, UK.

Ironically, animal abuse in St Petersburg was a contributing factor to the establishment of the USA's main animal-protection organisation. Henry Bergh, a wealthy American socialite, was sent to St Petersburg as Abraham Lincoln's legate, to serve under ambassador Cassius Clay in the early 1860s. One snowy day, as Bergh was making his way through St Petersburg's streets, he came upon a Russian peasant who was mercilessly flogging his fallen horse. Bergh leapt off his coach and disarmed the man, but the incident affected Bergh profoundly.

Soon after, Bergh resigned his position (he and Clay had never got on). He stopped in London on his way back to the USA and met there with members of the RSPCA, which had been founded in 1824 by Richard 'Humanity Dick' Martin. Bergh was so impressed that on his return to New York he set about using his social and political connections and in 1866 established the American Society for the Prevention of Cruelty to Animals. ■

Just north of the zoo is a new permanent **Amusement Park**, complete with bumper cars, a couple of small roller coasters, and the like; rides cost about US$0.25.

East and behind the museum is **Lenin Park**, cool in summer but too close to traffic to be peaceful. At the back, the **Planetarium/Baltiysky Dom** theatre complex keeps post-Communist youth off the streets by throwing wild raves, all-night dance parties and drink-a-thons in summer. There's also a shrewdly positioned Baskin Robbins ice cream shop.

East of the park across Kamennoostrovsky prospekt (Kirovsky prospekt) is a working **mosque**, built in 1912

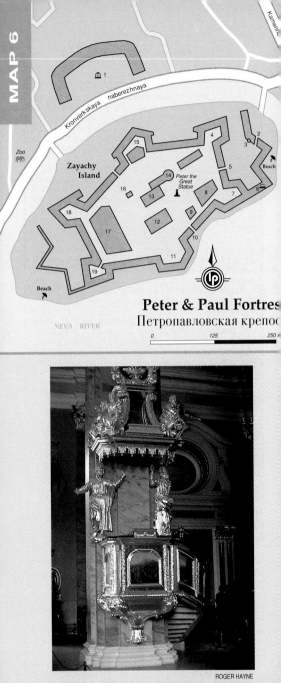

MAP 6

Kronverkskaya naberezhnaya

Zoo

Zayachy Island

15

16

14 *Peter the Great Statue*

13

8

7

9

12

18

17

10

19

11

4

3

2

Beach

5

6

Beach

NEVA RIVER

Peter & Paul Fortres
Петропавловская крепос

0   125   250

ROGER HAYNE

Interior, Peter & Paul Cathedral

Map 6   Peter & Paul Fortress

1 Artillery Museum
Артиллерийский музей
2 St John Gate
Иоанновские ворота
3 Ticket Office
Касса
4 Menshikov Bastion
Меншиковский бастион
5 St Peter Gate
Петровские ворота
6 Summer Rooftop Café
Летнее Кафе
7 Peter I Bastion
Петровский бастион
8 Engineers' Building
Инженерный корпус
9 Senior Officers' Barracks
Гауптвахта
10 Nevsky Gate
Невские ворота
11 Naryshkin Bastion
Нарышкинский бастион
12 Commandant's House
Обер-комендантский дом
13 SS Peter & Paul Cathedral
Петро-Павловский собор
14 Grand-Ducal Mausoleum
Усыпальница
15 Golovkin Bastion
Головкинский бастион
16 Boat House
Домик ботика
17 Mint
Монетный двор
18 Zotov Bastion
Зотовский бастион
19 Trubetskoy Bastion
Трубецкой бастион

and modelled on Samarkand's Gur Emir Mausoleum where Timur (Tamerlaine) is buried. Its fluted azure dome and minarets have been under renovation for years – the crane would seem to be a permanent fixture behind the fortress's spire.

Museum of Political History

East of Kamennoostrovsky prospekt at ulitsa Kuybysheva 4 is the Kshesinskaya Palace containing the Museum of Political History in Russia (Muzey Politicheskoy Istorii Rossii; ☎ 233 71 13), which is more interesting than it sounds. The Bolsheviks made their headquarters, and Lenin often gave speeches, from the balcony of this elegant Art Nouveau palace that once belonged to Matilda Kshesinskaya, famous ballet dancer and one-time lover of Tsar Nicholas II. Even if you can't read Russian go in to see the house itself, the paintings and photos from the lead up to the revolution, and the glossy dioramas and mini-films. It's open from 10 am to 5.30 pm, closed Thursday. Admission is US$0.80.

Perhaps best of all, the **Wax Museum**, accessible through the east-side entrance (under the arch and to the left), is a hoot; if you ever thought that maybe the Russians were telling a little stinky one about Lenin's body being 'preserved' in that glass box, you'll know for sure after you see this. You'll also see a quite senile-looking Krushchev, Brezhnev holding a bent cigarette, a preternaturally sober-looking Yeltsin pointing at a Gorbachev who appears to be saying, 'Calm down, everything will be all right ...' and Vlad himself looking quite chipper. The wax museum is open daily from 10 am to 6 pm; the US$0.50 admission is supposed to include a sombre Russian-language tour by an unusually dolorous guide, but you can slip that and just look at the display, which only takes a couple of minutes.

In mid-1995 the wax figures were moved out and temporarily relocated to the Municipal Cultural Centre at Nevsky prospekt 41, with an admission fee of US$3. The 20th-century figures were not included in the new exhibit, and it's up in the air as to whether the whole thing will stay there or move back. Check when you're in town, because this exhibition is worth seeing.

Peter's Cabin

In a patch of trees east of the fortress at Petrovskaya naberezhnaya 6 is a little stone building. In here is preserved St Petersburg's first residence, a log cabin where Peter lived in 1703 while supervising the construction of the fortress and city. Peter's Cabin (Domik Petra; ☎ 232 45 76) is open from 10 am to 8 pm, except Tuesday and the last Monday of the month. Admission is about US$1.50 (US$0.75 for ISIC holders, children and pensioners). It feels more like a shrine than a museum.

Cruiser *Aurora*

In the Nevka opposite the Hotel St Petersburg is the *Aurora* (or *Avrora*), a mothballed cruiser from the Russo-Japanese War. From a downstream mooring on the night of 25 October 1917, its crew fired a blank round from the forward gun, demoralising the Winter Palace's defenders and marking the start of the October Revolution. During WW II, the Russians sank it to protect it from German bombs. Now, refloated, restored and painted in awfully pretty colours, it's a museum, free of charge and open from 10.30 am to 4 pm, closed Monday, Tuesday and the last Wednesday of the month. It's swarming with kids on weekends.

S M Kirov Apartment-Museum

Sergei Mironovich Kirov, one of Stalin's leading henchmen after whom countless parks, plazas, squares and a town are named, spent the last days of his life (before his death at the hands of Stalinist lynch mobs) at his decidedly unproletarian apartment at Kamennoostrovsky prospekt (Kirovsky prospekt) 26-28. Now open as a museum (☎ 233 38 22), the apartment is a quick journey back to the days of Soviet glory, right down to the sombre and reverential babushki who lead you through each room, describing in detail all the great guy's artefacts.

If you have a half hour or so, it's worth stopping in to see his lovely study (with its enormous polar and brown bear rugs) if only to see the choice examples of late 1920s Soviet technology on display. Kirov had several telephones (including a hotline to the Kremlin), and you can also see typewriters, a nice scale, binoculars and cameras, among other things. And he had a lot of books (120,000 of them) and medals, which are all on display as well. The museum is open from 11 am to 5.30 pm daily except Wednesday; admission is practically free (less than US$0.05). The museum is on the 4th floor and the coat checkroom is on the 5th floor. Be polite to the babushka-guards – some of the last defenders of the Soviet Union.

The Wannabe Hotel

On the corner of Kamennoostrovsky prospekt (Kirovsky prospekt) and the Karpovka River (see the Kirovsky Islands map) sits a piece of real estate that will probably someday be a top-end hotel. Begun in the late 1980s, the construction – a Soviet-Yugoslav joint venture – was doomed from the start. When the coup in the former and the war in the latter took hold, the site was abandoned.

ROGER HAYNE

Cruiser *Aurora*

But these were the high-flying, heady days of the early 1990s. Intourist immediately stepped in and boldly offered the project (which was a bit more than one-third completed) to any foreign firm willing to pay what Intourist considered to be quite a reasonable sum – about US$50 million! Today construction crews (Turkish ones this time) are humming again ('it says something that Russians consider the Turkish lira to be hard currency' – P J O'Rourke). We're watching ...

Botanical Gardens

This quiet jungle in eastern Aptekarsky (Apothecary) Island, just north-east of the Petrogradskaya metro station and across the Karpovka River, was once a garden of medicinal plants which gave the island its name. The botanical gardens on the site today offers one of St Petersburg's most peaceful strolling grounds. The Dutch-built greenhouse is difficult to get into but the lovely gardens are, for now, free. The entrance is at ulitsa Professora Popova 2, but if they decide to start charging, there are holes in the fence near the intersection of the Karpovka River and Aptekarskaya naberezhnaya, on the river side.

TV Antenna

Here's a weird one – the Leningrad Radio-Tele Broad-casting Centre's antenna (☎ 234 78 87), at the northern end of Petrograd Side, is open for tours by arrangement with Peter TIPS (see Tourist Offices in the Information section earlier in this chapter). The 50,000-watt transmitter tower stands 310 metres over the city, and it has just recently been allowed to let the public inside. It's a great place to bring kids (hang on tight); it offers excellent views of the entire city and environs, and you can take photos.

The tower was the first of its kind in the Soviet Union when constructed in 1963, so they weren't thinking about revolving restaurants or other amenities yet (the Ostankino tower in Moscow is modelled on this one), but these days there's a bar/café on the 2nd observation level (200 metres). It was originally 316 metres (taller than the Eiffel Tower), but they had to lop off the last six due to stress from high winds.

The itty-bitty lift (once the fastest in the country) makes the trip from ground level to the first viewing platform (197 metres) in a minute and three-quarters; from there you can walk up to the café level, where you can access the outside catwalk. The tower sways up to 50 cm on windy days, and you can feel it! A fun fact: the tower's construction was supervised by an all-female crew; the forewoman still lives in St Petersburg.

All the city's TV and radio signals originate here, but residents within almost a km around the antenna still get bad reception, as the signal goes right over their heads.

Peter TIPS (☎ 279 00 37) will take foreigners for US$10 a head, Russians for US$1.20, and needs at least a day's notice. To reach the TV antenna start at Petrogradskaya metro, take trolleybus No 31 north up Bolshoy prospekt

NICK SELBY

TV Antenna, Petrograd Side

from the stop in front of Teatr Experiment for two stops; get off when you see the tower (if you cross the big bridge you've missed it). Walk down to naberezhnaya Kantemirovsky, turn right and walk to the city centre gates facing the river.

KIROVSKY ISLANDS

This is the collective name for the outer delta islands of Petrograd Side – Kamenny, Yelagin and Krestovsky (Kamenny's impossible to pronounce Soviet-era name, Trudyashchikhsya – meaning 'Of the Workers' – is on some older maps but nobody *ever* uses it). Once marshy jungles, the islands were granted to 18th and 19th-century court favourites and developed into elegant playgrounds. But they're still mostly parkland, huge leafy venues for picnics, river sports and white nights cavorting.

Kamenny Island

Kamenny (Stone) Island's charm, seclusion and turn-of-the-century dachas, combined with winding lanes and a series of canals, lakes and ponds, make a stroll here pleasant at any time of year (though the walk across the bridge from the Aptekarsky side gets a mite chilly in winter). At the east end of the island the **Church of St John the Baptist** (Tserkov Ioanna Predtechi, 1778) seems to have found better use as a basketball court. Behind it the big, classical **Kamennoostrovsky Palace**, built by Catherine the Great for her son, is now a weedy military sanatorium.

Extending across the island in an upside-down 'v' from the roundabout off Kamennoostrovsky prospekt in the centre of the island's eastern side, 2-ya Beryozovaya alleya sports some lovely dachas, including former party and KGB retreats, which now rent out space to wealthy Russians and foreigners, as well as some of the upper strata of St Petersburg Mafiagentsia.

The island also boasts a government retreat, used by the president when he's in town, and by other big wigs when he's not. Look for the **tree**, said to have been planted by Peter the Great, almost blocking naberezhnaya reki Krestovki just west of its intersection with 2-ya Beryozovaya alleya.

The centre of the island has lots of turn-of-the-century summer houses. A pretty example is a wooden ginger-bread mansion with high gables like hats. It's at the end of Polevaya alleya, next to the kindergarten, and is guarded by uniformed security personnel. A grander example on the north-west shore is the lavish mansion of one **Senator Polovtsev**, who had barely moved in when the Bolsheviks took it away. Nearby is an ungainly, though sweet, wooden **Kamenny Island Theatre** first put up in the 1820s, and a footbridge to Yelagin Island. The **Danish Consulate-General** has, hands-down, the coolest diplomat property in town: a massive dacha on Bolshaya alleya, towards the centre of the island.

Kamenny Island is a short walk from Yelagin island, 15 minutes walk north of metro Petrogradskaya and 10 minutes south of metro Chyornaya Rechka.

Yelagin Island

This island's centrepiece is the **Yelagin Palace** (Yelaginsky dvorets), built for his mother by Tsar Alexander I, who had architect Carlo Rossi landscape the entire island while he was at it. The palace is to your right as you cross the footbridge from Kamenny Ostrov.

The very beautiful restored interiors of the main house include old furnishings on loan from the Europe and Astoria hotels; don't miss the stupendous 1890s carved-walnut study ensemble from Europe and the incredible inlaid-wood floors. The house is open from 10 am to 6 pm, closed Monday and Tuesday. Other nearby estate buildings sometimes have exhibitions too. Admission is US$1 for foreigners, US$0.10 for Russians, US$0.05 for students and children. Other nearby estate buildings sometimes have exhibitions, too.

The rest of the island is a lovely network of paths, greenery, lakes and channels – you can rent rowing boats – and a plaza at the west end looking out to the Gulf of Finland. It's all now the **Central Park of Culture & Rest** (named after, still, Kirov), two km long and pedestrian only. Several small cafés are open in summer.

The rowing boat rental stand is at the northern end of the island, at the 3-ya Yelagin bridge, which runs between the island and Primorsky prospekt to the north. The water bicycle rental stand is almost due south of the Yelagin Palace. Rates are about US$1 per hour, and you can explore the network of canals and lakes on the island. If you stop for a picnic, keep the boat in sight!

Krestovsky Island

Krestovsky Island, the biggest of the three, consists mostly of the vast **Seaside Park of Victory** (Primorsky Park Pobedy), dotted with sports fields and the 100,000-seat

Kirov Stadium, where you can see St Petersburg's reprehensible football team, Zenit, suffer crushing, humiliating defeat to whatever team it's taking on (OK, OK, in 1995 they did a bit better, but ... still).

Bus No 71a from metro Petrogradskaya goes the length of Krestovsky Island to Kirov Stadium. Bus No 71 from near metro Petrogradskaya, Bus No 45 from inner Nevsky prospekt and the Hermitage, and tram No 12 from metro Gostiny Dvor or metro Gorkovskaya all terminate on Krestovsky near the footbridge to Yelagin.

Buddhist Temple

From Yelagin Island a footbridge crosses north to the mainland. There, at Primorsky prospekt 91 by Lipovaya alleya, is a Buddhist *datsan* (temple), of all things. (Russia's Buddhist community is centred in the Buryatia Republic in Siberia.) A neglected but handsome and richly coloured three-storey building with walls sloping in Tibetan style, it was built from 1900-15 at the instigation of Pyotr Badmaev, a Buddhist physician to Tsar Nicholas II.

Enter the datsan from the door on the east side of the building; walk up the stone staircase to the right, avoiding the unbelievably smelly toilet under the staircase. There's an exhibition in Russian on Buddhism and the Dalai Lama. A small kiosk sells incense and pamphlets.

From anywhere but Yelagin Island, take any tram or trolleybus west from metro Chyornaya Rechka to the Lipovaya alleya stop.

VYBORG SIDE

Peter the Great had no apparent interest in the far side of the Neva, and today, beyond the embankment and Finland Station, among the factories and railway lines, there are few attractions, though if you're looking for a fur hat, the **Krondatevsky Market** at Polyustrovsky prospekt is just the ticket.

Finland Station

Finland Station (Finlyandsky vokzal) is where, in 1917, Lenin arrived from exile in Switzerland (having ridden in a sealed railway carriage through Germany, Sweden and Finland) and gave his legendary speech from the top of an armoured car, in the square where his statue now stands. After fleeing a second time he again arrived here from Finland, this time disguised as a rail fireman, and the locomotive he rode in is displayed on the platform. It's not really the same station, having been rebuilt following WW II. There's a statue outside, Vlad's pointing across the Neva to the Big House – former KGB headquarters! The Ploshchad Lenina metro station is next door.

Kresty Prison

Kresty is St Petersburg's main holding prison; if you're busted here, Kresty's where they take you to await whatever it is that awaits you (it's conveniently located just next door to the Holiday Hostel). But what distinguishes Kresty from, say, New York's Riker's Island, is that Kresty is located on a main boulevard, and prisoners can get to the windows. Russian families are quite close, and with true Russian exuberance, the families of the accused line the street outside, bonding with their inmates.

On any given day you can see dozens of these well wishers lining Arsenalnaya naberezhnaya. Mothers, fathers and sometimes even drunken friends stand crying. Wives and girlfriends stand close to the concrete fence, moving their arms in what may look like complicated dance moves, but what is in fact a crude code, known to inmates and prison guards alike.

The prisoner, let's call him the receiver, makes himself known by holding an article of clothing out the window (they stick their arms through the bars or through holes in the steel mesh). When the sender, down on the street, identifies their man, they start waving their arms about, tracing Cyrillic characters in the air.

The receiver waves up and down to signal 'I understand', and side to side to signal 'repeat'. Under this method, after three or four minutes of waving, one can clearly discern the message, 'I c-a-l-l-e-d y-o-u-r f-r-i-e-n-d M-i-s-h-a'!

The process, understandably, is time consuming (a message like 'I called your lawyer but he was out to lunch' could take a good while), but the family and friends on the street below (again in true Russian style) bring along sausage, bread, cheese and thermoses filled with hot tea. Of course, some bring along a bottle of vodka just to pass the time.

The best time to go is in the early evening; bring along a snack, and try not to be obtrusive or rude.

Inside the prison itself, there's said to be a **Police and Crime Museum** containing gruesome exhibitions like embalmed severed limbs and the usual murder weapons. It's only open to law enforcement types (forget about it).

Piskaryovka Cemetery

For two and a half years during WW II the Germans besieged Leningrad and between half a million and one million people died, mostly of cold and starvation. Almost half a million were buried in mass graves in this cemetery (Piskaryovskoe memorialnoe kladbishche). With acres of slightly raised mounds marked by year, it's a sobering place. At the entrance is an exhibit of photographs that need no captions. Here you'll understand the Russian obsession with that war.

The cemetery is way out; about a 40-minute trip from the city centre on public transport. From Ploshchad Muzhestva metro station turn left, cross prospekt Nepokoryonnykh and take bus No 123 about seven minutes east to the square granite pavilion.

St Sampson's Cathedral

Peter the Great defeated the Swedes at Poltava in 1709, on the feast day of St Sampson. In commemoration a wooden church (Sampsonevsky sobor) was built at what is now prospekt Sampsonevsky 41, and the five-domed stone church that replaced it in the 1730s is now among the city's oldest buildings. The comely church, with galleries on either side and a kerb-side bell tower, is closed and in the hands of a team of Polish restorers.

ST PETERSBURG WALKS

These are some basic orientation walks through the centre and a bit south. They're not meant to take you through everything, but they do pass by much of St Petersburg's most stunning or at least landmark architecture, sights and points of interest. They also afford some great photo opportunities.

Walk 1: Dvortsovaya Ploshchad to Ploshchad Iskusstv

To start this walk, refer to the Central St Petersburg map (front gatefold). Time: about an hour, more if you stop for a snack or a drink.

After standing around and cursing the difficulty of photographing the Hermitage, which refuses to fit into frame until you're far enough away to make the rooftop statues look like gold smears, start this walk with Photo Op from Heaven No 1. Walk north-east to the start of Millionaya ulitsa, and from there into the porch covering the south entrance of the **New Hermitage** (Novy ermitazh). This is one of several buildings in the city that has a façade supported by musclemen: if you play this right you can get a shot from the north-east corner of the porch that includes a healthy slice of St Isaac's Cathedral past the Winter Palace and some of its statuary, including the three musclemen.

Tip: a good way to get a photo of the Hermitage is from the river – catch a late-evening river cruise or water taxi; the Hermitage exterior has recently been fitted with floodlights.

Walking north-east again, make the first right turn and walk along the **Zimny Canal** the short block to the **Moyka River**. This is one of its loveliest stretches: to your right, Nevsky prospekt is crossed by the **Norodny Bridge**, and across Nevsky, catch a glimpse of the **Stroganov Palace**.

Along the Moyka Hope you enjoyed the glimpse, because that's not where you're going to turn left. On the left side of the Moyka embankment is the **Japanese Embassy**, and directly opposite that is one of the St Petersburg Philharmonia's two concert halls – the **Glinka Capella** (Akademicheskaya khorovaya kapella imeni M I Glinki). Cross the little footbridge to the west side of the river, turn left and walk past **Pushkin's last home**, diagonally opposite the French Consulate at naberezhnaya reki Moyki 12, to the little Konyushennaya pereulok, which brings you to one of Imperial St Petersburg's flashiest streets, Bolshaya Konyushennaya ulitsa. This street has been, at various times, home to Turgenev, Rimsky-Korsakov and Chernyshevsky, and the former location of the court stables (from which the street's name is taken). On the west side of the street is **DLT**, one of St Petersburg's best department stores, and opposite it, the little **Finnish Church** (1803-05).

The Konyushennayas There are two options as to the next leg of the walk: do a little browsing at DLT and maybe grab a snack in the upstairs Melita Café or at the excellent doughnut shop next door; or walk around to Nevsky prospekt and have a beer at the outdoor Koff Beer Garden in front of the **Lutheran Church**; in either case (by walking down Shvedsky pereulok or down to Nevsky and making two lefts) walk to the northern end of **ulitsa Malaya Konyushennaya** one block east, and turn into the tiny alley that runs between it and naberezhnaya Kanala Griboedova.

The Griboedova As you emerge onto the embankment, to your right will be Nevsky prospekt and the golden colonnades of the **Kazan Cathedral**, past which you can just make out the **Bankovsky Bridge** with its golden-winged griffins, before the canal twists south-west. To your left is the spectacular **Church of the Resurrection of Christ** (Khram Voskresenia Khristova, 1887-1907), built on the spot where Alexander II, despite his actually caving in and doing exactly what they wanted (the establishment of an elective assembly), was blown up by the People's Will terrorist group in 1881. If you didn't stop for a bit of something back near DLT, walking north on the west side of the canal, you'll pass the little café adjacent to the Restaurant St Petersburg, famous for its inexpensive and wonderful mushrooms in cream sauce. Otherwise, turn south, towards Nevsky prospekt, and cross the canal on the lovely little 22-metre **Italyansky Bridge**. From the middle of this bridge is 'Perfect Photo Op No 2', of the cathedral and the canal.

Walk towards the cathedral on the east side of the canal (being sure to turn before you reach the fur hat and military watch purveyors) and turn right onto Inzhenernaya ulitsa. This short block opens into **ploshchad Iskusstv** (Arts Square), where this walk concludes. If you haven't been into the **Russian Museum** now's the perfect time to do it.

NICK SELBY

Bankovsky Bridge

NICK SELBY

Dostoevsky country

Walk 2: Crime & Punishment

To start this walk, refer to the Central St Petersburg Map.
Time: about an hour

Looking at **Sennaya ploshchad** today, it's not hard to
imagine that in Dostoevsky's time it was a teeming
madhouse, filled with drunks, layabouts and gutter-
snipes. Though the present-day metro station is built
on the site of the former Church of the Assumption,
the major landmarks of the day were seedy pubs and
inns of which there were more than there were street
corners.

The border between reality and fantasy has been
smudged irrevocably here: Petersburgers will point
out where Dostoevsky lived as quickly as they will the
home of Raskolnikov and the old pawn broker. And
snatches of the grim reality of slum life in the mid-19th
century can still be had during an hour's walk. The
omnipresent stray cats, as permanent a fixture in St
Petersburg courtyards as dim light, foul odours and
pockmarked cement, are the gatekeepers to a
neighbourhood whose gloominess and squalor has
been preserved well enough to make it instantly
recognisable, even to Fyodor himself.

For *Crime and Punishment* fans, even those with
limited time, the area is a wonderful opportunity to get
a better feel for the neighbourhood in which it was set.
Die-hard fans argue to this day about where the '730
steps' would place Raskolnikov's attic, and it's come
down to two addresses.

Raskolnikov's Flat(s) From Sennaya ploshchad, walk north on Grivtsova pereulok, across the canal, and turn left onto ulitsa Grazhdanskaya. On the far right hand corner of ulitsa Przhevalskogo is **No 5**, one of the two possible locations of Raskolnikov's attic. Coincidentally, the building also bears marble plaques in Russian and German marking the waterline reached by the great flood of 7 November 1824, immortalised in Pushkin's poem, *The Bronze Horseman*. Unfortunately, the door to the stairwell is locked. Those who say that this is the place go further, saying that Rodya (the diminutive of Raskolnikov's first name, Rodyon) retrieved the murder weapon from a street-sweeper's storage bin inside the tunnel leading to the courtyard.

From that corner, turn south, onto ulitsa Przhevalskogo (formerly Stolyarny pereulok, or 'S ... lane', from the book), where at **No 9**, you can enter the building of the second possible address (which I believe is the one, as in the first paragraph of the book it clearly says '... the cubicle sublet to him in S ... lane'). Walk through the tunnel, turn right and use entrance 2 (up the crumbling stone steps) and walk up four flights until the stairwell ceiling opens upward. Graffiti on the wall sometimes reads, 'Don't Kill, Rodya'. Rodya's flat would be the padlocked attic on the left hand side of the fifth floor.

Dostoevsky's Flats Back on Przhevalskogo, turn south again and walk the 50 metres to the corner of **ulitsa Kaznacheyskaya**. Dostoevsky lived in three flats on this street alone: from 1861-63 at **No 1**, far down and on the left at the Griboedova, and from 1864-67 at **No 7**, at the northeast corner of Przhevalskogo and Kaznacheyskaya. It was from this flat that he wrote *Crime and Punishment*. Dostoevsky spent one month living in the faded red building, **No 9**, before moving to No 7.

The Murder Route From whichever flat Raskolnikov lived, he walked out and down Przhevalskogo towards the canal. He crossed the **Kokushkin bridge**, where he would stand and gaze into the canal, deep in thought. Looking at the canal today you'd never guess it used to be very dirty (that was a joke).

Murderer yes, orienteering student no; the route to the pawn broker's house taken by Rodya is circuitous. After you cross the canal, head straight, to ulitsa Sadovaya, then turn right. Make your first right turn into **ulitsa Rimskogo Korsakova**. Cross Voznesensky prospekt, and continue past Bolshaya Podyacheskaya and

Srednyaya Podyacheskaya; the pawn broker's building sits between there and the canal embankment.

For a good look at the building, cross the street and stand at the southern side of the Komsomolsky bridge. The entrance to the courtyard is a bit north on the embankment, at **naberezhnaya Kanala Griboedova 104**. Enter the dank, pot-holed tunnel, and head straight for **entrance No 5** (flats 22-81).

The building's residents are very used to people entering the building to get a look. In fact, brass balls at the corners of the iron banisters are there specifically for visitors, and they end just after the third floor, where her flat (74) is on the right hand side. For you law enforcement types: after the murder, the suspect ran through the tunnel leading to **Srednyaya Podyacheskaya**.

Walk 3: From the Kazan Cathedral to Ploshchad Ostrovskogo

To start this walk, refer to the Nevsky prospekt (west) map. Time: about two hours

The **Kazansky sobor** is a quintessential St Petersburg landmark due to its unique form (despite the fact that it's heavily based on St Peter's in Rome) and its absolute prime location. Almost equidistant from The Grand Hotel Europe and the former Duma to the east, the Church of the Resurrection of Christ to the north, the Bankovsky Bridge to the south and the Admiralty and the Hermitage to the west, it is a perfect starting point for this walk through the very heart of the city.

Directly across the street, **Dom Knigi**, housed (as you'll hear over and over again) in the former Russian headquarters of the Singer Sewing Machine company, is definitely worth a browse, especially the map and poster sections upstairs. The view north from Nevsky prospekt to the **Church of the Resurrection of Christ** is spectacular, but if you missed Photo Op 2 from Walk No 2, hold out a few more minutes and it gets even better. Begin the walk facing the Kazan Cathedral: cross to the left side of the building and walk south along naberezhnaya Kanala Griboedova; there may be a beer garden set up almost outside the side entrance to the **Museum of the History of Religion** housed inside the cathedral. Keep walking south along the canal until you reach the **Bankovsky Bridge** one of St Petersburg's loveliest, suspended from chains emerging from the mouths of golden-winged griffins, and cross this little footbridge. From the middle, turn north and *now*'s when to snap that picture of the cathedral, with Nevsky prospekt and the Italyansky Bridge in the foreground.

Unless you want to get an education in economics (the school right in front of you) or buy a train ticket (the centre's just up the street to the left), let's keep going from here; turn left on the other side of the embankment and then make the first right turn onto Lomonosova ulitsa. This is, at this point, a quiet and somewhat dirty little street that serves as the rear end of one of the city's biggest shopping malls, which we'll get to shortly.

Make the first left turn onto ulitsa Dumskaya. On the left, at the corner of Dumskaya and Nevsky prospekt, is the former **Town Duma** (the pre-Revolutionary municipal government's headquarters, 1799-1804), and the adjacent **Silver Stalls** (1784-87). The Duma's tall Western European-style clock tower is a landmark easily seen from most of Nevsky prospekt. In the centre of the street is a small building, housing a theatre ticket office. In warmer months, there's an outdoor café in front (north) of that building serving beer, soft drinks and snacks. Across Nevsky is the **Grand Hotel Europe** and, further down ulitsa Mikhailovskaya, ploshchad Iskusstv (see Walk No 2).

Gostiny Dvor To your right is St Petersburg's answer to Moscow's GUM and any North Carolina K-Mart. These days Gostiny Dvor is worth a browse – more and more shops are filled with more and more things. There's an entrance on ulitsa Dumskaya, but the main entrance is around on Nevsky prospekt towards ulitsa Sadovaya. The stalls have varying quantities of varying supplies, but a walk through the ground floor is usually interesting enough of its own accord. The 2nd floor holds more in the way of clothing, the ground floor in practicalities like stationary, photo equipment and accessories, some art supplies and children's toys. At the southern end of the ulitsa Sadovaya side, there's a pizza slice bar doing decent mushroom and ham pizzas.

Passazh Gostiny Dvor's more sophisticated cousin is directly across Nevsky prospekt. At the turn of the century, Passazh (1846-48) was the arcade of choice for discerning Imperial Petersburgers, and recently it's become far easier to see why. As in GUM, the main shopping area consists of stalls under a magnificent translucent arched ceiling with catwalks all around and balconies crossing here and there. The ground floor is worth a stroll, and the basement level has a blowout fully fledged Western-style supermarket. From the main entrance on the ground floor (actually up a small flight of stairs), continue straight through to the rear of Passazh, through the exit and down the stairs; we're walking out to Italyanskaya ulitsa along the south-east corner of ploshchad Iskusstv, and north-east from there.

The Winter Stadium to the Engineer's Castle

Turn right onto Italyanskaya ulitsa where you're likely to see stage trucks shuttling scenery to the nearby Musical Comedy and Komissarzhevskoy Drama theatres and lots of other loading/unloading activities, as well as track-suited gentlemen of dubious occupation barking into cellular phones. You'll pass through **Manezhnaya ploshchad** and its odd **Winter Stadium**. Make that left turn onto the 400-metre stretch of the divided **Klenovaya alleya**. Dead ahead (no, past the remnants of that 'tourist art market') is the **Engineer's Castle** (1797-1800), the evil-looking red-brick building built by the lunatic Tsar Paul I – in an attempt to insulate himself from assassination he went so far as to surround the place with moats (they're long since filled in).

Along the Fontanka Standing on ulitsa Zamkovaya facing the castle, turn right and walk the short block to the Fontanka River. From here, if you look left, about 400 metres down towards the Neva is the **Summer Garden**, with its little Summer Palace of Peter I, tea house and statuary, worthy of a trip on its own but not included in this walk. Turn right and walk south along the east side of the river. At the next intersection is the **St Petersburg Circus**, and two blocks further south brings you to another great Photo Op: The **Anichikov Bridge** with its statues of four rearing stallions and their trainers and the fabulously lavish Baroque **Beloselsky-Belozersky Palace**, a bright red building whose façades are supported by Atlases. If you want to take a break from this walk, you're passing the **River Cruise Pier** right now; tickets are available from the little kiosk near the bridge.

Nevsky Prospekt to Ploshchad Ostrovskogo

Turn right back onto one of Nevsky prospekt's most thriving stretches. While there are many shops and boutiques between here and ulitsa Sadovaya, the hands-down landmark is **Yeliseevsky Food Shop** at Nevsky prospekt 58.

Just across the street is **ploshchad Ostrovskogo**, a Carlo Rossi designed park that is somehow both right on a bustling stretch of Nevsky prospekt and also quiet and peaceful, and a very good place to conclude this walk. There's a lovely statue in the centre of **Catherine II** surrounded by her lovers; this is, in turn, surrounded by street artists, chess and backgammon players and is swarming with tourists in summer. To the right, facing the statue, is the **Saltykov-Shchedrin Library**, to the left is the **Anichkov Palace** and directly behind the statue is the enormous **Pushkin Theatre** (1828-32), with its Corinthian columns and relief of Apollo's horse-drawn chariot. Behind the Theatre is ulitsa Zodchego Rossi, a perfectly proportioned street that's home to the **Vaganov School of Choreography** (where the Kirov trains its dancers); beyond that, the four-tiered **Lomonosov Bridge** crosses the Fontanka.

Walk 4: A St Petersburg Pub Crawl

The Crawl starts north of metro Chyornaya Rechka (see the Kirovsky Islands map), then cuts through the Inner Petrograd side and Central St maps. Time: about four hours.

St Petersburg's pub scene has a decidedly 'island-nations west of the continent' tone, with Irish and English pubs holding the most prominent positions in ex-pat's hearts. There are a couple of other noteworthy entries: the Belgians have been making great inroads with beer distribution if not actual pub management, and the Swedes over at the Grand Hotel Europe have run the most successful of pubs with Sadko's since the place re-opened in late 1991.

Because of the far-flung nature of the Crawl, taxis and the metro play a key role in getting from some pubs to others. Once you're in the centre, though, you could easily walk between all the places – actually it would probably help you keep your head on straighter! Purists: while beer from many nations is the focus here, all the following places serve Russian vodka, and for drivers and other non-drinkers, there is a full line of soft drinks, coffee/tea and fruit juices. If you skip the nightclub, you can get away with all this for well under US$50.

Your Conscience: The Brits are Here to Help If

you're going to blow a stack of dosh on booze, you may as well start out at a place that donates some of the proceeds to charity: we begin the crawl at the not-too-inconveniently located **Dog & Fox** (count your blessings – they could have called it the Magpie & Stump). From metro Chyornaya Rechka, walk north about 200 metres, across the canal (that's Chyornaya rechka, or 'Black River'), then turn right and the very comfortable, convincingly English pub is 400 metres ahead, on the 3rd floor at naberezhnaya Chyornaya Rechka 41 (corner of ulitsa Grafova). The British partners donate 50% of their profits directly to the Red Kidz charity, involved in a host of worthy projects in town, mainly involving abandoned and disfigured children as well as homeless shelters. Don't panic; they also have beer, cider and lagers on tap.

The Belgians Finish up your pint and walk back to metro Chyornaya Rechka; take the metro two stops towards the centre to Gorkovskaya station. Across the street is a curious entry – the **Grand Cafe Antwerpen**. It's really a restaurant, but they do have a very nice and very chic bar: turn right as you enter, bear left and the circular bar is near the back. Service isn't as friendly as it could be, but the reason you're here is the draft Belgian beer and bottles of Duvell – don't linger too long (you may notice that no one else does).

The Fighting Irish: Part One The battle of the Irish pubs has been raging for a while now and no ex-pat is neutral on the subject. The relative newcomer is a short taxi ride from metro Gorkovskaya at **Teatralnaya ploshchad**, perfectly located just across the street from the **Mariinsky Theatre**. Here, in this cosy, vaulted-ceiling hang-out called the **Shamrock**, have a pint of Guinness. Remember that taste: Shamrock management claims that their Black Stuff comes direct from Dublin, while 'other' pubs use 'English muck'. Don't be put off by these allegations; that 'other' pub would be **Mollies Irish Bar**, four pubs down the line, which is a great and popular place.

The Swedes From Teatralnaya ploshchad, get a taxi (tell the driver 'Gostiny Dvor', not the 'Evropa' and the price will stay lower) to the Grand Hotel Europe. At the corner of Mikhailovskaya and Nevsky prospekt is a staple of St Petersburg nightlife, **Sadko's**. There's live music and on weekends Karaoke (always a hoot) and lots of young people – foreign and Russian, business people and students. It's a very fun and popular place. It's also probably a good idea to get some protein at this point; the food here is good though it gets a bit pricey. Service is very friendly.

Not all Brits are Philanthropists From Sadko's, cross Nevsky through the underpass and enter the Gostiny Dvor metro; you're heading one stop east to Mayakovskaya. From the station, cross ulitsa Marata, and walk east on Nevsky one block to the **John Bull Pub** on the corner of ulitsa Pushkinskaya. One of the earliest entries in the Foreign Pub Wars, the JBP took a beating early on because, while it's a lovely little pub (they trucked the whole thing, knick-knacks, trinkets and all, from the UK), at the end of the day you have to drink John Bull, and (not quite) pints are US$5! While fun to look at and nice for a while, this stop is definitely optional.

The Finns What would drinking in Russia be without Finns? A lot less crowded for one thing. From the Mayakovskaya metro exit or from the John Bull Pub, cross Nevsky prospekt and turn left (west) back towards the Admiralty. Behind No 86, almost directly opposite the Nevskij Palace Hotel, is a courtyard **Beer Garden** owned and operated by a Finnish gentleman of exquisite taste and honourable intentions. It's a lovely place to sit on a summer evening, but don't drink too much of that Lapin Kulta – gives everyone I know a headache. They also do grilled shashlyk.

The Irish Again Cross Nevsky, turn right and make your second left onto Rubinshteyna ulitsa. Two and a half long blocks down on the left hand side of the street is **Mollies Irish Bar**, a bastion of civility and civilisation. As you taste their Guinness (wherever it may be from), stand back and watch as bartender Christian Walsh occasionally launches into a bottle-twirling, glass-tossing, fruit-throwing, drink-mixing spectacle. It's worth hanging out here for a while – it may be the city's most popular watering hole, and there's a happy hour (hours change) when drinks are half price. That's when I ran into Ireland's Minister of Education. Smart lady.

Still Standing? If you're still on your feet you should probably be using them; from Mollies turn right onto Rubinshteyna back towards Nevsky. Almost directly across the street is your final destination: **Domenico's**, one of St Petersburg's most popular and expensive nightclubs. The place gets packed on weekend nights, and as the evening progresses, it's easy to forget where you are. If you do, by the way, forget where you are, the HI St Petersburg Hostel, Nevskij Palace Hotel and Grand

Hotel Europe are very close by and any would be happy to set you up with a bed for the night.

ACTIVITIES

For classic entertainment and sporting events, see the Entertainment section; for special events listings while you're in town, check *The St Petersburg Press* and *Pulse*.

Rowing Boat Rental

In summer, a lovely way to while away a day (or to keep the kids somewhat amused) is paddling through the canals and lakes on Yelagin Island. The rowing boat rental stand is at the northern end of the island, at the 3-ya Yelagin bridge, which runs between the island and Primorsky prospekt to the north. Water bicycles are also available, the stand is due south of the Yelagin Palace. Rates are about US$1 per hour, and you can explore the network of canals and lakes on the island. If you stop for a picnic, keep the boat in sight!

Working Out

The Summer Hostel's health club has free-weights and aerobics classes that cost about US$1.50 per hour.

The Grand Hotel Europe, Nevskij Palace and Astoria Hotels have health clubs that allow visitors. Prices range from about US$10 to 20 per day.

Banya

Tired? Overworked? A good beating may be all you need, and St Petersburg's public banyas are as good a place as any to get one! Here are a few of the better public banyas:

Banya 13 (☎ 550 09 85), Karbysheva ulitsa 29A (metro: Ploshchad Muzhestva), has a large outdoor heated pool
Banya 50 (☎ 233 50 92), ulitsa Malaya Passadskaya 28, is a nice, clean and friendly place
Nevskie Bani, ulitsa Marata 5/7 (metro: Mayakovskaya), the largest in town, is smack in the city centre

Hash House Harriers

A 'drinking club with a running problem', the HHH started in Kuala Lumpur, Malaysia, and has since spread to British consulates all over the world. The runs are usually of five km or less, followed by a 'down-down' chug-a-lug session during which you wear practically as

A Russian Banya

There's a level of clean that can only be attained, Russians say, through the rigorous action of a ritual Russian *banya*. A combination of dry sauna, steam bath, massage and plunges into ice-cold water, the banya is a weekly event that is as much a part of Russian life as, say, bowling in Bedrock. The word 'banya' has come to mean far more than its dictionary definition, which is 'bathhouse'.

Preparation begins at home, where thermos flasks are filled to their cork-plugged brims with specially brewed tea. These teas are peculiar to the banya; a mixture of jams, fruits, spices, tea and heaps of sugar. Armed with this brew, the bather heads out. (A couple of beers picked up along the way is not unheard-of either.)

Based on any number of scheduling concerns, people usually go to the banya on the same day each week and, with others there on the same day, a close circle is formed; the closest equivalent in the West would probably be your work-out buddies.

After a 'warm up' in the dry sauna (the word's the same in Russian, pronounced 'SA-oo-na'), where the tempera- ture is in the low 100's Celsius (lower 200's Fahrenheit), you're ready for the *parilka* – the dreaded steam room.

The parilka will have a furnace that's heating rocks. Onto these, bathers throw water, usually mixed with euca- lyptus oil, with a long-handled ladle-like implement made specially for the purpose. When the room's got a good head of steam going, the bathers grab hold of bundles of dried birch leaves *(vennki)*, dip them in hot water and, well, beat each other with them. The beating (which isn't violent, and feels a lot better than it sounds) is said to rid your body of toxins.

As you might suspect, all that steam makes the air even hotter; bathers continue to throw water on until visibility is nil and the room is unbearably hot, at which point everyone runs out coughing. And as if the relatively cold air outside the parilka isn't enough of a shock to one's system, the next step is a plunge into the icy cold waters of the *basseyn* (pool), whose health benefits I've yet to work out (they're probably incredibly important).

After the plunge, it's out to the locker rooms wrapped up in sheets (available from the attendant or somewhere in the locker room), where the events of the world are discussed over the tea (or whatever). Then the process begins again; sessions can go on for two or three hours.

Every Russian town has a public banya, larger towns and cities have several. Baths are segregated by sex, and depending on the size of the place, there are either separate sections for men and women or the baths admit different sexes on different days. One more thing. Alcohol affects you faster in a banya, so if you do partake, be careful and do it slowly. It's considered bad form to lose your lunch in a steam room! ∎

much beer as you drink. It can be great fun in a football-hooligan sort of a way. They meet every Sunday at 2 pm near the statue of Pushkin in ploshchad Iskusstv – bring running gear, and, if you like, new running shoes. For more information contact Lesley Saunderson at the British Consulate (☎ 119 60 36).

Tanning

Sallow? St Petersburg's full of tanning salons, usually costing about US$6 for half an hour. Try Luda (☎ 275 53 82) on Nevsky prospekt 18, Casa Antonio (☎ 114 37 55) on Soyuza Pechatnikov ulitsa, or the salon at Leninsky prospekt 115 (☎ 153 94 63). There are also tanning beds at the Summer Hostel and the Nevskij Palace Hotel.

Religious Services

See Religion in the Facts about St Petersburg chapter.

Gambling

Casinos have popped up all over town. Mainly these are sleazeball magnets, but there are a couple of more civilised places where you can try your luck (though I think that staying home and flushing dollar bills down the toilet one at a time is just as exciting and perhaps less expensive). There are more civilised casinos in the Hotel Astoria, above the Shanghai Chinese and Nevsky Melody restaurants.

Places to Stay

FINDING ACCOMMODATION

St Petersburg's accommodation scene has improved to the point that it's unrecognisable to returning visitors. And the changes have affected every price range; it's not just that big money moved in and built luxury places (which it did) but there are now no fewer than three youth hostels, as well as several companies that arrange B&B. Even the former state-run places have begun performing heretofore unheard-of acts such as smiling, cleaning the rooms, charging on the basis of value and so on.

But the increase in available bed space does not by any means imply that St Petersburg accommodation is a big bargain – it's not, at least when compared with that in the rest of the country outside Moscow.

Camping

Camping – not a good option in St Petersburg – will cost you at least US$15 a double. See the Bottom End – Outskirts section later in this chapter for details.

Private Flats

It's possible to pay the price Russians pay for staying in a private flat – about US$7 to 10 a night – by going with one of the people who approach travellers arriving off major trains at Moscow Station, or finding a *kvartirnoe byuro*, which is an agency that places short-term guests in private flats. You'll want to be sure that you can trust someone who approaches you at a station (many of them really are genuine folks just in need of some extra cash) and establish how far from the city centre their place is before accompanying them. It's better to avoid committing yourself before you actually see the place.

Lloyd Donaldson, editor of the *St Petersburg Press*, wrote of a very nice experience with one of these women when he was finding a place to stay for a friend. The woman approached them in Moscow Station with a hand-written sign around her neck, and ...

was offering hotel rooms for US$5.50 in the northern suburbs. When I said we were looking for something in the centre with a family, she said 'Come with me, I'll take you to the despatcher.'

When we got there we discovered that the system that operates in Budapest is now also operating in a very small way here in St Petersburg – the idea of a little bureau in the railway stations that acts as an agent for people with rooms to rent in their apartments.

The despatcher had 14 places on her list. One of the landladies spoke English. The price was US$11 a night, without meals, to be paid each day. When I said we were looking for something for a month, she said, 'well, we normally only do stays for up to 10 days ... but if you and the landlady like each other then you could extend it.'

The bureau is in Dom Kultury (the House of Culture) which is on Ligovsky Prospekt, next to Moscow Station. To find the bureau (which is literally just one woman at a shabby desk stationed in one corner of a corridor) go in the main entrance, turn right, and walk about four metres. It's on your right near the window.

My feeling about the whole deal, as an experienced traveller and someone who has lived three years in Russia, was that it was totally OK. There was no question at all of foreigners' discrimination in terms of pricing, and I had no hesitation in dealing with either women. They both seemed very decent, very ordinary women. (The one on the platform was a pensioner who gets 120,000 roubles (US$27) a month.)

B&Bs

If you choose very carefully and aren't concerned about being far from the centre, you may be able to find a B&B for as little as US$20 a double. The average, however, is US$25 to US$35 a couple.

There are several agencies advertising in the Russian and Western press that will find B&B accommodation for you.

The Traveller's Guest House Moscow (☎ (095) 971 40 59; e-mail tgh@glas.apc.org) finds flats in St Petersburg for as little as US$10 per person per night. *Peter TIPS* (See the Information section in the Facts for the Visitor chapter) offers B&Bs for US$20 a night or US$400 a month. It also offers apartment rentals in the centre. One-room flats cost US$25 a day or US$300 a month, while two-room flats cost US$35 a day or US$450 a month.

We've received numerous favourable letters about the *St Petersburg Host Family Association* (HOFA) (☎ /fax 275 19 92, 395 13 38; e-mail alexei@hofak.spb.stu.su); there have also been several more positive reports on CompuServe's travel forums; we've communicated with travellers who have used the service and they say it's a good deal. It has been around, they say, for four years, and originated at St Petersburg (then Leningrad) University.

HOFA places travellers with Russian families, generally academics and professionals, in their apartments around town. You'll usually get a private room and a shared bath, and breakfast is included. HOFA says that at least one member of the family will speak English. The basic price is single/double US$25/40 per night or US$150/240 per week for an apartment near the centre. This includes a business visa invitation that HOFA will register with OVIR on your arrival. Payment is made in cash to the family you're staying with.

Shakti (☎ 279 51 98; e-mail cas@spectron.spb.su) is a younger company that can arrange similar homestays with similar types of families. The basic price is US$30/45 per night for apartments near the centre. This also includes a business visa and OVIR registration, though be sure to insist on registration, as they tend to think little of the authorities. The flats we saw were quite nice and very clean.

The Peter TIPS, HOFA and Shakti companies also offer guides, excursions, Russian lessons and other add-ons; contact them directly for more information.

Other Types of Accommodation

Youth hostels charge from US$7 to US$15 for a bed. For a traditional hotel room, playing it straight (admitting you're a foreigner and using a Western passport), the rock-bottom price is about US$12/17 a single/double, but you'd have to get out of the centre to find it.

All the above hostel prices include breakfast. There are, of course, ways to get into hotels for cheaper prices, but you'd need help from a Russian friend or, better, a Russian company.

PLACES TO STAY – BOTTOM END

City Centre

Russia's first and to date only Hostelling International (HI) member hostel, the *HI St Petersburg Hostel* (☎ 329 80 18; fax 329 80 19; see next paragraph for e-mail) has the cheapest rooms in the centre at US$15 per bed in rooms with two to six beds. The hostel's been open since early 1992, and is run by an American and his two Russian partners. It's about a five-minute walk north-east of Moscow Station and ploshchad Vosstania, and the rooms are very clean and comfortable. Breakfast is included, the staff is preternaturally friendly, and the hostel's visa support service is one of the best around (see the Facts for the Visitor chapter). There's a video-café downstairs showing movies a couple of times a week. It also has a ticket-booking service for domestic and international train travel (face value plus a US$5 surcharge) and plane travel.

Reservations can be made by faxing directly on (7 812) 329 80 19, through any HI hostel on the International Booking System (IBN), or, in the US, through Russian Youth Hostels & Tourism (RYHT ☎ (1 310) 618 2014; fax (1 310) 618 1140). You can e-mail the hostel at ryh@ryh.spb.su for general questions about the hostel, and at bookings@ryh.spb.su to book. It will also accept reservations for Holiday Hostel and others in the Russian Youth Hostel Association (RYHA). If you have an Internet browser, http://www.spb.su/ryh/ gets you to the hostel's home page.

Unless you feel like spending upwards of US$300 per night, you can't get a much better location than that of the *Student Dormitory* (☎ 314 74 72) at ulitsa Plekhanova 6, 120 metres behind the Kazan Cathedral, but this is an iffy proposition. Technically, you should be allowed to get into its clean, comfortable singles and doubles for US$12/14.50, but management runs from a bit unpredictable to downright dodgy, and availability is very tight, especially in summer. Calling first may help. If you just try showing up, be friendly.

The *Bolshoy Teatr Kukol Hotel* – yes, that does mean the 'Big Puppet Theatre Hotel' – (☎ 273 39 96) at ulitsa Nekrasova 12, has singles/doubles at US$15/22. Said to be OK.

The *Oktyabrskaya* (☎ 277 63 30) at Ligovsky prospekt 10, a crumbling old place smack in ploshchad Vosstania, boasts a terrific location. With comfortable, but well-worn, singles/doubles at US$24/28, it's a fair deal. Rumour has it that it's being taken over by Holiday Inn, and slated to be gutted and converted to a luxury hotel, but for the moment it's still an option to be considered. It's opposite Moscow Station.

The *Hotel Rus* (☎ 273 46 83, 272 66 54) is a large, modern and popular place not far at all from the centre, and it's a good bet at US$28 for a single, US$40 for a double, with bath included, and US$50 for a two-room 'suite' (with a couch that sleeps a third person comfortably, if on an angle). It's at ulitsa Artilleryskaya 1, a one-block street just south of Preobrazhenskaya ploshchad (formerly ploshchad Radishcheva), near metro Chernyshevskaya. END

Petrograd & Vyborg Sides

The *Holiday Hostel* (☎ & fax 542 73 64) at ulitsa Mikhaylova 1, 3rd floor, became St Petersburg's second western-style youth hostel in 1994. Its location, just south of Finland Station (see the Central St Petersburg map), has its pros and cons. The pro is definitely the river view in summer – the rooftop café offers the classic 'Peter & Paul Fortress against the backdrop of raised drawbridges' panorama. Among the cons is that, aside from Finland Station, there's not much out there, and that incessant shouting you hear is the families of inmates calling to loved ones being held at Kresty Prison, which is right next door (see the Things To See & Do chapter). The hostel itself is clean and fun. It doesn't offer as much in the way of services as the HI St Petersburg Hostel, though the staff is very friendly and they try hard. It has two to five beds to a room (no surcharge if you're lucky enough to get a double); a bed is US$12 (US$14 in summer), and there's a US$10 fee for the visa invitation. From Finland Station (metro Ploshchad Lenina) make a left, walk to Mikhaylova ulitsa, turn right, cross the street; the entrance to the yard is on the left (you'll see the big red-brick prison wall), the entrance in the south-west corner of the courtyard. The code for the front door is 1648, and the hostel's on the 3rd floor.

The small, old *Hotel Druzhba* (☎ 234 18 44) at Chapygina ulitsa 4 (see the Kirovsky Islands map), at the foot of the city's TV antenna, would be a great place with a great location, but they say that they don't take foreigners, and thank God: the lobby is patrolled by Kalashnikov-carrying guards and management is cold but polite. If they were to let you stay, the price would be US$17/20. It's a pleasant 10-minute walk or a quick bus ride down Kamennoostrovsky prospekt (Kirovsky prospekt) to metro Petrogradskaya.

If there is a room to spare at the *Dvorets Molodyozhy* (Palace of Youth (☎ 234 32 78) at ulitsa Professora Popova 47 (index 197022), it's only because it hasn't yet been rented out by some fly-by-night company as office space. It's in a very quiet location (see the Kirovsky Islands map), but bus No 25 to Nevsky prospekt doesn't come by often, and it's a 25-minute walk to metro Petrogradskaya. It's big and Soviet-modern outside, plain inside. If you can get in, it has singles for US$13.50 and doubles for US$30 to US$50 not including breakfast (which might be a good thing; breakfast consists of a bowl of glop). Double and triple rooms have attached showers (some baths). There is one pleasant guests-only restaurant without music, and a forlorn gril-bar.

The following three hotels are on the main St Petersburg map.

On the mainland, north of Petrovsky Island, is the *Vyborgskaya* (☎ 246 91 41, 246 23 19) at Torzhkovskaya ulitsa 3 (index 197342). Its three buildings have singles/doubles/suites from US$14/24/50, some with attached bath, some with communal bath. There are two restaurants, both with bands, a bufet and a cheap sauna that fits three. Nearby metro Chyornaya Rechka makes it convenient to get to the centre.

The *Hotel Sputnik* (☎ 552 56 32) at prospekt Morisa Toreza 34 (index 194021), is in a quiet neighbourhood of apartment blocks, a 10-minute walk (or a short bus ride) north-west from Ploshchad Muzhestva metro. Foreigners get singles or doubles with attached bath, a restaurant with live music, and three bufety. It's not a bad place, though it's getting pricey. Singles are US$30 to US$40, while doubles are US$40 to US$50.

The crumbling *Hotel Karelia* (☎ 226 35 15/19) at ulitsa Tukhachevskogo 27/2 (index 195253) is a dump for the money and worth avoiding. Plain, quiet rooms with attached showers are US$26/38.50 the first night, US$20.50/31 each additional night. The staff is pretty slack and the location lousy, several km from the centre. It's a dreary 25-minute ride by trolleybus No 3 or 19 to metro Ploshchad Lenina.

South & East of the City Centre

The *Summer Hostel* (☎ 252 75 63; fax 252 40 19), the newest entry to the hostel scene, is not exactly centrally located (it's about a 10-minute metro ride from ploshchad Vosstania), but it's the cheapest hostel bed in town at

NICK SELBY

Narva Arch, commemorating Russia's victories in battle

US$7 per person (US$8 per person in the renovated wing) including tax and breakfast, and it's a nice place at twice the price.

Part of the state-run Industrial Teachers' College, the hostel employs English-language students as staff to keep costs down. There are two wings, both on the 3rd floor. The renovated wing has a much nicer common area (with a television and a pool table) and kitchen (three refrigerators and four hot plates) though both wings are clean and the rooms perfectly adequate – as adequate as in hotels costing 10 times as much! There are two very good Western supermarkets very nearby (see the Self-Catering section of the Places to Eat chapter).

The building also has a sauna, health club and hair-dresser, all available (at extra fees of about US$1 to US$3) to guests.

It's at ulitsa Baltiyskaya 26 (see the main St Petersburg map); from metro Narvskaya walk left (south), down prospekt Stachek away from the Narva Arch to ulitsa Baltiyskaya, where you turn left. The hostel is 300 metres ahead on the left hand side. As you enter, fight past the babushka/door guards, turn left down the hallway, right into the stairwell and up to the 3rd floor.

The hostel is a member of the Russian Youth Hostel Association, so reservations may be made through the HI International Booking Network (IBN), the RYHA, the RYHT office in Redondo Beach, California (see HI St Petersburg Hostel earlier in this chapter), or directly with the hostel.

The following three hotels are on the main St Petersburg map.

The dumpy but cheerful *Kievskaya Hotel* (☎ 166 04 56) is at Dnepropetrovskaya ulitsa 49 (index 192202), and the *Hotel Zarya* (☎ 166 83 98) a block away at Kurskaya ulitsa 40. Both are city-run under a single management, and both charge a reasonable US$18/28. The Kievskaya has attached showers, the Zarya baths. Each has a bufet and a plain guests-only restaurant without music. They're out in a boring neighbourhood on the Obvodny Canal, though transport is easy. Bus No 25 from the local bus terminal next door is a mini-tour to Gostiny Dvor metro, Nevsky prospekt and Petrograd Side. Between nearby Ligovsky prospekt and metro Ploshchad Vosstania, take anything except bus No 14; the nearest stop is Obvodny Canal.

Far south at ulitsa Gastello 17 (index 196135), staff members at the last-resort, down-at-heel *Hotel Mir* (☎ 118 51 66) spend most of their time on the phone. Half the rooms have attached toilets and showers, half don't. Avoid it, but if you fail, the closest metro is Moskovskaya,

or take bus No 16 from Park Pobedy metro. Rooms are
US$24/33.

Outskirts

Unless you're driving from Finland and are so tired you
can't possibly go a km further, skip the *Motel-Camping
Olgino* (☎ 238 35 50), about 18 km north-west of the
centre at Primorskoe shosse 59 (index 197229). It's far
away, inconvenient for public transport, and is not a
completely safe part of town. Breakfast may run out
before you get it and the only place for dinner has
unwilling waiters and a desperately loud band. At least
you can walk through the pine woods to the Baltic shore
to clear your head.

A taxi to the city (they know you need to get there)
will be at least US$10. By public transport count on at
least 1½ hours. The nearest metro is Chyornaya Rechka,
about nine km away by country bus No 411 or 416
(US$0.50) or city bus No 110. From the metro station,
walk north across the park and over the road to the bus
stop. The last bus at night leaves here at about 10.45 pm.
At Olgino, the stop is about 400 metres towards St
Petersburg from the motel entrance. Oh, yeah, doubles
are US$15.

PLACES TO STAY – MIDDLE

City Centre

The *Hotel Moskva* (☎ 274 30 01, 274 20 51) is, like the Hotel
St Petersburg, a big three-star place not far from the
centre. It's at ploshchad Alexandra Nevskogo 2 (index
143317), just opposite the Alexandr Nevsky Monastery,
at the end of Nevsky prospekt, but it comes second to
the St Petersburg in everything except access (Ploshchad
Alexandra Nevskogo metro is right under the hotel).
Service is slacker, the lobby dimmer, rooms smaller
(though comfortable and clean) and the feeling more
institutional. For what you get, the rack rate of US$67/82
(it accepts Visa, MasterCard, Eurocard and American
Express) is a bit steep, but a lot of package tours use the
Moskva, and then the price drops considerably. Try for
a room at the back where it's quiet.

Downstairs in the lobby, the Neva Star, formerly a
hard-currency shop, is a welcome feature. The restaurants and caf,s are so-so, and there's an all-you-can-eat
buffet (see the Places to Eat chapter).

The big *Hotel Helen-Sovietskaya* (☎ 259 25 52) at
Lermontovsky prospekt 43 (index 198106) is only three

km south-west of the Hermitage, along the Fontanka River, but is poorly served by public transport. The hotel is a Finnish-Russian joint venture. Rooms are about three-star standard, and come with TV, telephone and bath; service is decent, and there is a big shop, an almost-real and not-very-expensive Bierstube, three restaurants and three cafés. Singles/doubles cost US$66/102, and it accepts Visa, MasterCard and Eurocard.

The nearest metro is Baltiyskaya, 750 metres south, but if you're already paying the price, you won't mind getting a US$3 taxi ride from the centre. Trolleybus Nos 3 and 8 follow Zagorodny prospekt to Nevsky prospekt; bus No 49 and tram No 1 go to the Mariinsky Theatre en route to ploshchad Truda. Reservations can also be made through its joint-venture partner, Arctia Hotels in Helsinki (☎ (358 0) 694 80 22).

Vyborg Side

The big three-star *Hotel St Petersburg* (☎ 542 90 31, 542 95 60) has standard post-Intourist accommodation and facilities, with clean but dull rooms. It's opposite the Cruiser Aurora at Vyborgskaya naberezhnaya 5/2 (index 194300), which gives the front rooms great views over the Neva towards the Hermitage but also traffic noise if you open the windows. Eating facilities are good, the service bureau big but erratic in attitude. At US$75/95, it's not a bad deal, though the staff is still struggling to crawl out from under the rock of Intourist training (*'Get stuf ... er ... May I help you?'*). It has a good restaurant, a beer hall and even a concert hall downstairs. It takes Visa, MasterCard, Eurocard and American Express.

The place just about burned down in 1991 after a Russian-made television set popped its cork and torched a couple of floors, but it's been renovated back to standards. The extension may some day be finished.

On the down side, public transport is mediocre for a place so close to the centre. It's a 15-minute walk to the nearest metro, Ploshchad Lenina; and you may wait 20 minutes on Finlyandsky prospect behind the hotel for the westbound tram No 6 or 63 to take you across the Sampsonevsky Bridge over to metro Gorkovskaya. Tram No 63 continues to the Strelka. There are also buses and trams from ploshchad Lenina.

The *Hotel Okhtinskaya* (☎ 227 44 38), across the Neva from the Smolny Cathedral, is an under-publicised French-Russian joint venture that has been made absolutely inconvenient due to the closing of the Bolshoy Okhtinsky Bridge that connected it to the eastern half of the centre at the Smolny. The bridge is scheduled to reopen in 1997. The Okhtinskaya, at ulitsa Okhtinskaya 4 (it's really on Sverdlovskaya naberezhnaya, about 200 metres south of the Nevsky Melody restaurant) is a fine business-class hotel, with very clean and modern rooms affording river views (though the views aren't exactly of St Petersburg's finest sections).

What's good about it is the staff, the dining rooms and the saunas. What's bad is its location, and due to that, the US$88/90 seems a bit out of line.

Vasilevsky Island

The *Hotel Gavan* (☎ 356 85 04), Sredny prospekt 88 (see the main St Petersburg map), is reasonably modern inside, with two restaurants (one with live music), two bufety and a bar. Rooms – mostly doubles with attached bath – are old and plain but clean. Aside from a small park the neighbourhood is featureless. From the hotel, bus No 30 goes to the Hermitage and outer Nevsky prospekt; tram No 63 goes to the Hermitage and the Strelka.

South & East of the City Centre

The expensive *Hotel Deson-Ladoga* (☎ 528 56 93), prospekt Shaumyana 26 (see the main St Petersburg map), is a dreary block in a sea of dreary blocks, across the Neva from the Alexandr Nevsky Monastery. Single and double rooms have attached showers (US$78/104), and there's a restaurant with live music. It's one block east of metro Novocherkasskaya (take exit stairs No 8). The only bright spot in the neighbourhood is the Shvabsky Domik restaurant by the metro.

The Best Western-managed *Hotel Neptune* (☎ 315 48 51) is in a pretty odd location, but its rooms are nice and clean and not outrageous at US$80 to US$100. It's at naberezhnaya Obvodny Kanala 93A, about a five-minute walk from Bus Station No 2, and 10 minutes from Bus Station No 1 and Warsaw and Baltic railway stations.

PLACES TO STAY – TOP END

City Centre

St Petersburg's luxury hotels are now truly luxurious. The appearance of foreign-owned and run hotels has resulted in a fundamental improvement in service levels in the city. The luxury hotels all offer heaps of amenities, which include at the very least a health club, satellite television, telephone, business centres, shops, newsstands, drinkable coffee, and a concierge desk to take the hassle out of buying tickets (this last, to be sure, at a premium price).

All the top-end hotels are in the centre, and all accept major credit cards and offer several categories of rooms.

Top of the Russian-owned line and most inexpensive in the luxury category is the *Hotel Astoria* (☎ 210 57 57; fax 315 96 68; telex 121213 ASTOR SU), ulitsa Bolshaya Morskaya (ulitsa Gertsena) 39 (index 190000), right in front of St Isaac's Cathedral. It too has been renovated; the original Astoria appears in its Art-Nouveau glory, and period furniture that wasn't stolen, looted or damaged can be seen in some of the more expensive rooms.

The hotel is in two sections, new and old (the old wing flanks the corner of ulitsa Bolshaya Morskaya (ulitsa Gertsena), and you'll have to walk outside to get to either from the other. The entrance is on Voznesensky prospekt. The old wing's grand rooms and suites are large and luxurious, while the new wing's rooms are large and comfortable.

Give the hotel's restaurants a big swerve; the lobby bar is actually quite nice for business drinks, and there's a nice little café on the 3rd floor and in the lobby of the old wing. Service is desperately fighting its Intourist upbringing (with a good amount of success) – it's clearly the best of the non-joint-venture hotels. Singles are US$170 to US$220, doubles US$210 to US$300, two-room suites US$370 to US$400, and three-room apartments (these are *nice*) US$600.

The *Nevskij Palace Hotel* (☎ 275 20 01; telex 121279 herms su), run by the Austrian Marco Polo Hotels & Resorts chain, is a fantabulously renovated place, with about as much luxury as one can stand. All rooms are what you'd expect from any Austrian luxury hotel, and their lobby is a great place to hang out on rainy days; it's a gold and marble multi-level atrium, with chi-chi shops, a Bierstube, and a general feeling of opulence. The hotel offers full conference facilities.

The hotel's restaurants are perhaps the best in town (see the Places to Eat chapter), and the service is excellent all around – if it's not, grab a manager and they'll set it right immediately (as they did when a slightly uppity reception desk clerk wouldn't give us an envelope!). The concierge service is good. Singles are US$280, doubles US$334, a small suite of two rooms US$365, a regular suite US$456, and a presidential suite US$851 (one bedroom) or US$1155 (two bedrooms); prices include breakfast and VAT. Reservations can be made directly with the hotel, through Steigenberger Reservations System agents, or by contacting Marco Polo International in

Vienna (☎ (43 1) 1213 31200). The hotel's address is Nevsky prospekt 57, and the nearest metro is Mayakovskaya, 200 metres east.

The *Grand Hotel Europe* (☎ 119 60 00; fax 119 60 01; telex 64 121073) – the *Yevropeyskaya* in Soviet times – is perhaps the finest property in town if you go by location and architecture. It's certainly the most expensive.

A joint venture between Reso Hotels, SIAB construction and the City of St Petersburg (totally irresponsible local scuttlebutt says that the partners squabble and continually threaten to back out), the original and breathtaking Art-Nouveau interiors, along with a Baroque façade designed by Rossi, have been completely restored to their turn-of-the-century glory.

Restaurant Europe's ceiling has got to be seen, even if that's the only reason you set foot in the hotel. The vaulted affair is covered with phenomenally beautiful and intricate stained glass, perhaps as a foil to keep your eyes off the prices, which are stellar. The atrium coffee bar is pleasant; the lobby bar would be nice if they had some higher bar stools and some lower prices. The hotel has a total of four restaurants, a bar, a caviar bar, a 'nightclub' and an atrium café.

Rooms are comfortable, but a bit smaller than you'd think, and service is about as good as you get in Russia. The address is Mikhailovskaya ulitsa 1/7 (postal code 191073). Singles are US$295 to US$335, doubles US$335 to US$375, belle chambre or terrace singles/doubles US$375/415, penthouses US$415 to US$530, two-room suites US$530 to US$710, an executive suite US$850, and 'Lidvall' or 'Rossi' suites US$975. These prices, by the way, do *not* include breakfast (which is only another US$20!) but do include VAT. In case you don't have your own limousine, Nevsky Prospekt metro is around the corner.

Inner Petrograd Side

On the corner of Kamennoostrovsky prospekt (Kirovsky prospekt) and the Karpovka River (see the Inner Petrograd Side map) sits a piece of real estate that will some day be a top-end hotel. See the Things to See & Do chapter for a brief description of this heretofore doomed property.

Vasilevsky Island

The *Hotelship Peterhof* (☎ 213 63 21), moored off naberezhnaya Makarova (see the Central St Petersburg map), just north of the Tuchkov Bridge, is a Swiss-managed, Russian-staffed hotel-ship that certainly has staying power. Billing itself as 'A Little Slice of Switzerland in St Petersburg', it's kind of a fun place, not too inconveniently located from the centre. It's about five blocks from metro Vasileostrovskaya, which is one stop from the Gostiny Dvor/Nevsky Prospekt metro stations.

The rooms aren't huge – in fact, they're cabins – but they're certainly clean and the ship has a good restaurant downstairs (it does 'theme nights', and its Italian food is darn good) and a full bar and sort of disco-ette upstairs. The staff is very courteous and helpful. Whether the good service justifies a US$115/190 price tag is a toss-up, but they certainly try. It takes Visa, MasterCard and Eurocard.

The *Pribaltiyskaya Hotel* (☎ 356 41 35, 356 45 63) is an Intourist-built behemoth on the Gulf of Finland (see the main St Petersburg map), at ulitsa Korablestroyteley (Shipbuilders' St) 14 (index 199226). It's very popular with package-tour groups (perhaps you caught its movie debut, in *The Russia House*) and has fair service and big, clean rooms (no singles) with stunning views of the Gulf of Finland if you're lucky (ask). The rack rate of US$155 for a double is laughable; no-one ever pays that, and it can be a very economical place to stay if you're here on a package. It accepts MasterCard, Eurocard and American Express.

The good news is that perhaps because it's a bit inconvenient, it has a lot of extras – like a bowling alley, a Baltic Star shop (formerly a hard-currency shop), a good business and conference centre, moneychangers and an in-house (though pricey) taxi service.

The huge service bureau, though, appears to be staffed by female androids, and oh yeah, they charge you extra for CNN. Its four restaurants all serve food, and their maîtres d' possess hearts of stone. But it's blessed with a good three-meals-a-day Swedish table, a bufet on almost every floor, and close proximity to the Venezia Italian restaurant and a pizzeria. If you're lucky, you can wash your clothes in the washer-dryer of one of the US Consulate employees who live in the diplomat apartment building diagonally across the street. Three bars keep the folks sloshed. Flanking the hotel on both sides is St Petersburg's biggest beryozka.

It's far away on the Gulf of Finland, at the windy (whoo!) end of Vasilevsky Island, half an hour from the city centre. From Nevsky prospekt, the fastest way is to metro Primorskaya, and then a bus No 41 to the hotel.

South of the City Centre

The main advantage of Intourist's modern *Hotel Pulkovskaya* (☎ 264 51 22), eight km south of the centre (see the St Petersburg map) at ploshchad Pobedy 1 (index 196143), is its proximity to the airport, 15 minutes away by bus No 13, which stops right in front of the hotel. A taxi ride costs US$3 (don't take the in-house taxi service – walk a little north, away from the hotel, and flag one down on Moskovsky prospekt to avoid paying a 'tourist price'). No doubt the four-star rates are to pay for all those Finnish lighting fixtures, but the rooms (all with baths) are comfortable and clean, at US$120/140, and service is good.

Two cavernous restaurants with floor shows are no good for a quiet meal, though the food isn't bad. There's a good lobby bar with cheap Heineken beer. The hotel is about 750 metres south of metro Moskovskaya by the Defenders of Leningrad Monument; bus Nos 3 and 39-Э (not 39) go to ulitsa Bolshaya Morskaya (ulitsa Gertsena) via Nevsky prospekt.

Places to Eat

Television news images of bread queues, meat shortages and empty shelves are as dated as junk bonds, Duran Duran, power ties and Charles and Diana.

Restaurants in St Petersburg are civilised and plentiful. The Soviet way of doing things (where a thug standing in a restaurant doorway asks a couple dressed for dinner, 'what do *you* want?!?') has mostly gone the way of the five-year plan. You won't have to make reservations except in very popular places, and if you're told there are no seats, there probably aren't any.

Undeniably, an increase in price has come with the increase in quality; you can still eat cheaply at *stolovayi*, unpretentious cafés and Russian snack bars, but if you patronise the chic new eateries, bistros or cafés you'll pay near Western prices and the shock value of a bill from some of the city's finer restaurants is as worthy of a *'Mon Dieu!'* as any eatery that Paris has to offer. But with all of this, the wide range of choice can only be good news. Whatever you fancy – from Uzbek to Arabian, Chinese to Italian, Georgian to fast food, Western European to good ol' Russian home cooking – it's here and in abundance.

FOOD

Breakfast

Breakfast or *zavtrak* (*'ZAHF-truk'*) in hotels can range from a large help-yourself buffet spread to bread, butter, jam, tea and a boiled egg (or, worse, a pair of cold meatballs). Items you might find include:

Блины
  (*'blee-NIH'*) – *bliny* or leavened buckwheat pancakes; as блинчики, *blinchiki*, they're rolled around meat or cheese and browned
Каша
  kasha or Russian-style buckwheat porridge
Сырники
  (*'SEER-ni-ki'*) – fritters of cottage cheese, flour and milk
Творог
  (*'tva-ROK'*) – cottage cheese
Яйцо
  (*'yai-TSOH'*) – egg

всмятку
    ('FSMYAT-ku') – soft-boiled
крутое
    ('kru-TOY-eh') – hard-boiled
омлет
    ('ahm-LYET') – omelette
яичница
    ('yuh-EECH-nit-suh') – fried
кефир
    ('kyi-FEER') – yoghurt-like sour milk, served as a
    drink

Bliny, kasha and syrniki can be delicious if topped with some combination of jam, sugar and the universal Russian condiment, сметана *('smi-TA-nuh')*.

Lunch & Dinner

Russians often like a fairly heavy early-afternoon meal, *obed ('ah-BYET')*, and a lighter evening meal, *uzhin ('OO-zhin')*, but a night-out supper can go on and on.

Meals (and menus) are divided into courses:

Закуски
    zakuski or appetisers, often grouped into холодные
    закуски (cold zakuski) and горячие закуски (hot
    zakuski)
Первые блюда
    first courses, usually soups
Вторые блюда
    second courses or 'main' dishes, also called
    горячие блюда (hot courses)
Сладкие блюда
    sweet courses or desserts
Мясные
    meat
Рыбные
    fish
Из птицы
    poultry
Овощные
    vegetable

Appetisers The fancier appetisers rival main courses for price. Of course try the caviar, икра *('ee-KRA')*. The best is black (sturgeon) caviar, *ikra chyornaya*, also called *zernistaya*. Much cheaper and saltier is red (salmon) caviar, *ikra krasnaya*, also called *ketovaya*. Russians spread it on buttered toast or bliny and wash it down with a slug of ice-cold vodka. There's also ersatz caviar made entirely from aubergine or other vegetables.

A few other zakuski worth trying include:

Блины со сметаной
('blee-NIH sa-smi-TA-noy') – pancakes with sour cream
Грибы в сметане
('gree-BIH fsmi-TA-nyeh') or жульен из грибов ('zhool-YEN eez gree-BOF') – mushrooms baked in sour cream, obscenely good
Рыба солёная
('RIH-buh sahl-YO-nuh-yuh') – salted fish
Сёмга копчёная
('SYOM-guh kahp-CHO-nuh-yuh') – smoked salmon

Salad, салат ('suh-LAHT'), is an appetiser too. Most likely you will be offered one with tomatoes, из помидоров ('eez pa-mi-DOR-uf'), or cucumbers, из огурцов ('eez a-goort-SOF'), or the ubiquitous салат столичный ('suh-LAHT sta-LEECH-ni'), comprised of vegetable and beef bits, potato and egg in sour cream and mayonnaise.

Soup Rich soups may be the pinnacle of Slavic cooking. There are dozens of varieties, often served with a dollop of sour cream. Most are made from meat stock. The Russian word sounds the same, суп.

Among the most common soups are:

Борщ
('borshch') – beetroot soup with vegetables and meat
Лапша
('LAHP-shuh') – chicken noodle soup
Окрошка
('a-KROHSH-kuh') – cold or hot soup made from cucumbers, sour cream, potatoes, egg, meat and kvas (a beer-like drink)
Рассольник
('rah-SOL-nik') – soup of marinated cucumber and kidney
Солянка
('sahl-YAHNK-uh') – thick meat or fish soup with salted cucumbers and other vegetables
Уха
('OO-khuh') – fish soup with potatoes and vegetables
Харчо
('khar-CHOH') – garlicky mutton soup, Caucasian-style

Щи
  ('shchi') – cabbage or sauerkraut soup (many varieties)

Poultry & Meat Poultry is птица *('PTEET-suh')* – usually chicken, курица *('KOO-rit-suh')* or цыплёнок *('tsi-PLYOH-nuk')*. Meat is мясо *('MYA-suh')*; in particular:

Говядина
('gav-YA-di-nuh') – beef
Свинина
('sfi-NEE-nuh') – pork

Cooking Styles Words you might spot on the menu are:

Варёный
  ('var-YOH-ni') – boiled
Жареный
  ('ZHAR-ih-ni') – roasted, baked or fried
Отварной
  ('aht-var-NOY') – poached or boiled
Печёный
  ('pi-CHOH-ni') – baked
Фри
  ('free') – fried

Poultry & Meat Dishes The list of possible dishes (and possible names) is huge, but following are some common ones:

Антрекот
  ('ahn-tri-KOHT') – entrecôte, boned sirloin steak
Бефстроганов
  ('byef-STRO-guh-nof') – beef stroganoff, beef slices in a rich sauce
Бифштекс
  ('bif-SHTEKS') – 'steak', usually a glorified hamburger filling
Голубцы
  ('ga-loop-TSIH') – golubtsy, cabbage rolls stuffed with meat
Жаркое
  ('zhar-KOY-eh') – meat or poultry stewed in a clay pot; the commonest seems to be жаркое по-домашнему *('... pa-da-MAHSH-ni-mu')*, 'home-style', with mushrooms, potatoes and vegetables

Котлета
('kaht-LYET-uh') – usually a croquette of ground
meat; котлета по-пожарски ('... pa-pa-ZHAR-ski') is
minced chicken
Котлета по-киевски
('kaht-LYET-uh pa-KEE-iv-ski') – chicken Kiev, fried
boneless chicken breast stuffed with butter (watch
out, it squirts!)
Осетрина отварная
('a-si-TREE-nuh aht-VAR-nuh-yuh') – poached sturgeon
Осетрина с грибами
('a-si-TREE-nuh zgree-BUH-mi') – sturgeon with
mushrooms
Пельмени
('pil-MYEN-i') – *pelmeni* or Siberian-style meat
dumplings
Плов
plov or pilaf, rice with mutton bits, from Central Asia
Цыплёнок табака
('tsi-PLYOH-nuk tuh-buh-KAH') – chicken tabaka,
grilled chicken Caucasian-style
Шашлык
shashlyk, skewered and grilled mutton or other
meat, adapted from Central Asia and Transcaucasia

Fish Fish is рыба ('RIH-buh'). Some common varieties
are:

Омуль
('OH-mool') – omul, like salmon, from Lake Baikal
Осётр
('a-SYOTR'), осетрина ('a-si-TREE-nuh') or севрюга
('siv-RYU-guh') – sturgeon
Сёмга
('SYOM-guh') – salmon
Судак
('su-DAHK') – pike perch
Форель
('far-YEL') – trout

Vegetables Vegetables are овощи ('OH-va-shchi');
greens are зелень ('ZYEH-lin'). Any vegetable garnish
is гарниры ('gar-NEE-ri'). Common vegetables include:

Горох
('ga-ROKH') – peas
Капуста
('kuh-POOS-tuh') – cabbage

Картошка
  ('kar-TOSH-kuh'), картофель*('kar-TOF-il')* – potato
Морковь
  ('mar-KOF') – carrots
Огурец
  ('a-gur-YETS') – cucumber
Помидор
  ('pa-mi-DOR') – tomato

Fruit Fruits are фрукты *('FROOK-ti')*. In the market (or if you're lucky, in a restaurant) you might find:

Абрикос
  ('uh-bri-KOS') – apricot
Арбуз
  ('ar-BOOS') – watermelon
Виноград
  ('vi-na-GRAHT') – grapes
Груша
  ('GROO-shuh') – pear
Дыня
  ('DIN-yuh') – melon
Яблоко
  ('YA-bla-ka') – apple

Other Foods On every table are stacks of bread, Хлеб, *('khlep')*. Best is Russian 'black' bread, a vitamin-rich sour rye.
  Russians are mad about wild mushrooms, грибы *('gree-BIH')*; in late summer and early autumn they troop into the woods with their buckets. Other items:

Рис
  ('rees') – rice
Сыр
  ('seer') – cheese
Масло
  ('MAHS-la') – butter
Перец
  ('PYER-its') – pepper
Сахар
  ('SA-khar') – sugar
Сметана
  ('smi-TA-nuh') – sour cream
Соль
  ('sol') – salt

Desserts Perhaps most Russians are exhausted or drunk by dessert time, since this is the least imaginative course. Most likely you'll get ice cream, мороженое ('ma-ROH-zhi-nah-yuh'). Other possibilities are:

Блинчики
('BLEEN-chi-ki') – pancakes with jam or other sweet filling
Кисель
('ki-SEL') – fruit jelly (jell-o to Yanks)
Компот
('kahm-POHT') – fruit in syrup (probably from a tin)
Оладьи
('a-LAH-dyi') – fritters topped with syrup
Пирожное
('pi-ROZH-na-yuh') – pastries

Vegetarian Meals

St Petersburg can be rough on a vegetarian – though some private restaurants have caught on with salad bars and vegie dishes. The new wave of chi-chi sandwich shops, like Bon Jour and Minutka (formerly Subway) have begun offering all-vegie sandwiches, so in a pinch, head for one of these.

Main dishes are heavy on meat and poultry, vegetables are boiled to death and even the good vegetable and fish soups are usually made from meat stock.

If you're vegetarian, say so, early and often. You'll see a lot of tomato and cucumber salads, and will develop an eagle eye for the rare good fish and dairy dishes. Zakuski include quite a lot of meatless things like eggs, salted fish and mushrooms. If you spot обоши свежие, fresh (raw) vegetables on the menu, you're in luck!

Menus often have a category like овощные, молочные, яичные, мучные блюда (vegetable, milk, egg and flour dishes) – but don't get your hopes up. You may have to just run down the names of things you can eat, rather than relying on the waiter to think of something.

By the way, potatoes (kartoshka, kartofel) aren't filed under 'vegetable' in the Russian mind, so you must name them separately: 'potatoes and vegetables'.

I'm a vegetarian. (f)
  ya vi-gi-ta-ri-AHN-ka   Я вегетарианка.
I'm a vegetarian. (m)
  ya vi-gi-ta-ri-AHN-yets   Я вегетарианец.
I cannot eat meat.
  ya ni yem myis-NOH-va   Я не ем мясного.
without meat
  bis MYA-suh   без мяса

only vegetables
  TOL-ka OH-va-shchi   только овощи

Some Other Food-Related Language

Many restaurants in town will have menus in English, though many others don't.

waiter, waitress	
ah-fit-si-AHNT ,	официант,
ah-fit-si-AHNT-kuh	официантка
menu	
min-YU	меню
hot	
gar-YA-chi	горячий
cold	
kha-LOHD-ni	олодный
another	
yee-SHCHO	ещё
May we order?	
MOZH-na zuh-kuh-	
ZAHT?	Можно заказать?
Please bring ...	
pri-nyeh-SEE-tyeh,	Принесите,
pa-ZHAHL-stuh ...	пожалуйста ...
That's all.	
vsyo	Всё.
Bon appetit!	
pri-AHT-ni ah-pih-TEET!	Приятного аппетита!

When you're done you'll have to chase up the bill, счёт ('*shchyot*'). If there's a service charge, noted on the menu by the words за обслуживание (for service), there's no need to tip further unless the service has been exceptional (see the Money section of the Facts for the Visitor chapter).

DRINKS

'Drinking is the joy of the Rus. We cannot live without it.' With these words Vladimir of Kiev, the father of the Russian state, is said to have rejected abstinent Islam on his people's behalf in the 10th century. And who wouldn't want to bend their minds now and then in those long, cold, dark winters? Russians sometimes drink vodka in moderation, but more often it's tipped down in swift shots, with a beer, with the aim of getting legless.

The *average* Russian drinks more than 12 litres of pure alcohol a year – equivalent to over a bottle of vodka a week – and men drink much more than women.

There are dozens of pubs and bars in town, and more opening all the time. If it's vodka that's being drunk, they'll want a man to down the shot – neat of course – in one (women are usually excused). This can be fun to start with as you toast international friendship etc, but vodka has a knack of creeping up on you from behind and if that happens just after you've started tucking into steak, chips and fried egg, the consequences can be appalling. A slice of heavily buttered bread before each shot, or a beer the morning after, are reckoned to be vodka antidotes.

Refusing a drink can be very difficult. Russians may continue insisting until they win you over, especially on some train rides. If you can't manage to stand quite firm, take it in small gulps with copious thanks, while saying how you'd love to indulge but have to be up early in the morning etc. And if you're really not in the mood, the only tested and true method of warding off all offers (as well as making them feel quite awful) is to say 'Ya alkogolik' ('alkogolichka' for women) – 'I'm an alcoholic'.

Alcohol

You can buy it everywhere. Kiosks, shops, bars, restaurants, you name it. Foreign brands as well as Russian are common. But be very suspicious of kiosk spirits. There's a lot of bad cheap stuff around that can make you ill, or worse. Only buy screw-top – never tin-top – bottles. Always check to see that the seal is not broken. Taste carefully any liquor you've bought at a kiosk to make sure it's really what it's supposed to be, and that it hasn't been diluted or tampered with. Err on the side of caution. People have been hospitalised after drinking tainted kiosk vodka - this is no joke.

In a restaurant you can order drinks by the bottle (which could be half a litre, three-quarters of a litre or one litre) or, for smaller quantities, by weight: 50 grams, equal to 50 ml, for one shot, maybe 200 grams in a small flask for a few shots.

Vodka Vodka is distilled from wheat, rye or occasionally potatoes. The word comes from *voda* (water), and means something like 'a wee drop'. Its flavour (if any) comes from what's added after distillation. Two common 'plain' vodkas are Stolichnaya, which is in fact slightly sweetened with sugar, and Moskovskaya, which has a touch of sodium bicarbonate. Tastier, more colourful and rarer are Zolotoe Koltso (Golden Ring), Pertsovka (pepper vodka), Starka (with apple and pear leaves), Limonnaya (lemon vodka), and Okhotnichya (Hunter's), which has about a dozen ingredients, including peppers, juniper berries, ginger and cloves. Zubrovka, one of God's gifts to mankind, is flavoured with bison grass but is unfortunately very hard to find outside Poland.

Sure enough, the fashion for Western products has extended even unto vodka. The more popular imports are Smirnoff (made in Connecticut, USA), Absolut (and all its varieties), Gorbachow, Rasputin and New Yorkskaya. An export-quality, orange-flavoured Stolichnaya may be available as well – swoop it, it's terrific.

Supermarket and liquor store prices range from around US$2.50 for a half-litre of Stolichnaya or Moskovskaya to US$18 for the most exotic ones. Average kiosk prices in 1995 were Russkaya US$1, Stolichnaya US$1.50 to US$3, Absolut Citron US$13.50, Absolut Kurant US$15, Absolut plain US$10.

Beer Ordinary Russian beer is hoppy. It's also not pasteurised, so after a couple of days those hops try to start a little hop farm of their own right in the bottle – the date on the bottle is the date of production, not the sell-by date. Beer's safe for about three days after its production.

Regular brands are generally named after the cities they come from – Moskovskoe, St Petersburgskoe, Zhigulevskoe (from Zhigulevsk on the Volga) – and a bottle of these is around US$0.25 to US$0.40 in shops or kiosks. But new joint-venture brewers are starting up all over the country, and bringing quality and taste up to Western norms. Probably the best of the brews is St Petersburg's Baltika, a fresh, slightly bitter Pilsner-type beer that's obscenely good, believe it or not, with a crushed clove of garlic added to it. Baltika is sold at kiosks and from wire baskets in front of metro stations, as well as in shops. There are several grades – you only want grades 3, 4 or 6. Another St Petersburg brewery, a joint venture, is Piterbir.

Champagne, Wine & Brandy Soviet champagne (it's still called this – isn't it interesting that two of the things that Russians hold most dear, passports and champagne, still say 'Soviet'?) comes very dry (*bryut*), dry (*sukhoe*), semidry (*polusukhoe*), semisweet (*polusladkoe*) and sweet (*sladkoe*). Anything above dry is sweet enough to turn your mouth inside out. A three-quarter-litre (750-

NICK SELBY

Beer stand: bring your own container

gram) bottle is about US$6 in a restaurant and US$5 in a
supermarket, kiosk or liquor store. Most other wine
comes from outside the former USSR (Eastern European
brands are the cheapest), though you can still find Georgian, Moldovan or Crimean wine.

Brandy is popular and it's all called *konyak*, though
local varieties certainly aren't Cognac. The best non-
Western konyak in Russia is Armenian (and simply
labelled Konyak), and Five Star is fine.

Kvas & Mead *Kvas* is fermented rye bread water,
dispensed on the street for a few kopecks a glass from
big wheeled tanks with 'kvas' printed on the side. It's
mildly alcoholic, tastes not unlike ginger beer, and is cool
and refreshing in summer.

Mead *(myod)*, brewed from honey, is a great winter
warmer. It crops up here and there.

Some Alcohol-Related Language

alcohol
   al-ka-GOHL   алкоголь
glass
   stuh-KAHN   стакан
bottle
   bu-TIL-kuh   бутылка

50 grams	*pit-dis-YAHT grahm*	пятьдесят грамм
200 grams	*DVYES-t i grahm*	двести грамм
750 grams (three-quarter litre)	*sim-SOT pit-dis-YAHT grahm*	семьсот пятьдесят грамм
litre	*LEE-tr*	литр
vodka	*VOHT-kuh*	водка
Soviet champagne	*sav-YET-ska-yuh sham-PAN-ska-yuh*	Советское шампанское
very dry	*brYUT*	брют
dry	*soo-kha-YEH*	сухое
semidry	*pah-loo-soo-kha-YEH*	полусухое
semisweet	*pah-loo-slat-kah-YEH*	полусладкое
sweet	*SLAT-kah-yeh*	сладкое
wine	*vi-NOH*	вино
white wine	*BYEL-ah-yuh vi-NOH*	белое вино
red wine	*KRAHS-na-yuh vi-NOH*	красное вино
dry (wine)	*soo-KHOY*	сухой
sweet (wine)	*SLAT-ky*	сладкий
brandy	*ka-NYAK*	коньяк
beer	*PEE-vah*	пиво
beer bar	*piv-NOY bar*	пивной бар
kvas	*kvahs*	квас
mead	*myoht*	мёд
takeaway	*sa-BOY*	с собой
To your health!	*za VA-sheh zda-ROH-vyeh!*	За ваше здоровье

Nonalcoholic Drinks

Water & Mineral Water Stick to mineral water, which is ubiquitous and cheap (see the Health section in the Facts for the Visitor chapter for more on tap water, which you shouldn't drink or get involved with at all).

Tea & Coffee The traditional Russian tea-making method is to brew an extremely strong pot, pour small shots of it into glasses and fill the glasses with hot water from the *samovar*, an urn with an inner tube filled with hot charcoal. The pot is kept warm on top of the samovar. Modern samovars have electric elements, like a kettle, instead of the charcoal tube. Putting jam, instead of sugar, in tea is quite common.

Coffee comes in small cups and is supposed to be thick, but quality – and sometimes supplies – are erratic. Almost any café, restaurant or bufet, and some bakery shops, will offer tea or coffee or both.

If you're a serious coffee or tea drinker, carry a thermos, mug, your own tea bags and/or coffee, and powdered milk and sugar if you use them. It's easy to get the thermos filled with boiling water by your *dezhurnaya* (floor lady) or at a hotel bufet.

Sok, Napitok & Limonad *Sok* is juice, of a kind, usually sweetened, flavoured and heavily diluted. It never resembles the original fruit, but a jugful with a meal often goes down a treat. *Napitok* means beverage but in practice it's often a fancy sok, maybe with some real fruit thrown in. *Limonad* is a fizzy drink apparently made from industrial waste and tasting like mouthwash.

Other Jugs of *kefir*, liquid yoghurt, are served as a breakfast drink. Milk is common and sold cheaply in dairy shops *(molochnaya)* – but often not pasteurised. Pepsi, Coke and their relatives are widely available.

Some Language for Nonalcoholic Drinks

water
  va-DAH   вода
boiled water
  ki-pya-TOHK   кипяток
mineral water
  mi-ni-RAL-nuh-yuh
    va-DAH   минеральная вода

soda water
  ga-zi-ROH-va-nuh-yuh
    va-DAH
	газированная вода

coffee *KOF-yeh*	кофе
tea *chai*	чай
with sugar *s SAKH-ar-am*	с сахаром
with jam *s far-YEN-yim*	с вареньем
juice *sohk*	сок
apple juice *YAHB-luch-n y sohk*	яблочный сок
orange juice *ah-pil-SIN-ah-vy sohk*	апельсиновый сок
grape juice *vi-na-GRAD-ny sohk*	виноградный сок
beverage *na-PEET-ak*	напиток
lemonade *li-ma-NAHD*	лимонад

soft drink
  biz-al-ka-GOHL-ni nuh-
    PEE-tuk
	безалкогольный
	напиток

milk *ma-la-KOH*	молоко

SELF-CATERING

Self-catering is now not only possible but plausible. The city has seen an explosion in food shops, and Western-style supermarkets are popping up like weeds all over the place. Teeming with fresh meats, cheese, vegetables, tinned goods, frozen prepared foods (like pizza, some dinners and even fresh-frozen prawns) and usually booze, in many of these places you'd swear you'd been transported back home to a Safeway or Coles. Chain shops, like *Babylon*, *Kosmos* and *Holiday*, have many extended or 24-hour grocery shops in several areas of the city; there are several along Nevsky alone, and a good one for quick snacks at ploshchad Vosstania, just east of Moscow Station.

Food Shops & Supermarkets

The biggest supermarket in the centre is called – surprise, surprise – *Supermarket*, in the basement of Passazh shopping centre, open 9 am to 9 pm. Another good bet in the centre is the *Babylon* opposite the corner of Nevsky prospekt and ulitsa Mayakovskogo, which has a collection of tinned and packaged foods, Western soft drinks and a varying stock of other stuff, and accepts credit cards. The Frukti Conservi vegetable shop at the corner of Marata and Nevsky prospekt has a great many of vegies, Finnish drinking water, Western booze, and a Russian juice bar (about US$0.05 a glass).

Yeliseevsky Food Shop, on Nevsky prospekt opposite ploshchad Ostrovskogo, is Russia's most beautiful, if not most famous, food shop. A turn-of-the-century rich-people's food court, the place has now been mostly restored to its pre-Soviet Art-Nouveau splendour, with enormous stained-glass windows and chandeliers. Meat, chicken and fish are found through the right-hand entrance, while Western and high-end Russian packaged and bulk dry goods are to the left.

Lower on Nevsky prospekt, the *Antanta Market*, in a basement on ulitsa Malaya Konyushennaya 9, is a sprawling labyrinth of imported foods and enough varieties of booze to look like a US liquor store; prices are going northward, however. It's open Monday to Friday from noon to 10 pm and Saturday from noon to 8 pm.

Out at the Petrogradskaya side, *Babylon Super* has a terrific selection of exotic (for Russia) fresh vegies, like fresh ginger root and avocado, as well as frozen vegies and a French-inspired bakery section that makes wonderful breads and awesome pastries several times daily. It also has lots of wines and beers. It takes Visa, MasterCard, Eurocard and American Express, and if you'll be in town for long, you can set up a Babylon Super credit card. It's at Maly prospekt 54, and is open Monday to Saturday from 10 am to 9 pm and Sunday from noon to 8 pm. And while you're out there on the Petrograd Side, check out the florist (☎ 238 19 15) at Kamennoostrovsky prospekt (Kirovsky prospekt) 5. It sells flowers, plants and, oh yes, a full line of Mercedes Benz sedans. It's open daily 9 am to 7 pm.

The Kalinka Stockmann's, behind the Hotel St Petersburg at Finlandsky prospekt 1, is a smaller affair, with good Finnish milk supplies. It's a good place to buy decadent Western luxuries to cook up at the Holiday Hostel. It also sells some international newspapers and magazines.

And if you're in that Finnish-food mode, head for one of *Spar Market*'s two locations: Slavy prospekt 30 (way out in southern nowhere; take metro Moskovskaya then trolleybus No 27 or 29 east – it's just past the Kupichinsky department store), and at the much more central, but smaller, prospekt Stachek 1 (metro Narvskaya) location, at which there is also a small café doing very nice pastries and coffee for about US$1.50. If you're staying at the Summer Hostel, the prospekt Stachek location is ideal; if it hasn't got what you're after, try diagonally across the street towards the hostel on ulitsa Baltiyskaya, 30 metres past the corner of Stachek, where a *VIT St Petersburg* superette has fruit, vegies, frozen foods, beer, wine and other booze.

Bakeries

Even in the old days the standard Russian *bulochnaya* (bakery) turned out some terrific, rich, sour brown bread. There are bread shops in every neighbourhood (almost always marked by a sign that just says булочная, as well as speciality and joint-venture bakers. *Karavay Bakery*, just across from the City Children's Park (formerly Tauride Gardens), has sumptuous bread, cakes and buns; it's at Tavricheskaya ulitsa 33 (see the Smolny Region map) and is open from 8 am to 8 pm. *Nevsky 27*, across from the Grand Hotel Europe, is another joint-venture place doing exceptionally good bread; there are long queues before it closes for its lunch-time break. It's open from 8 am to 1 pm and from 2 to 7 pm. The *Bahlsen Bakery*, next to Bahlsen – Le Cafe at Nevsky 142, does good bread and cakes. It's open Monday to Saturday from 8 am to 8 pm.

Markets

With the advent of widespread supermarket and 24-hour store trading, St Petersburg's markets (*rynky*; singular *rynok*) no longer cause St Petersburgers to drop their jaws to pavement level and drool in envy, but

NICK SELBY

Yeliseevsky Food Shop

they're still fascinating places to visit and fabulous sources of fresh produce, meats and other food.

In buildings large enough to house small football fields, the markets are held daily, and food and produce from all over the former Soviet Union can be had, including exotic fruits and vegetables that you may never have seen before (and sometimes wish you never had!). Most of the markets also feature fresh meats, as in so fresh they're still in the process of being hacked off the carcass. Markets are also a good place to pick up honey and honey products (try before you buy – it's free), cottage cheese, heavy cream and sometimes even flowers.

Two of the liveliest and most central (and most expensive) are the *Kuznechny* on Kuznechny pereulok, two minutes walk from Vladimirskaya metro, and the *Maltsevsky* at ulitsa Nekrasova 52 (metro Ploshchad Vosstania). Some others are the *Sytny*, at Sytninskaya ploshchad 3/5 (metro Gorkovskaya, behind Alexandrovsky park and up towards Kafe Tbilisi); the scary *Torzhkovsky* at Torzhkovskaya ulitsa 20 (metro Chyornaya Rechka), noted as much for its selection of fine poultry as its gangland slayings; the *Krondatevsky* at Polyustrovsky prospekt 45 (metro Ploshchad Lenina, then tram No 6 or 19, bus No 100, 107, 136 or 137 or any trolleybus except No 8), with its terrific fur (as well as pet) market out back, where there are great hats; the *Moskovsky* at ulitsa Reshetnikova 12 (almost opposite Elektrosila metro); the *Sennoy* at Moskovsky prospekt 4 (Ploshchad Mira metro); and the more inexpensive *Vasileostrovsky* at Bolshoy prospekt 18 on Vasilevsky Island (Vasileostrovskaya metro).

RESTAURANTS

City Centre

1001 Nights (☎ 312 22 65) is an Uzbek place near the Hermitage that has good Central Asian food, a very nice atmosphere and, considering its prime location, very reasonable prices, with main courses averaging US$3.35 to US$4.75. Definitely try the manty, which are enormous spicy dumplings, for US$1.90, and the very tasty kebab garshochke at a steeper US$4.30. Service is slow, but that's because you're expected to relax and take awhile – tell the staff if you're in a hurry! There's belly dancing in the evenings. The restaurant's at Millionnaya ulitsa 21/6, downstairs. It's open from 11 to 1 am.

Nearby, at ulitsa Furmanova (which runs parallel to and on the west of the Fontanka), *Russky Bliny* does just those in a cosy setting for incredibly cheap prices –

US$1.10 for a minced chicken pancake is as high as things go. It's only open for lunch and an early dinner, Monday to Friday from 11 am to 6 pm.

The *Korean House* serves up what may be the best Korean food in Eastern Europe, and after some problems with the last location, it has resettled at Izmailovsky prospekt 2, near Tekhnologichesky Institut. There are signs in both English and Russian on the street, but the entrance itself is not very conspicuous – go through the building's entrance and on the right you'll see the Korean House sign. At its last location the food was awesome, with a decidedly heavy hand on the garlic and spices, and the staff was incredibly friendly. Specialities were Korean-style beef (marinated and cooked at the table), marinated carrots, and kim chi. They also did darn good cold and hot noodle soups and dishes for both vegetarians and carnivores. Main courses were priced from US$3 to US$5.

Another excellent food spot on the move is *Restaurant Shen Yan*, a (you guessed it) Chinese place at Rubinshteyna 12. The move was being planned at the time of writing, but they hadn't quite figured out where they were going; find out when you get here. The food was exquisite, plentiful and cheap, with sweet and sour pork (US$6.50), the interesting 'squirrel made out of fish' (US$7), and sumptuous roast vegetables (US$4.50). It closes for one month in winter when the staff heads home to China to see the family (see Nevsky Prospekt East map).

Metekhi (☎ 272 33 61) at Belinskogo ulitsa 3, near the Belinskogo Bridge, does Georgian specialities at reasonable prices. Main courses are priced from US$3 to US$6, starters from US$1 to US$4. It offers good vegie dishes and fine service. It's closest to metro Gostiny Dvor.

Tandoor (☎ 312 38 86) is *the* Indian place in town, with a full traditional Indian menu at about US$2.50 for starters and US$5 to US$9 per main meal and a limited wine list. The only drawback I found was a tendency to undercook chicken dishes – specify that you want yours well done. It has a number of vegetarian items on the menu, as well as a good selection of traditional Indian breads and desserts. If you like things spicy, insist on *spicy*. The restaurant is worth going to at least once, maybe more often. It's at Voznesensky prospekt 2, just off Isaakilevskaya ploshchad, and is open from noon to 11 pm.

Shanghai (☎ 314 31 38), a big, old Soviet-style eating palace, has surprisingly good food, though it's erratic – it's hard to predict which dish will be good on which day. It's generally a dodgy bet (one Austrian diner was overheard saying, '*Das Fleisch ist sehr gut, aber die Suppe ist fuü den Hund!'*). There's a casino upstairs. Why bother? The restaurant's at Sadovaya ulitsa 12/23, just around the corner from the Nevsky prospekt metro. Main courses are priced from US$4 to US$10, and it's open from noon to midnight.

Saigon's (☎ 315 87 72) Asian interior (complete with a bamboo bridge) belies its Russian menu; its steaks for US$7, chicken tabaka at US$4.75 and salmon for $6 are all fine. It's at ulitsa Plekhanova 33 and is open from noon to 10.30 pm.

St Petersburg's *Pizza Hut* (☎ 315 77 05), at naberezhnaya reki Moyki 71/76, does nine varieties of pizza (medium plain US$5.50, medium vegetarian US$7.50, medium super supreme US$11), sells beer, wine and cappuccino, and has a salad bar. It also delivers to a very limited area. It's a very nice place to sit, though the 'thin and crispy' pizza dough tastes a little like a Saltine cracker – get the pan style and pig out.

There's a decent Armenian restaurant, the *Nairy* (☎ 314 80 93), on ulitsa Dekabristov 6, near metro Sadovaya/Sennaya ploshchad, open from 11 am to midnight.

Bahlsen – Le Cafe (☎ 271 28 11) at Nevsky prospekt 142, just east of ploshchad Vosstania (see Smolny Region map), is both an inexpensive stand-up café serving hot dogs, pizzas and snacks for less than US$3 and a sit-down bistro with Swiss-style prices. It's a good place for a chat, and it does a good spaghetti bolognaise for US$7.80, a Spanish omelette for US$5.80 and a cheeseburger with fries and a salad for US$7.85. It's open from noon to midnight (though the later it gets, the worse the service), and it takes Visa, MasterCard, Eurocard, American Express, JCB and Diners Club.

Chopsticks (☎ 119 60 00), at the Grand Hotel Europe, has dependable Chinese food in a stylish setting. Its main courses are priced from US$8 to US$22, it takes Visa, MasterCard, Eurocard, American Express, JCB and Diners Club, and it's open from 1 to 11 pm. It's at the entrance closest to Nevsky prospekt – the restaurant to the right as you enter.

Nikolai (☎ 311 14 02), in the House of Architects (Dom Arkitektora) at Bolshaya Morskaya 52, does its best to serve up European and even Brazilian food. It has a nice layout, and its main courses average from US$10 to US$15.

Bistro Le Francais (☎ 210 96 22, 315 24 65) is just that – the genuine French chef greets guests with a jaunty *'Bonjour'* – but *sans* surly maître d' pretending not to speak English. It has very nice, very rich specialities priced from US$8 to US$20, and hey, you know what they call *Pulp Fiction* in a French bistro? 'Two bucks'. There's a video-rental place inside that does free screenings (see the Entertainment chapter), and in the back there's a pool table. This is a nice place. It's at ulitsa Galernaya 20 and takes all major credit cards.

The *Restoran Nevsky* (☎ 311 30 93), at Nevsky prospekt 71, above metro Mayakovskaya, seems to be doing its best to keep up the traditions of the Communist Dining Experience. If you haven't yet experienced overpriced, mediocre food and poor service, you might stop in for a bite. It's open from noon to 11 pm, and it has several theme rooms to choose from.

Bella Leone (☎ 113 16 70) is a cheerful and very Western place serving Italian and European food. Make reservations, as it's very popular. It's at Vladimirsky prospekt 9, and it accepts American Express.

Queen (☎ 314 07 18) at ulitsa Gorokhovaya 27 (near metro Sennaya ploshchad) is a quiet and small but excellent spot for Russian and European food. The service is terrific, and the food quite good. The sturgeon and salmon for US$10, veal Toscano at US$19 and fillet of chicken at US$16 are all fine, but a portion of butter is US$1 – that's getting greedy. It's open until midnight, but call ahead for reservations, as it's small.

Montreal Steak (☎ 310 92 56) is a staggeringly expensive steakhouse on the Fontanka River (US$25 to US$30 for steaks), but its steaks are pretty darn good, if that's the sort of thing you like. It's not very busy, but it definitely has the right atmosphere – the towering host with the black cowboy hat speaks very good English. It's a block north of the American Medical Center at Apraksin pereulok 22, on the corner of naberezhnaya reki Fontanki.

Club Ambassador (☎ 272 91 81), at naberezhnaya reki Fontanki 14, is a slick place, with lovely, cosy rooms and good food. It's unfortunate that a high number of cellphone-carrying types have discovered this. However, it's a very nice place for a meal, and it prepares Russian and French food quite well. It's open from 1 pm to midnight and has a fixed-price lunch from 1 to 4 pm.

Syurpriz is in fact *syurpriz*ingly good – with a café to the left (see Cafés, Bistros, Fast Food & Snack Bars later in this chapter) and full restaurant to the right. It's a modern place with friendly service at Nevsky prospekt 113 (which is technically Staryi Nevsky). The shrimp and beef dishes are good, though they cost, respectively, US$12 and US$15. It's open from 10 am to 10 pm.

The *Senat Bar* (☎ 314 92 53), at Galernaya ulitsa 1-3, is a first-class Russian place, with an odd, but interesting, interior designed by local artists and a beautiful vaulted ceiling. The food is good (at about US$15 for a main course), and beer lovers will love the extensive beer list. It's open from 11 am to 5 am.

Afrodite (☎ 275 76 20) at Nevsky prospekt 86, just across the street from the Nevskij Palace Hotel, specialises in seafood, but it has a good all-round menu and an extensive wine list. It has a pleasant setting, good food and good service, and it can afford it; at US$12 to US$18 for main courses, it's pricey, but it's good for a treat, and it takes Visa, MasterCard and Eurocard. Behind it, in summer, the Beer Garden is a very cool place to hang out (See Pubs, Bars & Beer Gardens, later in this chapter).

The Brasserie (☎ 119 60 00) is the Grand Hotel Europe's casually elegant dining option; it has a more relaxed atmosphere than the Restaurant Europe, but hasn't let its hair down so low that it's become Sadko's (see Cafés, Bistros, Fast Food & Snack Bars later in this chapter). With excellent food and service, it's good for a business lunch. Its main courses are priced from US$12 to US$18, starters from US$4 to US$10. It takes Visa, MasterCard, Eurocard, American Express, JCB and Diners Club and is open Monday to Saturday from 11 am to 11 pm and Sunday from 3 to 11 pm.

Restaurant St Petersburg (☎ 314 49 47), opposite the Church of the Resurrection of Christ on the Griboedova Canal, has a nice setting, though the whole thing feels a bit like a tourist trap; during dinner (beef and lamb from US$17 to US$20; chicken US$15 and fish from US$14 to US$20), a floor show occurs in which Peter the Great flounces about the place ... it's too much! The food's good, and the service is fine. It's open from noon to 2 am, and the floor show begins at 9 pm. If you do go, the glass and tile work, done by local artists, is worth looking at.

Ariran (☎ 274 04 66), at 8-ya Sovietskaya ulitsa 20 (see the Smolny Region map), is a Korean restaurant that has had good reviews, but when we went the place smelled pretty stale and the prices were outrageous – main dishes (beginning with stir-fried vegies) were priced from an unforgivable US$15 to US$40. If its prices come down, it'll be worth a shot.

The Grand Hotel Europe's flagship, *Restaurant Europe* (☎ 119 60 00), has the most beautiful setting in town, if not the country. This extravagantly luxurious place, with its stained-glass ceilings and luminous history (you want celebrities, we got celebrities, from the King of Siam to Krushchev to Buzz Aldrin to Michael Caine ... the list goes on and on!), serves spectacular food at celestial prices – so celestial, in fact, that they're spelled out: 'thirty two dollars' etc. It also serves a luxuriously sumptuous Sunday Jazz Brunch ('thirty dollars') from noon to 3 pm. If someone well off is taking you out to dinner, this is the place to have them take you. It's open for breakfast ('twenty dollars') from 7 to 10 am and for dinner from 6 to 11 pm.

Dinner at The Nevskij Palace's *Imperial Restaurant*, where guests also have their buffet breakfast, is a superb buffet affair, with continental and international specialities and live music on most evenings. Here is where it also holds its blow-out Sunday Jazz brunches (US$32). On the 2nd floor, the *Admiralty Restaurant* has fine Russian and seafood specialities, in a sort of 'Ahhhr, matey' setting, with ship models from the St Petersburg naval museum. Main courses are priced from US$23 to US$28, starters from US$10 to US$21 and salads from US$9 to US$15. It's not quite as sexy as the rooftop *Landskrona*, thought by many to be St Petersburg's finest restaurant. The European and Russian specialities are served in a gorgeous setting, and there's dancing and live music; in summer, an open-air terrace offers panoramic views of the city. Main courses are priced from US$29 to US$34, starters from US$15 to US$21 and salads from US$7 to US$9. In all of these restaurants the service is impeccable, and they all accept Visa, MasterCard, Eurocard, American Express, JCB and Diners Club.

South of the City Centre

Pizza House, formerly Pizza Express (☎ 316 26 66), has been serving up Finnish-style pizzas and decent Italian food for several years now. It also has a huge wine list and tonnes of liquor. And it delivers. It's near metro Tekhnologichecky Institut at ulitsa Podolskaya 23, and its pizzas cost an average of US$8 to US$10. Prices are in Finnish markka and it accepts Visa, MasterCard and Eurocard. Delivery's free if you order five dishes or more. It's a comfortable place to sit.

Daddy's Steak Room (☎ 298 95 52) is a bit out of the way, south of the centre at Moskovsky prospekt 73 (just next to metro Frunzenskaya) but the trip is worth it. St Petersburg's first Western-style steakhouse, this Finnish-run Godsend serves up great slabs of beef at very reasonable prices; you can get a good, large steak, garlic potatoes and a couple of trips to the salad bar for about US$10, and it has an extensive wine list, though that can get pricey. It's also starting to do a limited Mexican menu. The place gives you good value for money. It accepts Visa, MasterCard and Eurocard, and prices are in Finnish markka.

Troyka (☎ 113 53 43), a Swiss-Russian joint venture, is like a night at an execrable variety show – in fact, it's so awful

it might even be worth the US$45 set price. There's
Russian food and a lot of red and gold and sort of pseudo
exotic dancers and big hats. It's in the basement at
Zagorodny prospekt 27, which is about equal distance
from the Pushkinskaya and Vladimirskaya metro stations.

Petrograd Side

The Grand Café Antwerpen (☎ 233 97 46) at Kronverksky
prospekt 13/2, just opposite the Gorkovskaya metro
station, is a stylish place with fantastic stuffed mushrooms (US$5), decent Russian/European food (starters
US$3 to US$10, main courses US$8 to US$15) and darn
good Belgian beer on draught and in bottles. It has an
atrium café attached to the main dining room, and it's
open noon to midnight.

Kafe Tbilisi (☎ 230 93 91), St Petersburg's first coopera-
tive, serves up great Georgian food – most of the time.
Definitely try the home-made cheese, and its lavash and
khachipuri breads. Its satsivi chicken is usually great, as is
its shashlyk. Main courses range from about US$2 to US$4,
starters from US$1 to US$3. It's at Sytninskaya ulitsa 10 and
is open from noon to 10 or 11 pm, depending on the crowd.
Dig the crazy doorman in traditional Georgian garb. It also
has a tiny bar, and service is very good.

Kafe Tet-a-Tet (☎ 232 75 48), Bolshoy prospekt 65, is a
perfect name for this place; all the tables are quiet, cosy
and for two. The food's fine, and there's a pianist tin-
kling away while you dine – worth it on a date. It's open
from 1 to 5 pm and 7 pm to midnight.

Khaibei (☎ 233 20 46) at Bolshoy prospekt 61 has average
Chinese meals, give or take the occasional pebble in your
food. Prices are heading up: at the time of writing, main
courses averaged from US$4.75 to US$6. The restaurant is
upstairs from the Express Kafe (see Cafés, Bistros, Fast
Food & Snack Bars, later in this chapter).

Petrogradskoe (no telephone) at Bolshoy prospekt 88/1
has perfectly ordinary food in a pleasant place. Beef and
chicken cost up to US$6.50. The nearest metro is
Petrogradskaya.

Demyanova Ukha (☎ 232 80 90) has quietly remained
one of St Petersburg's more reliable seafood places for
years. It has a very relaxed, and newly refurbished,
atmosphere (lots of wood) and pleasant staff. Seafood
dishes range from about US$5 to US$9, while shashlyk
costs US$6. It's behind the Peter & Paul Fortress, at
Kronversky prospekt 53. It may pay to book.

Petrostar (☎ 232 40 47), at Bolshaya Pushkarskaya
ulitsa 30, is said to have a good selection of Russian

cuisine, at reasonable prices (under US$10 for main courses). It's open from 1 pm to midnight.

Pirosmani (☎ 235 46 66), at Bolshoy prospekt 14, has excellent Georgian food in a ... well, in a unique setting. It's not advisable to go if you're subject to hallucinogenic episodes – the rear wall of the restaurant is psychedelically sculpted in what's billed as a tribute to the Georgian artist's work, and there are rivers flowing through the restaurant. When all's said and done, though, the food is what brings you back, even though the average meal will cost you US$14 (its basturma is US$7.95, shashlyk US$7.15 and khachipuri bread US$1.90). It's not convenient to public transport: from metro Petrogradskaya take any trolleybus south along Bolshoy prospekt. It's open from noon to 11 pm.

The Imperial restaurant, not to be confused with the Imperial Restaurant at the Nevskij Palace Hotel (☎ 234 17 42), has excellent Russian food, good service and a tasteful dining room, though you'll need to get past its Soviet-style doorman to discover this (just be polite and keep saying 'Dinner'). It's popular, so be sure to book. It has a good bar and a very nice dining room; try the baked mushrooms (US$15) and the Surovsky beef (also US$15), which are among the cheapest dishes. It's at Kamennoostrovsky prospekt (Kirovsky prospekt) 53 (see the Kirovsky Islands map), just across the Karpovka River on Aptekarsky Island, about a 10-minute walk from metro Petrogradskaya.

Vasilevsky Island

Svir (☎ 213 63 21) is the Hotelship Peterhof's restaurant, and it's quite a nice place to spend an evening. The dining room is on the lower level of the ship, moored off naberezhnaya Makarova just west of the Tuchkov Bridge at the north-east end of Vasilevsky Island (see the Central St Petersburg map), so there's a nice Neva view, and the food and service are both very good. It runs food festivals, rotating monthly, during which it highlights specific cuisines. Main courses cost from US$12 to US$25, starters from US$4 to US$10.

Restoran Kalinka (☎ 213 37 18) has Russian romance, guitar-strumming and Russian food: good baked mushrooms 'po-Tolstovsky' (US$11), interesting pancake nests with heavy cream and caviar at US$13, shchi and borsch at US$6 and more expensive seafood. It's at Sezdovskaya 9, north of Bolshoy prospekt and it's open noon to midnight. Don't panic – the wolf in the front entrance is stuffed.

The *Venezia* (☎ 352 14 32), at ulitsa Korablestroyteley 21 near the Prebaltiyskaya Hotel (see the main St Petersburg map), has two distinct sections; downstairs it sells takeaway pizzas for about US$2, and upstairs it's a more formal Italian restaurant with fair service and good enough food, though it gets pricey. Main courses are priced from US$8 to US$25 and it accepts Visa, MasterCard and Eurocard. It's open from 12.30 to 11.30 pm, and the nearest metro is Primorskaya. You can phone in orders to pick up; it's flirting with the idea of delivery but ...

The restaurants in the Pribaltiskaya hotel are none too spectacular.

Vyborg Side

People say great things about *Staraya Derevnaya* (☎ 239 00 00), a family-run traditional Russian restaurant at ulitsa Savushkina ulitsa 72. (The nearest metro is Chyornaya Rechka, from which you can take tram No 2, 31 or 37.) It's said to have great service, and because it's small, it's very intimate and cosy – make reservations. On weekend evenings, there's musical entertainment in the form of traditional Russian ballads. Main courses are priced from US$4 to US$7, starters from US$2 to US$5.

Schvabsky Domik (☎ 528 22 11) at Novocherkassky prospekt 28 (see the main St Petersburg map), at metro Novocherkasskaya, was one of the earliest joint-venture restaurants in town. The Bavarian décor is pushing the hokey barrier but it's still fun, and the food – schnitzel, sauerkraut, sausage and roast pork – is good. There are two entrances: the one on the left is the former hard-currency place that it is hoped Westerners will use, while the one on the right is for Russians and is cheaper.

CAFÉS, BISTROS, FAST FOOD & SNACK BARS

Practically every street in the centre has several places where you can grab a bite of something. This list is not by any means complete, though it does cover the major bases and will help you to keep your stomach quiet until time for dinner.

In addition to these places, the standard Russian blinnayi, bistros, kafe morozhenoe, kafeterii, stolovayi and bufety are all over the place, and these days most of them have what they say they have! Nevsky prospekt, for example, has something every 100 metres or so, and it's really a question of what you're *craving* as opposed to what you *can* have.

City Centre

Nevsky Prospekt (West) At the Admiralty end of Nevsky, the *Kafe Druzhba*, at Nevsky prospekt 15, has good chicken and bliny from US$1.50 to US$3. There's also a small disco in the evening from 7 to 11 pm. It's open from 11 am to 11 pm. This lower Nevsky area, west of Griboedova Canal, is also home to several good kafe morozhenoe. We like the one at Nevsky prospekt 3 (open from 10 am to 9 pm). These ice-cream cafés can be spotted throughout the entire stretch of Nevsky prospekt.

Balkany (☎ 315 47 48) is a pita/felafel café that also changes money and sells T-shirts (you figure it out) at Nevsky prospekt 27. You can buy Middle-Eastern goodies through its street window or go inside, where the little café sells only snacks and drinks. The felafel is good at about US$1, and it has a good deal on moussaka for three people at US$4.50.

The *Pyshki-Pyshechnaya* doughnut shop just near the DLT department store on ulitsa Bolshaya Konyushennaya serves up some great plain doughnuts (covered with confectioners' sugar when it's around) and drinkable coffee from 9 am to 8 pm. Inside DLT itself, on the 2nd floor in the south wing, *Melita Cafe* serves up some good coffee, small pizzas (US$1.25), sandwiches (US$0.60) and hot dogs (US$0.60).

A bit higher on the culinary chain, the *Kafe St Petersburg* two blocks east, adjacent to the Restaurant St Petersburg across the Griboedova Canal from the Church of the Resurrection of Christ is an incredibly popular place with great food for very reasonable prices. You may have to queue amongst all the foreign students trying to grab a portion of the splendid baked mushrooms in cream sauce, for about US$1.50. It's open from 9 am to 11 pm (break between 1 and 2 pm).

We list *Kafe Literaturnoe* because it's in so many other guidebooks you might wander in thinking it's a good place. It may have had its day back in Pushkin's time (his last meal was eaten here) but today, despite the lovely setting and the very civilised string quartet playing away in the back, the Lit Caf is nothing more than a highly priced tourist trap, with terrible food, sloppy service and variable prices.

Nevsky 27 is a stand-up café/bakery/pastry shop right near the Grand Hotel Europe, with decent coffee and dirt-cheap pastries.

Inside Gostiny Dvor on the Sadovaya side, the cunningly named *Pizza Holl* serves up terrific pizza by the slice – thick crust, gooey cheese and several toppings for about US$1.40 a slice. It also has hot dogs for about US$0.80.

With the opening of *Grillmaster* (☎ 110 40 55) at Nevsky prospekt 46 in the summer of 1994, the Germans officially beat out the US McDonald's as St Petersburg's first Western-style *schnell*-food hamburger joint. If Ray Kroc were alive he'd be going McGreen with envy watching the crowds fight to get at the US$2.10 jumbo burgers, US$1.35 hot dogs and US$2.05 chicken fillet sandwiches. It's open from 8.30 am to 10 pm and also has fish, pizza and ice cream, but no toilet.

The Transcarpathian Kafe (☎ 110 69 97) is a classy kind of place in a sleazeball sort of way just off Nevsky prospekt on ulitsa Bolshaya Morskaya. Funky booths, nasty staff; meat main courses US$4.30 to US$4.50, soups at US$2.50 to US$3. Next door, the *Bistro* is still a good option, a standard Russian stand-up with cheap chicken, salads and sandwiches.

Kafe 01 (☎ 312 11 36), at Karavannaya ulitsa 15, was an unpretentious and little-known bistro, serving up great food at great prices, but it's been out of the bag for a couple of years now and it's very hard to get a seat, what with all those henchmen in there flexing their muscles and making cell-phone calls. The food's still very good, as are the prices: fried pike or perch at US$4 and pork 'po-Karsky' at US$5. Make reservations or forget about it.

The tiny *Kafe* at Dvortsovaya naberezhnaya 28 does cheap hamburgers, hot dogs and hot chocolate. It's open from 11 am to 5 pm.

We passed by the *Priboy Kafe* (☎ 311 82 85) at naberezhnaya reki Moyki 19; it looked worth trying out. It has bliny (jam and sour cream US$1.40; caviar US$3.35), a pork grill at US$3.50 and chicken dishes at around US$2.85. It's open from 11 am to 10 pm.

Gino Ginelli's (☎ 312 46 31) is an Italian ice and ice-cream place next to the Chayka bar that also does microwaved pizza and burgers. It's open from 10 am to 1 am, at naberezhnaya kanala Griboedova 14.

If you're in the mood for some microwaved pizza for about US$6, head for *Nevsky 40* (☎ 312 24 57), a place whose location is far better than it deserves, just opposite Gostiny Dvor. It also has a lovely café/bar in the easternmost entrance – lots of wood and mirrors. Nice for a rest.

For its first year, *Sadko's* (☎ 119 60 00) at the Grand Hotel Europe was so popular that it became unmanageable (it charged in roubles but looked and felt like a Western bar). It seemed that every business deal – dirty or otherwise – involving foreigners that went down in

NICK SELBY

Sidewalk café, central St Petersburg

town was discussed here, and speculators used to hop from table to table to schmooze. In 1992, when it turned to hard currency in an attempt to flush out the riffraff, it was such a big deal that it was written up in *Newsweek*. Today, Sadko's is a huge, Texan-inspired barn of a bar, still popular but by no means what it was. It serves decent, though pricey, food (burger and fries US$10, starters US$8 to US$10) and it has a great beer selection (US$3 to US$9), but its 'speciality cocktails' – like a piddle of whisky at the bottom of a cup of coffee – are getting out of line at US$10. It has karaoke and good live bands on weekends, when the place really starts jumping. It's open till midnight and accepts Visa, MasterCard, Eurocard, American Express, JCB and Diners Club.

Sandwich fans who heard about the Subway sandwich shop that opened at Nevsky prospekt 20 in December, 1994, may be disappointed to know that intrigue, embezzlement and management clashes closed that venture. Fortunately, the Russian partners of the venture have reopened the doors, under the name *Minutka*, which serves the same kind of food at lower prices. All the submarine-style sandwiches they make come with cheese, onions, lettuce, tomato, pickles, green peppers, olives, salt and pepper at no extra charge. Prices for the new venture weren't available as we went to press, but Subways were on the high side: the cheapest six inch sandwich was vegie & cheese at US$2.25; the most expensive was roast beef at US$3.85, and in between there was tuna, turkey, meatball and ham. They're open 10 am to 10 pm daily. Best new feature: the trash bins now have a sign reading 'Spasibo' in addition to the English 'Thank You'.

Just across ulitsa Plekhanova from the Kazan Cathedral, at No 3, is *Bon Jour Fast Food* (☎ 219 47 89), doing burgers, sandwiches and fries at decent prices. Le Burger with cheese is US$2.60, and le vegie and cheese roll is US$1.45. It's open from 9 am to 10 pm daily.

Nevsky Prospekt (East) *Baskin Robbins* (☎ 164 64 56) at Nevsky prospekt 79 is just one of the US ice-cream parlour chain's locations in St Petersburg (it also has a branch out by the Planetarium behind the Peter & Paul Fortress, and kiosks here and there) and it's spreading throughout the country. Killer ice creams are about US$0.50 per scoop.

Another fast food joint (which many say is the best so far) selling burgers and the like is *Carrols* (☎ 279 17 36), an enormous Finnish-run place doing fast-food set meals for under US$5; a plain burger with salad is US$1.25, while a fishburger is US$2.20. It's at ulitsa Vosstania 5, just north of metro Ploshchad Vosstania, and is open 9 am to 11 pm daily. Another Carrols is set to open on Nevsky at ulitsa Rubenshteyna (see Nevskij Prospekt Eat map).

Kafe Vienna (☎ 275 20 01) at the Nevskij Palace Hotel is, well, a Viennese café, though it's gaining popularity with the short-neck cell-phone crowd. It has good pastries, coffee and hot chocolate, accepts Visa, MasterCard, Eurocard, American Express, JCB and Diners Club and is open from 10 am to 11 pm.

Bahlsen – Le Cafe (☎ 271 28 11) at Nevsky prospekt 142, just east of ploshchad Vosstania, is an inexpensive stand-up café, serving hot dogs, pizzas and snacks for less than US$3. It's open from noon to midnight and takes Visa, MasterCard, Eurocard, American Express, JCB and Diners Club.

Guess what's cooking at *Kafe Hot Dog*, downstairs at Nevsky prospekt 103? You're right! They're sizzling, along with burgers, from 11 am to 9 pm, with a break from 2 to 3 pm.

There's a nice and very cheap *Roast Chicken Kafe* at Nevsky prospekt 147, up towards the Hotel Moskva. It has very cheap roast chicken and fountain Coke, Fanta and Sprite. It's open from 8 am to 8 pm, but takes a break from 1 to 2 pm.

And speaking of the Hotel Moskva, its *Russian Kafe* at the north-east end of the hotel does decent pastries, ice cream and coffee (see Central St Petersburg map).

Syurpriz Kafe, next to Syurpriz restaurant at Nevsky prospekt 113, is a nice little sit-down pizza joint that does very good pizzas (US$2.40 to US$5) and other snacky things including a good chicken Kiev for US$3.60. It also has Tuborg on draught, and it's open from 10 am to 10 pm.

North & East of Nevsky Prospekt *Bagdad Kafe* (☎ 272 23 55) is still cookin' and cooler than ever. With its excellent huge and tasty manty dumplings (US$2.40), shish kebab (US$3.60), soups and plov (US$1.90), this basement café is an old stand-by. Open from noon to 11 pm, it's at Furshtadtskaya ulitsa 27.

Hostellers go for the *Bar Don Kikhot*, at naberezhnaya reki Fontanki 21, a Spanish-Russian joint venture doing grilled chicken (US$3.35), burgers (US$1.40) and Polish sausage (US$1). The sign in the window is in English. It's open 10 am to 6 pm.

North-east of the hostel, at Suvorovsky prospekt 43, the *Verona Pizzeria* (☎ 275 77 62) does decent pizzas for US$2.25 to US$3.20; it's open from 10 am to 10 pm and it also has soft drinks and beer (see the Smolny Region map).

Kafe Maksim (☎ 312 26 12) at Millionnaya ulitsa 10 does kotlet (US$3.10), pelmeni (US$3.10) and other café food, in a pleasant, two-room setting. It's open from 11 am to 10 pm.

The *Springtime Shwarma Bistro* is our favourite Middle-Eastern place in town because it's so darn cheap and good. You can get a gyro or felafel for under US$1 (though they are a bit on the small side) and it has a large selection of other Middle-Eastern specialities, especially vegetarian ones. It's at the corner of Radishcheva ulitsa and Nekrasova ulitsa at Radishcheva ulitsa 20, four long blocks east of Liteyny prospekt (see the Smolny Region map). Of course, when it comes to Middle-Eastern food, there's always dissenting opinion: the *St Petersburg Press*' editors argue that *Shakherezada*, at Razeszhaya 3, has the best felafel and hummus in town. You decide. It's pretty good for vegetarians and is open from 11 am to 11 pm. It's near metro Dostoevskogo.

Vechernee Kafe is an OK basement affair with hot dogs (US$2.40), kotlet (US$1.90) or steak (US$3.35) served mainly to wash down various blue and pink liqueurs and Western beer with. It's at ulitsa Chaykovskogo 75 (see the Smolny Region map), just a bit east of ... you guessed it, the Finnish Consulate. Around the corner, *Kafe Medved* calls itself a business-club/saloon; it's in the basement of ulitsa Potyomkinskaya 7, and it does cheap snacks, beers etc. It's good if you're trying to renew your

German passport and they've made you wait for hours. Next door, the *Kafe Saloon* has draught De Koninck beer and a seedier atmosphere.

South of Nevsky Prospekt *Iveria* (☎ 164 74 78) at ulitsa Marata 35 has awfully good Georgian fast food; choose from the samples on the counter, and pick up your food through the hole in the wall. It has nice service. The restaurant's in the basement and is open from 11 am to 10 pm, with a break from 2 to 3 pm.

Petrograd Side

If you're peckish at metro Petrogradskaya, there's the *Sandwich Kafe* (☎ 232 70 28) just across the street, through the spooky tunnel. This little bastion of civility does very good sandwiches, salads and ice cream, and the highest price is about US$1.90. It's open from 11 am to 8 pm. A bit closer to the metro (adjacent to it, in fact) and even flashier is *2 + 2*, which has sandwiches, salads, pizzas and other snacks, nuked to your liking. It's open from 10 am to 9 pm.

If only there were a *Gril Diez* (☎ 232 42 55) everywhere; this wonderful place does whole spit-roast chicken (though on some days they can be a tad scrawny) for about US$2.50. It's at Kamennoostrovsky prospekt (Kirovsky prospekt) 16, on the roundabout. One frustrating aspect is that it seems to wait until all chickens are sold before putting up another broiler-full, which creates huge and stagnant queues – and the guy in front of you (the one with the huge rucksack) is going to buy the last seven. It also sells Middle-Eastern pita bread for US$0.35 for a pack of eight. It's open from 10 am to 8 pm. Just outside Gril Diez, a stand sells vegetarian felafel (deep fried balls of mashed chick peas in pita bread with salad) for US$0.35.

Heading south from metro Petrogradskaya, all vegetarians will kindly form a line and hit *Troitsky Most*, aka the *Hare Krishna Kafe* (☎ 232 66 93), which does excellent vegetarian dishes, herb tea, mind-washing potion ... er ... pizzas etc. You can sample small dishes of everything on the menu (mainly lentil and white beans in curry sauce, curried rice with clove and sultanas, and kasha) for under US$2, and what's more there's minimal chanting required. It's at Malaya Posadskaya ulitsa 2, near metro Gorkovskaya, and is open from 11 am to 8 pm (break from 3 to 4 pm).

Way down at the south-west end of Bolshoy prospekt next to Pirosmani Restaurant is the *Pirosmani* pavement café, doing lavash bread, pastries, hot dogs and hamburgers. Everything's less than US$1 except the copious quantities of booze available.

Someone should speak with the owner of the *Kafe Grot*, (☎ 238 46 90) in Admiraltiysky Park behind the Peter & Paul Fortress, about the way that name sounds in English. The Grotto, which is what it means, actually looks like one, and is a very nice place for a mid-afternoon coffee if you sit outside (inside it smells a bit like spilled beer). It's open from 11 am to 9 pm, and no smoking is allowed inside.

The *Kafe* at Kamennoostrovsky prospekt (Kirovsky prospekt) 50, just north of the Karpovka River (see the Kirovsky Islands map), has hot chocolate, cakes, coffee and a really nice cat; it's open from 9 am to 9 pm (break between 1 and 2 pm). And on the opposite side of the street, the *Kafe* at Kamennoostrovsky prospekt (Kirovsky prospekt) 54, near the Hotel Druzhba (actually under a sign that says Druzhba – see the Kirovsky Islands map), is very cheap and has good coffee and hot chocolate. It's even a pleasant place to sit. It's open from 7 am to 8 pm (break between 1 and 2 pm).

Chick-King (☎ 232 49 22) at Kamennoostrovsky prospekt (Kirovsky prospekt) 54 (see the Kirovsky Islands map), near the Hotel Druzhba, is a fast-food chicken place doing decent schnitzel (US$2.50), fried chicken (US$2) and great deep-fried potato chunks and fried onions (US$0.60). In front there's a Koff bar doing pints for US$2.

The *Express Kafe* (☎ 233 20 46), just downstairs from the Khaibei restaurant at Bolshoy prospekt 61 (see the Inner Petrograd Side map), is cheap and serves fast Chinese and Russian food. Pick from the samples on the counter – everything's less than US$2.40, and almost everything is tasty, especially the dumplings. It's open from 10 am to 7 pm.

Vasilevsky Island

The tiny *Sirin Bar & Restaurant* (☎ 213 22 48, 213 72 82) at Vasilevsky Ostrov 1-ya Linia 16, has surprisingly good and cheap Russian food, including chicken dishes and 'Hungarian Meat' for US$2.60. It's open from 11 am to midnight.

Kafe Grilette at 1-ya Linia 40 has ice cream and hot sandwiches for less than US$1.

Kafe Nika (De Koninck) (☎ 213 22 79), at Bolshoy prospekt 8, is yet another café to sport this Belgian beer logo. Some substantial café food is served here, like a pork grill (US$3.10), hunter's sausage (US$2.15) and a beef grill (US$2.85). It's a nice place.

The food at the *Gril-Bar Vo Dvore* (☎ 213 24 21), just next to Nika (under the arch), looks pretty good; it has pita-kebabs (US$1.20), chicken dishes at US$1.90, and a big pork cutlet for US$2.15. It's open from 11 am to 11 pm.

Salon Best at 6-ya Linia 9 is a little shop that also sells good grilled chickens for US$2.85 a piece. It also has bottled beer and draught Coke, Sprite and Fanta and is worth a shot if you're starving on the Strelka. Panic not if you think the beer's too expensive – there's a *pivo kiosk* just outside serving up the suds, and it even has beer mugs.

The *Sun Deck Kafe* (☎ 213 63 21) at the Hotelship Peterhof (see the Central St Petersburg map) is, in summer anyway, a pleasant deck-top café serving hot and cold snacks, sandwiches, drinks etc at Swiss prices. It's on board the hotel-ship, moored along naberezhnaya Makarova just north-west of Tuchkov Bridge.

PUBS, BARS & BEER GARDENS

In 1994 most foreign residents here danced a wee jig, when *Mollies Irish Bar* (☎ 319 97 68) brought a bit o' the black to the City on the Neva: draught Guinness pints for US$4 and lagers for US$3. This place became hugely popular very fast for its great beer, classic pub decor, friendly service, and Christian Walsh, who trained at the school Tom Cruise went to for the movie *Cocktail*. He stands back there twirling bottles, breaking hearts and making management nervous ('Only twarl the cheap stoof, laddy ...'). It serves pub food (sandwiches for about US$4 to US$5, soups for US$2). It's at Rubinshteyna ulitsa 36 and is open from 11 to 3 am every day. You never know who might turn up – one night Nick met Ireland's Minister of Education!

The cool and cavernous *Shamrock* (☎ 219 46 25), at ulitsa Dekabristov 27 just across the street from the Mariinsky Theatre, is claiming that its Guinness is shipped straight from Dublin, while 'other' pubs use English stuff. Its location couldn't be better; we'll see how the battle of the Irish pubs goes. US$5 pints, US$3 bottles. Just down the street is the *Klub*, which has US-style pool tables.

The *Dog & Fox* (☎ 242 22 68), on the 3rd floor at naberezhnaya Chyornaya Rechka 41 (corner of ulitsa Grafova), serves imported beer and cider, as well as pub and vegetarian food. The place looks and feels like a large English pub (lots o' Union Jack, though switch the flags and it could be a Texas two-step joint).

Management knows that its location could be a lot more central, but a good reason to go out of your way to have a pint here is that 50% of the profits go directly to the Red Kidz charity, which is involved in a host of worthy projects in town, helping abandoned and disfigured children and constructing shelters for the homeless. The ladies' room in this pub is one floor down from the bar area, the men's two (blimey).

From metro Chyornaya Rechka (see the Kirovsky Islands map), walk north about 200 metres, across the canal (that's Chyornaya Rechka, or 'black river'), then turn right and the pub is 400 metres ahead on the left hand side of the street. It has live music on some nights and is open from noon to 3 am daily.

The Beer Garden, behind Afrodite restaurant (Nevsky prospekt 86) and opposite the Nevskij Palace Hotel, is a great summer spot. It's in a secluded courtyard, there's music, Finnish beer, blue liqueurs and Finnish snacks, and it's a very enjoyable place in which to spend an evening. It's popular, it seems, with everyone – expats, Russians and travellers alike.

If you're wondering how *The John Bull Pub* (☎ 164 98 77), at Nevsky prospekt 79 near metro Mayakovskaya, managed to get an English pub to St Petersburg, the answer is: on a truck. The whole kit and caboodle. And after going to all that trouble, it goes and serves John Bull bitter and Skol lager at US$4 for a bit less than a pint. Still, it's a fun place to sit and have a beer after a long day of walking up and down Nevsky. Don't try to steal any of the knick-knacks – they're nailed down! It's open from noon to midnight and has an adjacent restaurant serving Russian food.

On the weekend, *Sadko's* (☎ 119 60 00) huge, Texan-inspired barn of a bar gets packed, people have a great time and one can glean why it used to be the most popular place in town (well, it was fun, cheap and the *only* place in town for a while, but that's nit-picking, isn't it?). It has karaoke and good live bands on Friday and Saturday, a huge selection of booze and beer, snacks and full meals in the adjacent restaurant section. It is open till midnight and accepts Visa, MasterCard, Eurocard, American Express, JCB and Diners Club.

Warsteiner Forum (☎ 277 29 14) at ploshchad Vosstania isn't very popular, but it's a nice place with good German beer and schnitzel. Beers cost about US$5, and the schnitzel is US$12; its 'peasant breakfast' (sausage, eggs, toast) is US$7, and a plate of sausages is a mean US$6. It's open from noon to 2 am.

The Bierstube in the Nevskij Palace Hotel is pretty much what you'd expect; waitresses in dirndl, an Austrian setting, snacks and good but dear beer. Draughts (0.5 litre) are US$6. It accepts Visa, MasterCard, Eurocard, American Express, JCB and Diners Club and is open from 10 am (for those in need of a *Frühschoppen)* to 11 pm.

The Grand Hotel Europe's *Lobby Bar* is a very civilised place, best visited if you're on an expense account. It has beer for US$7 a bottle, and mixed drinks get expensive! It also serves coffee, espresso and cappuccino. It accepts Visa, MasterCard, Eurocard, American Express, JCB and Diners Club. There's piano entertainment in the evenings, and you can walk through the archway into the library to read the paper.

The *Marine Bar* at the US Consulate (☎ 274 86 89) isn't really open to the public, but it does have Friday night get-togethers, barbecues, movie nights etc that are open to citizens of most Western – and even some Eastern European – countries by invitation only. The bar itself is kind of cool, and there's a pool table. You'll have to check at the consulate to see if anything's happening, and you will need to be invited by one of the marines – don't just show up.

On any given night, the *Chayka* (☎ 312 46 31) bar is filled with foreign businesspeople, German tour groups singing *Schunkellieder*, and swarms of prostitutes who'll sidle up to you at the bar and say something coolly seductive like, 'I want peanuts. Buy me beer'. In the past there have been suggestions that customers who stayed late may have been overcharged by having imaginary beers tacked onto the punch-cards that are used to cal-

ROGER HAYNE

Streetside beer stalls

culate the bill (and if you lost the card you had to buy it for DM60). This place is worth avoiding if you're picking up the tab. It's at naberezhnaya Kanala Griboedova 14, near the corner of Nevsky prospekt.

The Nightclub on the top floor of the Grand Hotel Europe has a small dance floor – and large bills.

There are a couple of *Koff* beer gardens in the centre: one opposite the Grand Hotel Europe, between the former Duma and Gostiny Dvor, and one in front of St Peter's Cathedral. Both have draught and bottled beers, for about US$2.85 and US$2.15, respectively.

A Final Word on Beer The queues you see early in the morning at places around town – at the corner of naberezhnaya reki Fontanki and ploshchad Lomonosova, for example – are folks waiting to fill up their jars at *The Odd Stray Beer Cart*, a fine tradition that should be experienced at least once during a stay in St Petersburg. The beer is fresh and usually ... well, it won't kill you. Bring your own jar. It's dirt cheap, which is fitting.

Entertainment

St Petersburg is the entertainment equal of many Western cities, and Intourist no longer requires you to like opera or ballet. Sure, the classical entertainment in the city is amongst the best on the planet – ballet, opera, classical music and theatre – but there's a new world here of rock clubs, jazz joints and discos that has St Petersburg nightlife soaring to heights never before witnessed in Russia.

But because of the precarious nature of everything here, clubs come and go faster than in other places. Both *Pulse* and the *St Petersburg Press* have comprehensive weekly club and pub listings, as well as names and addresses of new clubs and venues.

For other listings, being able to decipher Cyrillic is a huge advantage. St Petersburg has proper listings magazines in Russian, such as *To Da Vsyo (This and That)*. A huge amount of information, including some about rock and sports events, is published on posters. Check what's-on charts in hotel service bureaus, at concierge desks and in the central ticket kiosks (they can be identified by the words *teatralnaya kassa* Театральная касса or just *teatr* Театр). For performances listed on posters look for words like Продажа *prodazha* (sale) and билети *bileti* (tickets).

Tickets

Face-value tickets are sold at the venues themselves (usually from 11 am to 3 pm and 4 to 6 pm, and best bought in advance) or through the combined booking offices. The Kirov apart, the dearest tickets are rarely more than US$2.

Peter TIPS sells tickets to almost every event in town at the Russian face price plus a 10% commission; it's a great source of tickets and information (see the Facts for the Visitor chapter for more information).

The best booking office at which to buy tickets is the Theatre Ticket Office (Teatralnaya kassa ☎ 314 93 85) at Nevsky prospekt 42, opposite Gostiny Dvor, and in the middle of Dumskaya ulitsa on the west side of Gostiny Dvor. Here you can get tickets for everything, including the Kirov, but they sell out quickly. Offering to buy tickets *s nagruzkoy*, or along with a bunch of other tickets to must-misses no-one wants to see, can help otherwise unavailable tickets to appear, and this usually works out to be cheaper than any other option. In May 1995, good tickets were available for a performance of Swan Lake at the Mariinsky Theatre for US$2.60 each at this office (s nagruzkoy was unnecessary), but in the high season ticket prices and demand increase.

Concierge desks at the better hotels will be only too pleased to sell you Kirov tickets for upwards of US$60. They do, however, get some of the best seats in the house, so if you've got a limited amount of time, you may be happy to pay their price. The HI St Petersburg Hostel and Holiday Hostel will try to get you tickets at a less breathtaking mark-up.

When all else fails, remember here, as in many cities, there are also touts – usually young speculators hanging out in front of the venue before a performance. If you want to buy a ticket from one of them, go along to the venue an hour or so before the performance. A standard tout price you shouldn't feel fleeced paying (even though you're being fleeced) is US$30. And when you get the ticket, make sure it's for the date and section you want: ground floor is the *parter*; the mezzanine is the *beletazh*; and the balcony is the *balkon* or *yarus*.

Sometimes people sell tickets from tables in pedestrian subways; check the underpasses at Nevsky prospekt and Gostiny Dvor metros.

Wherever you decide to buy your tickets, good seats will go fast! Most theatres and concert halls are closed on Monday. There are usually matinees on Sunday and sometimes on Saturday.

BALLET, OPERA & CLASSICAL MUSIC

September to early summer is the main performing season – the cultural scene goes into neutral for the rest of the summer, with companies away on tour. An exception is the last 10 days of June, when St Petersburg stages the White Nights Dance Festival. Extra events of variable quality are mounted through the summer tourist season at halls like the Lensovieta Culture Palace at Kamennoostrovsky prospekt (Kirovsky prospekt) 42 (metro Petrogradskaya) and the Oktyabrsky Concert Hall at Ligovsky prospekt 6 (metro Ploshchad Vosstania).

Ballet & Opera

St Petersburg was the birthplace of Russian ballet back in 1738; the Kirov Ballet premiered Tchaikovsky's Sleeping Beauty and Nutcracker, and nurtured Nijinsky, Pavlova, Nureyev, Makarova and Baryshnikov. Today, under director Oleg Vinogradov, the Kirov has a reputation for more varied and sensitive productions than Moscow's Bolshoy. Don't miss it. The Kirov Opera can also be a treat, though sometimes it's truly awful. Both are at the Mariinsky Theatre at Teatralnaya ploshchad 1. Russian and international classics are in the repertoire, and about five ballets and five operas are performed each month. The operas are performed (murdered?) in Russian.

The companies tend to go away on tour for about two months in the summer and unpredictably the rest of the year. The ballet's home shows are nearly always booked out (ticket sales from the theatre usually start 20 days in advance). Be sure it's the Kirov company itself, and not the Russian Ballet, that you're paying to see; sometimes visiting ensembles perform here too.

Cheaper and easier-to-get-into ballet and opera performances are staged at the Maly (Small) Theatre (Peterburgsky Gosudarstvenny Akademichesky Maly Teatr Opery i Baleta imeni M P Mussorgskogo), at ploshchad Iskusstv 1. It stages more contemporary works than the Kirov and standards are respectable. The Conservatory, on Teatralnaya ploshchad, also stages some operas.

Classical Music

The St Petersburg Philharmonia's symphony orchestra is particularly renowned. It has two concert halls: the Bolshoy Zal (Big Hall ☎ 311 74 89) on ploshchad Iskusstv, and the Maly Zal imeni M I Glinki (Small Hall, named after M I Glinka and not to be confused with the Maly Theatre, or the Maly Dramatic Theatre, or the Glinka Capella) nearby at Nevsky prospekt 30. The Glinka Capella (Akademicheskaya Khorovaya Kapella imeni M I Glinki ☎ 314 10 58), at naberezhnaya Reki Moyki 20, also has high standards, focusing on choral, chamber and organ concerts. Other venues include Smolny Cathedral (☎ 271 91 82), which usually features choral works, and the Peterburgsky Concert Hall at ploshchad Lenina 1.

THEATRE

The premier drama theatre is the Pushkin, at ploshchad Ostrovskogo 2, which stages (in Russian) the likes of Shakespeare, Aristophanes and even Arthur 'Aeroport' Hailey as well as home-grown plays. The Lensoviet Theatre, at Vladimirsky prospekt 12, and the Gorky Bolshoy Dramatic Theatre, at naberezhnaya Reki

Fontanki 65, are the other top mainstream drama thea-
tres. For experimental fare, try the Maly Dramatic
Theatre at Rubinshteyna ulitsa 18 or the Komsomol
Theatre at Park Lenina 4. Music-hall variety shows are
staged at the Komsomol Theatre and the Teatr Estrady
at ulitsa Zhelyabova 27. Teatr Experiment, at the corner
of Kamennoostrovsky prospekt (Kirovsky prospekt)
and Bolshoy prospekt (Petrograd Side), stages performances and is a gay and lesbian nightclub on weekends.

JAZZ

A really fun time can be had at The New Jazz Club (☎ 275
60 90) on the east side of the Tauride Gardens (see the
Smolny Region map), near the City Children's Park. It
has good bands (not only jazz) and a good bar, and it's
a comfortable place to hang out for a while. From metro
Chernyshevskaya, make a right to Furshtadtskaya
ulitsa, then a right to the park; the club's in the yellow
opera house at the far right-hand corner. It's open from
7.30 to 11 pm and admission is US$1.90. Down at
Okoshki Art Cafe, the setting is by far the most, er, laid
back in town – it seems pretty thrown together, and the
jazz and blues entertainment is inconsistent. It's at ulitsa
Bolshaya Morskaya (ulitsa Gertsena) 58, just across the
street from the American Business Center – use the small
door on the left.

The Jazz Philharmonic Hall, formerly the Jazz Club,
is a weird place for Russia in that it prohibits smoking.
It has two bands – a straight jazz and an attempt at
Dixieland (it's not bad, and can be fun) – plus guests
doing mainstream and modern jazz, all hosted by the
co-founder, David Goloshchyokin, who runs about
being seen. Tickets for foreigners are US$3.80 (US$4.75
on Sunday), for Russians US$1.40/2.85. The club is at
Zagorodny prospekt, a 10-minute walk to the south-
west of metro Dostoevskaya (see the Central St
Petersburg map).

Also in that neighbourhood, the clubbier Kvadrat Jazz
Club at Pravdy ulitsa does traditional and mainstream
jazz; from metro Dostoevskaya, head for Bolshaya
Moskovskaya and take it south-west until it turns into
Pravdy.

ROCK

St Petersburg can lay a strong claim to being the Russian
rock capital, having produced in the 1980s top bands
like Akvarium, Alisa, Kino, DDT, AVIA, Televizor and

Populyarnaya Mekhanika. And now that the government's out of the creative process, the rock scene in St Petersburg is far less bleak than it used to be. It's not Amsterdam or London yet, but it's got the attitude of the early CBGBs and ever more venues in which to let off steam. Check The *St Petersburg Press*' weekly 'Music Scene' and 'Club Guide' or *Pulse* for listings of who's in town.

The TaMtAm Club, at the corner of Maly prospekt (Vasilevsky Side) and 16-ya Linia, is the ticket for head-bashing rock 'n' roll; it goes in and out of fashion, but low prices keep the place full of interesting people and few thugs – the latter don't bother going to places where they can't flaunt their wealth. Admission's a paltry US$1, and it's open Thursday to Saturday from 8 to 11 pm.

Another good obstreperous venue is the Ten Club, out in the middle of nowhere at Obvodnovo Kanala naberezhnaya 62 (from the nearest metro, Pushkinskaya, walk south to the canal, then east for about seven minutes; it's in the yellow building just past the factory), which charges US$2.40 admission. More convenient (just) to the centre is the Wild Side (☎ 186 34 66), a couple of blocks from metro Narvskaya. It has live rock and pop shows and disco, for a US$4.75 admission fee. It's at 12 Bumazhnovo Kanala naberezhnaya.

The Archwall Club at Pravdy ulitsa 10 (metro Dostoevskaya) has live rock concerts, but it's a bit tame; it also has a disco night on Saturday. Admission is $1.90 to US$2.85 for concerts. Rock Around The Clock (☎ 310 12 16) at Sadovaya ulitsa 20, between Nevsky prospekt and metro Sennaya Ploshchad, is a bar/restaurant that also has classic rock from 9 pm to 6 am. Admission from Sunday to Wednesday is US$4.75, while from Thursday to Saturday it's anyone's guess up to US$19.

NIGHTCLUBS & DISCOS

Check the *St Petersburg Press* and *Pulse* for listings. I guarantee there will be new places open, and some closures, by the time you visit. (See, also, the Pubs, Bars & Beer Gardens section of the Places to Eat chapter.)

The Western influence has taken its toll here; most new clubs are decidedly Western, and many import DJs from cities renowned for their nightlife – Paris, and New York come to mind – and sometimes from more unlikely places like Ouagodougou, Lagos and London. St Petersburg's raves are all-night affairs, usually in a con-verted theatre or sport complex, where thousands of young Russians and a smattering of foreigners party to acid-house and trance, replete with laser shows, naked people, the works. The ones that were held at the sport complex on the Petrograd Side (near the corner of Malaya Posadskaya ulitsa and Konny pereoluk) had all this, and the added bonus of an Olympic-sized swimming pool and an upstairs solarium! There's usually a high enough door fee to keep the riffraff out. Check the radio for ads or ask Russian friends.

St Petersburg's nightclubs seem to run through a definite life cycle: inception; buzz and hype; 'what-a-place'; discovery by gangsters, thugs and hoodlums; discovery by tourists; decline. That said, there are more than enough places to boogie in, and the list grows all the time. Most large hotels offer some sort of night bar, possibly with disco.

Domenico's (☎ 272 57 17) opened in 1994 and became very popular with expatriates and Russians alike. It's teamed up in the past with Mollies Irish Pub's management to do joint promotional nights (like midwinter beach blowouts awarding free drinks to those showing up in swimming trunks). It's also a class-act disco and nightclub. The address is Nevsky prospekt 70, between the Fontanka River and Rubinshteyna ulitsa. Admission is free before 9 pm and US$30 after 9 pm, and beers are US$4 to US$5. The food is rich but good: steak, a speciality, is US$11, pasta dishes are US$7 to US$9 and fish is US$11 to US$13.

The Tunnel (☎ 233 25 62) is popular and based in a bomb shelter, where it plays house and trance music. It is open Thursday to Saturday from midnight to 6 am. It's on Lyubyansky pereulok at Zverinskaya ulitsa (the closest metro's Gorkovskaya). Joy (☎ 311 35 40) is a popular place with Mercedes-Benz owners; it's perfectly located and we love that polyester look. Admission is about US$14, and it's open from 10 pm to 5 am at 1/27 Lomonosova ulitsa (it's the round thing) on the corner of naberezhnaya Kanala Griboedova.

Nevsky Melody (☎ 227 26 76) would be more popular if it were closer to the centre; it's out on Sverdlovskaya naberezhnaya, opposite the Smolny Cathedral and across the closed Bolshoy Okhtinsky bridge. But if you don't mind shelling out a lot, it's an interesting place to spend an evening. It has a disco downstairs, along with a casino, and it does erotic shows at about 1 am (it also runs an amateur strip night that's sometimes good for a laugh). It's open from 10 pm to 4 or 5 am.

The Stardust Nightclub at the Planetarium just behind the Peter & Paul Fortress is, depending on the night, fantastic fun or perfectly fine. It's huge and jammin' and it has live rock concerts, disco nights and some erotic evening shows. It's in Alexandrovsky Park, five minutes walk from Gorkovskaya metro.

Stiers Club (☎ 186 95 22) at ploshchad Stachek, opposite the Narvskaya metro station, is a pretty standard disco/nightclub that charges US$14 to get in. It has two bars, and is open Wednesday to Sunday 10 pm to 6 am.

Courier Disco (☎ 311 46 78), next to the Okoshki Art Cafe, is a traditional meat market, with ladies' nights on Saturdays, when women pay US$3.80 and men pay US$7. They play dance and house music; ulitsa Bolshaya Morskaya (ulitsa Gertsena) 58.

GAY & LESBIAN VENUES

Don't expect these listings to stretch on for pages: there were, at the time of writing, only three bars/clubs that catered to gays and lesbians, and they weren't exactly advertising heavily. To get in, either say you're *ya goluboy* (gay) or *ya lesbianka* (lesbian) to the hulking goon at the door; foreigners will probably be allowed in regardless of sexual orientation. Back rooms, called *chyornaya komnata* (black rooms), are not common, and are frowned upon by gay-rights activists because their legality is iffy at best.

The Klub/Disco at ulitsa Galernaya 33 is a weekend disco with a US$4 entry fee.

There's another weekend nightclub/disco downstairs at Teatr Experiment just near metro Petrogradskaya, and a small daily nightclub at ulitsa Mokhovaya 15.

CINEMA & VIDEO

Most of the cinemas in St Petersburg play US or other foreign movies that have been heinously translated and dubbed using a single male voice (the man is called a *lektor*) for all characters, which is only amusing during love scenes. The French recently lost their title as the world's worst translators (the line: 'Shot of rotgut – in a dirty glass'; the subtitle: *'Un apéritif, s'il vous plaît'*) when the Russian team, translating the movie *Wayne's World*, learned the Americanism 'hurl'. Cinemas charge less than US$1 for entry and films run continuously from about 1 to 10 pm.

When you tire of trying to pick out the English from beneath the lektor's voice, you can either attend a video screening or rent an English-language video.

The VideoStar Club (☎ 210 96 22 or 315 24 65) at Bistro le Francais, ulitsa Galernaya 20, screens a movie on

Wednesday and Thursday evenings and two on Sunday
(Sunday afternoons are going to be family movies). The
screenings are free and you can buy café snacks (great
chocolate truffles), beer and soft drinks; it also rents
English-language videos to club members. Membership
is US$30 per year, a US$50 security deposit and US$3 for
one film, US$5 for two and US$7.50 for three; rentals are
for 48 hours. It'll rent you a video player as well at a cost
of US$20 for two days. If you're in town for a while, it
has a home delivery service available, for which a US$2
charge is added to the rental price. It's open from noon
to midnight daily.

The HI St Petersburg Hostel has weekly video screenings in its lounge, which is open to the public; it charges
US$2 for Coke and popcorn.

CIRCUS & PUPPETS

The St Petersburg State Circus (☎ 210 46 49) has a permanent building at naberezhnaya Reki Fontanki 3, half
a km south of the Summer Garden. There are shows on
Tuesday, Wednesday and Friday at 7 pm and Saturday
and Sunday at 3 and 7 pm. It's closed Monday and
Thursday. The season runs from September to June.
Tickets bought here cost from US$0.60 to US$3, although
the foreigners' price is US$10.

For puppets, the main venue is the Bolshoy Teatr
Kukol (☎ 272 88 08), at Nekrasova ulitsa 10, with shows
on Saturday and Sunday at 11.30 am and 2 pm; tickets
for everyone (Russian or not, kid or not) cost between
US$0.30 and US$0.60. The Teatr Kukol-Marionetok, at
Nevsky prospekt 52 (☎ 311 19 00), does, as the name
suggests, puppet and marionette shows on a varying
schedule. Tickets cost between US$0.20 and US$1.

Shopping

No-one comes here specifically for the shopping, but a lot of people leave with their wallets a lot lighter, now that St Petersburg has almost everything you'd want – oftentimes cheaper than at home.

Most St Petersburg shops are open from 11 am to 7 or 8 pm, but Western-style shops, beryozki and department stores give you an extra hour or two at both ends. Virtually everything shuts for lunch from 2 to 3 pm and some places also close all day Sunday.

WHERE TO SHOP

Along Nevsky Prospekt

Russia's most famous avenue, Nevsky prospekt, is rapidly becoming one of St Petersburg's grandest shopping streets; as things are renovated and restored and new businesses open and old ones shape up, the strip between the Admiralty and Moscow Station is rapidly becoming the chic thoroughfare it was at the turn of the 20th century.

Optika Exclusive (No 13) is good for Western glasses and frames. There are a couple of good pharmacies along Nevsky – see under Health in Facts for the Visitor.

An Art Books shop selling maps and with an exchange office is at No 20. For other bookshops see Books & Maps in Facts for the Visitor.

Nike's shop at No 34 sells running shoes and accessories at high European prices. It's open from 11 am to 8 pm and takes cash only.

Barbie at No 63 is the place to go to get that special something for that special someone: a fountain mermaid Barbie is US$17, a magic change hair set US$5.20. It also has Ken dolls, and turbo colour Hot Wheels at US$5.40. It's open from 10 am to 7 pm.

Original Levis at Nevsky 102 has just that, at Western European prices.

See also Self-catering in the Places to Eat chapter.

Western Speciality Shops

Throughout the city, Western-owned shops (or shops appearing to be Western) pop up now and then, the most obvious examples being Barbie, Nike and Reebok on Nevsky prospekt. There are many more opening every day: Bally's mind-blowingly expensive accessories and trinkets shop (sports jacket – US$709) on Bolshoy prospekt (Petrograd Side) comes to mind. A miscellany: Lancôme, Yves Rocher and Nina Ricci all have shops along Nevsky prospekt selling designer perfume, trinkets, cologne etc; Diesel and Marco Pizzo at the Petrogradskaya metro sell, respectively, jeans, sweaters and casual wear and (decent) shoes; and just across the Karpovka, Rifle Jeans sells a great selection of out-of-season stock.

The Dutch-run Babylon chain has shops all over town, and each specialises in something: look on Liteyny prospekt (housewares) and Sadovaya ulitsa (men's clothing). There are also three along Bolshoy prospekt (Petrograd Side): at Kamennoostrovsky prospekt (Kirovsky prospekt) (women's clothing), north of Rybatskaya ulitsa (children's toys) and south of Rybatskaya ulitsa (photo supplies, film and cameras). There's also a 24-hour Super Babylon food shop at Maly prospekt 16.

Department Stores

The city's dotted with department stores; service and supplies are better than ever and it's great fun to join the thronging crowds in the big ones. Gostiny Dvor on Nevsky prospekt between ulitsa Dumskaya and Sadovaya ulitsa is St Petersburg's answer to Moscow's GUM, though its selection and service just aren't up to those of its big brother across the street, Passazh. Both of these stores are covered in the Things to See & Do chapter.

DLT at Bolshaya Konyushennaya ulitsa 21/23 began as a children's department store but now has a great supply of everything. It's still, however, the best place to start looking for imported and Russian-made toys and games, children's clothing etc. It also has a great selection of sporting goods at the back of the store.

All the department stores in the city have moneychanging offices, and many let out space to Western firms like Littlewoods, which sell a variety of Western goods (usually, though, not the best).

Kiosk Cities

Throughout the city, usually (though not always) adjacent to metro stations, dozens of kiosks group en masse selling generally the same stuff – counterfeit clothing from China, Finnish juice drinks, Western beer, cheap vodka, blue liquors, bootleg video cassettes, and Western cigarettes (the average price for a pack of 20 Marlboro and Winston

NICK SELBY

Shoppers' R&R outside Passazh

in 1995 was US$1.20, L&M US$0.85). Some, like the ones near Petrogradskaya, Chernyshevskaya, Ploshchad Muzhestva and Ploshchad Vosstania metros, are reliable suppliers of staple items, music cassettes and other goods, while others, like the one at metro Primorskaya, are just a blight on the landscape. The City of St Petersburg has passed regulations forcing kiosks to conform to aesthetic standards, so the kiosk cities are getting, albeit marginally, prettier.

Be *extremely* careful when buying alcohol in kiosks: make certain that the cap is an untampered screw-top (never the foil seal), and taste carefully before taking a full drink; err on the side of caution.

Markets

Markets are mainly for food, but the Krondatevsky fur market (see, unfortunately, the Places to Eat chapter) has some fantastic buys, though they're getting pricey. Always check the inside for mismatched fur, poor stitching etc.

WHAT TO BUY

Arts & Antiques

There are dozens of art and antique shops throughout the city, but only some of them – generally the more expensive – will walk you through the customs clearing procedures. See the Customs section in the Facts for the

Visitor chapter for complete details on what you can take out of the country and how to do it.

Palitra (☎ 277 12 16) is a gallery owned and operated by St Petersburg artists, and it's the real thing. It's at the end of Stary Nevsky, at No 166, and is open Tuesday to Saturday from 11 am to 7 pm. It serves coffee.

Dimion (☎ 275 34 94), at Nevsky prospekt 3, has a good selection of groovy rock-crystal items; It's open Monday to Friday from 10 am to 5 pm and Saturday and Sunday from 11 am to 7 pm.

The Exhibition Hall at the Union of Artists (☎ 314 30 60) displays some of the finest art works in St Petersburg, though prices here are higher and the artists give up a cut to the union. It's at ulitsa Bolshaya Morskaya (ulitsa Gertsena) 38, near Isaakilevskaya ploshchad, and is open Tuesday to Sunday from 1 to 7 pm.

Ananov at the Grand Hotel Europe (☎ 119 60 00) has that Fabergé egg you've been planning to buy to add elegance to the study; its prices are high enough to ensure that you'll have no problems clearing customs on the way out. It's open from 11 am to 8 pm.

There's an artists' market for tourists on both sides of Nevsky prospekt, near the Nevsky Prospekt metro station entrance at ulitsa Mikhailovskaya. On the south side of the street portrait artists sit beneath the arches, while purveyors of matryushka and other crapola wind around the corner opposite Gostiny Dvor. Opposite, the space just west of the Grand Hotel Europe's Sadko's restaurant is reserved for 'painting' and other locally produced 'art'.

Petersburg (☎ 273 03 41) is an antique salon with an exquisite selection of antique furniture, almost none of which you'll be able to get out of the country under normal circumstances. If you'll be living in town for awhile, or if you've got connections, it's a great place to shop. It's at ulitsa Furshtadtskaya 42, and is open Monday to Saturday from 11 am to 2 pm and 3 to 5 pm.

Na Liteynom antiquarian bookshop (☎ 275 38 73), in the courtyard at Liteyny prospekt 61, has a good selection of old books, as well as a small antique collection. It's open daily except Sunday from 11 am to 7 pm.

Film & Photographic Equipment

Russian photographic equipment can be a real bargain; see Film & Photography in Facts for the Visitor

Music & Video Cassettes

Copyright? Huh? You can find bootlegged music cassettes at kiosks around the city. Usually labelled in

Russian or bad English, the tapes are of varying quality. For higher quality, try Garmonia Lyuks, downstairs next to the florist at Shpalerna ulitsa 44 (☎ 272 16 88). The walls are covered with computer print-outs of the selections available. Pick what you want, either give the staff a tape or buy one from them and come back in about a week to pick up your cassette.

Mir Muzika at ulitsa Furshtadtskaya 42 has a small collection of CDs at US prices (about US$11 to US$14). For works rejected by the rest of the world, head for the Kodak shop on upper Nevsky prospekt, which has the very best of ABBA, Tom Jones and the meaningful ballads of Mr Julio Iglesias priced from US$15 to US$20; Melodia is still around at Nevsky prospekt 47, though these days it stocks more blenders than record albums; a real Melodia (☎ 232 11 39), which stocks a great selection of CDs and LPs of mainly Russian musicians (Russian CDs US$11; CDs by Western artist US$17 to US$21; LPs US$1.50 to US$3) still exists at Bolshoy prospekt (Petrograd Side) 47, and is open from 11 am to 7 pm daily.

Excursions

Between 25 and 45 km from central St Petersburg lie five splendid old tsarist palaces surrounded by lovely parks, all fine outings from the city. The time to see Petrodvorets *('petradvahr-YETS')* on the coast is summer, when its famous fountains are flowing and it can be reached by hydrofoil from St Petersburg. Pushkin has another glorious palace, and Pavlovsk has probably the loveliest park. These last two, lying close together south of the city, can be combined in one trip. Then there's Lomonosov, beyond Petrodvorets, and Gatchina, further south than Pushkin and Pavlovsk. All except Lomonosov suffered varying degrees of damage in WW II and some are still being restored.

Best of all, you don't need to book a tour or hire a guide; all of these obscenely lavish estates are open to the public and easily accessible by inexpensive public transport. A great option is the tours that leave from in front of the Kazan Cathedral on Nevsky prospekt; look for the person with the megaphone and book your tickets with them.

Tickets can also be booked at the excursion booth just outside Gostiny Dvor on ulitsa Dumskaya. Both of these places charge less than US$3 for a tour including transport. Peter TIPS and The St Petersburg Travel Company and hotel concierge desks offer coach tours to all the palaces for about US$20 per person or more.

The most frequently visited places are Petrodvorets, Pushkin and Pavlovsk. It's a good idea to take your own snacks to the palaces; most of them only have minimal (none, in the case of Lomonosov) offerings. For longer hauls, visitors to Petrozavodsk can get a quick ferry to the open-air museum on Kizhi island, featuring the dazzling 220-gabled Cathedral of the Transfiguration.

Finally, an overnight trip to the monastery at Valaam can make a very rewarding experience that not many take the time to enjoy.

PETRODVORETS

ПЕТРОДВОРЕЦ

Peter the Great had a cabin 29 km west of St Petersburg on the Gulf of Finland, to oversee construction of his Kronstadt naval base. He liked it so much there that he built a villa, Monplaisir, and then a whole series of palaces across an estate originally called Petergof, which has been called Petrodvorets (Peter's Palace) since 1944 (there was a brief attempt to rename the place Petergof in 1992, but it fizzled). All are set within a spectacular ensemble of gravity-powered fountains that are now the site's main attraction. This 'Russian Versailles' is probably the most impressive of St Petersburg's suburban palaces.

Petrodvorets was completely trashed by the Germans in WW II and is largely a reconstruction from photos, drawings and anecdotes.

There will almost always be something closed while you are there because, inexplicably, each site has its own closing days: Grand Palace, Monday and last Tuesday of the month; Marly, Tuesday and last Wednesday; Monplaisir, Hermitage and Catherine Building, Wednesday and last Thursday; Cottage, Friday and last Thursday. The estate is open 9 am to 10 pm daily, while the museums are open from 11 am to 8 pm from the end of May to the end of September. The Lower Park and Alexandria Park are open every day.

Because of the confounded opening hours, it's only possible to take in all the museums and palaces in a single day during weekends, when, naturally, the place is swarming with visitors. All the attractions charge separate admissions. Admission to the grounds is payable at the cash booth on the jetty.

Grand Cascade

The uncontested centrepiece is the Grand Cascade & Water Avenue, a symphony of fountains and canals partly engineered by Peter himself. The central statue of Samson tearing open a lion's jaws celebrates, as so many things in St Petersburg do, Peter's victory over the Swedes. All of the over 140 fountains run on gravity-pressured water.

To the disappointment of visitors since 1990, the Cascade has been shut down for restoration. With luck it will be squirting again by the time you see it, though it's difficult to say for certain. Other fountains are functional, and the trick fountains triggered by hidden switches (hidden, that is, by hordes of kids jumping on them) are designed to squirt passers-by. Normally the fountains play from 11 am to 8 pm daily from May to September.

Grand Palace

Between the cascade and the formal Upper Garden is the *Bolshoy dvorets* (Grand Palace). Peter's modest project,

ROGER HAYNE

Petrodvorets: outlook to Gulf of Finland

finished just before his death, was grossly enlarged by
Rastrelli for Empress Elizabeth and later redecorated for
Catherine the Great. It's now a vast museum of lavish
rooms and galleries – a monument above all to the craft
of reconstruction (which is still going on). Anything not
nailed down was removed before the Germans arrived,
so the paintings, furniture and chandeliers are original.

Highlights include the Chesma Hall, full of huge
paintings of Russia's destruction of the Turkish fleet at
Çesme in 1770, all by the same German artist. After the
battle Catherine arranged for a ship to be blown up so
he could paint it properly. In its pathological single-
mindedness, the room is not unlike a Lenin museum.
Two 'Chinese' rooms have walls of rich lacquered wood.
Between them is another bizarre gallery: 360 portraits of
eight young girls by the Italian Pietro Rotari, sold *en bloc*
to Catherine by his widow, who managed to slip in a few
elderly subjects too.

Of some 20 rooms, the last, without a trace of Catherine, is the finest – Peter's simple, beautiful study,
apparently the only room to survive the Germans. It has
14 fantastic carved-wood panels, of which six reconstructions (in lighter wood) are no less impressive; each
took 1½ years to do.

This palace should not be missed and would be best
viewed with a guide. Peter the Great still looks like the
tsar with the best taste.

You'll need to join a tour group to enter (US$5.50 for
foreigners, US$1 for Russians; photos US$2.15, video
US$5.50). Tickets are sold inside, near the lobby where
you pick up your tapochki.

Monplaisir

Peter's outwardly more humble villa, with study and galleries facing the sea, remained his favourite and it's not hard to see why: wood-panelled, snug and elegant, peaceful even when there's a crowd – which there used to be all the time, what with Peter's mandatory partying ('misbehaving' guests were required to gulp down huge quantities of wine). The main hall has marble floors and a richly painted ceiling; the kitchen is Dutch style, a little study is Chinese. Admission for foreigners/Russians is US$4.50/0.19 while photos/videos are US$1/2.

To the left is an annexe called the Catherine Building because Catherine the Great was living here – establishing an alibi? – when her husband Peter III was overthrown. Catherine Building admission is US$2.75/0.19, and US$1/2 for photos/video. Tickets are sold around the east side of the building.

Lower Park & Other Pavilions

Along the gulf is the Lower Park, with more fountains big and small, elegant and silly (watch out for the trick fountains), and more pavilions.

Near the shore, and finished soon after the Grand Palace, is a two-storey pink-and-white box called the Hermitage, which features the ultimate in private dining on the second floor. Special elevators hoist a fully laid table into the imperial presence, thereby eliminating any hindrance by servants. The elevators are circular and directly in front of each diner, whose plate would be lowered, replenished and replaced. Admission for foreigners/Russians is US$2.85/0.09, while photos/videos are US$1/2.

Further west is Marly, another of Peter's mini-palaces and guesthouses. To the east an old Orangery – which would appear to be a rest house for Russian tourists – houses the Historical Museum of Wax Figures, containing 49 figures of big-wigged Russians (from Peter I to Nicholas II) from the 18th and 19th centuries. Admission to the museum is US$2.85/0.09 while photos/videos are US$1/2.40. Get tickets in the small shack outside. It's open every day from 11 am to 6 pm.

Alexandria Park

Even on summer weekends, the rambling, overgrown Alexandria Park is peaceful and empty, and ideal for a leisurely walk. It was built for Tsar Nicholas I (and named for his tsarina) and it looks like his heart wasn't in his royal work. Besides a mock-Gothic chapel, its diversions include the Farmer's Palace (1831), which vaguely resembles a stone farmstead and is currently in ruins, and the Cottage (1829), which is modelled on an English country cottage.

Now a museum, the Cottage's rooms – neo-Gothic, Rococo or Art Nouveau depending on later renovations – are full of imperial bric-a-brac and hundreds of works by minor Russian artists. In the boudoir is a clock with 66 faces, one for each pre-Revolutionary province.

On the way back, what looks like a Gothic college campus was once the imperial stables and is now a retirement home (for humans, we suspect).

Petergof Palace Pharmacy

This peculiar tourist attraction is a brand-new, old-style apothecary shop with drawers full of medicinal plants – it looks (and smells) like the real thing. The staff will whip up a herb drink for you, and if your Russian's good enough you can talk to them about your ingrown whatsit. They've also got a fair selection of Western remedies, like Panadol. The Pharmacy is open from 8 am to 8 pm and closed Saturday. It's just east of the Upper Garden.

Petrodvorets Town

Outside the grounds is Petrodvorets town. Don't overlook the five-domed SS Peter & Paul Cathedral across the road, in traditional style but built only at the turn of the century. If you're around at 9.45 am and 4.45 pm you'll hear the church bells play a lovely tune. The cathedral holds evening services at 5 pm, and closes at 6 or 7 pm except on holidays, when night services are held.

Six km east of Petrodvorets is Strelna, another estate with parklands and two palaces built for Peter (later enlarged for Empress Elizabeth by Rastrelli).

Places to Stay

There's a dorm in the middle of all this – the *Sanitoriya Petrodvorets* (no telephone) – that has double rooms in a rest home for US$7.50 a person. It's at ulitsa Avrora 2.

Places to Eat

Just across from the pharmacy, the *Kafe Trapeza* (☎ 427 93 93) is a nice and cosy place doing veal with fried potatoes and chicken Kiev for about US$3.80. There's a newish

Galereya Kafe (☎ 427 98 84) in the back of the Bolshoy Palace – a stylish place doing snacks and light lunches from US$2 to US$4, and beer for about US$2. It's open from 10 am to 8 pm (closed Monday). The round pavilion near the boat landing has an adequate café, gril-bar and canteen, open from noon to 8 pm (closed Saturday).

Getting There & Away

Suburban trains take 40 minutes from Baltic Station to Novy Petrodvorets (not Stary Petrodvorets), departing every 30 to 60 minutes until early evening. Buy tickets from the cash desk for US$0.70. From Novy Petrodvorets Station, take any bus but No 357 to the fifth stop (the fourth is a church), which takes about 10 minutes, to the park; ask for 'fontana'. As you enter, arrowed signs direct you to the lower park, Monplaisir, Marly and the booking office.

For beating queues, a coach tour is a good idea, but be sure of what you'll see besides the grounds. An individual excursion with guide and rental car is a complete waste of money.

By road it's about an hour; there's plenty of street parking outside the grounds. You can get an official taxi for about US$35 to US$40 to take you there, wait for you and bring you back; alternatively, you can negotiate with any other taxi for a bit more.

From May to September, a fine alternative is the *Meteor* hydrofoil from the Hermitage Landing in front of St Petersburg's Hermitage, which goes every 20 to 30 minutes from 9.30 am to at least 7 pm. A ferry, which is much slower, leaves every 20 to 40 minutes from Morskaya pristan (Sea Landing) near Tuchkov Bridge on naberezhnaya Makarova, Vasilevsky Island. The trip takes half an hour and costs US$4, plus the US$1 park entry fee (US$0.05 for Russians) payable on the way out from St Petersburg.

To tour the grounds with the locals, queue at the ticket kiosks and join a tour narrated in Russian.

LOMONOSOV

ЛОМОНОСОВ

While Peter was building Monplaisir, his right-hand man, Alexandr Menshikov, began his own palace, Oranienbaum, 12 km farther down the coast. Menshikov never saw the finished product; following Peter's death and Menshikov's exile, the estate served briefly as a hospital and then passed to Tsar Peter III, who didn't much like ruling Russia and spent a lot of time at Oranienbaum. After doing away with him, his wife Catherine (the Great) made it her private pleasure ground.

Oranienbaum was not occupied by the Nazis. After WW II it was for some reason renamed for the scientist-poet Mikhail Lomonosov and now doubles as museum and public park, with boat rentals and carnival rides alongside the remaining buildings.

The park is open from 9 am to 10 pm all year, but the palace-museums are open only from 11 am to 6 pm (to 5 pm Monday), and closed Tuesday, the last Monday of the month, and in winter.

Things to See

Biggest of all, with semicircular galleries and lower garden, is Menshikov's **Grand Palace**, which is (still) under restoration, though a finishing date of 1996 has been given. A canal once linked it to the gulf. Beyond the pond is **Peterstadt**, Peter III's boxy toy palace, with rich, uncomfortable-looking interiors and some Chinese-style lacquer-on-wood paintings. It's approached through the **Gate of Honour**, all that remains of a toy fortress where he amused himself drilling his soldiers.

But most worth seeing is Catherine's over-the-top **Chinese Palace**, Baroque outside and extravagantly Rococo inside, a private retreat designed by Antonio Rinaldi with painted ceilings, fine inlaid-wood floors and walls, and decoration probably unequalled in any of the other St Petersburg palaces. The most blindingly sumptuous is the **Large Chinese Room**, designed in the 'Oriental' style of the day. The house, though restored, is not a reconstruction but the real thing. The nearby kitchen house has a small exhibition of furnishings. The Chinese Palace is open Monday and Wednesday to Friday from 11 am to 6 pm, and Saturday and Sunday from 10 am to 6 pm (closed Tuesday and the last Monday of the month).

The building that looks like a blue-and-white wedding cake is the **Coasting-Hill Pavilion**, the launching pad for Catherine's private roller coaster, a multistorey wooden slide down which courtiers would fly on little carts or toboggans. The slide is gone but the pavilion's extravagant inner rooms are worth a look. Tickets are sold inside the main entrance (US$2 for foreigners, US$0.10 for Russians) to the Porcelain Room and the White Room.

Perhaps Lomonosov's best feature is the several km of quiet paths through pine woods and sombre gardens, with relatively small crowds – a rarity on the Russian tourist trail. The town of Lomonosov has nothing to offer, not even food.

Getting There & Away

The suburban train from Baltic Station to Petrodvorets continues to Lomonosov; a ticket is US$1.10. Get off at Oranienbaum-I (not II) Station, an hour from St Petersburg. From the station, walk past a church and then cross prospekt Yunogo Lenintsa to the park entrance, a small stone gatehouse by a Lenin statue.

From May to September, hydrofoils come here from the Morskaya landing at naberezhnaya Makarova (near the Hotelship Peterhof) and the Tuchkov Bridge on Vasilevsky Island every 30 minutes, from about 7.30 am to at least 6 pm, for US$5. The route is Morskaya, Kronstadt, Lomonosov, Morskaya. Note that in 1995 this service was not available due to renovation of something or other at Lomonosov, and it is unclear when it will be reinstated.

PUSHKIN & PAVLOVSK

ПУШКИН И ПАВЛОВСК

The sumptuous palaces and big, beautiful parks at Pushkin and Pavlovsk, neighbours 25 km and 29 km south of St Petersburg, can be combined in a day's visit, but since they're both good places to relax, you might want to take them more slowly.

Pushkin's palaces and parks were created under empresses Elizabeth and Catherine the Great between 1744 and 1796. The centrepiece is the vast 1752-56 Baroque Catherine Palace (Yekaterininsky dvorets), designed by Rastrelli and named after Elizabeth's mother, Peter the Great's second wife. Pushkin used to be called Tsarskoe Selo (Tsar's Village) but was renamed after Russia's favourite poet, who once studied here, in 1937. The country's first railway opened in 1837 to carry the royal family between here and St Petersburg.

Pavlovsk's park of woodland, rivers, lakes, little valleys, avenues, classical statues and temples is one of the most exquisite in Russia, while its Great Palace (Bolshoy dvorets) is a classical contrast to the Catherine Palace. Palace and park were originally designed by Charles Cameron between 1781 and 1786, on Catherine the Great's orders, for her son, the future Paul I.

Information

At both places, getting into the parks and lesser exhibitions is little or no problem, but tickets for the two main palaces are zealously guarded by stern babushki who, like their comrades in the Hermitage, can smell Reeboks at 1000 metres: expect to pay the foreigner price (US$7.25, as opposed to US$0.50) unless your Russian is good. Russian-language tours (lose the group and wander freely amidst the luxury) run at set times between noon and 5 pm, and tickets for these are sold from 10 am until they run out, which they may do in an hour or two on busy days. So if you're keen to see the inside of a palace, you may avoid disappointment by taking an excursion – separate trips for the two places are usually available, each lasting about four hours. You could make your own way back to the city if you wanted to stay on afterwards.

The interior of the Catherine Palace is the more sumptuous, if you have to choose between the two. Count the breasts on the ceiling and see if you come up with an even number.

The parks are open every day, but the Catherine Palace is closed on Tuesday and the last Monday of the month, while the Great Palace at Pavlovsk is closed Friday and the first Monday of the month. The Catherine Palace is open 11 am to 6 pm in summer and until 5 pm in winter.

Catherine Palace

As at the Winter Palace, Catherine the Great had many of Rastrelli's original interiors remodelled in classical style. Charles Cameron, reputedly an aristocratic Scot but probably a London builder's son with a flair for long-term acting, was her chief redesigner. The palace was used in varying degrees by different tsars until 1917, but was ruined by the Germans in WW II. So far, most of Rastrelli's wonderful exterior and 20-odd rooms of the interior have been restored with no mean skill – compare the results with the photographs of the devastation left by the Germans and you shall be suitably impressed. The palace is 300 metres long, with the golden domes of its chapel rising at its north end, and outbuildings enclosing a courtyard on the west side. The visitors' entrance and ticket office are in the middle of the courtyard side.

All the rooms on show are upstairs. Visits normally start with the white State Staircase, an 1860 addition. South of here, only two rooms, both by Rastrelli, have been restored: the Gentlemen-in-Waiting's Dining Room (Kavalerskaya stolovaya) and, beyond, the Great Hall (Bolshoy zal), which is the largest room in the palace, all light and glitter from its windows, mirrors and gilded woodcarvings.

North of the State Staircase on the courtyard side come the State Dining Room, then the Crimson and Green Pilaster Rooms, and then the Portrait Room and the Amber Room (Yantarnaya komnata). This last was decorated by Rastrelli with gilded woodcarvings, mirrors, agate and jasper mosaics, and exquisitely engraved amber panels given to Peter the Great by the King of Prussia in 1716. But its treasures were plundered by the Nazis and went missing in Kaliningrad (then Königsberg) in 1945. Next is the large, sumptuous Picture Hall (Kartinny zal).

Most of the north end is Cameron's early classical work. The elegant proportions of the Green Dining Room (Zelyonaya stolovaya) on the courtyard side are typical. Also on the courtyard side are three rooms with fabulous patterned silk wall-coverings: the Blue Drawing Room (Golubaya gostinaya), the Chinese Blue Drawing Room (Kitayskaya golubaya gostinaya) – a severely classical design enlivened by the 18th-century fashion for Oriental motifs, all re-created since WW II from photos – and the Choir Anteroom (Predkhornaya), whose gold silk, woven with swans and pheasants, is the original from the 18th century. The anteroom leads into the Choir (Khory) itself and the chapel, designed by Rastrelli – both are painted blue and gold. On the park side, next to the Chinese Blue Drawing Room, is an elegant monarchical bedroom.

On the ground floor beneath the chapel are rooms used for temporary exhibitions, entered from the road outside, across which is the entrance to a branch of the Pushkin Museum. It has more than 20 rooms, and the only way to get in is to queue for a guided tour – it's mainly for enthusiasts of poetic paraphernalia and 19th-century Russia!

Pushkin Parks

Around the south and east of the Catherine Palace extends the lovely Catherine Park (Yekaterininsky park). The main entrance is on Komsomolskaya ulitsa in front of the palace.

The park's inner, formal section runs down terraces in front of the palace to Rastrelli's blue-and-white Hermitage building. Just off the south-east corner of the palace, Cameron's Cold Baths building, containing his extravagant Agate Rooms (Agatovye komnaty), is sometimes open. His Cameron Gallery next door, with a display of 18th and 19th-century costumes and carriages, is open daily except Tuesday. Its upper arcade was made for Catherine the Great to enjoy the views from. Between the gallery and the palace, notice the south-pointing ramp which Cameron added for the ageing empress to walk down into the park.

The park's outer section focuses on the Great Pond, where you can rent a boat in summer. This section is dotted with an intriguing array of structures ranging from the 'Pyramid', where Catherine the Great buried her favourite dogs, to the Chinese Pavilion (or Creaking Summerhouse), the Marble Bridge (copied from one at Wilton, England) and the Ruined Tower, which was built ready-ruined in keeping with a 1770s romantic fashion – maybe an 18th-century empress's equivalent of pre-faded jeans!

A short distance north of the Catherine Palace along ulitsa Vasenko, the classical Alexander Palace was built by Quarenghi in 1792-96 for the future Alexander I. It isn't open to the public. Nor officially, it seems, is the wild and empty Alexander Park, which extends on three sides of it, adjoining the Catherine Park in the south. But usually you'll find the odd gate open or a section of fencing missing, enabling people to wander into the park without any problems. One such gate is behind the Catherine Palace.

Pavlovsk Great Palace

Cameron's original palace was a three-storey domed square with single-storey wings curving only halfway round the existing courtyard. Paul loathed his mother, and with his wife, Maria Fyodorovna, wanted a more restrained, more French approach to building than Cameron's. The Englishman was replaced by his assistant Vincenzo Brenna, who disproportionately enlarged the wings and, along with other noted architect/designers like Quarenghi and Rossi, completed the inside. The palace, a royal residence until 1917, burnt down in WW II but was fully restored by 1970.

The finest rooms are on the middle floor of the square central block. Cameron designed the round Italian Hall beneath the dome, and the Grecian Hall to its west, though the lovely green fluted columns were added by Brenna. Flanking these are two private suites mainly designed by Brenna: Paul's along the north side of the block, and Maria Fyodorovna's on the south. The insane, military-obsessed Paul's Hall of War – he's also responsible for the Engineers' Castle in St Petersburg – contrasts with Maria's Hall of

Peace, which is decorated with musical instruments and flowers. Cameron's Egyptian Vestibule is on the ground floor at the foot of the stairs.

On the middle floor of the south block are Paul's Throne Room and the Hall of the Maltese Knights of St John, of whom he was the Grand Master. Also in the palace is an exhibition on 19th-century Russian interiors, for which tickets are sold separately.

Getting There & Away

Take one of the frequent suburban trains from the Vitebsk Station in St Petersburg. They usually go from platform 1, 2 or 3, and you can get tickets from the cash desk. They go to Detskoe selo Station (zone 3, US$0.50) for Pushkin, and to Pavlovsk Station (zone 4, US$0.60) for Pavlovsk. It's about half an hour to either place.

A five-minute ride on bus No 370, 371, or 378 from outside Detskoe Selo Station takes you to within two minutes walk of Pushkin's Catherine Palace. From Pavlovsk Station, you can reach the Great Palace either by bus No 370, 383, 383A or 493 (five to 10 minutes); or by entering the park across the road from the station, and walking 1.5 to two km across it to the palace. Walking at least one way across the park is a good idea. Bus No 370 also runs to and from Pushkin (two blocks from the Catherine Palace), so it's easy to get between Pavlovsk and Pushkin.

GATCHINA
ГАТЧИНА

Catherine the Great's lover Grigory Orlov had a palace and park created at Gatchina, 48 km south of St Petersburg, between 1776 and 1782. Later, Paul I moved here from Pavlovsk to remodel it as a medieval castle with drawbridges and battlements. Post-WW II renovation is still going on, but about half the place is up and running. There's also an exhibition of firearms and weaponry from the 17th to the 19th centuries. In the lovely palace park is the **Birch House**, an imperial joke that looks like a stack of logs from outside, but opens up to reveal a suite of palatial rooms lined with mirrors. There's also Black Lake, with a **priory** on its shore, and White Lake, with a **Temple of Venus** on its Island of Love.

Getting There & Away

Frequent trains go to Gatchina from St Petersburg's Baltic Station. There aren't regular group coach trips to

Gatchina: a car and guide from The St Petersburg Travel Company costs around US$100 for up to three people, for about four hours including the drive there and back.

VALAAM

ВАЛААМ

The Valaam Archipelago, which consists of Valaam Island and about 50 smaller ones, sits in north-western Lake Ladoga *('LAH-da-ga')* south of south-western Karelia and north of St Petersburg. The main attractions here are the 14th-century **Valaam Transfiguration Monastery** (Spaso-Preobrazhenskii Valaamsky monastyr), its cathedral and buildings, and the pleasant town that surrounds it.

There is some dispute about the identity of the first settlers – some sources say that they were 10th-century monks – but most agree that the monastery was first settled in the late 14th century as a fortress against Swedish invaders, who managed to destroy it completely in 1611. Rebuilt with money from Peter the Great, the monastery doubled as a prison.

Many of the monks and much of the monastery's treasure were moved to Finland, which controlled the territory between 1918 and 1940, when it fell back into Soviet hands. The Soviet authorities closed the monastery, took whatever was left and built what they referred to as an 'urban-type settlement' here.

Today the buildings are protected architectural landmarks, but neglect has taken its toll. Many of the buildings are decrepit and in need of immediate repair. Concerned people are trying hard, but in many cases arguments about how to proceed with the restoration have impeded progress, and lack of funding compounds the difficulties.

There are about 600 residents on the main island, including army service personnel, restoration workers, guides and clergy, most of whom get around in horse-drawn carriages or motorboats.

The most common way to get here and, once here, to get around is on tour boats which leave from St Petersburg at night, arrive in the morning, do about a six-hour tour of the islands, and then head back, arriving in St Petersburg the following morning. Getting here from Karelia, while less common, can be a more satisfying adventure.

Getting There & Away

Cruise ships leave the St Petersburg River Terminal frequently, but on uncertain schedules; check with Sindbad Travel (☎ 327 83 84) or Peter TIPS (☎ 279 00 37) to see when they'll go during your stay. The river terminal (☎ 262 02 39, 262 13 18) is at prospekt Obukhovskoy oborony 195, near metro Proletarskaya. It's open daily from 9 am to 9 pm. The cruise, which lasts for two nights and one day, costs from US$54 to US$78 including full board. If you add Kizhi, the trip becomes one of four nights and three days and costs from US$145 to US$208 including full board.

These prices are the same for Russians and foreigners, though foreigners are required to buy a 'voucher' – essentially a surcharge – which costs US$30 for Valaam, US$60 for Valaam and Kizhi. Tickets can be booked at the river terminal or through Sindbad Travel, which charges a service fee of US$10 per ticket.

KIZHI ISLAND

КИЖИ ОСТРОВ

An old pagan ritual site, Kizhi Island, 55 km north-east of the Karelian city of Petrozavodsk across Lake Onega, made a natural 'parish' for 12th-century Russian colonists, though none of the earliest churches remain.

Its centrepiece is the fairy-tale **Cathedral of the Transfiguration** (Preobrazhensky sobor, 1714), with a chorus of 22 domes, gables and ingenious decorations to keep water off the walls. Even so, it's now so rickety that it's been closed, and in spite of UNESCO protection nobody can agree on how to restore it. Next door is the nine-domed **Church of the Intercession** (Pokrovskaya tserkov, 1764). The icons from the cathedral are on display here and in the Petrozavodsk Fine Arts Museum.

The other buildings in the collection were brought from the region around Lake Onega. Rich and poor 19th-century peasant houses are nicely restored inside. The little 14th-century **Church of the Resurrection of Lazarus** may be the oldest wooden building in Russia. The **Chapel of the Archangel Michael** has an exhibit on Christianity in Karelia, and music students from Petrozavodsk play its bells in the summer.

There are more wooden churches outside the 'museum', and a hamlet with houses like the ones inside, but occupied. From the landing it's three km north to another village and five km to the end of the island. The silence, fresh air and views on a sunny day are reason enough to come here (but beware of poisonous snakes in the remoter parts).

Museum entry fees are steep for foreigners (though we paid the Russian price simply by saying *'odin bilet, pazhalsta'*, meaning 'one ticket, please') at US$9.50; Russians pay about US$0.50, and Russian students pay less than US$0.05. Karelian residents enter free.

A restaurant is near the landing, but it seems to want to sell drinks more than food. Just opposite the pier is a small kiosk cluster, including an 'art shop' selling heinously overpriced souvenirs, and a café that has some snacks. There's a map of the museum and island 50 metres south-east of the kiosk cluster.

NICK SELBY

Cathedral of the Transfiguration, Kizhi Island

Getting There & Away

Cruise ships from St Petersburg stop here as part of the St Petersburg-Valaam-Kizhi circuit. (For more information, see the Getting There & Away section of Valaam earlier in this chapter). You can only go during 'navigation season', which is mid-May to mid-November.

Glossary

aeroport – airport
aerovokzal – air terminal in city
apteka – pharmacy
avtobus – bus
avtovokzal – bus station
babushka – grandmother
banya – bathhouse
benzin – petrol
bilet – ticket
bufet – snack bar, usually in a hotel, selling cheap cold meats, boiled eggs, salads, bread, pastries etc
bulochnaya – bakery
buterbrod – open sandwich
dacha – country cottage, summer house
deklaratsia – customs declaration
Detsky Mir – Children's World (department store name)
dezhurnaya – hotel floor lady
dom – house
duma – parliament
elektrichka – suburban train
etazh – floor (storey)
GAI – State Automobile Inspectorate (traffic police)
gazeta – newspaper
glavpochtamt – main post office
gril-bar – grill bar, often limited to roast chicken
gorod – city, town
gostinitsa – hotel
ikra – caviar
izveshchenie – notification
kafe – café
kassa – ticket office, cashier's desk
khleb – bread
klyuch – key
kniga – book
krazha – theft
kreml – kremlin, a town's fortified stronghold
kvartira – flat, apartment
kvitantsia – receipt
magazin – shop
manezh – riding school
marka – postage stamp or brand, trade mark
marshrutnoe taxi – minibus that runs along a fixed route
mashina – car
matryoshka – set of painted wooden dolls within dolls
mesto – place, seat

militsia – police
mineralnaya voda – mineral water
morskoy vokzal – sea terminal
most – bridge
muzey – museum
muzhskoy – men's (toilet)
naberezhnaya – embankment
novyy – new
obed – lunch
obmen valyuty – currency exchange
ostanovka – bus stop
ostrov – island
pereulok – lane
plan goroda – city map
ploshchad – square
pochtamt – post office
poezd – train
poliklinika – medical centre
prospekt – avenue
rechnoy vokzal – river terminal
reka – river
remont – closed for repairs (a sign you'll see all too often)
restoran – restaurant
rubl – rouble
rynok – market
sanitarnyy den – literally 'sanitary day'; the monthly day on which establishments shut down for cleaning
schyot – bill
sever – north
sobor – cathedral
staryy – old
stolovaya – canteen, cafeteria
teatr – theatre
tserkov – church
tsirk – circus
tualet – toilet
tuda i obratno – 'there and back', return ticket
ulitsa – street
uzhin – dinner
vkhod – way in, entrance
voda – water
vokzal – station
vostok – east
vorovstvo – theft
yug – south
zal – hall, room
zaliv – gulf, bay
zapad – west
zhenskiy – women's (toilet)
zheton – token (for metro etc)

Index

319
Notes

Notes

321
Notes

Maps

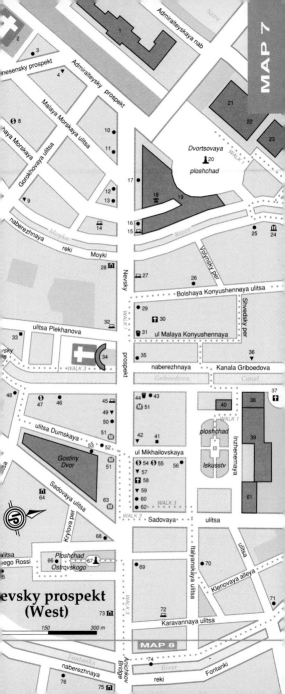

MAP 7

Admiralteyskaya nab

Neva

1

2

3

nesensky prospekt

Admiralteysky prospekt

4

Malaya Morskaya ulitsa

haya Morskaya

8

Gorokhovaya ulitsa

10

11

17

12

13

9

14

16

15

Dvortsovaya
20
ploshchad

WALK 1

18

19

21

22

23

25

24

naberezhnaya

Moyka

reki   Moyki

28

River

27

Volvinsky per

26

Nevsky

Bolshaya Konyushennaya ulitsa

Shvedsky per

29

30

ul Malaya Konyushennaya

31

32

ulitsa Plekhanova

33

34

35

prospekt

36

naberezhnaya   Kanala Griboedova

WALK 3

sky
e

WALK 3

Griboedova   Canal

48

37

47   46

45

44   43

40

38

M 51

49

50

ulitsa Dumskaya

51   M

ploshchad

39

42   41

53   52

Gostiny
Dvor

M
51

ul Mikhailovskaya

54   55   56

Iskusstv

Inzhenernaya

Sadovaya ulitsa

63

M

57

58

59

60

62

WALK 3

61

64

WALK 3   Sadovaya   ulitsa

68

ulitsa
ego Rossi

66

Ploshchad
Ostrovskogo

67

69

70

Italyanskaya ulitsa

ulitsa

Klenovaya alleya

71

evsky prospekt
(West)

73

72

WALK 3

Karavannaya ulitsa

150   300 m

MAP 8

Fontanka

naberezhnaya

76

75

Anichkov
Bridge

74   River   reki   Fontanki

Map 7   Nevsky Prospekt (West)

PLACES TO STAY

5   Hotel Astoria
    Гостиница Астория
33 Student Dormitory
    Обшежитье
41 Grand Hotel Europe
    Европа Гранд Хотел

PLACES TO EAT

4   Tandoor Indian
    Restaurant
    Ресторан Индиский
    Тандор
9   Pizza Hut
    Пицца Хат
14 Transcarpathian Café
    Кафе Закарпатское
15 Kafe Literaturnoe
    Кафе Литературное
27 Minutka
    Минутка
32 Bon Jour Fast Food
36 Restaurant\Café St
    Petersburg
    Ресторан и Кафе Санкт
    Петербург
42 Sadko's
    Ресторан Садко
44 Chayka Bar
    Бар Чайка
45 Balkany Café
    Балканы кафе
49 Nevsky 27 Bakery
    Невский 27
    булочная-кондитерская
57 Nevsky 40
    Невский 40
59 Grillmaster
    Грилмастер
69 Yeliseevsky Food Shop
    Гастрономая Елисеевский
72 Kafe 01
    Кафе 01

OTHER

1   Admiralty
    Адмиралтейство
2   St Isaac's Cathedral
    Исаакиевский собор
3   Finnair Office
    Финнаир
6   Air France
    Аир Франц
7   Airline Offices
    Конторы авиа-компании
8   Bank
    Банк
10 Beryozka
    Берёзка
11 Aeroflot
    Аэрофлот
12 Bookshop
    Книги
13 Bookshop
    Книги
16 Staraya Kniga
    Старая книга
17 Nevsky Prospekt 14
    Невский проспект 14
18 Central Telephone Office
    Телефон
19 General Staff Building
    Здание Главного штаба
20 Alexander Column
    Александровская
    колонна
21 Winter Palace
    Зимний дворец
22 Little Hermitage
    Малый Эрмитаж
23 Large Hermitage
    Великой Эрмитаж
24 Pushkin Flat-Museum
    Музей-квартира А.С.
    Пушкина
25 Glinka Capella
    Хоровая капелла имени
    М.И. Глинки
26 DLT Department Store
    Д.Л.Т. Универмаг
28 Stroganov Palace
    Строгановский дворец
29 24-Hour Pharmacy
    Аптека (24-Часа)
30 Lutheran Church
    Лутеранский церковь
31 Koff Beer Garden
34 Kazan Cathedral
    Казанский собор
35 Dom Knigi
    Дом книги
37 Church of the
    Resurrection of Christ
    Храм Воскресения
    Христова
38 Benois Building
    Корпус Бэнуа
39 Russian Museum
    Русский музей
40 Maly Theatre
    Малый театр
43 Gino Ginelli's
46 Central Train Ticket
    Office
    Железнодорожные
    билетные кассы
47 Bank
    Банк
48 Joy Nightclub
    Джой
50 Central Art Salon
    Центральный
    художественный салон
52 Theatre Booking Office
    Театральная касса

JOHN NOBLE

Beleselsky-Belezersky Palace

Map 8 Nevsky Prospekt (East)

PLACES TO STAY

14 Nevskij Palace Hotel
  Гостиница Невский Палац
28 Hotel Oktyabrskaya
  Гостиница Октябрьская
32 HI St Petersburg Hostel & Sinbad Travel

PLACES TO EAT

5 Shen Yen Restaurant
7 Carrols
16 Afrodite Restaurant
  Ресторан Афродите
20 Restoran Nevsky
  Ресторан Невский
23 John Bull Pub
  Джон Булл Пуб
24 Baskin Robbins
  Баскин Роббинс
26 Carrols
30 Warsteiner Forum
  Варштайнер Форрум
33 Bahlsen-Le Café & Bakery

OTHER

1 Anichkov Bridge Landing
  Аничковская пристань
2 Beloselsky-Belozersky Palace
  Белосельский-Белозерский дворец
3 Cultural Centres
4 Maly Dramatic Theatre
  Малый драматический театр
6 Cop Shop
8 Domenico's
  Клуб Доменико
9 Sporting Goods
  Спортивний магазин
10 Babylon
  Вавилон
11 Cosmos Supermarket (24-hour)
  Супермаркет Космос
12 Bank
  Банк
13 Vladimir Church
  Владимирская церковь
15 Westpost and Peter TIPS
17 Afrodite Beer Garden
  Афродите пивной бар
18 Federal Express
19 Babylon Market
  Рынок Вавилон
22 Arctic & Antarctic Museum
  Арктический и Антарктический музей
25 Pharmacy
  Аптека
29 24-Hour Supermarket
  Супермаркет (24-часа)
31 Phillips

METRO STATIONS

21 Mayakovskaya
  Маяковская
27 Ploshchad Vosstania
  Площадь Восстания

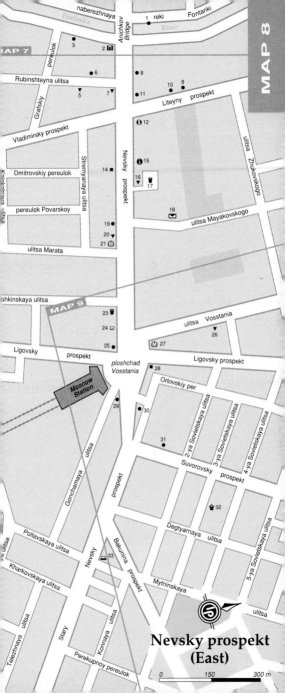

MAP 8

naberezhnaya

Fontanka

Anichkov
Bridge

1 reki   Fontanki

River

MAP 7

3

2

6

Rubinshteyna ulitsa

8

pereulok

Gratskiy

5   7

10   9

11

Liteyny   prospekt

12

Vladimirsky prospekt

15

Stremyanaya ulitsa

ulitsa Zhukovskogo

16

Dmitrovskiy pereulok

14

17

Nevsky   prospekt

pereulok Povarskoy

18

ulitsa Mayakovskogo

19

20

ulitsa Marata

21

shkinskaya ulitsa

MAP 9

23

ulitsa   Vosstania

24

26

Ligovsky   prospekt

25

27

Ligovsky prospekt

ploshchad
Vosstania

28

Moscow
Station

Orlovskiy per

29

30

2-ya Sovietskaya ulitsa

3-ya Sovietskaya ulitsa

4-ya Sovietskaya ulitsa

31

Suvorovsky   prospekt

Goncharnaya   ulitsa

prospekt

32

Degtyarnaya   ulitsa

Poltavskaya ulitsa

5-ya Sovietskaya ulitsa

Bakunina   prospekt

Kharkovskaya ulitsa

33

Nevsky

Mytninskaya

Telezhnaya   ulitsa

Stary

Kontnaya   ulitsa

Perekupnoy pereulok

ulitsa

Nevsky prospekt
(East)

0   150   300 m

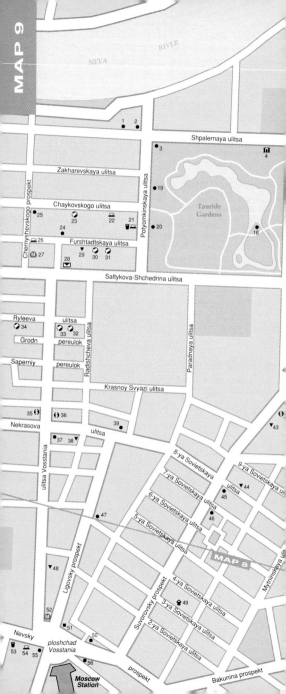

MAP 9

RIVER

NEVA

1 2

Shpalernaya ulitsa

3

4

Zakharevskaya ulitsa

19

Chaykovskogo ulitsa

25

23

22

21

Tauride
Gardens

24

20

26

Furshtadtskaya ulitsa

16

M 27

28

29 30 31

Saltykova-Shchedrina ulitsa

Ryleeva

34

ulitsa

Grodn

33 32

pereulok

Saperniy

pereulok

Krasnoy Svyazi ulitsa

35

36

39

43

Nekrasova

37 38

ulitsa

8-ya Sovietskaya

9-ya Sovietskaya ul

7-ya Sovietskaya ulitsa

ulitsa

44

45

6-ya Sovietskaya ulitsa

47

5-ya Sovietskaya ulitsa

46

MAP 8

48

4-ya Sovietskaya ulitsa

49

3-ya Sovietskaya ulitsa

52
M

2-ya Sovietskaya ulitsa

Nevsky

51

50

ploshchad
Vosstania

53 54 55

56

prospekt

Bakunina prospekt

Moscow
Station

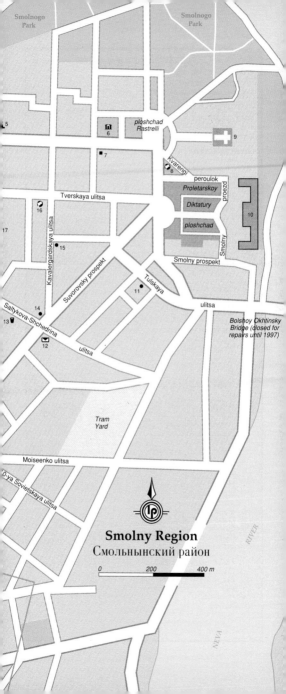

Smolnogo
Park

Smolnogo
Park

5

6

ploshchad
Rastrelli

9

7

Kvareng

8

peroulok

Tverskaya ulitsa

Proletarskoy

16

Diktatury

17

ploshchad

10

15

Smolny proezd

Smolny prospekt

Tulskaya

11

ulitsa

*Bolshoy Okhtinsky
Bridge (closed for
repairs until 1997)*

14

13

12

ulitsa

Saltykova-Shchedrina

Kavalergardskaya ulitsa

Suvorovsky prospekt

Tram
Yard

Moiseenko ulitsa

D-ya Sovietskaya ulitsa

RIVER

Smolny Region
Смольнынский район

0   200   400 m

NEVA

Map 9   Smolny Region

PLACES TO STAY

7 Student Dormitory
   Обшежитье
49 HI St Petersburg Hostel & Sindbad Travel
51 Oktyabrskaya Hotel
   Гостиница Октябрьская

PLACES TO EAT

17 Karavay Bakery
   Каравай Булочная
21 Kafe/Saloon
   Кафе/Салон
22 Vechernee Kafe
   Вечернее Кафе
25 Kiosks
   Киоски
26 Café (Summer only)
   Кафе
29 Kafe Bagdad
   Кафе Баглад
38 Springtime Shwarma Bistro
   Шварма
43 Verona Pizzeria
   Верона Пищериа
44 Ariran Restaurant
   Ресторан Ариран
48 Carrols
50 Warsteiner Forum
   Варштайнер Форум
54 Baskin Robbins
   Баскин Роббинс

OTHER

1 Garmonia Lyux
   Гармония Люкс
2 Flower Shop
   Интерфлора
3 Flowers Exhibition Hall
   Выставочный зал
4 Tauride Palace
   Таврический дворец
5 Dzerzhinsky Statue
   Памятник Ф Дзержинскому
6 Music School No 2
   Музыкальная школа No 2
8 British Consulate
   Консульство Велико-Британии
9 Smolny Cathedral
   Смольный собор
10 Smolny Institute
   Смольный Институт
11 Supermarket
   Супермаркет
12 Post & Telephone Office
   Почта и Телефон
13 Sidewalk Bar (open 24 hours)
   Бар
14 Pharmacy
   Аптека
15 Supermarket (24 hours)
   Супермаркет (24-часа)

MAP 10

To Peter & Paul Fortress
& Petrograd Side

Birzhevoy Bridge

STRELKA

Dvortsovy Bridge

MALAYA NEVA RIVER

naberezhnaya Makarova

1

2

4

5

6

3

7

Birzhevoy prospekt

Birzhevoy prospekt

Tamozhyonny
pereulok

Mendeleevskaya linia

8

Birzhevaya linia

9

ST PETERSBURG
STATE UNIVERSITY

10

Filologichesky pereulok

Strelka, Vasilevsky Island
Стрелка, остров Василевское

0   200   400 m

Universitetskaya naberezhnaya

NEVA RIVER (BOLSHAYA NEVA)

11

To Morskaya
Pristan Landing

Sezdovskaya & 1-ya linii

12

13

Ploshchad
Shevchenko

ulitsa Repina

Bolshoy

ulitsa Repina

2-ya & 3-ya linii

2-ya & 3-ya linii

16

14

prospekt

15

4-ya & 5-ya linii

4-ya & 5-ya linii

17

Leytenant
Shmidta
Bridge

Bugsky per

21

22

20

19 18

6-ya & 7-ya linii

6-ya & 7-ya linii

Map 10 Strelka, Vasilevsky Island

1 Rostral Column
Ростральная колонна
2 Rostral Column
Ростральная колонна
3 Institute of Russian Literature
(Pushkin House)
Институт русской литературы
(Пушкинский дом)
4 Museum of Agriculture
Музей сельского хозяйства
5 Central Naval Museum
Центральный военно-морской музей
6 Museum of Zoology
Зоологический музей
7 Museum of Anthropology
& Ethnography (Kunstkammer)
Музей антропологии и этнографии
(Кунтскаммер)
8 Lomonosov Statue
Памятник Ломоносову
9 Twelve Colleges
Двенадцать коллегий
10 Philological Faculty
Филологический факультет
Государственного Университета
11 Menshchikov Palace
Дворец Меншикова
12 Church of St Catherine
Церковь св. Екатерины
13 Sirin Bar & Restaurant
Ресторан Сирина
14 Kafe Nika (De Koninck)
Кафе Ника
15 Academy of Arts Museum
Музей академии художеств
16 Sphinx Monument
Свинкс
17 Sphinx Monument
Свинкс
18 Salon Best
Салон Бест
19 Pivo Stand
Пиво
20 Market
Рынок
21 St Andrew's Cathedral
Андреевский собор
22 Church
Церковь

To Television
Tower

Professora Popova ulitsa

Medikov prospekt

Aptekarsky prospekt

Aptekarskaya naberezhnaya

Botanical
Museum

Botanical   Gardens

Karpovka River

naberezhnaya   reki   Karpovki

13
14

15
16

Lva Tolstogo pereulok

**Inner Petrograd
Side**
Петроград, внутренняя
сторона

0   200   400 m

Chapaeva ulitsa

Rentgena ultisa

66

Monetnaya Bolshaya   ulitsa

Kotovskogo ulitsa

65 ★

64

63 ★

ulitsa Mira

Mat Monetnaya ul

62 ▼

Divenskaya ulitsa

61

Bol Posadskaya ulitsa

55

60
59
58

57

Malaya

56

54

Posadskaya ulitsa

Kronverkskaya ulitsa

Sytny
Rynok

52

53

Kamennoostrovsky prospekt

50

41
42

0

MAP 6

51

49
48

47

ulitsa Kuybysheva

46

45

44

naberezhnaya

43

Kronverkskaya

Petrovskaya naberezhnaya

To Cruiser
Aurora (400 m)

Peter & Paul
Fortress

Trotsky Bridge

NEVA   RIVER

Zayachy Island

Map 11   Inner Petrograd Side

PLACES TO STAY

4 Future Hotel Site

PLACES TO EAT

1 Chick-King
Чик-Кинг
2 Kafe
Кафе
3 Imperial Restaurant
Ресторан Империал
12 Sandwich Café
Кафе Сандвич
13 2+2 Café
Кафе 2+2
18 Restaurant
Petrogradskoe
Ресторан Петроградское
19 Kafe Tet-a-Tet
Кафе Тет-а-тет
21 Khaibei and Express
Café
Хаибеи и Экспресс Кафе
35 Pirosmani Restaurant
Ресторан Пиросмани
36 Pirosmani Pavement
Café
Кафе Пиросмани
38 Demyanova Ukha Res-
taurant
Ресторан Демьянова уха
39 Kafe Tbilisi
Кафе Тбилиси
41 Baskin Robbins (Ice
Cream)
Баскин Роббинс
47 Kafe Fortetsia
Кафе Фортеция
51 Kafe Grot
Кафе Грот
56 Grand Café Antwerpen
Кафе Антверпен
61 Troitsky Most (Hare
Krishna Kafe)
Троицкий мост
(Харе Кришна Кафе)
62 Gril Diez
Грил Диез

OTHER

5 Church
Церковь
6 Bank
Банк
7 Post Office
Почта
8 Telegraph/Telephone
Office
Телеграф и Телефон
9 Popov Statue
Памятник Попову
10 Cinema
Кино
11 Book Shop
Книжний Магазин
15 Teatr Experiment
Театр Эксперимент
16 Bank
Банк
17 Babylon
Вавилон
20 Photo Shop
Фото
22 Kodak One-Hour Photo
Кодак 1-Час
23 Kodak One-Hour Photo
Кодак 1-Час
24 Lenin Statue
Памятник В. И. Ленину
25 Melodiya
Мелодия
26 Bank
Банк
27 Babylon Super
Вавилон супер
28 Bally
Баллы
29 Babylon Toys
Вавилон игрушки
30 Babylon Photo Express
Вавилон фото экспресс
31 Bank
Банк
32 Everything For
Fishermen
Всё для рыболовова
33 Staraya Kniga
Старая Книга
34 Newton (Electronic Dept
Store)
Нютон (Электронный
магазин)
37 Zoo
Зоопарк
40 Music Hall
Мюзик Хол
42 Planetarium
Планетариум
43 Artillery Museum
Артиллерийский музей
44 Petrol Station
Бензо-колонка
45 GAI Booth
ГАИ
46 Peter's Cabin
Домик Петра Великого
48 Diana Sporting Goods
Спортивний магазин
Диана
49 Museum of Political
History
Музей Русской
Политической Истории
50 Mosque
Мечеть
53 GAI Booth
ГАИ

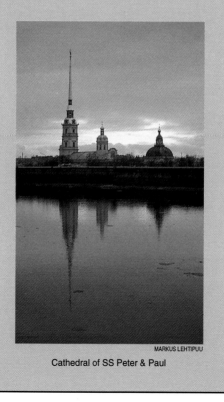

MARKUS LEHTIPUU

Cathedral of SS Peter & Paul

Map 12   Kirovsky Islands

PLACES TO STAY

25 Dvorets Molodyozhy Hotel
   Гостиница Дворец молодёжи
29 Hotel Druzhba
   Гостиница Дружба
37 Future Hotel Site

PLACES TO EAT

4 Kafe
   Кафе
19 Kafe
   Кафе
24 Restaurant Tryum
   Ресторан Трюм
33 Kafe
   Кафе
34 Chick-King
   Чик-Кинг
35 Kafe
   Кафе
36 Imperial Restaurant
   Ресторан Империал

OTHER

1 Buddhist Temple
   Буддистский дацан
2 Boat Rental
   Прокат лодок
3 Amusement Park
   Аттракционы
5 Stables
   Конюшни корпус
6 Kitchen Building
   Кухонный корпус
7 Yelagin Palace
   Елагинский дворец
8 Polovtsev House
   Дом Половцева
9 Danish Consulate General
   Генеральный консул
   Дании
10 Sports Hall
   Спортывний зал
12 Military Naval Academy
   Военно-Морская
   Академия

13 Kamennoostrovsky Palace
   Каменно-Островский
   дворец
14 Church of St John the Baptist
   Церковь Иоанна Предтечи
15 Sphinx Monuments
   Свинкс
16 Peter's Tree
   Дуб Петра I
17 Kamenny Island Theatre
   Каменный остров театр
18 Water Bikes
   Водный велосипед
20 Ferry Landing
   Пристань,
21 Kirov Stadium
   Стадион имени С. М.
   Кирова
22 Ferry Landing
   Пристань
23 Dinamo Stadium
   Стадион Динамо
26 Petrograd Central GAI Station
   ГАИ

27 Church
   Церковь
28 Market
   Рынок
30 Bank
   Банк
31 Rifle Shop
   Магазин Ружьё
32 Bank
   Банк
38 Post Office &
   Telephone Office
   Почта и телефон
39 Bank
   Банк
   Bank
   Банк

METRO STATIONS

11 Chyornaya Rechka
   Чёрная Речка

MAP 12

Kirov Islands
Острова Кировские

To Olgino, Repino,
Vyborg & Helsinki

Yelagin
Island

Krestovsky
Island

Kamenny
Island

Aptekarsky
Island

Ushakovsky
Bridge

Kamennoostrovsky
Bridge

Kamennoostrovsky prospekt

Professora Popova ul

MAP 11

Primorsky

Nevka River

Bolshaya Nevka River

Malaya Nevka River

Srednyaya Nevka

Kirov Park

Seaside Park

Betozovaya

Betozovaya

2ya alleya

1ya alleya

Kamennoostrovsky prospekt

Pesochnaya naberezhnaya

Bolshaya

Konstantinovsky pr

Krestovsky prospekt

Matrjova

Morskoy prospekt

Kemskaya ulitsa

ulitsa Ryukhina

nab

M10

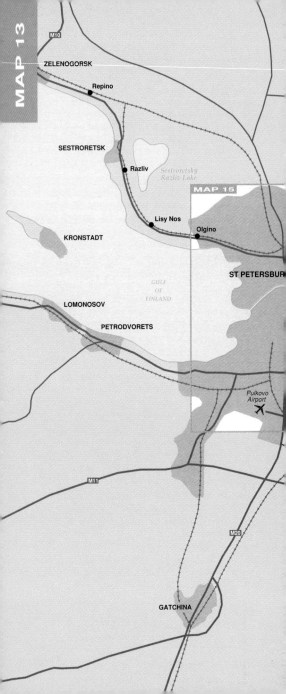

MAP 13

M10

ZELENOGORSK

Repino

SESTRORETSK

Razliv

*Sestroretsky
Razliv Lake*

MAP 15

Lisy Nos

Olgino

KRONSTADT

*GULF
OF
FINLAND*

ST PETERSBUR

LOMONOSOV

PETRODVORETS

*Pulkovo
Airport*

M11

M20

GATCHINA

St Petersburg
Excursions

0   5   10 km

Lake
Ladoga

Ladozhskoe
Ozero

Vsevolozhsk

Petrokrepost

M16

Neva

River

KOLPINO

PUSHKIN

PAVLOVSK   M10

NICK SELBY

Petrodvorets - with the water off

MAP 14

St Petersburg Metro
Санкт Петербургское метро

LEGEND

Transfer Stations
Станции пересадок

Metro Stations
Станции метро

Railway Stations
Железнодорожные вокзалы

1 — Kirovsko-Vyborgskaya Line
Кировско-Выборгская линия

2 — Moskovsko-Petrogradskaya Line
Московско-Петроградская линия

3 — Nevsko-Vasileostrovskaya Line
Невско-Василеостровская линия

4 — Pravoberezhnaya Line
Правобережная линия

Please note: Map not to scale

Devyatkino
ДЕВЯТКИНО

Grazhdansky Prospekt
ГРАЖДАНСКИЙ ПРОСПЕКТ

Akademicheskaya
АКАДЕМИЧЕСКАЯ

Politekhnicheskaya
ПОЛИТЕХНИЧЕСКАЯ

Ploschad Muzhestva
ПЛОЩАДЬ МУЖЕСТВА

Lesnaya
ЛЕСНАЯ

Vyborgskaya
ВЫБОРГСКАЯ

Finland Station
ФИНЛЯНДСКИЙ ВОКЗАЛ

Ploshchad Lenina
ПЛОЩАДЬ ЛЕНИНА

Chernyshevskaya
ЧЕРНЫШЕВСКАЯ

Parnasskaya
ПАРНАССКАЯ

Prospekt Prosveshchenia
ПРОСПЕКТ ПРОСВЕЩЕНИЯ

Ozerki
ОЗЕРКИ

Udelnaya
УДЕЛЬНАЯ

Pionerskaya
ПИОНЕРСКАЯ

Chyornaya Rechka
ЧЁРНАЯ РЕЧКА

Petrogradskaya
ПЕТРОГРАДСКАЯ

Gorkovskaya
ГОРЬКОВСКАЯ

Neva River

Primorskaya
ПРИМОРСКАЯ

Vasileostrovskaya
ВАСИЛЕОСТРОВСКАЯ

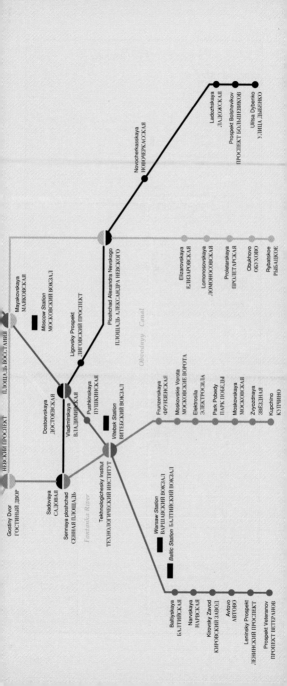

Gostiny Dvor
ГОСТИНЫЙ ДВОР

Mayakovskaya
МАЯКОВСКАЯ

Moscow Station
МОСКОВСКИЙ ВОКЗАЛ

Ligovsky Prospekt
ЛИГОВСКИЙ ПРОСПЕКТ

Ploshchad Alexandra Nevskogo
ПЛОЩАДЬ АЛЕКСАНДРА НЕВСКОГО

Novocherkasskaya
НОВОЧЕРКАССКАЯ

Ladozhskaya
ЛАДОЖСКАЯ

Prospekt Bolshevikov
ПРОСПЕКТ БОЛЬШЕВИКОВ

Ulitsa Dybenko
УЛИЦА ДЫБЕНКО

Elizarovskaya
ЕЛИЗАРОВСКАЯ

Lomonosovskaya
ЛОМОНОСОВСКАЯ

Proletarskaya
ПРОЛЕТАРСКАЯ

Obukhovo
ОБУХОВО

Rybatskoe
РЫБАЦКОЕ

Obvodny Canal

ПЛОЩАДЬ ВОССТАНИЯ

НЕВСКИЙ ПРОСПЕКТ

Dostoevskaya
ДОСТОЕВСКАЯ

Vladimirskaya
ВЛАДИМИРСКАЯ

Pushkinskaya
ПУШКИНСКАЯ

Vitebsk Station
ВИТЕБСКИЙ ВОКЗАЛ

Sadovaya
САДОВАЯ

Sennaya ploshchad
СЕННАЯ ПЛОЩАДЬ

Teknologichesky Institut
ТЕХНОЛОГИЧЕСКИЙ ИНСТИТУТ

Frunzenskaya
ФРУНЗЕНСКАЯ

Moskovskie Vorota
МОСКОВСКИЕ ВОРОТА

Elektrosila
ЭЛЕКТРОСИЛА

Park Pobedy
ПАРК ПОБЕДЫ

Moskovskaya
МОСКОВСКАЯ

Zvyozdnaya
ЗВЁЗДНАЯ

Kupchino
КУПЧИНО

Fontanka River

Warsaw Station
ВАРШАВСКИЙ ВОКЗАЛ

Baltic Station
БАЛТИЙСКИЙ ВОКЗАЛ

Baltiyskaya
БАЛТИЙСКАЯ

Narvskaya
НАРВСКАЯ

Kirovsky Zavod
КИРОВСКИЙ ЗАВОД

Avtovo
АВТОВО

Leninsky Prospekt
ЛЕНИНСКИЙ ПРОСПЕКТ

Prospekt Veteranov
ПРОСПЕКТ ВЕТЕРАНОВ

Map 15   St Petersburg

PLACES TO STAY

2 Hotel Sputnik
   Гостиница Спутник
3 Vyborgskaya Hotel
   Гостиница Выборгская
4 Hotel Karelia
   Гостиница Карелия
10 Pribaltiyskaya Hotel
   Гостиница Прибалтийская
12 Hotel Gavan
   Гостиница Гавань
14 Hotel Deson-Ladoga
   Гостиница Десон-Ладога
23 Summer Hostel
   Летний Хостел
26 Hotel Mir
   Гостиница Мир
29 Hotel Pulkovskaya
   Гостиница Пулковская

PLACES TO EAT

9 Venezia Restaurant
   Ресторан Венеция
15 Shvabsky Domik Restaurant
   Ресторан Швабский домик

OTHER

1 Piskaryovka Cemetery
   Пискарёвское кладбище
5 Krondatevsky Market
   Крондатевский Рынок
6 St Sampson's Cathedral
   Самсоновский собор
7 Vyborgsky Culture Palace
   Выборгский дворец культуры
8 Finland Station
   Финляндский вокзал
11 Passenger Sea Terminal
   Морской вокзал
13 Kirov Culture Palace
   Дворец культуры имени С.М. Кирова
16 Moscow Station
   Московский вокзал
17 Vitebsk Station
   Витебский вокзал
18 Warsaw Station
   Варшавский вокзал
19 Bus Station (Avtovoksal) No 1
   Автовокзал No 1
20 Baltic Station
   Балтийский вокзал

NICK SELBY

Narva Arch

MAP 15

St Petersburg
Санкт-Петербург

A128

ulitsa Rustaveli

Piskarovsky prospekt

■ 4

● 5

prospekt

Polyustrovsky

Vyborg Side

Lesnoy prospekt

■ 2

● 6 ✚

7 ✚

Bolshoy Sampsonevsky prospekt

A22

■ 3

MAP 11

Pirogovsky prospekt

MAP 12

Kirovsky Islands

0   1.5   3 km

To Motel-Camping
Olgino & Vyborg

M10